Minimum Deterrence and India's Nuclear Security

SERIES EDITORS

Muthiah Alagappa
Director, East-West Center Washington

Itty Abraham
Social Science Research Council

Victor D. Cha
Georgetown University

Amitav Acharya
Nanyang Technological University

Alastair Iain Johnston
Harvard University

INTERNATIONAL BOARD

Dewi Fortuna Anwar
Indonesian Institute of Sciences

Chung-in Moon
Yonsei University

Thomas J. Christensen
Princeton University

Sukh Deo Muni
Jawaharlal Nehru University

Stephen P. Cohen
Brookings Institution

T. V. Paul
McGill University

Aaron L. Friedberg
Princeton University

Christian Reus-Smit
Australian National University

G. John Ikenberry
Princeton University

Sheila Smith
East-West Center

Miles Kahler
University of California-San Diego

Yoshihide Soeya
Keio University

Peter J. Katzenstein
Cornell University

Ramesh Thakur
United Nations University

Khong Yuen Foong
Oxford University

Wang Yizhou
Chinese Academy of Social Sciences

Michael Mastanduno
Dartmouth College

Wu Xinbo
Fudan University

Mike Mochizuki
George Washington University

Studies in Asian Security

A SERIES SPONSORED BY THE EAST-WEST CENTER

Muthiah Alagappa, Chief Editor
Director, East-West Center Washington

The aim of the Asian Security series is to promote analysis, understanding, and explanation of the dynamics of domestic, transnational, and international security challenges in Asia. Books in the series will analyze contemporary security issues and problems to clarify debates in the scholarly and policy communities, provide new insights and perspectives, and identify new research and policy directions related to conflict management and security in Asia. Security is defined broadly to include the traditional political and military dimensions as well as the non-traditional dimensions that affect the survival and well being of political communities. Asia, too, is defined broadly, to include Northeast, Southeast, South, and Central Asia.

Designed to encourage original and rigorous scholarship, books in the Asian Security series seek to engage scholars, educators, and practitioners. Wide-ranging in scope and method, the series welcomes an extensive array of paradigms, programs, traditions, and methodologies now employed in the social sciences.

* * *

The East-West Center is an education and research organization established by the U.S. Congress in 1960 to strengthen relations and understanding among the peoples and nations of Asia, the Pacific, and the United States. The Center contributes to a peaceful, prosperous, and just Asia Pacific community by serving as a vigorous hub for cooperative research, education, and dialogue on critical issues of common concern to the Asia Pacific region and the United States. Funding for the Center comes from the U.S. government, with additional support provided by private agencies, individuals, foundations, and corporations and the governments of the region.

Minimum Deterrence and India's Nuclear Security

Rajesh M. Basrur

SPONSORED BY THE EAST-WEST CENTER

Stanford University Press • Stanford, California 2006

Published with the partial support of the
Sasakawa Peace Foundation (USA)

Stanford University Press
Stanford, California

© 2006 by the Board of Trustees of the
Leland Stanford Junior University
All rights reserved

No part of this book may be reproduced or transmitted in any form or by any means, electronic or mechanical, including photocopying and recording, or in any information storage or retrieval system without the prior written permission of Stanford University Press

Printed in the United States of America

Library of Congress Cataloging-in-Publication Data

Basrur, Rajesh M.
 Minimum deterrence and India's nuclear security / Rajesh M. Basrur.
p. cm. — (Studies in Asian security)
"Sponsored by the East-West Center."
Includes bibliographical references and index.
ISBN 0-8047-5255-9 (cloth : alk. paper) —
ISBN 0-8047-5256-7 (pbk. : alk. paper)
 1. India—Military policy. 2. Nuclear weapons—India. 3. Deterrence (Strategy). I. Title. II. Series.
UA840.B265 2006
355.02'17'0954—dc22   2005021505

This book is printed on acid-free, archival-quality paper.

Original printing 2006

Last figure below indicates year of this printing:
15 14 13 12 11 10 09 08 07 06

Typeset at Stanford University Press in 10/13 Bembo

To STEPHEN P. COHEN
with appreciation, admiration, and respect

Acknowledgments

I owe thanks to many individuals and institutions for their assistance and contribution to this work. Among the institutions that enabled me to undertake the research incorporated in this book are: in the United States, the Brookings Institution, the Cooperative Monitoring Center at Sandia National Laboratories, the Henry L. Stimson Center, and the Center for International Security and Cooperation at Stanford University; and in India, the University of Mumbai and the University Grants Commission. My deepest debt is to the individuals who were instrumental in giving intellectual shape to the final product, for which I alone am responsible. These include Itty Abraham, George Baldwin, Kent Biringer, Stephen P. Cohen, Sunil Dasgupta, Sumit Ganguly, Michael Krepon, Amir Mohagheghi, George Perkovich, Gaurav Rajen, Hasan-Askari Rizvi, Scott Sagan, Friedrich Steinhausler, Brian Woo, and three anonymous reviewers for Stanford University Press. I am grateful to Muthiah Alagappa and his colleagues at the East-West Center Washington and to Mary Bearden, Muriel Bell, John Feneron, Kirsten Oster, and their colleagues at Stanford University Press for their encouragement and patience. But for the unstinting support of my wife, Swati, who bore the burden of my preoccupation in research and writing and was yet a constant source of encouragement and inspiration, and likewise our children, Siddharth, Shravan, and Tara, this book would not have gone beyond initial conception.

Contents

1	Introduction: Nuclear Weapons in World Politics	1
2	The Essentials of Minimum Deterrence	25
3	Strategic Culture	49
4	Compellence in a Nuclear Environment	80
5	Missile Defense	102
6	Nuclear Terrorism	122
7	Minimum Deterrence and Democracy	148
8	Conclusion: Shaping the Uncertain Future	169
	Notes	185
	Index	235

Minimum Deterrence and India's Nuclear Security

1

Introduction: Nuclear Weapons in World Politics

In May 1998, India shook the world with a series of nuclear tests accompanied by a declared strategy of "credible minimum deterrence." More than half a decade later, the contours of the strategy are not entirely clear. In essence, the Indian conception of minimum deterrence encompasses the understanding that it is not necessary to have large numbers of sophisticated weapons to deter nuclear adversaries; that nuclear "balances" are not meaningful; and that weapons need not be deployed and kept in a high state of readiness in order that deterrence be effective. Beyond this, important questions remain. While the development of capabilities in technology and organization proceeds apace, nobody is quite clear about what minimum deterrence means. How many weapons are adequate, and of what kind? Might deployment become necessary at some point of time, and if so, under what circumstances? Is war still possible, and if so, how? What kind of arms control is feasible? These and many other questions have been the subject of much discussion since the tests. Perhaps the best thing about the tests is that such questions are now being asked, for they scarcely ever were before the 1998 tests, though the weapons had long been built. This book attempts some answers by examining the fundamentals of nuclear weapons and deterrence in the Indian context.

This is neither a history nor a blueprint. Rather, it is a critique of Indian nuclear thinking and practice based on an inquiry into the basic assumptions and principles that underlie an optimal nuclear weapons posture. The book's central concern is with the hitherto inadequately defined conception of "minimum deterrence" officially adopted by India in 1998, and with the need to clarify its parameters so as to arrive at a cost-effective nuclear strategy. It seeks to comprehend the nature of the world around us, the place of nuclear weapons in it, and the strategic framework that is appropriate to this world.

The character of world politics makes the possession of military nuclear capability a reasonable choice in certain circumstances. Yet the extraordinarily destructive quality of nuclear weapons makes their possession problematic, creating new dimensions of insecurity that can never be eliminated. What minimum deterrence can do is reduce them significantly without sacrificing security. The main objective of this book is to spell out the parameters of minimum deterrence, assess India's nuclear-strategic thinking and practice, and help correct the flaws discovered in the process.

Policy makers choose diverse doctrines because they fail to understand that minimum deterrence is the most cost-effective. A nation's actual choice of posture depends on the historical context in which the decision is made, on its technical and financial prowess, and on its normative preferences about the use of force in general and nuclear weapons in particular. India's adoption of an official doctrine of minimum deterrence is embedded in its historical experience and ethical predisposition, but has tended to lose its moorings because of an inadequate understanding of its fundamental assumptions. This is evident from India's search for a variety of capabilities in nuclear hardware, the recent failed experiment with coercive diplomacy or compellence vis-à-vis Pakistan, and the lack of clarity as to why missile defense is perfectly compatible with minimum deterrence. This book also examines a largely neglected area in the nuclear weapons discourse: the relationship between nuclear terrorism and nuclear strategy. Minimum deterrence, it is argued, is the optimal strategy for a country that faces a significant threat from nonstate actors with an interest in acquiring the capability for mass destruction. Finally, the implications of nuclear weapons for democracy are assessed, and the case is made that minimum deterrence keeps to tolerable proportions the moral and political costs that the possession of these weapons entails.

In the pages that follow, the gray areas between opposite trends and realities that affect India's still evolving nuclear posture are explored. These contradictions encompass the tensions between:

Anarchy and interdependence in world politics—between the self-help character of the world of states, in which power and the use of force are still the bases of national survival, and the increasing integration of this same world, succinctly described by the term "globalization." In the uncertain space between them lies the realm of decisions about the extent to which armed force, and nuclear weapons specifically, must be thought of and organized. The fundamental question is how best we can reduce threats and promote cooperation in such a world.

The possession and non-possession of nuclear weapons—between the sense of insecurity that nations experience when, under threat, they do not have the means to exercise deterrence, and the sense of insecurity they feel even after they *do* have them because there is no guarantee that deterrence will always work.

Nuclear weapons as usable instruments and as unusable instruments of state power—between the fact of their actually having been used and the possibility of future use, on one hand, and, on the other, the powerful practical and moral constraints on their use for more than half a century. Here, we grapple apprehensively with the dilemma of possessing instruments of mass destruction that we never want to use, and yet threaten to use for the sake of our own survival.

The defensive character of one's own weapons and the offensive character of those possessed by others—between the security nations seek when they acquire (or attempt to acquire) nuclear weapons, and the insecurity they experience when others do so while citing the same reasons.

Democracy and deterrence—between the decentralizing tendency, openness, and respect for human life that characterizes democracy, and the centralizing tendency, secrecy, and indiscriminate destructiveness that adheres to nuclear weapons.

This is a holistic examination of these areas, encompassing three types of relationship. First, the study investigates the domain of interstate interaction, which is characterized by coexisting patterns of cooperation and conflict. Here, Indian policy must simultaneously optimize threat reduction and promote cooperation—not an easy task, since measures taken to offset threats, such as the acquisition of nuclear weapons, generate new tensions. The problem is to maximize security while at the same time restraining the negative impact of measures taken to do so. In this respect, the fundamental question to ask in organizing nuclear weapons for the purpose of deterrence is not how much is enough, but how *little* is enough.

The second relationship investigated is that between the external and internal realms of the state. Policy decisions as to how to respond to external threats are made in the latter. The ways in which Indians think about nuclear weapons and their preferences about how to organize their responses to nuclear threats are different from the ways in which others, for instance Americans and Russians, think about them. The reasons for this are historical, but also "cultural," though in a political-strategic rather than a social-anthropological sense. Like everyone else, Indians are not always very clear or consistent in their thinking (not least because of the contradictory nature of the weapons themselves), which opens the door to uncertainty about what is appropriate, and potentially, to a needless expansion of nuclear capabilities. The book presents a line of reasoning that fortifies the historically restrained character of India's minimum deterrence posture.

The third relationship examined is that between the state and civil society. The centrality of this relationship, marked as it is by the last set of opposites mentioned above, is unquestionable. Ultimately, the security of the citizen is indivisible: protection against internal threats is an integral part of the security needs of the individual. And if, as is evident in the case of nuclear weapons, the search for external security detracts from the citizen's everyday security within the state, that is a serious problem that needs to be acknowledged and dealt with. Here too, minimum deterrence must be understood in the most comprehensive way, not only as a means to augment the security of a democratic society by countering external threats, but as a doctrine that minimizes the erosion of that democratic society by curtailing the inherently anti-democratic character of nuclear weapons.

The book journeys across territory that is intensely contested. It seeks to draw attention to optimal choices, but without laboring under the illusion that these choices are unambiguous. There is no scientific model here, only an attempt to navigate a difficult political course through perilous waters. Above all, this is a work about the fundamental politics of choice. It is about the conditions in which nuclear decisions are made, and about how, in a context in which these decisions inevitably have profound positive *and* negative effects, we might make them in such a way as to maximize the former and minimize the latter. The process of making choices must spring from Indians' own understanding of contemporary world politics. In a sense, this already exists. No other single fact better illustrates the uniqueness of the Indian position than that nearly a quarter-century elapsed between the first nuclear test of 1974 and the series conducted in 1998. India's eminently political conception of nuclear weapons, much derided by critics, has not been adequately explained, has indeed been imperfectly understood, by its own adherents. Hence, the choice of a minimalist nuclear posture lacks a sound conceptual basis in the ongoing discourse. This work is an attempt to fill the spaces between the theory and the practice of India's nuclear stance, an effort to create a stronger strategic discourse that is distinctively Indian in its strategic language and understanding, but within a framework of universal principles.

An important underlying thread running through the book is the understanding that the politics of nuclear weapons is conducted at two levels. At the primary level, there is a direct relationship between the existence of nuclear weapons and state behavior. The weapons, regardless of the strategies woven around them, produce patterns of caution and war-avoidance among states that possess them. From time to time, states strain at the leash, but inevitably they draw back, sobered by the prospect of mass annihilation. At the secondary level, there is an overlay of symbolic strategic politics in which states engage in moves and countermoves that have no real basis in the politics of the primary level. Nonetheless, this behavior has the potential to subvert the essential stability of the primary level. This is evident, for instance, in the politics of "bean counting," where much emphasis is placed on "balances" between numbers and types of weapons grossly in excess of the requirements of deterrence. This type of politics produces nuclear arms races that spiral upward toward ever higher levels of confrontation, thereby creating the very instability they seek to avoid. The secondary level includes the politics of prestige, which is about the self-image of nations as well as about the image that other nations have of them. This type of politics may motivate states to acquire nuclear weapons, or be unwilling to relinquish them, and hampers arms control. The Cold War embodied both types of nuclear politics, with the secondary level exercising an excessive influence on the policies of its contestants. The persistence of secondary nuclear politics, in part a game played for the benefit of corporate and bureaucratic players, accounts for some of the slowness of post-Cold War arms control. In India's case, the primary level has been dominant, and the secondary one restricted to image consciousness. An important purpose of this book is to contain the secondary level of nuclear politics, which produces no benefit (other than to vested interests) but invariably carries costs. These are not only economic costs—the price of large arsenals—but, more seriously, security costs—the rising levels of risk related to "vertical" proliferation and arms racing.

The question of motivation is not the focus of this work. That has been discussed at length in numerous scholarly works, all of them centering on one or more of Scott Sagan's three causal models: security, bureaucratic politics, and normative concerns.[1] Rather, the purpose, while acknowledging the diverse reasons why states choose to go nuclear, is to provide a sound intellectual basis for minimum deterrence as the optimal nuclear doctrine and posture for the attainment of national security objectives. The central issue today is not whether India's actual decision to go nuclear was for the right reasons or not, but how to think about maximizing stability once the choice has been made. This involves a degree of optimism, since much that goes by the name of doctrine is devoid of substantive intellectual content. Nor is it assumed that doctrine is the necessary progenitor of nuclear posture, for politics often privileges parochial motives and uncontrollable processes.[2] But hope springs eternal. The project is worthwhile because it may bring a modicum of clarity and effectiveness to an enterprise that is inherently hazardous in the extreme.

Outline of the Book

In this chapter, nuclear weapons are placed in the context of global politics. Any effort to develop a coherent nuclear strategy must begin with a cogent worldview. What is the appropriate conceptual framework for understanding the world around us? To what extent is it a world of cooperation and interdependence, and to what extent a world of conflict? What is the role of force in this world and, more specifically, what is the place of nuclear weapons in it? Such questions call for an assessment of alternative "paradigms" or ways of understanding the world. Within the broad canvas of the worldview that emerges, I discuss the fundamental characteristics of nuclear weapons and their role in the attainment of national security. These characteristics are often contradictory, which makes the formulation of policy difficult. What can nuclear weapons do and what can they not do? What have nuclear weapons done to politics and what is the politics of nuclear weapons? The answers to these questions set the parameters of cost-effective choice.

Chapter 2 focuses on the concept of minimum deterrence. Though Chapter 1 narrows the range within which optimal choices can be made, actual choices may and do vary considerably, from very large arsenals (the United States and Russia) to small ones (India and Pakistan), and beyond to what might be labeled "proto-arsenals" (Japan, Sweden). It is shown why minimum deterrence, which itself encompasses a range of potential postures, is optimal. Its various facets—deployment, delivery vehicles, targeting, and perennially debated questions about escalation, preemption, stability, and damage limitation—are analyzed in terms of the pivotal calculation of potential risk in relation to strategic objectives. Less, it is argued, is invariably better.

Chapter 3 focuses on the evolution of India's deterrence thinking and practice, and the crystallization of India's strategic culture of nuclear minimalism. This approach to nuclear weapons is the most conducive to the rational requirements of minimum deterrence as understood through the discussion in Chapter 2. However, strategic culture is not static. It evolves over time and needs to be reinforced if it is not to lose its bearings and carry strategy away from cost-effectiveness. Indian strategic culture has a tendency to drift toward operational conceptions whose implications are not very well understood, and hence toward the expansion of capability without a clear conception of what is sufficient. The critique ends with a call for self-awareness, balance, and consistent observance of the precepts of minimum deterrence.

Chapter 4 underscores the lack of clarity in Indian thinking in a different respect. Though it is often said that nuclear weapons are meant only to deter, they may also be used—and on numerous occasions have been—more "proactively" to induce specific behaviors in an adversary. The chapter examines at length the shift in Indian strategy from deterrence to compellence vis-à-vis Pakistan. This shift carries intrinsic difficulties, however, because compellence is a difficult objective to achieve, and because the risks of escalation are considerable. The analysis concludes that minimum deterrence overrides compellence, and that the latter is not a viable strategy for India.

Chapter 5 is focused on missile defense. Every nuclear strategist recognizes the possibility that deterrence may fail. While the built-in restraint peculiar to nuclear weapons makes deterrence failure unlikely in a "normal" strategic relationship between states, there is nevertheless a small chance of failure owing to miscalculation, misperception, technical breakdown, or the acquisition of nuclear capability by extreme radicals. In that event, missile defense comes into play. What are the strategic implications of missile defense? The chapter analyzes from the standpoint of minimum deterrence the Indian debate over the strategic implications of the ongoing development of the U.S. missile defense system, and India's own interest in missile defense. The discussion makes it clear that missile defense is fully in accord with the tenets of minimum deterrence and that, for India, it is both strategically unexceptionable and morally desirable.

The threat of nuclear catastrophe comes not only from adversarial states, but also from nonstate actors. Terrorism has a nuclear dimension that is almost as dangerous as the specter of nuclear war. Chapter 6 examines the ways in which nuclear/radiological terrorism affects security. Nuclear weapons and the infrastructure surrounding them are potential targets for terrorists, specifically those whose objectives are not local, but universalistic. Furthermore, acts of nuclear terrorism have the potential to spark off interstate conflict. Nuclear terrorism brings together the external and internal dimensions of security. Minimum deterrence helps to curtail the threat by reducing risks in both dimensions.

In Chapter 7, the relationship between nuclear deterrence and India's democratic political system is discussed. Nuclear deterrence is ethically disturbing, since the security of one's own people is sought by threatening to decimate noncombatants in another society. For a democratic society, which is ultimately founded on the recognition of universal human rights, this imposes a serious moral dilemma. While there is no escaping the responsibility that a democratic system places on the shoulders of ordinary people, the painful nature of this dilemma can be minimized by the successful practice of minimum deterrence. Nuclear weapons also tend to undermine democratic values by placing a premium on centralized power and secrecy, which in turn erodes citizenship, accountability, and the rule of law. It is argued that, while some loss of freedom is inevitable and necessary in the interest of security, minimum deterrence best constrains these threats to democratic life.

Chapter 8 draws together the main threads of the book and looks at the uncertain future. The possibilities are diverse, for there is a wide array of factors that could turn strategy this way or that. This offers some perspective on the value of minimum deterrence. It ends with a set of pointers based on the concept of "reassurance" that could help shape the future and induce strategic stability. There are no guarantees, but neither are there better alternatives.

The Nature of World Politics: Competing Paradigms

Notwithstanding the remarkable changes that have occurred around the turn of the century—the accelerated process of globalization, the end of the Cold War—there is an essential continuity in world politics. The conditions which make power a decisive political currency still persist. For at least some countries, particularly those whose adversaries possess nuclear weapons, nuclear deterrence is an attractive option. The end of the Cold War was not as transformative an event as it appeared at first. The demise of one of its principal combatants, the Soviet Union, marked a profound change in global politics, as the United States became the undisputed superpower of the new millennium. What would be the contours of the post-Cold War world? Would there be a dramatically different world order? Was this indeed the end of history in a Hegelian sense, with liberal democracy and capitalism henceforth to reign unchallenged in a fundamentally stable world?[3] Not many were convinced. To some, the new era was already marked by a very different kind of struggle, again conceived, if not quite expressed, in Hegelian terms: the clash of civilizations.[4] Following the dramatic terrorist attacks of September 11, 2001 (hereafter referred to as "September 11"), there emerged a widespread perception that terrorism is the defining feature of the present age.[5]

At a more mundane level, political leaders struggled to cope with the redrawing of strategic maps, the end of the Soviet Union, the collapse of its vast Eurasian empire, and the troubling question: What next? That question remains inadequately answered today. It is made more challenging not only by the current pervasiveness of terrorism, but by the other great phenomenon that has transformed the world in so many ways: the postindustrial revolution. The changes the latter has engendered in communication, production, and the global flows of information and money have occurred on an unprecedented scale. One might easily argue that this transformative process ushered in the end of the Cold War. After all, the reason Mikhail Gorbachev set into motion the restructuring (*perestroika*) of the Soviet system, thereby helping to destroy it with surprising rapidity, was that it was in danger of being left behind by technological change. The world was changing, and Gorbachev saw his country unable to keep pace. Globalization had rendered the Soviet system obsolete.[6] Nuclear weapons, the great symbols of Cold War confrontation, were threats to all in an interdependent world. The future lay in cooperation and stability, not in threatening mutual annihilation.

The early post-Cold War period was a time of hope. Many expected nuclear weapons to be relegated to the fringes of interstate politics, if not abolished. There was much rethinking about security, with calls for a shift from the prevailing state-centric, predominantly military-strategic conception to a new emphasis on "human security" in which people would be at the center, and the state came to be widely regarded as a part of the problem rather than as the provider of solutions.[7] But foreseeing the future is difficult: most projections are unreliable, partly because of the complexities of the world and its manifold interrelationships, and partly because the activities of human beings are subject to will, which is never quite predictable.[8] Today, we remain uncertain about the future. Nuclear weapons are still with us in the thousands, and the hope that they would be marginalized in the aftermath of the Cold War's end has faded. The existing nuclear powers show no inclination to denuclearize. While several states—Belarus, Kazakhstan, South Africa, and the Ukraine—have dismantled their nuclear capabilities, others—Iraq (until recently), Iran, North Korea—have shown a persistent interest in acquiring nuclear weapons. South Asia has two newly declared de facto nuclear powers with a constantly troubled relationship. At the same time, the process of globalization continues to integrate the world and make its constituents—states, societies, and individuals—increasingly interdependent. This steadily raises the cost of conflict and makes large-scale organized conflict between states less and less likely. As K. J. Holsti has shown, interstate wars have decreased significantly in frequency in the post-Second World War period.[9] How do we come to terms with these opposing realities? How do we comprehend the simultaneous decline of interstate war and the continuing existence of large stocks of nuclear weapons by countries which really have no one to point them at?

In order to understand the place of nuclear weapons in the world today, it is necessary first to understand the world as it is. For this, the tools of analysis that we select are important. In short, it is essential to have more than a passing acquaintance with the rarefied world of international relations theory. To begin with, we may ask whether it is useful to conceive of the world as a unified one or not. If it is not, we might need different analytical tools to analyze its diverse segments. Some scholars have argued that the world is bifurcated. The developing world is very different from the developed, and theories devised to study the latter may not be useful in understanding the former. From this standpoint, international relations theory, which claims to explain the world around us, has serious limitations because it is "essentially Eurocentric theory, originating largely in the United States and founded, almost exclusively, on what happens or happened in the West."[10] In K. J. Holsti's view, existing international relations theory is quite inappropriate for an adequate understanding of the politics of developing countries. European history, on which its edifice is constructed, was characterized by a politics of war, power balancing, and alliances among coherent state units. In contrast, Third World politics is one of intrastate rather than interstate conflict, with state units lacking in cohesion and legitimacy and plagued by substantial problems relating to economic, social, and political development. From this perspective, a proper understanding of the Third World requires a different kind of theory than that which currently prevails.[11] A related view is that because the two worlds are distinctive—the industrialized and democratic developed nations constitute a "zone of peace," and the economically and politically unstable and conflict-ridden developing countries a "zone of turmoil"—we should not view the world with unified lenses.[12]

The "different theories for different worlds" argument exaggerates the differences between the developed and the developing countries. Across historically comparable time frames, these differences are in fact not very great. Take nineteenth-century Europe, for instance. After 1815, interstate wars were relatively few, intrastate conflict more plentiful. Much of the conflict that occurred was caused by democratic and nationalist challenges to regime and state legitimacy, the incongruence of state and ethnic identities, and societal tension arising from problems of economic, social, and political "development" generated by the industrial revolution.[13] In short, the European politics of the nineteenth century bears a strong resemblance to the Third World politics of the present. The relatively low incidence (certainly not the absence) of balance-of-power and alliance politics in the latter is explained by the fact that most Third World countries have stronger vertical economic linkages with developed countries, which makes them weak and dependent. In any case, it remains true that while the overall incidence of war among developing countries has not been very high, there have been numerous armed conflicts between them, a fact that would have hardly escaped the notice of Indians and Pakistanis. My own earlier work has shown the utility of "Western" theory in explaining the patterns of India's external relations since Independence (1947).[14]

For all their obvious differences, developed and developing countries have much in common even today. Both struggle to manage the increasingly complex web of ties with other states. The task is often a difficult one even for developed states, as Canadians for instance know, because interdependence among unequal entities involves a substantial degree of dependence. Both developed and developing countries have also to grapple with the increasing penetration of state and society by transnational nonstate forces. They must cope with the economic effects of global flows of money, goods, and services; the cultural and identity-related effects of information flows; the problems created by global and regional environmental deterioration; and the destabilizing effects of cross-border migration. Hardly any nation is free from the threat of terrorism. The need to regulate and institutionalize interstate interdependence and transnational flows applies to both sets of countries. True, developed countries have a much greater capacity to shape outcomes than developing countries, but the difference is one of degree, not of substance.

A unified view of world politics requires an integrated framework that reconciles the main paradigms or schools of thought that seek to interpret global events and processes. How might such a framework, relevant to both developed and developing countries, be constructed? A paradigm may be defined in terms of three criteria: (1) the *problematique*, or essential behavior to be analyzed (e.g., the causes of war and the conditions of peace, or the causes of exploitation and the conditions of human freedom); (2) the essential actors or units of analysis (the state, multiple actors, world capitalism); and (3) the central image of the world (a system of conflict, a society of states, a global and unequal division of labor).[15] There are numerous ways of classifying the paradigms that seek to understand world politics.[16] The literature as a whole centers around four: realism, liberalism, the Marxian approach, and constructivism. In the postcommunist age, it is common to ignore Marxism as passé, but a better reason for doing so in the present context is that it is weak in its explanatory capacity with respect to war as a general phenomenon.[17] It certainly cannot tell us much about the India-Pakistan conflict. Hence, it is not particularly useful for the purpose of understanding the place of nuclear weapons in world politics. Constructivism, which stresses the central importance of identities and norms in determining what happens in international relations, has now become a standard "paradigm" in textbooks on international relations theory, but there is good reason to pass it over for present purposes.[18] It has little that is new to offer in terms of the criteria for the paradigms stated above, largely because it is not distinguishable from liberalism in its identification of the dynamics of transformation.[19] The realist-liberal divide, on the other hand, is central to the issue.

Realism has a rich history, its myriad practitioners since the beginning of history matched by erudite writings from the likes of Kautilya, Thucydides, and Machiavelli.[20] These and later thinkers viewed the selfishness of human nature as the source of perpetual conflict among states.[21] Contemporary "structural" realism (or "neorealism") has a different starting point. It holds that international politics is a system of self-centered states compelled by the lack of a sovereign above them to privilege self-interest over collective interest, which makes cooperation difficult, and to seek power for the sake of security, which periodically results in tensions and war. The anarchic structure of the system creates typical patterns of power balancing, arms racing, alliance formation, and competition for influence. What states do is determined largely by their external structural relationships, not so much by internal factors such as leadership, party politics, interest groups, ideological preferences, and so on. Much of the current literature dwells at length on the merit or otherwise of this structural explanation of international politics, which is widely attributed to the neorealist writing of Kenneth Waltz.[22] In fact, the structural realist perspective goes back at least to Jean Jacques Rousseau, who described the realm of nations as a "state of war" inherent in the condition of states, "the effect of a constant, overt, mutual disposition to destroy the enemy state, or at least to weaken it by all the means one can."[23] In this view, the lack of a sovereign to constrain them makes states prone to war, particularly because they come into conflict as a result of interdependence and inequality.[24]

Liberal theory, on the other hand, stresses cooperation and a growing sense of community on a global scale.[25] The notion of an essential harmony among states goes back to the eighteenth-century *philosophes*, and to James Mill and Jeremy Bentham.[26] The four main strands of liberal thought are commercial liberalism, which stresses the positive effects of free trade; democratic liberalism, which holds that democracies are essentially peaceable by nature; regulatory liberalism, which highlights the importance of rules and institutions in engendering cooperation; and sociological liberalism, which believes that expanding transnational contacts are changing national attitudes and interests.[27] Since the 1990s, the burgeoning literature on globalization has increasingly questioned the capacity of the state to function as an autonomous unit in a world characterized by rapidly accelerating transnational economic and cultural flows.[28]

The two theoretical traditions are not irreconcilable. Nor do they apply separately to different worlds, liberalism to the developed, realism to the developing. In important ways, states are powerful in both types of country. Individually, they maintain armed forces and sometimes fight, or engage in economic competition, which they influence through policies relating to taxation, interest rates, support for research, export subsidization, the imposition of nontariff barriers to trade, and so on. Collectively, they develop multilateral institutions to regulate economic life, the environment, and military conflict. To the extent that they enjoy autonomy and power, internally determined choices influence their behavior. Some states (the United States, Russia) choose to possess thousands of nuclear weapons; others (Sweden, Japan), none at all. Most prefer economic openness and integration, but some prefer relative isolation (Myanmar, Bhutan). Yet external constraints limit their options in two ways. The anarchic system often privileges self-interest and power politics and hinders cooperation. This means collective efforts for the common good may be slow to take effect, as with humanitarian intervention in Bosnia, and with the ongoing efforts to curb climate change. Where their autonomy is weakened by interstate interdependence or by the penetration of transnational forces, states are compelled to restrain their competition. Strategic interdependence forced the superpowers to negotiate on arms control; economic interdependence greatly limits the intensity of U.S. competition with Europe and Japan; resource interdependence compels India and Pakistan to jointly manage the Indus River system.

Neither paradigm fully explains the nature of world politics. While realists see conflict as intrinsic to an anarchic world, liberals focus on interdependence, which in their view impels nations toward cooperation. The conflict between the two paradigms is less sharp than we might at first think. As Robert Jervis has observed, realists focus on state power and conflict because they are more interested in military-strategic issues, whereas liberals tend to look more at nonmilitary issues, and hence stress interdependence.[29] In the absence of a high degree of interdependence, the realist argument holds good. The world does consist of relatively autonomous states existing in a condition of anarchy that may be described as a "self-help" system. Globalization notwithstanding, states continue to exercise a significant degree of power, making domestic and international rules and, most relevant for present purposes, wielding and sometimes utilizing to lethal effect diverse instruments of military power.[30] The condition of anarchy has not disappeared. States can never be sure of their security, and moreover, if that security is violated, can never be sure that others will come to their assistance. Consequently, the possession of military power is a necessity, which explains why virtually all states maintain armed forces, even those that have not experienced war for long periods. It may at best be said that states enmeshed in highly interdependent economic relationships are very unlikely to go to war. But the fact is that no state has such a relationship with all other states. Ergo, war remains a possibility for all.

The new focus on terrorism in the aftermath of the attacks on the World Trade Center and the Pentagon has not done away with the perceived need for nuclear weapons. One might argue that this is a new kind of war: neither a hot war nor a cold war, but a "Gray War, a war without fronts, without armies, without rules."[31] Expanding on his insightful work on the "risk society," Ulrich Beck notes, "if the military gaze was previously fixed upon others of its [the state's] kind—that is, upon other nation-state military organizations and their defence—it is now transnational threats of substate perpetrators and networks that challenge the collective world of states."[32] Perhaps, but terrorism has not marginalized nuclear weapons. There have certainly been significant changes in the relationships among major powers in the aftermath of the September 11 attacks. Russia and the United States have attained an unprecedented level of mutual understanding. China too appears to have reformulated its view of the United States.[33] For the first time in history, all the major powers are on the same side. Yet none is about to abandon its nuclear weapons. The reason is simple: the world remains anarchic, and nuclear weapons continue to be valued by states as the ultimate arbiters of their strategic fates.

However, a state's level of military preparedness depends on its perception of threat and its calculation of the cost of maintaining armed forces relative to competing demands on its resources. A state that feels threatened is likely to maintain larger and more active armed forces than one that is not. On the other hand, a state that is lacking in resources is less likely to maintain large forces in the face of threats. The calculus is also determined by related factors such as the availability of security assistance from allies. From this perspective, the possession of nuclear weapons is no different from the possession of non-nuclear forces. States that perceive nuclear threats are likely to desire the benefits of nuclear deterrence and states that do not are likely to forgo them.[34] Of course, the former may not acquire nuclear weapons if they do not have the technology or if they enjoy the protection of allies who do. But those who do have the technical capability tend to keep their options open by "hedging," which permits them to exercise the option should the need arise.[35] Thus, the condition of anarchy is a facilitating factor which provides the basis for the possession of weapons of war, including nuclear weapons. The actual choice of possessing nuclear weapons depends mainly on threat perceptions and the availability of resources.

It is important to recognize that the passing of the Cold War was a historical watershed in only a limited sense. It did not change the fundamentally anarchic character of world politics. It transformed the distribution of power within the anarchic system, but did not change the system itself.[36] The hope that nuclear weapons could be abolished or at least marginalized was a forlorn one.[37] There are many reasons why states are likely to retain their nuclear weapons for a long time to come.[38] These include the sheer practical difficulty of eliminating them in a time frame of less than several decades; uncertainty over whether old threats may reappear or new ones materialize; the need to deter chemical and biological weapons; and, above all, the knowledge that "there would always be a latent menace, even if nuclear weapons were no longer in existence at all, implicit simply in the fact that they could be rebuilt."[39] If anything, in the minds of many observers, the post-Cold War era is one of new uncertainties, with new threats around the corner.[40] There may be a nuclear confrontation between the United States and China over Taiwan, or a nuclear attack on the United States by a "rogue" state, and so on. Under the circumstances, it is not surprising that the United States, the sole superpower on whose shoulders many place the onus of taking the initiative to bring about denuclearization, or at least the marginalization of nuclear weapons, has shown great reluctance to do what is expected of it.[41] The *Nuclear Posture Review* of 1994 produced little change; that of 2001 declared a willingness to reduce the active U.S. arsenal significantly, but to retain the option to rearm by storing rather than dismantling nuclear weapons.[42]

Other states face similar problems. They may have to contend with nuclear rivals or adversaries with far superior conventional forces. From the Indian perspective, the existence of nuclear threats in an anarchic world cannot be discounted. So long as India is not enmeshed in highly interdependent economic relationship with other states, the possibility of military conflict remains. Even if highly interdependent economic relationships were to emerge with some states, the possibility of war with those states with which such a relationship does not exist would remain. Military power thus still counts for a great deal. It is often argued that motives other than security—the bureaucratic politics of bomb-producing scientists, the symbolic politics of modernity, and the electoral politics of nationalism—have driven India's nuclear weapons program.[43] While these factors have no doubt played some role, it is undeniable that the security threat has been a constant factor since the very beginning. From Jawaharlal Nehru onward, there was a constant awareness among prime ministers that the nuclear option could not be closed because there might be a need to exercise it at some point in time. As threat perceptions grew, Indian leaders inched closer to making the bomb, at least from as early as the mid-1960s, following China's first nuclear test.[44] It is often forgotten that the bomb was not a creature of the Bharatiya Janata Party (BJP), but was ready and in the basement long before the tests of 1998.[45] And the reason why politicians of very different hue, from Rajiv Gandhi of the left-leaning Congress to Atal Behari Vajpayee of the rightist BJP, felt the need to have it was the perception that India's security required it. The post-Cold War environment had deteriorated in several respects. India felt relatively isolated with the breakup of the Soviet Union and Russia's turn to the West. China, which seemed to be the next superpower in the making, was known to have a close nuclear and missile nexus with Pakistan. Pakistan itself was not only understood to have developed nuclear capabilities, but was active in supporting terrorists in India's Punjab and Kashmir. Finally, the United States was exerting increasing pressure on India to close the nuclear option.

Critics of the tests have decried what they call India's decision to swim against the tide of denuclearization, but the reality is different. In the new millennium, the world has not changed fundamentally. With the end of the Cold War itself a decade-old memory, the perceived need for nuclear weapons has not faded. The United States not only retains large stocks of nuclear weapons, but shows signs of interest in new and "better" weapons.[46] Russia has sought to modernize and streamline its nuclear forces.[47] Nations that are obliged to eschew nuclear ambitions altogether by virtue of their being signatories to the Nuclear Nonproliferation Treaty (NPT)—Iran, Iraq, North Korea—have attempted to develop nuclear capabilities.[48] Even Japan, for all its constitutionally mandated restraint and public opposition to nuclear weapons, has "quietly built up the capacity to make and deploy nuclear weapons, missiles and delivery systems very quickly if and when a new consensus should emerge that such a course was necessary for national security."[49] Most important, India's two adversaries are nuclear-armed, and their intentions cannot be said to be benign.[50] China has been modernizing its nuclear forces for some time.[51] While India-China relations have certainly improved, it is possible that this may change. According to one thoughtful analysis, China's current circumspection arises from its relative weakness. By 2020–2025, it will likely become stronger and more assertive.[52] Recent evidence of Chinese nuclear and missile assistance to Pakistan is evidence of animus on the part of China which India cannot ignore.[53] Pakistan is undoubtedly the most immediate threat, not least because of India's continual confrontation with it over Kashmir.[54]

From within India, objections to going nuclear have been widely expressed. The most common is that there is no strategic rationale to justify nuclear deterrence. The Pakistani nuclear program has always been a reactive one, and India should have taken the lead in nuclear abstinence because the Chinese threat has never been of a magnitude that India could not live with.[55] The Sino-Pakistani nuclear nexus, one argument goes, is no more than a commercial relationship.[56] These views underplay the historical record of India's conflicts with both countries, the continuing conflicts of interest with both, the political reality that arms transfer relationships are rarely without strategic implications, and the policy maker's fear that, in an anarchic system, the intentions of others can change faster than one's capabilities to counter them. Another argument is that deterrence has regularly broken down in the past, and will likely do so again, with horrendous consequences.[57] Here, the qualitative distinction between the prenuclear and nuclear eras is ignored, and no attempt undertaken to counter the deterrence theorist's obvious case for nuclear deterrence, to wit, that it has never broken down.

An additional criticism is that nuclear deterrence is unaffordable for a country where poverty abounds and resources are relatively scarce.[58] But this is one-sided. It assumes that huge amounts of money must necessarily be spent on a nuclear deterrent, which is not necessarily true if one adheres to a strictly minimalist conception of deterrence of the kind outlined in the next chapter. It is also an inadequate response to a perception of nuclear threat. By this logic, *all* defense expenditure is wasteful, and one need not have armed forces at all. Finally, it is a particularly popular belief that the 1998 tests were driven by an aggressive nationalism that sought to make political capital for the BJP, the leading constituent of the coalition government at the time.[59] This ignores the fact that the BJP crossed the nuclear Rubicon only in a limited sense. The bomb had already been constructed much earlier under Congress leader Rajiv Gandhi in the early 1990s, and related paraphernalia were developed under five subsequent prime ministers belonging to various political parties.

In the West, a spirited debate is still under way about the relative stability of new nuclear weapon powers.[60] Proliferation optimists make the case that deterrence at once brings security and produces caution and war-avoiding policies, while proliferation pessimists highlight the risk of deterrence breakdown owing to misperception, uncontrollable escalation from conventional conflict, and unauthorized launch. In essence, the debate is about *all* nuclear weapons, for the main arguments apply to nuclear weapons in general. There are, of course, some who try to show that there is something particularly problematic about new nuclear powers. They might be willing to accept high levels of damage, be inclined to unleash preemptive strikes, or, worse yet, be "undeterrable."[61] They might even be lacking the rationality required to maintain stability: there is, according to one expert, "a surplus of irrational actors in South Asia who would view the advent of crisis as an opportunity rather than as a problem to be contained."[62] One may be inclined to ignore such sentiment entirely but for the serious attention it is given in many quarters, echoed at times by eminent Indians worrying about dictators and "part-lunatics" in the subcontinent.[63] More meaningful criticisms that the new nuclear states are vulnerable to the problem of geographic proximity, or that their command and control systems are inadequate, fail to acknowledge that the U.S.-Soviet case was not different. Cold War nuclear forces were eyeball-to-eyeball in Europe, and frequently at sea. Their command and control systems remained highly vulnerable to technical failure throughout.[64]

In the end, none of this is helpful for policy makers confronted by threats which impel them to think seriously about acquiring nuclear weapons. Both the optimists and the pessimists have a reasonable case, but neither is or indeed can be fully correct. Peter Feaver makes the crucial point that even if rational deterrence theory can successfully predict peace 99.5 percent of the time, that is not good enough, for the remaining .5 percent is good cause for worry when the stakes are extremely high.[65] The argument is unexceptionable, and applies to all cases of nuclear possession. The problem for policy makers is that this argument may apply just as much to *not* possessing nuclear weapons. Where is the guarantee that a hostile state possessing nuclear weapons will not use it against a nuclear abstainer? The only historical cases in which nuclear weapons have been used have been those in which one side had them and the other did not. Notwithstanding the restraint that has prevailed since 1945, there is no assurance that it can never happen again. A rational decision to go nuclear, then, will not be influenced by the arguments of either proliferation optimists or pessimists, or their more general counterparts. That decision, for better or worse, will be determined by the weighing of factors such as threat perception, costs, and technical capability. The second-order choice that follows is: having made the decision to go or not go nuclear, how does one maximize its potential benefits and minimize its potential costs? Here, the proliferation debate, as a subset of the larger debate over all nuclear weapons, may be of some utility if it helps the policy maker assess the relative benefits and risks of nuclear possession. The argument in this book is that, given the dilemma that policy makers face—that both possession and abstinence carry inherent risks—minimum deterrence offers an optimal position.

The paradoxical reality is that when adversaries do possess nuclear weapons, they face a new and unprecedented difficulty. Nuclear weapons have a unique quality about them which makes their use extraordinarily difficult. Their destructive power is so enormous that it makes the resort to war counterproductive in most circumstances. Clausewitz, it is widely agreed, has been stood on his head: between nuclear weapons powers, war is no longer an instrument of state politics. Hence, Bernard Brodie's insight early in the nuclear era: "Thus far the chief purpose of our military establishment has been to win wars. From now on its chief purpose must be to avert them. It can have almost no other useful purpose."[66]

The acquisition of nuclear weapons creates a fresh source of insecurity for the state, leaving it caught in the midst of the "security dilemma."[67] Not arming leaves the state vulnerable to the threats or depredations of others at some unknowable point in time, and hence insecure. Yet, arming causes others to feel threatened and do likewise, which results in the insecurity of arms racing and rising threat perceptions. In short, states threatened by nuclear weapons tend to feel insecure when they do not possess such weapons and insecure when they do. What is the way out? One argument might be that if nuclear weapons have revolutionary effects that preclude rational war between their possessors, the security dilemma has in effect vanished. If two states deter each other, there is no reason to be insecure. But that may not end their insecurity. On the contrary, if they have large arsenals on hair-trigger alert, the chances of something going wrong are sufficiently high to make them both very insecure. And if their political disputes bring them close to armed conflict, the fear of deterrence failure would be very strong indeed.

To return to theory, to the extent that states can no longer see war as an option, the structural effects of systemic anarchy have been superseded. The role of structure is thus a function of the strategic interaction between states.[68] The effect of structure on a strategic relationship varies with the intensity of interaction, i.e., the extent to which one state impacts the interests and activities of another. When intensity of interaction (hereafter, for the sake of brevity, called "intensity") is low, structure has limited effects, and states have a high degree of autonomy. Thus, the distribution of power matters little when two states are not much "connected" by regular interaction. This may appear to be a pointless truism, but it is of significance in a real sense. For instance, weak states have frequently sought to minimize their economic relationships with strong ones in order to avoid dependence. As intensity increases, the effects of structure come into play. Relative power matters, and interests may clash. Strategies are devised to try and ensure security and the protection of interests. Middle-intensity interaction is the stuff of realist politics: power balancing, alliances, wars, and treaties. Structure reigns. When interaction reaches a very high level of intensity, resulting in mutual interdependence and vulnerability, structure recedes in significance. Notwithstanding clashes of interest, a significant degree of cooperation results. Between nuclear-armed states, war-avoidance becomes standard (though other maneuverings may persist). Similarly, in the case of economically interdependent states, even if there is intense competition, cooperative endeavors ensure that there is no systemic breakdown.

Let me briefly illustrate the dynamic effects of changing levels of intensity. Until the mid-nineteenth century, Russian-American relations were of low intensity. Their relative power did not matter, and their interests did not clash. Thereafter, as both expanded into the Pacific and toward each other, there was a rising intensity in their interaction, and tensions gradually emerged. After the Second World War, U.S.-Soviet relations intensified, and the Cold War represented their structural struggle for preeminence and security. However, the nuclear confrontation between them created the high-intensity interaction (mutual dependence and vulnerability) that mitigated the effects of structure to the extent that they were compelled to negotiate and institutionalize a process of arms control.

The theoretical antecedents for this formulation lie in less-noticed aspects of the writings of Thomas Hobbes and Immanuel Kant. Both admitted the possibility that interstate relations might be transformed by intensifying interactions. Hobbes held that states need not transcend the state of nature (anarchy) because people are relatively secure (as compared to the pre-Leviathan state of nature). But this does not necessarily condemn states to endless conflict, as is widely believed by critics of Hobbes. Rather, the implication is the opposite. As Stanley Hoffmann observes, "should the competition become more intense, should the risk of total destruction, affecting all citizens, become intolerable, we could also surmise that Hobbes's relative complacency would lose its justification; the same arguments he used to justify the Leviathan would have to be applied to establish a world-wide one."[69]

Hobbes, then, would have allowed that high-intensity military interaction is the harbinger of systemic transformation in the limited sense of ruling out war and seeking institutional alternatives to the unfettered states system. Similarly, Kant believed that from the destruction of war, good would ultimately come: "And at last, after many devastations, overthrows, and even complete internal exhaustion of their powers, the nations are driven forward to their goal which Reason might well have impressed upon them, even without so much sad experience. This is none other than the advance out of the lawless state of savages and the entering into a Federation of Nations."[70]

Thus, both Hobbesian realism and Kantian liberalism are compatible with the subsuming of structure as a consequence of high-intensity interaction. Whether a super-Leviathan created by a social contract among states or a peaceable federation will emerge some day, perhaps as a result of nuclear mishap, only time will tell. The fundamental point is that, with the advent of nuclear weapons, systemic transformation as a consequence of exhaustion from war is not a prospect to be anticipated with optimism. States and their citizens will not merely be "exhausted" by war; they may cease to exist. Nuclear weapons induce fundamental change in the behavior of states *before* they are used. As is evident from actual behavior during confrontations between nuclear-armed states, a kind of systemic transformation—an undiluted preference for war avoidance—is already evident in the strategic politics of the Cold War. The predominant feature of the Cold War was not so much a "balance of terror" as simply terror.

The consequence of this terror, and the need to forestall possible calamity, was the institutionalization of war-avoidance. There are prenuclear precedents approximating Kant's vision. In modern history, collective efforts to stabilize interstate politics as a result of exhaustion from war include the post-Napoleonic "Congress system" in Europe, the creation of the League of Nations after the First World War, and the establishment of the United Nations in the wake of the Second World War. The last did not prevent unregulated confrontation between nuclear powers in the form of repeated crises, with the Cuban Missile Crisis the high point. There is often a time lag between the advent of new social situations and the devising of institutions to regulate them.[71] The nuclear powers took some time to respond to the unprecedented difficulties posed by these new weapons and institutionalize safeguards to prevent nuclear disaster. This took the form of a combination of a managed system of deterrence (arms control) and a managed system of abstinence (the nonproliferation regime).[72] But this attempt to regulate nuclear power was imperfect at best, and tensions rose as Cold War antagonisms peaked in the 1980s, while nuclear capability spread gradually to more states, notably India and Pakistan. The problem with efforts to manage nuclear weapons is that the very process of management, by mitigating the potential effects of nuclear weapons, lowers the intensity of interaction from a very high to a middling level, thereby facilitating the resurgence of structural behavior which undercuts systemic management. The Congress system was eventually weakened by the wars of German and Italian unification; the League by another world war; the United Nations by the Cold War; and the 1970s détente by the high tensions of the 1980s. International politics in each era has been characterized by an undulating graph illustrating the constant tension between structurally driven adversarial behavior and intensity-driven cooperative behavior. There is no getting away from the security dilemma.

It may be possible, though, to minimize the security dilemma. Rousseau offers some guidance. From his pessimistic perspective, the only feasible course is for states to isolate themselves. By reducing their interdependence, they can hope to reduce conflict among themselves.[73] Hoffmann considers this a "utopian" solution in that Rousseau advocates "a return to an isolation that the march of history had proved impossible long before he wrote."[74] But perhaps what Rousseau suggests is not the reversal of history, only the reduction of interdependence or, to put it another way, a significant reduction in the intensity of interaction. What does this imply for nuclear politics? To recall, where there is low-intensity interaction, the role of structure in shaping interstate politics is limited. If one's weapons are less threatening to the adversary, intensity is in effect diminished, and structural pressures correspondingly reduced. This does not solve the problem of the security dilemma, but it does help lessen its gravity in a nuclear world.

Ironically, by reducing the risk of nuclear war, the end of the Cold War has undercut a vital source of structural pressure for arms control. The underlying reality of anarchy in world politics remains, making it difficult, as we have seen, to conceive of doing away with nuclear weapons altogether. The paradox of nuclear-strategic interdependence is that it tends to be nonlinear in its effects: the caution and stability-oriented policies it generates undermine the sense of mutual vulnerability that created the experience of interdependence in the first place. We are then left with the structure of the anarchic system, which militates against the elimination of nuclear weapons. This is not to say that nuclear arms reduction is ruled out, but it is to say that reduction must then be based on other calculations, such as whether one needs nuclear weapons to counter specific threats, and if so, how many are appropriate. Shifts in perceptions about adequacy may drive the process, but as reduction proceeds, the anarchic structure of the global system will inevitably make it more and more difficult to sustain the momentum.

The only way to lessen this dilemma is if one can feel relatively secure and at the same time minimize the adversary's insecurity. Conceptually, this requires that one adhere to a form of realism that is defensive rather than offensive.[75] Whereas "offensive realism" seeks absolute security through the expansion of power, "defensive realism" tries to maximize relative security without getting caught up in a competitive spiral. Anarchy compels states to pay close attention to their security, but does not tell them how to go about doing it. Offensive realists emphasize the accumulation of power under virtually all circumstances, whereas defensive realists assess threats and weigh costs in relation to competing demands for resources. In choosing specific policies, they frequently resort to cautious strategies that avoid creating insecurity for other states.[76]

In broad terms of military posture, defensive realism leans toward "non-offensive defense," which tries to maintain forces and force postures that are relatively less threatening to an adversary.[77] There are diverse facets to nonoffensive defense. One way of practicing it is by deploying troops away from a contested border, which is less threatening than if they are positioned at the border itself. In nuclear strategy, a minimum deterrence posture characterized by a small number of undeployed weapons is far less threatening than one which seeks security from large numbers of sophisticated weapons deployed on alert status. Minimum deterrence keeps the "strategic distance" between states at a safe level. The concept, as originally articulated by Quincy Wright, is "a function of the obstacles to attack by one state upon another," such as "geographic distance, natural barriers, fortifications, and defensive forces."[78] If time is included as a component, then deployment on a nonalert basis and nondeployment of nuclear forces increase strategic distance, keeping the intensity of interaction between nuclear adversaries to a low level. Minimum deterrence, in short, is conducive to stability because it offsets the influence of structure: it is satisfied with a posture that is relatively less threatening to an adversary and therefore does not invite a highly competitive and tense strategic relationship.

From the Indian perspective, the intensity of interaction between India and its adversaries is limited because of its adherence to a nondeployed posture (as is true of Pakistan). On the positive side, this means that the risks of a nuclear conflict or an active, spiraling arms race are kept under check. On the negative side, it does nothing in itself to curb political tensions or to impel India and its adversaries to manage their relationships through arms control. This is clearly not a satisfactory state of affairs, but in a nuclear context it is better than having to manage deterrence owing to the compulsions of high-intensity interaction, which would be the case if India were to adopt a posture of alert, deployed forces. India's current posture, then, by being relatively less threatening to its adversaries, narrows the ambit of the security dilemma, which is the best that a nuclear-armed state confronting nuclear-armed rivals can hope for. However, the present doctrine of "credible minimum deterrence," it appears, does not rest on a clear understanding of this, which leaves open the door to a shift toward a less optimal posture in the future. Hence the need for a carefully articulated exposition of the fundamentals of minimum deterrence.

Conclusion

The foregoing makes it clear that nuclear weapons have a place in world politics, and that, in general terms, minimum deterrence maximizes deterrence security and minimizes the risks and costs incurred. Notwithstanding the growth of interdependence, the world of states is constituted by anarchy, which necessitates the resort to arms to counter threats to security. In some instances, the acquisition of nuclear weapons may be seen as necessary, even if they are viewed with some trepidation because of their potential to wreak catastrophe. The nuclear version of the security dilemma allows no escape. The most we can hope for is that we might diminish the acuteness of the dilemma by adopting a strategy of minimum deterrence which is less threatening to an adversary than other strategies. This requires a nuanced and thorough understanding of what minimum deterrence is. Chapter 2 undertakes this task.

2

The Essentials of Minimum Deterrence

Minimum deterrence is predicated on the understanding that, where nuclear weapons are concerned, it takes very little to deter. Beyond a point, admittedly hard to pin down, neither number nor technological sophistication matters, and balances are unimportant. The capacity to inflict unacceptable damage—again, impossible to define precisely, but conceived in minimalistic terms—gives a state minimum deterrence capability. Because the key concepts of capability and damage are slippery, minimum deterrence admits only a broad definition, which is that "it threatens the lowest level of damage necessary to prevent attack, with the fewest number of nuclear weapons possible."[1] This lack of precision allows a wide margin of interpretation as to what constitutes "minimum." The position taken here is that minimum deterrence rests not so much on quantitative assessments of capability and damage, but on a more fundamental distinction. What deters is not one's own certainty of inflicting damage, but *the adversary's perception of risk*. Because nuclear weapons produce catastrophic damage, virtually no objective justifies even a low risk of their being used, and an adversary is easily deterred. This chapter explains why, of the range of choices available to nuclear-capable states, minimum deterrence is the most cost-effective. The revolutionary character of nuclear weapons pits their political aspect against their technological or operational one. Once the primacy of the political—the centrality of risk—is accepted, basic concepts such as "unacceptable damage," "credibility," "survivability," "escalation," and so on begin to take on a clear meaning in the search for an optimal strategy. A careful scrutiny of these concepts shows some of the flaws in Indian thinking.

Alternative Strategies

For a new entrant into the world of nuclear powers, there is a wide range of choices, determined not only by what it can afford, but by what it may aspire to. What are the alternative models it can choose from? There are a number of identifiable nuclear postures.[2]

Assured Destruction

American and Soviet/Russian strategy rests on the immense resources available to countries with continental economies, though the state of Russia's economy in recent years has raised serious questions about its capacity to sustain its large nuclear inventory.[3] Assured destruction assumes the possession of a very large, diverse, and sophisticated triad of air, land, and sea-based nuclear forces capable of destroying a substantial portion of the enemy's population and military and economic assets. The immensity of these forces has much to do with social-psychological factors (such as industrial society's belief that size does matter) and vested interests, but it is at root the product of the Second World War, which framed the historical context in which the first nuclear weapons were born. One "lesson" of the war was that adversaries could withstand enormous damage in military conflict. The Americans learned this from the failure of their fire-bombing missions in Germany and Japan to force the enemy to surrender. Only the use of the atomic bomb, it seemed, achieved the desired effect, that too at the fag end of the war, when Japan had virtually been defeated already. The Russians doubtless learned the same, not least from their country's ability to withstand colossal losses in not one but two world wars, and to recover from them and emerge as a superpower. Consequently, it is no surprise that both countries based their nuclear strategies on large forces with great destructive capacities. Nor is it remarkable that they should have believed that the stability of their antagonistic relationship during the Cold War years rested on their ability to destroy each other completely. What is remarkable is that, more than a decade after the end of the Cold War, both the United States and Russia continue to retain an interest in developing new nuclear weapons.[4]

Limited Deterrence

Limited deterrence, which is a restricted version of assured destruction, is espoused by China. In essence, this posture envisages a range of capabilities similar to those that characterize assured destruction, but is limited by resource constraints. It envisages a triad of weapons, as well as the capacity to fight at different levels from the local to the national.[5] Its historical setting—

the Second World War—is the same as that of assured destruction. The Chinese experience, it must be remembered, was similar to that of the United States and Russia: the pain of two Japanese invasions in the 1930s, the second leading into the Second World War. One assessment is that China maintains a lower-scale, minimum deterrence posture toward the continental United States and Russia, and limited nuclear deterrence with respect to its theater forces.[6] Another view is that China's interest in limited deterrence is more aspirational than actual.[7] Its aim is to make deterrence as effective as possible by maximizing the damage capability of a relatively small arsenal. In short, limited deterrence is an "affordable" version of assured deterrence. Continuing efforts to this end are reflected in the launch of a new nuclear submarine designed to fire intercontinental ballistic missiles (ICBMs) in December 2004.[8]

Minimum Deterrence

Minimum deterrence has been adopted in part by China, as well as by Britain and France, and is now the official doctrine of India and Pakistan.[9] Resource constraints have been an important reason for the emphasis on "minimum," though China, of course, has been able to envisage a shift toward limited deterrence because of its consistent economic growth. Britain and France have been able to maintain relatively small weapons inventories because of the security obtained from U.S. backing. (Of the two, France has the larger one because of its reluctance to depend heavily on the United States.) It is arguable that in the absence of U.S. support, both would have been inclined to build larger arsenals than they actually have. China, lacking such support, has aspired to a more powerful deterrent force in spite of resource constraints. All three, it should not be forgotten, have been deeply influenced by the experience of the Second World War.

India and Pakistan, on the other hand, have not had similar strategic histories. On the contrary, they have fought only short and limited wars (the India-Pakistan wars of 1947–48, 1965, and 1971; and India's war with China in 1962), none of which was very highly destructive, and in all of which the targeting of population centers was noticeably absent. Unlike the first two types of deterrence, this form is based on the assumption that deterrence may be achieved by a small force because a comparatively small quantum of damage is unacceptable to any adversary. At root, minimum deterrence rests on an existential foundation: the mere possession of a few weapons suffices to deter. However, it does not seem to have developed the solid intellectual basis it needs for its sustenance, which explains why it has become something of an umbrella concept, embracing varying quantities and types of forces, and nondeployed as well as deployed postures. Conceptual ambiguity makes it open-ended and subject to expansionary pressures arising from changed threat perceptions, the availability of greater resources, and domestic interests. That, of course, presents a problem with respect to India. Below, this lacuna is filled by an exposition of the fundamentals of minimum deterrence.

Opaque Deterrence

For about a decade before they officially declared themselves to be nuclear-armed states in 1998, India and Pakistan maintained an opaque status, as Israel still does today.[10] Its chief characteristics include absence of testing, denial of possession, eschewal of nuclear threats, and nondeployment.[11] In large part, opacity stems from the apprehension that transparency would invite negative consequences in the form of sanctions invoked under the Nuclear Nonproliferation Treaty (NPT) and other restrictions imposed by national laws and international agreements. But it is also based on some sense that overt nuclear deterrence is not central to national security, and that it can be achieved at a minimal level if the adversary knows—or merely has good reason to believe—that one has achieved nuclear weapons capability. It is, strictly speaking, a subcategory of minimum deterrence, resting on the assumption that relatively small numbers of nondeployed weapons are sufficient to deter. All three of the states mentioned in this category have similar backgrounds: limited resources and a history of short wars that caused relatively little damage. Hence, none believes that vast and sophisticated arsenals are necessary in order to deter. For Israel, relatively favorable static conditions—the absence of a nuclear challenge and the sustenance of conventional superiority over its adversaries—have encouraged continuity. There has long been neither a new and significant external security threat (though Iran may become one in the near future) nor significant pressure from the nonproliferation regime to roll back its nuclear capability. In contrast, India not only perceived rising threats, but was under great international pressure to abandon its opaque deterrent and chose as a result to go nuclear officially. Opaque deterrence is likely to be the favored choice for future proliferants. North Korea appears to be the latest instance.[12] The Indian example is a pointer to the difficulty facing the nonproliferation regime: while there is a strong desire to pressurize aspiring nuclear powers to reverse their policies, pushing them too hard may actually drive them to "come out."

Virtual Deterrence

Virtual deterrence involves the acquisition of some degree of technical capability without actually translating that capability into weapons.[13] India and Pakistan belonged to this category before the late 1980s, when they are both thought to have developed their respective nuclear weapons. India, in fact, acquired its wherewithal at least as early as 1974, when it carried out its first nuclear test. The achievement of rudimentary capability provides the basis for an existential form of deterrence, since adversaries are deterred by the possibility of nuclear retaliation. Some states may have the technical capacity without attempting to exercise it. Japan has developed the basic infrastructure of nuclear weapons capability in such a way as to be able to nuclearize within a reasonable time frame should the need arise.[14] The case of Sweden is similar, and Germany is not far behind.[15] Needless to say, all three have little incentive to go nuclear so long as they enjoy the benefits of the U.S. nuclear umbrella. For those who seek deep reductions in nuclear armaments, but understand that nuclear abolition is unlikely in an anarchic world, the concept of virtual deterrence is a beacon of hope. It may be possible eventually to bring deterrence to an existential minimum through a multilateral system of verified "virtual nuclear arsenals" consisting of segregated weapons components stored and monitored by common agreement. It is readily evident that there is no substantial difference between India's present posture of unassembled, undeployed weapons and the concept of virtual deterrence. Virtual deterrence may be viewed as one end of a minimalist spectrum, with the French and British arsenals at the other.

Where does India stand? The picture is an evolving one. Historically, India has adopted a hedging strategy since Independence in 1947.[16] In effect, its posture has incorporated significant elements of what might be called a reluctant deterrence that has evolved in stages. These are:

— Deterrence without testing, weapons, or organization (before the 1974 tests);
— Deterrence with a single test, no weapons, and no organization (1974 to the late 1980s);
— Deterrence with a single test, an unspecified number of unassembled weapons, and no organization (from the late 1980s to the 1998 tests);
— Deterrence with a few tests, a few unassembled weapons, and a gradually developing organization.

Nuclear threats—potential and real—are an inescapable reality that has grown over time. China, Pakistan, and future proliferants have to be contended with. Recently unearthed evidence of nuclear cooperation among Iran, Libya, North Korea, and Pakistan is an indication of how future threats may be completely unanticipated.[17] Whether there will be further policy change and if so, how much, is uncertain. India's nuclear doctrine and posture are no longer opaque, but neither are they transparent and clear. Arguably, this nuclear translucence is deliberate; but it may in part reflect a lack of clarity about fundamentals.[18] On one hand, its weapons are unassembled and undeployed, which positions it close to the idea of a virtual arsenal.[19] On the other, its missile program appears to be open-ended, with an ongoing effort to develop a full-fledged triad, and possibly an intercontinental ballistic missile (ICBM).[20] According to one report, the Executive Council—the operational component of the Nuclear Command Authority—has pressed for more delivery platforms.[21] Indian thinking is ambiguous. Official doctrine has been reticent in the extreme, restricted to a January 2003 press release that stressed no first use (NFU) and "massive retaliation."[22] An earlier document, the Draft Nuclear Doctrine (DND) of August 1999, was in part minimalist in its implied preference for "peacetime deployment" as opposed to "fully employable forces" in the event of a conflict situation arising, but maximalist in its call for, among other things, "multiple redundant systems" to ensure survivability.[23] While the DND has not been made official policy, it is said to play a significant role in strategic planning by the armed forces.[24]

The lack of clarity about minimum deterrence concepts is best exemplified in the writings of one of India's most articulate thinkers on nuclear weapons, the late General Krishnaswamy Sundarji.[25] Sundarji holds that the requirements for minimum deterrence are "finite," and India must not make the mistake of the United States' "obscene amassing of unusable weapons."[26] With nuclear weapons, absolute damage counts, not relative damage, and for that reason even conventional conflict should be avoided.[27] The use of tactical nuclear weapons (TNWs) should be shunned, because civilians will still be harmed if they are used.[28] On the other hand, Sundarji espouses the contradictory notion of employing TNWs "to deter the adversary from making first use of tactical nuclear weapons, and thus gaining the battlefield advantage."[29] He is not consistent on the need for rigorous testing to ensure the reliability of weapons and its implications for assured second strike capability. In one work, he regards it as a necessary.[30] In another, he does not.[31] He is also constantly concerned about operational aspects such as vulnerability and survivability (ubiquitous in U.S. debates), which are the primary drivers of force expansion.[32]

The need for a thorough exposition of minimum deterrence is evident. A major problem is the paucity of sources for guidance on its thinking and practice. It goes without saying that the superpower experience is only helpful in a negative way, illustrative as it is of the futility of maintaining large and diverse arsenals in the quest for combining security with stability. For India, it is not affordable anyway, but even a scaled-down version—limited deterrence—is not much better since it does not offer a more thoughtful basis for its recommendations. It is not widely known that minimum deterrence as a concept originated in the United States. But this was in the general context of assured destruction, with a specific focus on the efficacy of submarine-launched ballistic missiles (SLBMs) as survivable platforms capable of inflicting large-scale damage. Thus, a U.S. Navy justification for the Polaris system envisaged a fleet of 45 submarines capable of destroying "all of Russia" with about 720 warheads.[33] This clearly is not the sort of thinking that even the most maximalist of deterrence strategists in India subscribe to.[34] Much earlier, though, the United States had practiced a kind of minimum deterrence in the 1940s. At the time, President Harry Truman deliberately chose to build a small arsenal; warheads were kept under centralized civilian control and separated from delivery vehicles by a distance of about 100 miles; and warhead components were kept unassembled (the Hiroshima bomb was assembled only after take-off).[35] But this was during a time when the United States had a monopoly on nuclear weapons. After the Soviet Union acquired its bomb, the U.S. posture changed and its forces began to expand.

Consequently, there is not much that is useful in the mainstream U.S. literature on deterrence which dominates the field of strategic theory in the English language. Of the three main schools of thought in the United States, two—the punitive retaliation school and the military denial school—believe that assured destruction capability is a prerequisite for crisis stability, while the third—the damage limitation school—insists on nuclear superiority.[36] The punitive retaliation school stands closer to minimum deterrence than the others, but still rests its case on the assumption that it takes the ability to inflict very large-scale damage to deter. A preoccupation with the operational or "usable" aspect of nuclear weapons is ubiquitous in much deterrence-related thinking. Thus, though Bernard Brodie is widely credited for his insight on the revolutionary character of nuclear weapons, few notice that the same Brodie explicitly rejects minimum deterrence on the grounds that "it may require a large force in hand to guarantee even a modest retaliation"; that "if deterrence fails we shall want enough forces to fight a total war effectively"; and that "our retaliatory force must also be capable of striking first, and if it does so it had better be, as nearly as possible, overwhelming to the enemy's retaliatory force."[37] Similarly, Scott Sagan—hardly a believer in the efficacy of nuclear weapons for attaining security—argues his case against proliferation from the standpoint of the general operational requirements of stability. This requires, in his view, invulnerability from a first strike: "The United States and the former Soviet Union developed a large and diverse arsenal—long-range bombers, intercontinental ballistic missiles, cruise missiles, and submarine-launched missiles—and a complex network of satellite and radar warning systems, to decrease the risks of a successful first strike against their arsenals. Will new nuclear powers also construct invulnerable arsenals? How quickly?"[38]

The stability requirements of U.S. strategy are thus transposed into those of others who might have a very different conception of it. In the same vein, Michael Krepon believes that in South Asia, "*secure* second strike capability," a "core element of strategic stability," does not exist.[39] Likewise, Ashley Tellis, who views India's nuclear capability with considerable optimism, argues that an "important challenge" for India is ensuring its arsenal's "survivability against any first-strike temptations on the part of an adversary," for its "critical weakness" lies in "its potential inability to effectively reconstitute in the aftermath of a nuclear attack in order to carry out retaliation."[40] Tellis also argues that India's arsenal may suffice if present circumstances persist, but that greater capability may be required if the strategic environment changes, for instance if missile defenses become more effective, or India-China tensions rise sharply.[41] Below, we will see just how different the requirements of a true minimum deterrence strategy are. For the moment, suffice it to say that they do not include the need for one's forces to be "invulnerable." To deter, it is necessary to pose a risk of severe damage to the adversary, not to assure oneself that it will definitely occur.

For this reason, the British, French, and Chinese examples are inappropriate to minimum deterrence as it is conceived of here. The British deterrent is in any case a "minimal" one only because it piggy backs on the U.S. deterrent. Besides, like the latter, it focuses heavily on survivability as well as on penetrability, which is to say, on assuring itself of damage capability rather than depending on the adversary's risk perception.[42] The French deterrent is even less exemplary for two reasons. First, it has long emphasized the need for a triad of delivery vehicles, which is not intrinsic to minimum deterrence. Second, it has over the years flirted with counterforce strike capability, variously described as "prestrategic," "final warning," and "flexible weapons systems."[43] The Chinese deterrence posture is the least attractive because of its proclivity for limited deterrence. This is manifested in, among other things, a perceived need for redundancy for the sake of survivability in each leg of its triad, a growing interest in tactical weapons, and the maintenance of round-the-clock alerts.[44] In short, while the British, French, and Chinese deterrents may be described as minimum, they are not minimum enough. They are still relatively expensive, and do not minimize the security dilemma to the extent they might. The fundamentals of a true minimum deterrent are outlined below. The starting point for this is the nature of nuclear weapons and what they imply for deterrence.

The Revolutionary Effects of Nuclear Weapons

Despite the growing sense among many that nuclear weapons are not militarily "usable," there is by no means a clear consensus on the restricted role of nuclear weapons. On the contrary, there are at least three "models" of nuclear strategy that have been propagated over the years.[45] In the first, nuclear weapons are regarded as *regular weapons*. In this view, they are just another kind of military instrument, more powerful than others, which are usable in war and hence must be fully integrated into war planning. A second perspective is that they are *special weapons*, the use of which may be contemplated only in circumstances of great adversity. Here, the notion of winning a nuclear war is not ruled out. Last, nuclear weapons are no more than *explosive devices* which carry the constant risk of untold damage. The danger of escalation from even a single small use is too great to be acceptable, which makes the oxymoronic appellation "unusable weapons" appropriate. Hence, they should not be integrated directly into the military forces, but released for potential use only in the event of a truly severe threat. The last model appeals to our sense of caution and holds out the best hope of keeping nuclear weapons on a tight leash.

The stark fact about nuclear weapons is that, despite the strong taboo against their use, they were used, not once but twice, and there is no guarantee that they will never be used again.[46] How then should we conceive of them and the role they play in an anarchic world where the possibility of military force being used is still real? At the end of the Second World War, it was common enough to think of nuclear weapons as another sort of instrument of war—far more terrible than other weapons, but not revolutionary in character, for after all, this was a war in which some 40 million had died, half of them noncombatants. At the time, many believed that nuclear weapons could and would be used in the next war. Since the horrors of the First World War had not prevented the "gloomy logic" of the time, "the arrival of nuclear weapons simply meant that the next world war would finish off the destructive job the previous two had not quite completed."[47] Large-scale strategic bombardment continued to be the mainstay of military thinking, and even in the 1950s, the conception of "broken-backed war" in the wake of a thermonuclear exchange remained the basis for U.S. and Allied force posture and defense planning.[48] The view, indeed, was that "any future war in which America and Russia are the chief contestants . . . would certainly not be decided by atomic bombing alone. On the contrary, a long-drawn-out and bitter struggle over much of Europe and Asia, involving million-strong land armies, vast military casualties and widespread civil war, would be inevitable."[49]

But many thoughtful observers were convinced that the advent of nuclear weapons had fundamentally altered the relationship between war and politics. Even at the very beginning of the nuclear age, they recognized that these were devices that could do in one fell swoop what would take conventional weapons far more time on a much greater scale to do. Later studies have shown how catastrophic their effects can be, up to a possible "nuclear winter" in the event of an all-out nuclear war between major powers.[50]

In short, nuclear weapons are revolutionary in their effects: for the first time in history, weapons of war are "unusable" in any practical military sense.[51] Their sole purpose, it follows, is deterrence. Richard Harknett draws attention to the central point about these weapons: they not only cause destruction on an unprecedented scale, but do so at astonishing speed, so there is little one can do in response to their terrible effects once they have been unleashed. Conventional weapons can be contested, nuclear weapons cannot.

> Militaries and societies can adapt to the disruption and destruction possible with conventional weapons, even at severe levels. By contrast, nuclear weapons are capable of inflicting costs so quickly on such a vast scale, with lasting effect, that little adjustment can be made to blunt those costs to a significant degree. While conventional weapons allow for adaptation to costs, nuclear weapons permit little more than the absorption of punishment. Ultimately, the incontestable nature of nuclear weapons constrains the range of interaction between states in a military deterrence environment.[52]

It is this revolutionary character of nuclear weapons that rules out consideration of war as a rational option in national strategy if there is a risk of nuclear conflict. Given the potential impact of a nuclear war, even small risks that might lead to war are unacceptable. The relationship between the potential gain and the potential loss from such a conflict is inherently unequal: the latter will always outweigh the former.

The Political and Operational Facets of Nuclear Weapons

The problem with nuclear weapons is that their divergent military and political facets are hard to disentangle. On the one hand, they are *military* instruments that are, like other weapons, incorporated into national force structures. In this role, they have operational meaning for military personnel (and for many strategists) whose job is to think of their utility as instruments of war. Like other weapons, they are assessed in terms of their accuracy, speed, reliability, and so on. On the other hand, given their potential for massive destruction they are preeminently *political* instruments for decision makers whose paramount objective (at least, after Nagasaki) is to ensure that they are *not* used. This is what deterrence is all about. The two roles are inextricably linked: the political nonusability of nuclear weapons is the direct consequence of their operational usability. This inherent contradiction can never be resolved. But it would seem fair to say that politics does and should come first, and that even those who contemplate nuclear weapons in usable terms would prefer that they not be actually used.

Nuclear weapons *were* used by the United States against Japan. But once he had grasped the true horror of their character, President Harry Truman argued strongly for their nonusability. As he told David Lilienthal, a close advisor, "You have got to understand this isn't a military weapon. It is used to wipe out women, children and unarmed people, and not for military use."[53]

Similarly, President Dwight Eisenhower, who publicly espoused a strategy which envisaged the massive use of nuclear weapons against the Soviet Union, warned senior military officials against thinking of winning a nuclear war: "Gain such a victory and what would you do about it? . . . I ask you, what would the civilized world do about it? I repeat, there is no victory in any war except through our imaginations, through our dedication and through our work to avoid it."[54]

While the contradiction between the political and operational components of nuclear weapons is essentially beyond resolution, it can nonetheless be prioritized, and the way this is done has enormous consequences for nuclear strategy. Where the political meaning of deterrence takes precedence, nuclear weapons, regardless of their operational characteristics, are treated as uniformly dangerous, and the overwhelming emphasis is on war-avoidance. This perspective induces a minimalist strategy. The fewer the weapons and the less we rely on them, the better. If the operational constituent is accorded primacy, considerations of a "practical" character related to the usability of nuclear weapons powerfully influence strategy. This results in a strong focus on weapon characteristics, modes of deployment, vulnerability, reliability, and so on. Such considerations push strategy toward a maximalist position. Often, this translates into an inchoate sense that the bigger and more sophisticated the arsenal, the better. There is little evidence as yet that this complex and contradictory character of nuclear deterrence has been adequately grasped by policy makers and strategic thinkers. In consequence, both components of deterrence coexist uncomfortably. For instance, in the United States and Russia, political leaders strive to overlay operationally driven postures with a political approach to their strategic relationships. Actual variations in nuclear strategy among nuclear powers can be explained with reference to a quite different set of variables. The pushes and pulls of political and economic interests are played out over more deeply embedded causal factors: national economic and technological capabilities, historical experience (especially that just preceding the time nuclear weapons are acquired), and the symbolic value placed on nuclear weapons by strategic elites. It is vital that minimum deterrence be underscored by a clear understanding of the dual character of nuclear weapons, and that the political be prioritized.

This is not without attendant risks. An excessively political conception of nuclear weapons may encourage their possessors to think of them as political instruments of state policy. They may not be usable for fighting, but they might be seen as handy in other ways. Policy makers may resort to brinkmanship for bargaining purposes, and coercion to force an opponent to change policy. This, as we see in Chapter 4, is problematic at best, potentially catastrophic at worst. Minimum deterrence requires that the use of nuclear weapons for anything other than the threat of retaliatory punishment be ruled out.

The Centrality of Risk

The key to understanding the working of minimum deterrence is risk. This is the core of McGeorge Bundy's concept of "existential deterrence."[55] If, as we have seen, nuclear weapons are "incontestable," and if the risk attached to them is not worth the game, then what deters is not the particular strategy one adopts, but the sheer reality of the weapons themselves. The key elements of existential deterrence are that it rests on "uncertainty about what *could happen*, not [on] what has been asserted"; that no one knows what will actually happen if a nuclear conflict breaks out; that most changes in capabilities have no strategic effect because they do not radically alter the degree of risk; and, above all, that it "rests on one of the great realities of nuclear weapons: they are far more terrifying to adversaries than they are comforting to their possessors."[56] Arguably, the Cold War remained cold not because the contestants developed refined forces and sophisticated doctrines, but because the sheer existence of their weapons and the associated risk made them abundantly cautious.[57] As Kenneth Waltz points out, "The assumptions made in the effort to make a Soviet first strike appear possible are ridiculous. How could the Soviet Union—or any country, for that matter—somehow bring itself to run stupendous risks in the presence of nuclear weapons? What objectives might its leaders seek that could justify the risks entailed?"[58]

The last point is important. A decision to go to war involves an expectation of net gain. It is hard to think of any objective motivating a nuclear strike that might outweigh even a small risk of appalling damage, with the exception of national survival. Even in the case of national survival, the horrendous costs associated with nuclear use will have a powerful inhibiting effect on a decision maker contemplating a first strike to beat the enemy to the draw. Even if the probability of an enemy first strike appears significant, the risk of that happening cannot outweigh the near-certainty of colossal damage from launching one's own strike first. The balance of risk always favors restraint. This applies, of course, to the enemy as well, which reinforces restraint.

With nuclear weapons, risk confronts us in different ways. The most obvious risk, of course, is with respect to direct nuclear conflict. The prospect of a nuclear war invariably has an inhibiting effect on potential combatants. A second possibility is that of escalation from limited to full-scale nuclear conflict. It is conceivable that the former may be contained and that nuclear war may be fought on a very restricted scale, say with one or two demonstration explosions, or even a very limited "counterforce" exchange in which only military forces are targeted. But the most predictable thing about war is that it is not predictable, and it would take an extraordinary act of faith to believe that escalation from limited counterforce to unconstrained, city-busting "countervalue" war could be assuredly prevented. Once the first weapon has been launched, all bets are off, for who can be sure which way the action-reaction process of launch and counterlaunch will go?

A third form of risk relating to nuclear war arises from full-scale conventional conflict. Here again, there is a risk—lower than in the previous case, but still significant—of escalation from conventional warfare. For the side that is losing, or sees itself as losing, there is an incentive to use nuclear weapons. At the same time, the knowledge that the side that is losing has such an incentive is in itself an incentive to the winning side to launch first in the hope that it may minimize damage to itself. Unfortunately, the losing side must also be aware of the winning side's incentive to strike first, and so on. True, as argued above, nuclear weapons have a strong inhibiting effect. But the tensions raised by conventional war and the anticipation of nuclear strikes facilitate misperception, errors of judgment, loss of control through delegation of nuclear launch authority, and accidents. Whichever way we look at it, there is not much strategic space between conventional and nuclear war.

At a fourth plane—that of subconventional conflict—the level of risk dips considerably. Border skirmishes, for example, or covert infiltration may be considered "safer" in that they do not in themselves pose a serious enough threat to make resort to nuclear war likely. A "two-steps-short rule" applies to an adversarial relationship between nuclear powers.[59] In every confrontation, both stop two thresholds short of nuclear conflict. The first step would involve escalation from subconventional to full-scale conventional conflict, the second from conventional to nuclear conflict. It is readily evident that nuclear armed states have never allowed their confrontations to breach this rule. This is true of all adversarial relationships involving states with nuclear weapons: U.S.-Soviet Union, Soviet Union-China, India-Pakistan, and India-China.[60] In the Kargil conflict (1999) and in the ten-month-long military confrontation that followed the terrorist attack on the Indian Parliament on December 13, 2001, the threat of an India-Pakistan war appeared to be serious, but both sides always abided by the two-steps-short rule and remained below the threshold of conventional war. Nevertheless, it would be delusional to believe that such parrying short of conventional war is safe. In the Kargil case, large-scale Indian mobilization had begun to occur when the conflict came to an abrupt end. In the post–December 13 confrontation, there was large-scale mobilization by both sides, which meant that the threshold to conventional war came close to being crossed. The margin of safety was narrow. It is pertinent to ask: With each such face-off, does the risk of actual war not increase as both sides develop a sense of confidence that they can control escalation? The management of risk on a regular basis may foster the self-deception that risks will continue to be managed and encourage a tendency to play ever riskier brinkmanship games.

The pivotal role of risk in deterrence underlines the cost-effectiveness of a minimalist posture. Because of the high potential costs involved, nuclear deterrence rests not on the certainty of damage, but on its possibility (i.e., on the uncertainty of being able to avoid it). Minimum deterrence is strengthened by the weight of potential cost, which is at the heart of the concept of "unacceptable damage." This in turn greatly reduces the significance of the chief drivers of nuclear maximalism: credibility and vulnerability.

Unacceptable Damage

Minimum deterrence as conceived here goes beyond the conception of existential deterrence in two ways. First, it holds that the quantum of damage that is "unacceptable" and hence sufficient to deter an adversary is very low; and second, it regards relative damage as irrelevant. As regards the first, Bundy's conception of existential deterrence rests on the assumption that it requires the colossal damage potential of thermonuclear weapons to obtain deterrence.[61] But this need not be the case. Why should the threat of damage on a scale lower than that wrought by thermonuclear weapons not deter? U.S. and Russian strategic thinking is colored by the historical experience of the Second World War and the vast damage that it witnessed. To conceive of a level of damage as "unacceptable" required one to think of very large-scale destruction. This facilitated the notion that deterrence can only work at a very high level of damage expectancy, and hence the preoccupation with "mutual assured destruction" (MAD). It is hard to believe that the same level of damage is required to deter states today. It does not require the threat of virtual extinction to deter. Contemporary societies, one would think, are quite easily deterred by a relatively "low" level of potential damage (i.e., a level of damage that might be caused by a single small nuclear weapon). Which U.S. government would risk a war if there were even a small chance of a small nuclear weapon hitting a small American city? What conceivable objective would be worth the risk? From the Indian standpoint, the argument is exactly the same. Even small nuclear weapons have the potential to do harm of great magnitude. The logic applies to all societies. Bundy makes the point starkly: "If I kill a million and he kills a million, have I won or lost? No special national attitude is required for the right answer: I have lost, and lost overwhelmingly. It does not help me at all that *so has he*."[62]

One may go a step further and ask: How does it benefit me if my adversary loses ten million and I lose one million? Or, for that matter, a tenth of that? Minimum deterrence rejects the notion that relative damage is meaningful. Deterrence rests on the potential for absolute damage to the deterree regardless of the level of damage that may be suffered by the deterrer. In a nuclear confrontation, the logic applies equally to both sides. Minimum deterrence between hostile nuclear states is best conceived in terms of mutual unacceptable damage (MUD), not MAD. Relative capability (the ability to do more damage) does not matter, only absolute capability (to do unacceptable damage) does. In setting the appropriate parameters of such a strategy, the right question to ask is not how much is enough, but how *little* is enough. The answer cannot be precise, but is surely "not much."

Indian strategists of a minimalist persuasion recognize this. K. Subrahmanyam accepts that "deterrence is not to be measured in terms of any equation of damages each side can inflict on the other."[63] In absolute terms, "one bomb on one city is unacceptable."[64] How much damage that can do is also known.[65] Thus, "When we talk of deterrence between Pakistan and India, is Kashmir worth the loss of Lahore for the Pakistanis? . . . Will the Chinese risk Kunmin and Chengdu at present and even Shanghai and Guangzu later . . . for any conceivable political, military and strategic objective?"[66]

The implication is clear. Minimum deterrence does not require a calculation of the balance of capabilities in a nuclear relationship. Whether one side has more and/or "better" weapons does not matter. Equally, whether one's adversary actually subscribes to the tenets of minimum deterrence is of little significance. In practice, *all* deterrence is minimum deterrence because no one can afford to treat the risk of one bomb on one city as acceptable. The Cuban Missile Crisis of 1962 and the Soviet-Chinese border clashes of 1969 reflect this.[67] In both cases, the state which enjoyed an apparent qualitative and quantitative advantage *and* subscribed to an official doctrine basing deterrence on massive destruction thought it prudent not to cross the nuclear threshold. For India, it follows that the specific capabilities and doctrines of others do not matter much. Thus, neither the size of China's arsenal nor the specific doctrine espoused by its leaders has a significant bearing on India's capacity to deter that country.

Some strategists argue that different adversaries have different tolerance levels. Sundarji holds that factors such as the size of a nation, its "psycho-political calculation," degree of development, and level of democracy determine how much is required to deter a specific nation.[68] Gurmeet Kanwal uses a similar argument to assert that China and Pakistan are hard to deter because they are nondemocratic states, and, moreover, that China (for no reason that he cites) is harder to deter than Pakistan.[69] Such views, which do not reflect empirical evidence, encourage needless expansion of India's deterrent capabilities. Ironically, even offensive realists advocating a large deterrent force do not make this kind of argument.[70]

In principle, it is possible that tolerance levels may vary, but in practice such putative differences, if any, are impossible to determine. More to the point, where nuclear weapons are concerned, they are irrelevant unless one makes the absurd claim, for instance, that an adversary may tolerate a million dead, possibly two, but not three! Finally, the low threshold of unacceptable damage asserted here is not offset by the reality of actual historical wars, in which millions of casualties were "tolerated." Large wars invariably develop a destructive dynamic as they unfold. There is no evidence that leaders calculate in advance that a few million dead are acceptable damage. On the contrary, powerful nations sometimes lose small wars precisely because they have low thresholds of unacceptable damage. The U.S. withdrawal from Vietnam, the Soviet departure from Afghanistan, and the Indian decision to wind up its failed "peacekeeping" campaign in Sri Lanka are clear evidence of this.

Credibility and Survivability

Deterrence theorists place much emphasis on credibility.[71] Indian doctrine is said to be one of "credible" minimum deterrence, but what exactly is meant by "credible" has never been made clear. A fundamental difficulty inherent in the concept is that deterrence rests on the paradox of threatening to do precisely what one wishes to avoid, i.e., engage in nuclear conflict. Because deterrence involves a threat that is difficult to carry out, it is said to be more effective if one can communicate will or resolve. In India's Draft Nuclear Doctrine (DND), there is an emphasis on "will" and on communicating that will: "any adversary must know that India can and will retaliate."[72] But rather than basing credibility on the political logic of deterrence—the adversary's fear of any kind of nuclear conflict—the DND follows the well-trodden path of the operational logic of deterrence and, inevitably, makes the strategy itself the text of communication. Once weapons and their characteristics become the symbolic media of communication, conveying not only capability but also will, the expansionary logic of the operational component of deterrence becomes well and truly embedded. The DND's failure to separate the two logics of deterrence leads it into typically contradictory positions. For "credible" deterrence, it leans heavily on the operational component of deterrence; for facilitating deterrence stability, arms control and confidence-building, it shifts to the political component in the form of declaratory positions on no-first-use and on nonuse against nonnuclear states. No mention is made of credibility here, though declarations of intent are not, strictly speaking, credible. From an adversary's standpoint, one's stated intentions can be either deliberately misleading or subject to change at any time in the future.

Credibility is also frequently equated with the effectiveness of one's weapons. Deterrence is said to be effective if the adversary is "convinced" of one's ability to retaliate in sufficient numbers, and with sufficient power and accuracy.[73] There must be a "guaranteed second strike."[74] A minimum deterrent is defined in terms of "assured survivability against repeated attrition attacks."[75] This places a premium on survivability, which is an essential prerequisite for second strike capability.[76] For forces to be more survivable, they must be protected by means of hardened, hidden, dispersed, or mobile basing.[77] For maximum survivability, the SLBM is the preferred delivery vehicle.[78] These are strong requirements, but, as will be shown shortly, unnecessary ones.

The issue of credibility is really a problem of one's perception of one's *own* capability. Because the rationality paradox—threatening to do what one wishes to avoid (i.e., unleash nuclear weapons)—makes deterrence inherently problematic, national strategists have to convince *themselves* that deterrence is credible. This breeds a self-regarding logic that pushes strategic thought in the direction of the concrete characteristics of one's nuclear weapons. Numbers, reliability, accuracy, and survivability become important features determining credibility. This kind of thinking is an extension of thinking on conventional weapons. But nuclear weapons are different from conventional weapons: they are not straightforward Clausewitzian instruments of politics. As Waltz so concisely puts it, "contemplating war when the use of nuclear weapons is possible focuses one's attention not on the probability of victory, but on the *possibility* of annihilation," and hence "the problem of the credibility of deterrence, a big worry in a conventional world, disappears in a nuclear one."[79] Any potential attacker has first to think of, if not "the possibility of annihilation," at least the possibility of a calamity of colossal proportions. Thus, in considering a first strike, the potential attacker is inhibited by the possibility that even a small retaliatory strike will cause intolerable damage. From this perspective, a very small risk of failure is too great to be taken. For deterrence to be effective, one need not worry about the technical sophistication of one's forces, or about their vulnerability or survivability.

In fact, it is a very simple and useful exercise to consider deterrence from an other-regarding standpoint. What would it take, for instance, to deter Pakistan? According to one calculation, a single small nuclear explosion of twenty kilotons targeted only on the cantonment area of Karachi would, as per an estimate for 1990, result in 128,000 immediate deaths.[80] A bigger blast targeting the city center would cause far greater damage. In that case, how many weapons does India really need to deter Pakistan? And how sophisticated would they have to be? Above all, what political objective would Pakistan consider worth pursuing against even a very small risk of such levels of damage? The use of terms like "credibility," "survivability," and "effectiveness" has to be seen from this perspective. If the political component of deterrence is given priority over the operational, an other-regarding logic of the kind used above becomes the basis of deterrence strategy. This logic, which rests the calculus of credibility and effectiveness on the adversary's risk, induces restraint without sacrificing security.

Another means of enhancing credibility, it is said, is to convey the impression that one may not quite be in control of the situation. Thus, a state "can threaten to stumble into a war even if it cannot credibly threaten to invite one."[81] By conveying the impression that it is a "contingently unsafe actor," it can raise the risk of war, thereby reinforcing deterrence.[82] The notion that a contingently unsafe actor—or the impression of being one—deters more effectively is questionable. The adversary is deterred not by one's motivations or intentions, which cannot be gauged for certain, but by the *possibility* of a successful nuclear second strike. There is no need to manipulate that possibility by turning it into a greater probability. On the contrary, there is always some risk that the appearance of irrationality or loss of control may evoke responses that are unstable, thereby inducing actual loss of control. Whichever way one looks at it, credibility in a nuclear world is inherent in the possession of nuclear weapons. It follows that the requirements of minimum deterrence are very few indeed. One need only have a small number of weapons, and these need not be assuredly very accurate, highly reliable, or "survivable" in order to deter. Hardened silos, mobile missiles, and SLBMs are all superfluous. Even without them, an adversary has to contend with the risk of unacceptable damage. The simpler the deterrent, the more cost-effective it is.

From the discussion above, a number of elementary principles follow.

Size, Variety, and Technical Sophistication

Numbers do not matter. But Indian thinking is divided on this (see Chapter 3). It is frequently asserted that they do: that India must have sufficient numbers to make sure that its weapons "get through," or to be confident its deterrent is more than a "laughable flea-bite" for China.[83] One commentator calls for "overwhelming superiority" vis-à-vis Pakistan.[84] Others raise concerns about India's "two-front problem" since it has to contend with both China and Pakistan.[85] Size in terms of a bigger bang (high-yield weapons, usually thermonuclear weapons) also draws support from several strategists for its allegedly greater deterrence value.[86] With respect to delivery vehicles, there is wide support for a triad, mainly on the vulnerability grounds discussed above. Technical sophistication is also seen as an essential requirement to ensure reliability and penetrability.[87] For this reason, it is sometimes argued that further testing of warheads is desirable.[88] But minimum deterrence does not require any of this. Unless one contemplates actually fighting and winning a nuclear war, there is no need to have forces that are large, efficient, and survivable. These characteristics do not add anything to deterrence, which is based on the creation of a small risk with great consequences. Once that has been achieved through the possession of a small number of simple weapons, the marginal utility of additional investment in "improving" deterrence capabilities is zero.

Targeting, No First Use, and the Timing of Retaliation

Might there be exceptional circumstances in which a nuclear war is actually fought? There might. Deterrence, after all, cannot be guaranteed to work, as we have seen in Chapter 1. Minimum deterrence calls for a posture which sharply limits this possibility. On the question of targeting, almost all Indian strategists are opposed to counterforce options.[89] However, some do hedge their bets, leaving open the possibility of counterforce targeting for limited purposes.[90] The main reason for rejecting counterforce strategy from a minimum deterrence perspective is that it makes war per se more doable. There is also an unacceptable risk of escalation, particularly since many counterforce targets (such as airfields and cantonments) are close to population centers. Tactical nuclear weapons are a liability. They encourage the false perception that escalation to countervalue or "city-busting" war can be prevented. A limited nuclear war may be possible, but one cannot mortgage a nation's future on it.

No first use (NFU) has been a first principle of Indian strategy from the beginning and has been reiterated periodically over the years.[91] Prime Minister Vajpayee specified in 1998 that this included commitments against both nuclear and nonnuclear states.[92] This was qualified in the January 2003 press release, which stated that India reserved the option to respond with nuclear weapons to a chemical or biological attack. NFU means much symbolically, but not much strategically. It requires the adversary to take one's commitment on trust, which is hardly likely in a relationship between hostile nuclear-armed states. It is sometimes argued that NFU determines posture, making it more defensive. That is not true. If it were, Pakistan's refusal to adopt NFU should have led it to actively deploy its weapons, perhaps in a state of advanced readiness, at least during crises. That has not been the case. On the other hand, should conventional war break out, it is hard to believe that India will not deploy its weapons in much the same way as Pakistan would. If there is a crisis and weapons are in place, no country can set much store by its adversary's declaration of NFU.

Retaliation need not be immediate, as some strategists acknowledge.[93] The DND calls for a "rapid punitive response," but such a requirement also encourages a hair-trigger posture and launch-on-warning response. These in turn facilitate early delegation of launch authority. In short, a prompt retaliation strategy may hasten the onset of nuclear conflict. Minimum deterrence does not necessitate early response. On the contrary, since a potential attacker is aware that a response is possible at any time, whether early or late, and also has no certainty of 100 percent success in a first strike, that attacker is deterred.

Escalation, Compellence, and Preemption

The risk of escalation calls for abundant caution in several respects. First, it rules out counterforce strategy and the feasibility of limited nuclear war. Second, it eliminates conventional war as a rational strategy because the risk of escalation violates the two-steps-short rule. Sumit Ganguly and Harrison Wagner argue that because neither India nor Pakistan has an incentive to fight a nuclear war or even to respond to an accidental launch by retaliating instantly, escalation will not occur, and conventional war is still possible.[94] This represents a realist perspective, which sees escalation and bargaining as a rational, well-thought-out processes. But escalation is also influenced by psychological factors, and there is an empirical link between these and war.[95] The problem for decision makers is that they cannot know escalation will not take place, or that it is perfectly safe to go to conventional war. The risk involved is simply too great to be accepted with confidence, as Indian and Pakistani crisis behavior in 1999 and 2001–2 shows (see Chapter 4). By extension, between nuclear rivals conventional balances do not matter.[96] It follows that the acquisition of conventional hardware other than for border skirmishes and special operations is wasteful. Furthermore, the view that a limited conventional war is practicable may be on the right side of the two-steps-short rule, but hovers dangerously at its edges, for the adversary's conception of a limited war may differ significantly from one's own.

The risk of escalation makes the resort to coercive diplomacy or compellence problematic. Compellence strategy risks high tension, loss of control, and rapidly spiraling escalation.[97] Preemption or a so-called decapitating strike against a state's command and control centers is also ruled out because it cannot be guaranteed to be successful in preventing a retaliatory response.[98] However, it is sometimes argued that if a war is imminent, there is an incentive to strike first. "If one believes . . . that an attack is about to take place, then one might not require a guarantee of a perfect first strike, but merely a reasonable chance that one can destroy enough of the other side's force to make a meaningful difference in the damage one suffers."[99] An extension of this argument is the view that where two small and vulnerable nuclear forces are in confrontation, "both sides would have strong incentives to strike first to prevent preemption."[100] The "incentive to strike first" is questionable. One may "believe" that an enemy strike is imminent, but one cannot know. What matters is that one does have a good idea of the consequences of initiating war. As Alexander Cadogan, a senior British bureaucrat, is said to have remarked in 1938, "it would be very difficult to choose any course of action that might plunge Europe into war now to avert what might be a war later on."[101] In a nuclear world, the imperative not to act first and precipitate disaster is far more powerful. In any case, several crises have occurred in recent India-Pakistan relations without anything approaching a first-strike scenario, prompting P. R. Chari, whom one would be hard put to describe as a nuclear optimist, to dismiss the notion of preemption as a "myth."[102]

Deployment

Perhaps the most important feature of India's strategic posture is the absence of active deployment, sometimes referred to as "recessed deterrence."[103] Though the government has not chosen to make it official, India's weapons are known to be kept in a disaggregated state. Not only are the warheads stored separately from delivery vehicles, the warhead components themselves (nuclear cores and assemblies) are kept apart.[104] The result is that the "strategic distance"—conceived here in terms of time—between India's weapons and those of its adversaries is considerable. Pakistan's matching stance has brought a strong element of stability into their relationship. The margin of safety thus achieved does not detract from deterrence. As Sundarji puts it:

> "Weaponization" need not mean that the nuclear warhead has already been married to the bomb-casing or placed in the missile's bomb compartment. Likewise, "deployed" need not mean that the completely assembled missile has to be in or very near its launch pad. If the doctrine demands reaction within say six hours, the definition of "weaponized" and "deployed" would reflect the state of readiness which such doctrine demands.[105]

But there is a tradeoff here. The process of warhead assembly and mating of warheads with delivery vehicles is likely to occur, if at all, during times of tension, with a tendency to act speedily. This carries a significant risk with respect to safety. Besides, the process of deployment during a crisis is in itself likely to raise tensions because the adversary perceives it to be highly threatening.[106] That having been said, the balance in the tradeoff still favors the nondeployment side, especially considering the high level of tension that has prevailed between India and Pakistan since their official nuclearization. Ideally, an agreement to adhere to nondeployment would buttress this stability. But there does not seem to be sufficient incentive for it. First, the very fact that deterrence without deployment has existed for so long despite mutual tensions has given nondeployment the status of a convention that is already well established. India-Pakistan confrontations have not produced (so far) the kind of high-intensity interaction that might generate pressure for arms control. South Asia's crises have been serious, but they have not been comparable to the Cuban Missile Crisis. Ironically, the pressure for serious arms control is only likely to come *after* deployment, when the risks confronting India and Pakistan, or, less likely, India and China, become similar to those faced by the United States and the Soviet Union during the Cold War.[107]

Command and Control

Two aspects of a nuclear command and control system are particularly germane here.[108] One is the oft-stated problem of vulnerability. This is not as serious an issue as is widely believed. As we have seen, deterrence is based on the adversary's risk. Whether or not a command and control (C&C) system is highly efficient cannot have a significant impact on the calculation of risk, since the adversary cannot know how well one's C&C system works. More importantly, the adversary cannot risk launching a sudden "decapitating" strike since such a strike cannot be guaranteed to succeed completely. However, a well-organized C&C system is still necessary to ensure continuity and stability in case of an unexpected *internal* disaster, such as a natural calamity (say, a devastating earthquake) that disrupts the system or a terrorist strike against the leadership.

The second aspect relates to the so-called always/never problem.[109] For political leaders, it is said, there is a constant need to be sure that decisions are effectively made, and orders carried out, by both the personnel and instruments under them. This is the "always" side. On the "never" side, leaders worry about the possibility of unauthorized launch, whether deliberate or accidental. There is said to be a tension between the two, since the always side exercises a pull toward decentralization (delegation to avoid vulnerability) and the latter a pull toward centralized control. From the standpoint of minimum deterrence as conceived here, the problem is not a serious one. As shown above, vulnerability to a first strike, the main concern on the "always" side, is not really a problem because an attacker can never be sure of eliminating the risk of retaliation. On the other hand, the possibility of unauthorized launch—by accident or by renegades—is a major problem. Here, the weight of risk is on oneself, for one can never be sure of eliminating the risk of something going wrong internally. A nondeployed posture reduces much of the risk of unauthorized launch. In short, there is really no always/never problem, only a never problem. Extensive care has to be taken to ensure the safety of leaders and weapons, the reliability of personnel connected with nuclear weapons, and above all, the effectiveness of control systems, to ensure that an unauthorized launch does not occur. Delegation of launch authority must be avoided.

Conclusion

This chapter has outlined the basic contours of a theory of minimum deterrence on which an effective, inexpensive, and safe nuclear posture can be based. Key aspects—the relationship between nuclear and subnuclear conflict, and missile defense—are left for later discussion in full (Chapters 4 and 5). To reiterate, minimum deterrence rests on the risks one's weapons pose to an adversary, not on one's assurance that the weapons will be efficient, credible, or invulnerable. This does not resolve the security dilemma, but reduces its proportions. It keeps to a low level the requirements of deterrence, thereby gaining security, while incurring relatively little risk. Any recommendation on number and types would be arbitrary. Arguably, a couple of dozen unassembled warheads designed for land-based intermediate-range missiles will suffice to deter India's adversaries. More will not deter better. SLBMs would incur cost without adding to deterrence. Deployment would aggravate tensions. A missile defense system will do no harm and some good. As Chapters 6 and 7 show, a truly minimum deterrent will also be safer from the potential impact of terrorists and conducive to a healthy democratic polity.

On the whole, Indian thinking on nuclear weapons has been restrained, and many of the fundamentals delineated above are in fact part and parcel of Indian doctrinal thinking. But it is also self-contradictory and troubling in important respects. The emphasis on credibility is particularly problematic, since it facilitates a self-regarding, self-assuring, and open-ended conception of deterrence, whereas minimum deterrence is fundamentally rooted in an other-regarding and minimalistic approach associated with the risks faced by the adversary.

Political leaders need to think of nuclear strategy in strictly political terms. It is the task of military officials and some strategists to think operationally and to plan for the possibility of war. Such planning is akin to "fantasy planning."[110] It produces "fantasy documents" that are coherent and unambiguous, but are nevertheless "imaginative fictions about what people hope will happen after things go wrong."[111] Such plans are intrinsically fantastic because they can never be known to be fulfilled. In part, they are also "rhetorical devices" designed to convince others that the planners are capable of resolving a problem.[112] Such thinking turns out arcane designs for fighting a nuclear war, with attendant force requirements, which are far removed from reality. For those at the helm of national decision making, it is neither necessary nor wise to think much about the unthinkable. To think about operational aspects is more likely to produce the very outcomes that a political leader wants to avoid: forces and postures that invite tensions and the possibility of war.

The dilemma of deterrence remains. On one hand, because of the strategic environment, some form of deterrence is desirable. India cannot escape the imperatives of an anarchic world in which there are at least some interlocutors whose intentions toward it are less than benevolent. However abhorrent nuclear weapons may be, it would hardly be advisable to depend entirely on the morality of adversaries to feel secure from nuclear threats. On the other hand, the risks and costs attached to nuclear weapons are immense. While there is no escape from the dilemma, it can be minimized by adhering to the conception of minimum deterrence discussed here. Where will India go? The next chapter makes the argument that the element of restraint in Indian nuclear thinking and practice is strong and deeply embedded. But it is not without inconsistency, which underscores the need for a more thorough and nuanced understanding of the requirements of minimum deterrence.

3

Strategic Culture

The preceding chapter shows how minimum deterrence can be kept to the lowest possible level in both quantitative and qualitative terms. Actual national postures vary with capability, historical experience, and normative choices. Once a set of integrated choices is made, this often crystallizes over time into a pattern of thought and action that is called "strategic culture." Future thinking and behavior is then shaped by strategic culture, which inhibits drastic shifts from occurring in spite of significant changes in a state's external and internal environments. Strategic culture is a useful concept for understanding repetitive patterns of strategic behavior and for anticipating alterations in that behavior in response to environmental changes. Because it is not static, it does tend to change in response to shifting threat perceptions and motivations. This can be problematic. A clear understanding of minimum deterrence as a concept and awareness of one's strategic culture are necessary to optimize strategy.

This chapter demonstrates that Indian strategic culture with respect to the realm of nuclear weapons is broadly in accord with the precepts of minimum deterrence outlined above. But because Indian thinking and practice lack clarity on minimum deterrence as a concept, particularly with respect to the operational aspect, there is a tendency toward drift. An assessment of India's strategic culture under changing circumstances is important in determining how well strategy conforms over time to the principles of minimum deterrence delineated in Chapter 2. While radical shifts may not occur, gradual change—particularly change that draws away from the primarily political approach outlined earlier to a primarily operational one—may take strategy well beyond the requirements of principle. If the tendency toward operational drift is left unchecked, it could lead to a needlessly expansion-oriented and risk-laden posture that, mimicking Cold War deterrence strategies, is propelled by a search for more and more capabilities in order to achieve higher degrees of "credibility," "survivability," and "readiness."

The chapter begins with a brief review of the current position of Indian doctrine and practice to illustrate its ambivalence. This is followed by a discussion of strategic culture as a concept. Thereafter, a detailed examination of the formation and development of Indian strategic culture with respect to nuclear weapons is undertaken. Because this strategic culture is dynamic, it is open to change. An appraisal of recent developments in strategic thinking and practice reveals the tension between the political and operational components of Indian strategic culture. The chapter concludes with an assessment of the implications of this tension for minimum deterrence. Since defensive realism permits a range of choices in the way that a state responds to the perception of threat, it is my contention that Indian leaders have the option to reduce this tension by directing strategic thought and behavior, and in effect strategic culture, toward a stronger political position that ensures nuclear security while limiting its costs and risks.

India's Ambiguous Nuclear Posture

In Chapter 2, we have seen that Indian nuclear thinking is unclear and often contradicts the tenets of minimum deterrence. Officially declared strategy reflects this. The doctrine of "credible minimum deterrence," yet to be enunciated fully in public, has undergone significant changes between 1998 and the present. In the wake of the 1998 tests, Prime Minister Atal Behari Vajpayee made a very brief announcement in Parliament on the components of this doctrine. The statement declared that testing is not essential for credibility, affirmed India's commitment to the principle of no first use (NFU) of nuclear weapons, and made it clear that arms control and disarmament remained high on the national agenda.[1] Beyond that, nothing was said about threats, deployment, the kind and number of weapons sought, targeting, and other details which are thought to be the stuff of deterrence strategy. Much of the public understanding of India's minimum deterrence doctrine until recently was based on the Draft Nuclear Doctrine (DND) released by the National Security Advisory Board (NSAB) in August 1999.[2] Enumerating its objectives, the DND calls for "credible minimum deterrence" based on a capacity for "punitive retaliation with nuclear weapons to inflict damage unacceptable to the [nuclear] aggressor." For this, the requirements are "sufficient, survivable and operationally prepared nuclear forces" and the organization and will to employ nuclear weapons should deterrence fail. The document proclaims NFU as a central tenet and commits India to nonuse against countries that are not nuclear and are not allied with nuclear powers. Robust conventional forces are deemed necessary in order to raise the nuclear threshold.

The DND envisages a triad of air-, land-, and sea-based delivery systems whose "survivability will be enhanced by a combination of multiple redundant systems, mobility, dispersion and deception." It distinguishes between an unspecified "peacetime deployment" and a shift to "fully employable forces" in the event of a conflict arising. There is an emphasis on credibility—"any adversary must know that India can and will retaliate"—and on effectiveness based on "reliability, timeliness, accuracy and weight of attack." The DND goes on to outline the requirements for command and control, security and safety, and research and development, and concludes by focusing on disarmament and arms control. The document has been criticized for its lack of clarity and its open-endedness.[3] Its call for a triad of delivery systems, and its emphasis on credibility, effectiveness, and survivability go against the grain of a true minimum deterrence posture since they put a premium on one's own confidence rather than on the risks faced by adversaries. In short, the DND reveals a distinct proclivity for the operational rather than the political aspect of deterrence.

However, as Minister of External Affairs Jaswant Singh told an interviewer subsequently, the report was released in order to generate a national debate and was "not a policy document of the Government of India."[4] In fact, Singh's interview provides a much more political exposition of Indian nuclear thinking. There are, to be sure, a number of common elements in the DND and the interview. Both declare that India will not be the first to use nuclear weapons; that its retaliation-only posture will be based on the mobility and dispersal of assets as well as on an unspecified level of redundancy; that a distinction has to be made between peacetime and active deployment, implying the possibility of a normally de-mated disposition of warheads and launch vehicles; and that ultimate authority over the arsenal must be civilian.

But Singh's enunciation of nuclear doctrine differs from the DND in important respects. First, while noting that nuclear assets must be survivable, he does not echo the DND's stress on India's need for "multiple redundant systems" for survivability. The latter implies a discomfort with small numbers and a proclivity for arms racing because its points of reference are the operational characteristics of an adversary's inventory. Second, Singh explicitly states that "parity is not essential for deterrence," that India will not engage in arms racing, and that minimum deterrence is only a question of "adequacy," not relative size—a point not evident in the DND. Third, Singh makes the crucial point that retaliation need not be instantaneous. The implication for stability is clear: there is no need for Indian nuclear forces to be on high alert status, ready for instant retaliation. This allows a relatively stable nonthreatening nuclear posture. Again, this is a question that is not addressed in the DND. Fourth, whereas the DND does not dwell on the question of targeting, Singh observes that "we have discarded the Cold War reference frame of nuclear war fighting," and that "we do not see nuclear weapons as weapons of war fighting," which is an unambiguous rejection of counterforce doctrine. Fifth, while the DND calls for a nuclear triad, Singh holds that, though development in this respect will go on, it is "premature" to talk of a triad and, more important, that a triad is not a "pre-requisite for credibility."

The overall effect of the interview is to convey a relatively strong sense of commitment to minimum deterrence (as defined in Chapter 2) based on a relaxed posture with few weapons. In this respect, Singh is more reassuring than the DND. His delineation of nuclear doctrine is in keeping with a pattern of strategic preferences that treats nuclear weapons with great circumspection. This helps explain the early initiative taken by Prime Minister Vajpayee in February 1999 (less than a year after the nuclear tests of 1998) to travel to Lahore in Pakistan in an attempt to establish regional strategic stability. However, there are two contradictions in Singh's statement of doctrine: his emphasis on survivability to "ensure credibility"; and his assertion that the concept of "minimum" cannot be a "fixed physical quantification," but is a "dynamic concept" that is "firmly rooted in the strategic environment, technological imperatives and national security needs." Both statements leave open the door to an expansionary conception of adequacy that is incongruent with the general tenor of his views and the concept of minimum deterrence formulated in these pages.

The brief announcement on nuclear doctrine and on the establishment of a Nuclear Command Authority (NCA) in January 2003 added something to our understanding of official Indian thinking.[5] Its main points on doctrine were:

1. Reaffirmation of "credible" minimum deterrence;
2. Reiteration of NFU;
3. The threat of "massive" retaliation in response to a first strike;
4. Nonuse of nuclear weapons against nonnuclear weapon states;
5. The option to retaliate with nuclear weapons against a chemical or biological attack;
6. Adherence to strict export controls; and
7. Renewed commitment to arms control through participation in Fissile Material Cutoff Treaty (FMCT) negotiations, continued observance of the national moratorium on testing, and sustained commitment to universal disarmament.

Though these commitments do tell us something about India's deterrence posture, none of them has a direct bearing on the central character of *minimum* deterrence. No first use is not much use in this respect. It is a promise rather than a guarantee, and adversaries are hardly likely to take it seriously in their calculations of risk, which is the basis of deterrence. Besides, in comparison with earlier statements, it is diluted by the exceptions made with regard to chemical and biological weapons. Massive retaliation is a threat that will in any case be expected by an adversary. It is also basically unnecessary, since it does not take much to deter. "Unacceptable damage" can be caused even without it. The pronouncement nearest to conveying a commitment to minimum deterrence is the pledge not to test, since a sophisticated arsenal of diverse and "reliable" weapons would require testing. This may be regarded as making a virtue out of necessity, but the commitment is firm, with no hedging. The critical aspect of minimum deterrence that is not mentioned in the announcement is the perception that deterrence strategy is in place with few weapons, with weapons of relatively little variety and sophistication, and with weapons that are not deployed or even assembled. That this aspect has not been officially articulated does not mean that a minimum deterrence doctrine does not exist. Quite clearly, it does. That is evident in its practice. However, the search for diverse capabilities—land-, air-, and sea-based—shows that the concept of minimum deterrence is not consistent. Apart from the need to achieve retaliatory capability against China, the current crop of aircraft- and missile-deliverable weapons is adequate. The only argument for more would be that they are needed to minimize vulnerability. But, as has been shown in Chapter 2, vulnerability is not a meaningful issue in minimum deterrence. Sufficiency must be defined in terms of the risk of retaliation faced by the adversary in contemplating recourse to nuclear weapons, not one's own risk in being devastated by a first strike.

This brief review and the critique of Indian nuclear-strategic thought in Chapter 2 show the lack of consistency in India's minimum deterrence doctrine. If ambivalence is allowed to persist, the possibility of nuclear thinking and practice drifting toward an open-ended operational conception of deterrence will increase. On the positive side, as will be seen below, Indian strategic culture has sufficiently deep historical roots to restrain this possibility. But because change cannot be ruled out, its character and dynamics ought to be carefully assessed.

Nuclear Weapons and Strategic Culture

India's nuclear history is not a short one. The possibility of going nuclear and the awareness of India's potential were present since Independence in 1947.

Capability was achieved as early as 1974. Weapons were put together by about 1990. Deterrence was officially embraced much later in 1998. More than half a decade later, notwithstanding recurrent crises, its weapons are still not deployed. This history of restraint is best understood as a consequence of Indian strategic culture. While national leaders and strategists set much stock in doctrine, the basic parameters of nuclear posture tend to be set by normative preferences exercised in a specific historical context. These then become patterned over a period of time into set ways of doing things. Bureaucratic and interest-group pressures, the politics of symbolism, and technological imperatives are bound to play a role in pushing strategy this way and that, but the basic patterns are normally resistant to dramatic change. The concept of strategic culture provides useful insight into this reality and helps explain some puzzling aspects of Indian strategic behavior. Few analysts have been able to understand, for example, why, over the decades since Independence, India held fast to its nuclear option and yet refused to allocate sufficient resources to make that option more meaningful; why it was by all accounts a reluctant nuclearizer, given the passage of nearly a quarter-century between its first and second tests; and why, even well after announcing that it has become a nuclear power, it has been extraordinarily slow to develop its operational capabilities.

During the past decade or so, students of world politics and security have given considerable attention to various facets of culture.[6] The concept of strategic culture has helped shed considerable light on the singularities of national strategic behavior.[7] Strategic culture may be defined, in Colin Gray's words, as "the socially constructed and transmitted assumptions, habits of mind, traditions, and preferred methods of operation—that is, behavior—that are more or less specific to a particular geographically based security community."[8] This definition encompasses both habits of mind and habits of practice. Viewed as a set of structured preferences, strategic culture at one level entails fundamental understandings about the nature of the strategic environment, the role of force in that environment, perceptions of threat, and the framing of responses to perceived threats. At another level, it involves preferences relating to the operationalization of those responses in terms of the quality and quantity of military forces considered necessary in order to meet national objectives.

A focus on strategic culture need not be viewed as antithetical to a realist approach. Realists are culturalists too. As Gray points out, all behavior is cultural, so "there are, and can be, no uncultured realists."[9] In particular, defensive realism, by admitting the role of agency at the level of the state, provides conceptual space for strategic culture. Cultural explanations have their limitations, as Jack Snyder's review of anthropological studies of war shows, but their influence in shaping patterns of behavior (such as the frequency and intensity of war) is evident.[10] More broadly, state policies are an amalgam of the structural and the unit level (state/group/individual), and of material and ideational factors.[11] I take the position here that while state-level decisions about strategy in the context of systemic anarchy are made by conscious choice, strategic culture itself shapes policy in the long run. Once the seminal choices are made, thinking and practice tend to crystallize over time into a strategic culture that acts as an *intermediate structure* which molds the responses of the state to external and internal stimuli. Without being static, strategic culture narrows the range of outcomes when there is pressure for change. In the normal course, strategic culture changes slowly, but accumulated change over time may make a substantial difference. Because it is dynamic, it needs monitoring and appropriate social action to reinforce or change it as desired.

The concept of strategic culture has evolved over three generations of theorizing.[12] The first generation viewed strategic culture as the product of variations in macroenvironmental factors such as historical experience, geography, societal structures, and military institutions. It developed concepts such as "national character" and "style" to explain putative differences in state behavior, as between "weak" democracies like the United States and "tough" authoritarian regimes like the Soviet Union.[13] Such differences were also highlighted to stress the risks associated with misunderstanding the adversary.[14] The second generation perceived strategic culture as a hegemonizing tool used by elites to draw support for declaratory strategies masking actual operational strategies. The third and newest generation regards strategic culture not as deeply rooted in distant social and political history, but as the product of recent historical military-strategic experience. This encompasses a variety of concepts and behaviors. For instance, "national command philosophy" is a "unified structure of beliefs" that establishes, among other things, the "preferred attitude toward uncertainty and risk."[15] "Military culture" consists of "collectively held beliefs within a particular military organization" in relation to its internal workings as well as its external environment.[16] A nation's "political culture," similarly, consists of orientations on a larger scale. In the realm of nuclear strategy, for example, English, French, and German policy makers' decisions are said to display distrust of their own peoples and a desire to exercise political leadership.[17] In general, there is a stress on norm-driven strategic behavior, as opposed to the rational calculus emphasized by realists.[18] National proclivities continue to be adduced, such as the U.S. preference for low casualty rates, for reliance on technical and economic superiority, and for the belief that force should only be used if there is a clear and visible threat; or the Chinese partiality for the use of force to resolve disputes.[19]

The early approaches remain popular today. For example, nations are shown to have distinctive "negotiating styles": the Chinese are subtle, Russians relatively aggressive, Japanese rigid, and so on.[20] Distinctive regional modes of international behavior have been identified, such as an "Asian way" and a "Pacific way," which include a predilection for uniquely local forms of conflict resolution without the involvement of external powers.[21] It is evident from the foregoing that the concept is very broad, encompassing a wide range of preferences and behaviors. A central problem is the lack of theoretical rigor in demonstrating the linkage between identified cultural traits and actual behavior. This is particularly true when societal characteristics are held to be the primary determinants of behavior.

The latter failing is commonplace in the few studies that have tried to apply the concept to the Indian context. For instance, George Tanham paints a simplistic portrait of the alleged effects of culture on Indian thinking: "The acceptance of life as a mystery and the inability to manipulate events impedes preparation for the future in all areas of life, including the strategic. The Indian belief in life cycles and repetitions, in particular, limits planning in the Western sense."[22]

Betraying a less than cursory knowledge of the material aspects of Indian history and culture, such assertions confuse rather than illuminate. In an opposite and equally distorted view, Andrew Latham holds that Indian "security culture," drawing heavily upon the writings of the realist ancient thinker Kautilya, discourages the acceptance of confidence-building measures (CBMs) because "such measures operate on a premise that is directly contrary to the Kautilyan paradigm."[23] This is patently incorrect: India has agreed on a wide range of CBMs with China and Pakistan.[24] Besides, it is hard to see why a realist worldview should prevent arms control. It did not do so in the U.S.-Soviet relationship. Jaswant Singh makes similarly unsupportable generalizations on (Hindu) India's supposed religious pacifism and the resultant "emasculation of state power," and on the alleged absence of "a territorial consciousness and a strategic sense about the protection of the territory of residence."[25] Likewise, Sandy Gordon claims, among other things, that "the hierarchical nature of caste naturally leads to a propensity towards compartmentalization and exclusivity" which "undermines seriously coordination and planning."[26] Lacking methodological rigor, such assertions do not have much utility.

Perhaps the only systematic attempt to delineate the contours of Indian strategic culture has been undertaken by Kanti Bajpai.[27] However, Bajpai limits himself to a discussion of the divergent views of three streams of thought—identified by him as the Nehruvian, the liberal, and the hyperrealist—and does not attempt to examine set practices. Schools of thought by themselves do not constitute "cultures." Culture is an amalgam of thought and practice. One might speak of subcultures, but again, unless this incorporates variations in practice, such disaggregation has limited value. It is more methodologically sound as well as helpful to examine the overall pattern of thinking and behavior to define a strategic culture, with the proviso that variation in thought may be an agency of change.[28] Bajpai's useful essay, which throws much light on Indian thinking about strategic matters generally, and nuclear strategy in particular, is also hampered by a search for links to ancient history and the assumption that, in the absence of a corpus of classical thought on strategy, a "central strategic paradigm cannot be delineated with the kind of textual richness and rigor that Johnston was able to bring to bear in the Chinese case."[29] My position is different. It is not always necessary to dig deep into history for evidence of strategic culture. A specific strategic culture may be of relatively recent origin. The province of nuclear politics is historically limited. While the immediate historical context is important in understanding its genesis, the revolutionary character of nuclear weapons mitigates the need for more than a general knowledge of the distant past. The picture of "structured preferences" that a nuclear-strategic culture presents consists of relatively recent ideas about the strategic environment and its politics, ideas about how best to respond to it, and crucially, the actual behavior that is exhibited.

The concept of strategic culture employed here is precise and less prone to loose generalization than some of the work identified earlier. It applies to nuclear weapons alone and not to military strategy as a whole. It treats strategic culture as historically located within the time frame of the existence of nuclear weapons. It acknowledges that strategic culture is shaped by a specific congruence of factors: historical context, technological capability, the availability of economic resources, and, above all, ethical norms relating to nuclear weapons. It juxtaposes thought with action. There is no attempt to identify Indian strategic culture in its entirety even in this limited context. Nuclear weapons are a class unto themselves. Their revolutionary character makes only the immediate historical context of their genesis relevant and gives them a high degree of autonomy in shaping strategy. Thus, whether a nation's broad military culture in the realm of conventional warfare is inclined toward offensive or defensive strategy is largely irrelevant, as is the attitude toward risk. Given the watershed between prenuclear-strategic and nuclear-strategic culture, it makes sense to focus tightly on national habits of thought and practice as they coalesce into an integral whole in the nuclear era.[30]

Cultural theories generally distinguish between two categories: beliefs and practices. The present formulation goes further. Here, strategic culture has three components: idea, practice, and structure. The ideational component consists of two levels. The *level of basic assumptions and beliefs* relates to the nature of interstate relations, threat perceptions, and, in this setting, the role of nuclear weapons. The *operational level* relates to preferences about the state's responses to threats in terms of the nature of nuclear deployment, the number and types of weapons considered adequate, targeting doctrine, and some notion of conditions under which the use of nuclear weapons may be considered necessary. The component of practice consists of repetitive patterns of action over time. Practice is in constant interaction with thought and, in conditions of equilibrium, the two are mutually reinforcing. This is similar to the interaction in organization theory between the "substance" of culture, or shared belief systems, and cultural "forms" or observable expressions of culture.[31] When there is pressure for change, whether as a result of external or domestic factors or both, embedded thinking and/or practice restrains change, i.e., it contributes to either continuity or a preference for incremental over rapid change. Here, I introduce the concept of structure to highlight key overarching characteristics of nuclear-strategic culture. This has three facets: the mode of response to changes in the strategic environment (in terms of restraint versus precipitateness), tolerance of ambiguity (high versus low), and disposition toward arms control (positive versus negative). These give a distinctive quality and an element of continuity to the dynamic content of strategic culture.

Indian Strategic Culture in the Nuclear Context

Indian strategic culture in relation to nuclear weapons may be defined as *nuclear minimalism*. Its chief characteristics are: (1) very limited acceptance of the utility of nuclear weapons as a source of national security; (2) a political rather than a technical or operational understanding of nuclear weapons (nuclear weapons do deter, yet are "nonusable"); and (3) restrained responses to pressures either to enhance or reduce national nuclear capabilities. Indian nuclear minimalism acknowledges that power (by extension, nuclear power too) is a prerequisite for security in an anarchic international system. At the same time, it considers nuclear weapons both morally unacceptable and detrimental to security because of the risks associated with it. This nuclear minimalism was established at the time India gained independence (two years after Hiroshima) and crystallized over the next two decades. At the beginning of the new millennium, it is under some pressure, but its strength belies the warnings of those who stress the risks of arms racing and high spending allegedly inherent in India's decision to go nuclear.

Unlike most earlier formulations, the present one stresses the dynamism of strategic culture. Culture is viewed as a "collective subjectivity."[32] It is socially constructed and hence constantly subjected to change.[33] In the normal course, strategic culture changes slowly, which gives it the characteristic of a stable structure analogous to language.[34] Like language, it is at once restrictive in some respects and enabling in others. For instance, Indian strategic culture simultaneously constrains arms racing and facilitates arms control.[35] A structure of beliefs and practices crystallized over time, strategic culture constrains choices and induces relative continuity even when there is a changing environment, whether external, domestic, or both. But because it is dynamic, it is also vulnerable to pressure and needs to be carefully monitored for corrective social action.

Ideally, a study of strategic culture should engage in cross-national comparison over time to show variations in structured preferences. This book is restricted to comparisons of strategic preferences within a single state—India—over time and across objects of analysis. Four kinds of evidence, two official and two nonofficial, are examined here: (1) official preferences that relate to basic assumptions and beliefs; (2) state behavior expressed through policies and actions; (3) eight sets of nonofficial analyses and recommendations (seven by leading individual strategic analysts, and one in the form of the DND); and (4) interviews with members of the strategic elite. Nonofficial thinking has a significant bearing on Indian strategic culture because nuclear weapons in an operational sense are little understood within Indian officialdom, and because the Indian state is in the process of becoming decentralized and more open to nonofficial inputs.[36] Aside from determining a structure of preferences, the analysis will test for the role of strategic culture in shaping outcomes by comparison with predictions based on realist analysis. It will also control for the effects of other domestic variables: leadership preferences, party preferences, bureaucratic politics, parliamentary inputs, and public opinion.

Official Beliefs and Practices

The Foundations of Indian Strategic Culture—From Gandhi and Nehru to Indira Gandhi. Realist thought and practice has been an integral part of Indian history. As Bharat Karnad has shown, concepts of hegemony, balance of power, war and diplomacy were well established in ancient times.[37] In the nuclear era, Indian thinking has been shaped by both realism and a normative antipathy toward nuclear weapons. The basic contours of Indian strategic culture with respect to nuclear weapons crystallized during the long incumbency of India's first prime minister, Jawaharlal Nehru (1947–64). Nehru's attitude toward nuclear weapons reflected the ambivalent mix of realism and moral principle that permeated his foreign and defense policies.[38] Even Mahatma Gandhi, his political mentor, reflected this uncertainty. As Karnad has pointed out, Gandhi did not have an absolute commitment to nonviolence. While he often took an uncompromising position on issues of war and violence, he was aware of the practical problems involved in implementing his ideas.[39] On one hand, Gandhi rejected nuclear weapons and deterrence outright as immoral and declared that nonviolence was the only answer to the violence of the atomic bomb. On the other, he could not abandon the idea of using force for national defense. Late in his life, when questioned by an army general about the efficacy of nonviolence vis-à-vis an enemy who has no use for it, he admitted he had no answer:

> You have asked me to tell you in a tangible and concrete form how you can put over to the troops under your command the need for non-violence.
> I am still groping in the dark for an answer. I will find it and give it to you some day.[40]

As Karnad notes, Gandhi's apparently uncompromising morality in rejecting violence can be seen as a strategic "situation-dependent standard wielded by him only if it promised results."[41] Otherwise, he was willing to countenance the defensive use of force.

Nehru is sometimes regarded as an unrealistic idealist, but this is an exaggeration.[42] He was deeply influenced by Gandhi, but as a political steward exhibited a much greater pragmatism even in his grand vision of universal disarmament.[43] His view of nuclear weapons was that they were immoral and should be abolished, yet he was not ready to commit India to abstain from making them permanently. In contrast, his Defense Minister, V. K. Krishna Menon, was uncompromising in his rejection of nuclear weapons.[44] But Nehru remained ambivalent. His moral instincts recoiled from conceiving of nuclear weapons as usable instruments of state policy because "we know that the use of these weapons amounts to genocide."[45] He worried about the Cold War's potential for catastrophe—"one accident, one irrational decision, or one wrong move might very well spell an end for everything living"—yet he acknowledged the value of deterrence in preventing war between the United States and the Soviet Union.[46] Thus, while continually advocating universal nuclear disarmament, Nehru kept the door open for the possible development of nuclear weapons and refused to accept any agreement that might bring about its closure. In short, he adopted a passive hedging strategy. He held fast to this approach over a long period. In 1946, a year before Independence, he had expressed the "hope" that "Indian scientists will use the atomic force for constructive purposes," but added that if need be, India would "try to defend herself by all means at her disposal."[47] Shortly before his death in 1964, on a memorandum written by the pro-bomb nuclear scientist, Homi Bhabha, Nehru wrote that nuclear technology offered the "built-in advantage" of defense use should the need arise.[48]

The ideational and praxological foundations of Indian nuclear minimalism were firmly laid during the Nehru era. For seventeen years, consistent with Nehru's beliefs, India's strategic posture was characterized by a suspicion of nuclear weapons, strong advocacy of nondiscriminatory arms control and disarmament, and a high tolerance of ambiguity in the form of reliance on an open door policy to counter potential nuclear threats. But India's defeat in the 1962 war with China led to a greater realism and a renewed if still subdued interest in nuclear weapons.

Nehru's successor, Lal Bahadur Shastri (1964–66) responded guardedly to the enhanced threat from China, which tested its first nuclear device in 1964, just two years after inflicting a serious military debacle on India. In December 1965, the Prime Minister approved a secret research program, the Subterranean Nuclear Explosion Project (SNEP), to develop Indian nuclear weapons capability, but only to a level that would be three months short of an actual test. Publicly, Shastri resisted strong pressure from within his own Congress Party to embark on a policy of building nuclear capability for military purposes.[49] At the time, the nonproliferation regime had yet to acquire teeth in the form of the NPT. The reluctance to go nuclear clearly came from within.

Nehru's daughter Indira Gandhi (1967–77, 1980–84) was in many ways the quintessential realist. She engaged in a rapid conventional arms build-up and, in 1971, intervened in the civil war in Pakistan to play midwife to the birth of Bangladesh. But despite the threat of nuclear China's support for Pakistan during the 1971 war, and despite the deep anxiety caused by the United States' signaling of its displeasure in sending its nuclear-capable Seventh Fleet into the Bay of Bengal, Mrs. Gandhi's response was restricted to the symbolic. In 1974, India crashed into the nuclear club with a single successful test, but refrained from following this up with a weaponization program. Like her father, Mrs. Gandhi continued to stress the primacy of economic development and the inutility of deterrence, which she publicly rejected as "untenable."[50] After a brief hiatus (1977–80), she returned to power in 1980. In 1983, she launched the Integrated Guided Missile Development Program, but this was at best an expansion of the nuclear open door. No attempt was made to incorporate nuclear weapons even conceptually into the framework of national security policy.

Continuity until the 1990s. The prime ministership of Morarji Desai (1977–79) represented a normative shift in the other direction, and one would expect to see the nuclear door at least beginning to close. Desai was stubbornly opposed to nuclear weapons on moral grounds and began by publicly rejecting them. In his first press conference after coming to power, he declared, "I will give it to you in writing that we will not manufacture nuclear weapons. Even if the whole world arms itself with the bomb, we will not do so."[51]

But later, Desai returned to the established policy line of nuclear ambiguity by claiming with bland ingenuousness that he was against nuclear "explosions," not "blasts."[52] Furthermore, reacting to reports of a Pakistani effort to build nuclear weapons, Desai's cabinet approved the quiet resumption of India's nuclear weapons program in 1979.[53] Like his predecessors, he rejected as discriminatory the concept of a regional nuclear-weapon-free zone, refused to consider signing the NPT, and demanded the formulation of a time-bound program for the elimination of all nuclear weapons. In spite of his antipathy toward nuclear weapons, he remained within the ambit of a long-established practice circumscribed by Indian strategic culture.

Rajiv Gandhi (1984–89) revealed a new inclination toward the exercise of national power in the South Asian region. He embarked on a program of military modernization and naval expansion, compelled Nepal to be subservient by closing most of its access routes to the sea, forcefully intervened in Sri Lanka's civil war by sending in an unwelcome peacekeeping force, and raised fears of a war with Pakistan by conducting a massive military exercise—Operation Brasstacks—close to its western border. On the external front, growing evidence of Pakistan's nuclearization with Chinese assistance created an unprecedented nuclear threat. Yet Rajiv's *realpolitik* did not immediately extend to nuclear weapons. According to V. S. Arunachalam, his scientific advisor, he was "genuinely against the bomb," though he "did not want India to be found wanting in a crisis either."[54] Like his grandfather, Nehru, he pinned his hopes—quite unrealistically—on the possibility of ridding the world of nuclear weapons. At a five-nation conference on disarmament in early 1988, he pleaded: "They argue that nuclear weapons keep the peace. This is false. If nuclear weapons exist, they will one day be used, as they were in Hiroshima and Nagasaki, as weapons have been throughout history. There will be no going back, no survivor, no one to tell the tale. There will be no lessons for the future. For there will be no future."[55]

At the United Nations General Assembly's Third Special Session on Disarmament in 1988, he personally presented an ambitious grand design for universal and total nuclear disarmament. It was only the failure of this effort, combined with evidence of Pakistan's acquisition of the bomb, that led to Rajiv's authorization of a secret weaponization program.[56] Even then, there remained a high degree of continuity in India's nuclear posture. Despite the decision to weaponize, there was no move to incorporate deterrence doctrine into national security planning or to create the infrastructure for a nuclear force. On the contrary, Rajiv in late 1988 agreed with his Pakistani counterpart, Benazir Bhutto, that their countries would refrain from targeting each other's nuclear facilities in the event of war. In striking contrast to other nuclear powers, India began negotiating arms control agreements well *before* going nuclear officially.

During the 1990s, the pattern set earlier was continued by successive prime ministers: the Janata Dal's V. P. Singh (1989–90) and Chandra Shekhar (1990–91), the Congress Party's P. V. Narasimha Rao (1991–96), and his United Front successors, H. D. Deve Gowda (1996–97) and I. K. Gujral (1997–98), did not effect any major changes. The Prithvi missile was inducted into the army, but not deployed. Despite rising concerns over Pakistan's ongoing nuclearization (which finally prompted the United States to impose sanctions), fresh reports of Chinese nuclear and missile aid to Pakistan, the loss of the valuable "Soviet card" with the end of the Cold War, and India's increasing isolation amid intensifying nonproliferation pressures, nuclear posture continued to be characterized by restraint. The only significant changes were the go-ahead given by Rao for the resumption of testing for the intermediate-range Agni missile and for the construction of rail-mobile missile platforms in 1996.[57] Rao came close to testing, but refrained.[58] These developments represented a further opening of the nuclear door, an incremental response to the perception of growing external threat.

Vajpayee: Dramatic Shift or Marginal Change? The Bharatiya Janata Party (BJP) led a coalition to power in 1998 and almost immediately carried out a series of nuclear tests. Simultaneously, it enunciated its skeletal doctrine of "credible minimum deterrence." On the face of it, this was a dramatic policy shift: nuclear deterrence had now been officially adopted as a pillar of national security. In fact, the change was less substantial than it first appeared. Its central import was that it was a new *declaratory* position. Weaponization had already been initiated by Rajiv Gandhi in 1989.[59] As Vajpayee himself has acknowledged, in 1996, when he came briefly to power (for just thirteen days), outgoing Prime Minister Narasimha Rao had written to him that everything was in place, and he could go ahead and make India a nuclear power.[60] There was no effort to operationalize rapidly. While the process of putting nuclear strategy into practice was slow, initiative for arms control was not lacking. In February 1999, Vajpayee rode a bus to Lahore in an attempt to break new ground with Pakistan. The Lahore Memorandum committed the two countries to advance notification of missile tests and to negotiation on numerous measures to reduce nuclear risks. Though relations deteriorated sharply as a result of the Kargil conflict (1999), which brought India and Pakistan close to war, observance of the first provision continued. In 2001, the India-Pakistan summit meeting at Agra had nuclear stabilization on its agenda, but it ended in deadlock and subsequent confrontation in 2001–2 over Kashmir prevented forward movement.

The operationalization of nuclear strategy remained limited. Weapons were not placed under active deployment and organizational development was slow. Despite the widespread perception of the BJP as a party of hard-boiled realists, there was no significant demand for the deployment of nuclear weapons, or for the building of a large arsenal. Vajpayee himself is known as a moderate. His views on the value of nuclear weapons are far from unqualified. His reservations are expressed in his poetry:

> Those whose invention,
> Created the ultimate weapon . . .
> Do they even for a moment,
> Feel what was inflicted by them,
> Was monstrous?
> If they do then time will not put
> them in the dock,
> But if they don't,
> Then history will never,
> Ever forgive them.[61]

It has also been recently revealed that in 1979, during a meeting of the Cabinet Committee on Security, Vajpayee—then Minister for External Affairs—joined Prime Minister Morarji Desai in voting against reviving the Indian nuclear weapons program despite an intelligence input to the effect that Pakistan was making progress in uranium enrichment.[62]

Continuity under Manmohan Singh. The United Progressive Alliance, a coalition led by the Congress, assumed power under Prime Minister Manmohan Singh in 2004. The government has sought continuity on nuclear doctrine and explicitly stated that there is no change with respect to missile defense, on which the Congress had expressed reservations earlier.[63] In June 2004, Minister for External Affairs Natwar Singh reflected an old penchant for strategic stability through dialogue by calling for a "common nuclear doctrine" among India, China, and Pakistan so that they "might speak the same language on nuclear issues."[64] Extensive discussions initiated during the BJP-led government's tenure on a range of issues—including nuclear confidence building—have been carried forward. There is every indication of continuity in nuclear matters.

Quite clearly, there is a high degree of continuity and stability in India's nuclear posture. Neither enhanced threat perception nor change in domestic preference, whether in favor of nuclear weapons (Vajpayee) or against (Desai), has brought significant policy change. The strategic culture of nuclear minimalism, established in the initial years after Independence and reinforced by recursive practice, has restrained the response to changes in the internal and external environments of nuclear policy. Change, when it has occurred, has been incremental. Throughout, the need to deter has been acknowledged within a relatively narrow range from retaining an open door without developing military capability to the adoption of nuclear deterrence without deployment. In short, strategic culture has circumscribed India's nuclear posture to a significant degree.

Other Explanations

In assessing the role of strategic culture in shaping developments, it is useful to compare what happened with what one would *expect* to have happened had other factors been predominant. Indian nuclear strategy neither conforms to typical realist expectations of how states respond to rising external threats, nor accords with the range of domestic variables that normally explain policy. An offensive realist explanation does not offer an adequate understanding of Indian strategic behavior. Offensive realism stresses the preference for self-help in an anarchic international system. It leads us to expect that, in the event of enhanced threat perceptions, India should have accelerated its nuclear program significantly. On crucial occasions, it did not.

Following China's nuclearization in 1964, given the backdrop of defeat in the 1962 war, India should—from an offensive realist perspective—have made a serious effort to go nuclear, particularly since the constraints imposed by the nonproliferation regime were yet to become potent. But Prime Minister Shastri sanctioned only limited research. In 1967, Indira Gandhi revived the stalled weapons-oriented program only after failing to obtain nuclear guarantees from the United States, the Soviet Union, and Britain. This goes against offensive realism's expectation of a balancing response to threat in a self-help system. Indeed, India had sought no more than a U.S.-Soviet declaration of support. In any case, Mrs. Gandhi, as we have seen, did not attempt to go beyond the minimal demonstration of capability. Similarly, in the early 1980s, India's strategic position was distinctly uncomfortable.[65] There was growing evidence of a Pakistani bomb program aided by China and overlooked by the United States. India's strategic autonomy was compromised by its dependence on the Soviet Union. Responding to calls for nuclearization, Mrs. Gandhi, sanctioned another round of testing in 1982, but later changed her mind. When asked why, she told V. S. Arunachalam, "I am basically against weapons of mass destruction."[66] In the mid-1980s, India was convinced of a Pakistani bomb program and a Sino-Pakistani nuclear and missile nexus. Yet Rajiv Gandhi sanctioned the actual building of weapons only in 1989, after his plan for universal disarmament had been ignored by the nuclear weapon states.

From the beginning, the process of institutionalizing nuclear weapons—by incorporating them into the armed forces through the development of doctrine and military organization—has been leisurely. The establishment of the NCA was announced over four and a half years after the 1998 tests. George Perkovich believes that Indian politicians' and bureaucrats' deep-seated fear of the armed forces accounts for this.[67] This is only partly true. The armed forces have been periodically associated with nuclear planning from early on, even though they may not have got what they wanted.[68] The slow pace of infrastructure development is explained by the lack of a serious commitment to nuclear weapons on the part of a leadership constrained by strategic culture.

The significance of strategic culture is evident from a consideration of other variables:

Leadership (Nehru, Shastri, Indira Gandhi) was crucial in the creation of Indian strategic culture in the context of nuclear weapons. Nuclear minimalism was well established by the 1970s. Subsequently, however, shifts in leadership preferences, ranging from an explicit belief in nuclear deterrence (Vajpayee) to a strong antipathy for all things nuclear (Desai), did not bring appreciable discontinuity. Actual policy remained within a fairly narrow range providing for some measure of deterrence without deployment.

Party policy has also had no discernible impact. At one extreme, the BJP has long been a strident advocate of nuclearization, and one would have expected the party to push through a program of rapid operationalization, including deployment. This did not happen. At the other, the Congress in its early years was staunchly opposed to an operational nuclear weapons program, though some elements within the party favored it. Yet it was under the Congress that the first nuclear test in 1974 was carried out and, later, the bomb built. Actual policy, as already noted, has fallen within a restricted spectrum. By and large, no party has engaged in serious thinking (say, by means of a detailed committee report) over nuclear weapons.

Parliamentary inputs have been insignificant. Though broad political issues relating to nuclear weapons, especially in relation to disarmament, have been extensively discussed, the level of interest in, and knowledge about, the nitty gritty of nuclear weapons and deterrence has been very low.[69] In effect, Parliament has not contributed meaningfully to nuclear policy.

Bureaucratic inputs might be expected to have been substantial because the bureaucracy, particularly the atomic energy establishment, has been a major part of the small circle with access to nuclear policy. Some analysts have argued that a "strategic enclave" consisting mainly of atomic energy technocrats, played a pivotal role in India's nuclearization.[70] But careful investigation shows that they never exercised a decisive influence on the political leadership. Bhabha could not persuade Nehru to think seriously of weaponizing.[71] Indira Gandhi changed her decision to test in 1982 without consulting the so-called "strategic enclave."[72] In 1995, Narasimha Rao rejected strong technocratic pressures to test.[73] In 1996, even a relatively weak prime minister, Deve Gowda, overruled the atomic energy establishment's insistent demands for testing.[74]

Public opinion has not had a decisive impact either. Studies have shown that public opinion is broadly supportive of Indian nuclear policy.[75] In general, the nuclear issue has been very low on people's list of priorities in comparison to questions of domestic economic and political stability.[76] Thus, there is little reason to regard public opinion as a significant variable in determining nuclear policy other than possibly in a broad way by reinforcing decision makers' awareness of the need to curb excessive spending.

Technological weakness and poverty might be considered the primary reasons for the moderate pace of Indian nuclearization. In one sense, this is true: resource constraints have always been a serious problem. But it is only when such a program is normatively questioned and given relatively low priority that the weight of technological weakness and poverty overrides security considerations. In contrast, Chinese leaders, faced with similar conditions, chose to spend more on building nuclear capability.

Nonofficial Assumptions and Beliefs

Here, the preferences of only those who believe in the need for deterrence are examined. Arguably, a strategic culture need not contain a coherent set of beliefs. The pushes and pulls of contradictory beliefs (e.g., between pro-deterrence thinking and abolitionist thinking) might shape policy.[77] In the Indian context, though, absolute opposition to deterrence has been too insignificant to influence nuclear policy. Two sets of sources are examined below. The first consists of eight expositions by *strategic experts* on desirable nuclear strategy. Seven are individual works on nuclear strategy by Gurmeet Kanwal, Bharat Karnad, Raja Menon, Vijai K. Nair, Jasjit Singh, K. Subrahmanyam, and K. Sundarji.[78] The eighth is the National Security Advisory Board's DND, which is classified here as nonofficial because it consists largely of individuals working outside the government. The second category consists of extensive interviews, many confidential, with members of the *strategic elite*. These are serving and retired individuals, civilian and military, official and nonofficial. The interviews include questions designed to ascertain their basic assumptions and beliefs in relation to nuclear weapons. The findings are presented in general rather than statistical form for methodological reasons.

In both categories, an effort has been made to obtain preferences about three basic issues: the fundamental characteristics of world politics, the role of nuclear weapons in it, and the implications of nuclearization for India.

1. *The nature of world politics: is it primarily characterized by inter-state conflict, inter-state cooperation, or exploitation and inequality?* Six of the individual analysts and the DND offer no direct opinion on the fundamental nature of world politics. Only Menon in passing expresses an explicit realist worldview.[79] Karnad's book is unquestionably written on hard realist lines, though he does not essay an explicit consideration of this question. But, reading between the lines, it is clear that they are all realists who believe in the primacy of conflict. In contrast, the great majority of those interviewed believe that the primary characteristic of world politics is exploitation and inequality.

2. *The fundamental role of nuclear weapons in world politics: are they sources of risk, sources of security, or sources of national prestige?* All the detailed studies reflect a clear understanding that nuclear weapons are primarily sources of security. Among those interviewed, about two-thirds felt the same. Most of the remaining thought nuclear weapons to be associated with a greater element of risk than of security.

3. *The implications of nuclearization for India: will it bring greater security, less security, or increased bargaining power?* All the detailed studies hold the opinion that the possession of nuclear weapons will, above all, enhance India's security. Surprisingly, less than half of those interviewed echoed this view. A greater number were of the opinion that nuclear weapons are sources of bargaining power.

It is readily evident that there are significant areas of consensus in the assumptions and beliefs of the two sets of opinions, but also marked areas of divergence. On the nature of world politics, the realist understanding that world politics is primarily characterized by inter-state conflict does not enjoy strong articulation. The detailed studies do reveal a realist bias, but none gives thought to alternative worldviews. Those interviewed were specifically asked about the relative importance of welfare issues, and the majority does not see conflict at the top of a hierarchy of issues in the way that realists do. This accords with the defensive realist view that economic preferences set limits to the application of deterrence.

All eight of the detailed expositions reviewed agree that nuclear weapons are generally providers of security and, specifically, will augment India's security. In contrast, those interviewed are not unanimous that nuclear weapons are sources of security. They also tend to view nuclear weapons as sources of greater bargaining power rather than of greater security. Official policy reflects a slow shift over half a century from the Nehruvian perception that nuclear weapons are primarily sources of insecurity to the current opinion that they are pillars of national security. The significance of this shift is that it has brought the official view closer to that of the experts, on whom the government leans far more than before for policy perspectives on nuclear issues. A restraining effect may be imposed by the more qualified views of the wider strategic elite whose broad expertise is less enmeshed in the technicalities of doctrine. The perception among many of the strategic elite that nuclear weapons produce enhanced bargaining power is troubling, but on reflection, this may in part reflect ambiguity about the context. Bargaining power with respect to the nonproliferation regime is widely considered necessary. The interviews did not provide any indication that bargaining through the exercise of nuclear coercion is considered useful.

The overall picture that emerges is that nuclear weapons are viewed with less doubt and suspicion than in the past, but that their limitations are acknowledged. They are certainly not privileged as the principal providers of the nation's security.

Operational Preferences

Here, preferences are gauged with regard to the operational aspects of nuclear weapons and deterrence posture. The issues examined are deployment, numbers and types of weapons, targeting, and conditions necessitating the possible use of nuclear weapons.

Official Preferences. Official preferences are difficult to obtain because of government secrecy. Targeting appears to be restricted to countervalue and second-strike, as reflected in the 2003 statement on doctrine, which speaks of "massive" retaliation and NFU. Counterforce targeting is not mentioned in any official statement or in such information as can be gleaned unofficially. Deployment, we know, is not as yet considered a necessity even as delivery capability has been steadily upgraded from nuclear-capable aircraft to the development of surface-to-surface, airborne and sea-based surface missiles.[80] The preferred form of deterrence even after weaponization is through possession of non-deployed weapons in unassembled or nearly-assembled condition, kept concealed and not "mated" with delivery vehicles. Warheads and delivery vehicles are not co-located. The quantity of warheads remains small (around 60 warheads), and there is no evidence of an interest in increasing numbers significantly.[81] The range of weapons platforms conceived of is nevertheless wide. Long-range missiles and nuclear-powered submarines were the subject of feasibility studies as early as 1970.[82] Restricted to nuclear-capable aircraft during the 1970s, India commenced research and development on the short-range Prithvi and the intermediate-range Agni missiles in the early 1980s. The Prithvi (with a range of 300 km), the Agni-I (700 km) and Agni-II (2000 km) have been inducted into the Army.[83] The China-specific Agni-III is expected to be inducted by the mid-2000s. In 1985, the Indian Navy acquired on lease from the Soviet Union a nuclear-powered submarine, rechristened *INS Chakra*, for which the only rationale could have been the desire to gain experience on a vessel with nuclear-weapons potential. Two more for lease to India are under construction in Russia.[84] An SLBM—Sagarika—and a nuclear-powered submarine are under development.[85] In the meantime, the Dhanush, a sea-based version of the Prithvi with a range of 350 km, has been inducted as the Navy's first nuclear delivery vehicle for surface ships.[86] The development of the BrahMos cruise missile with Russian collaboration has opened up the possibility, not mentioned in official statements so far, of nuclear cruise missiles being developed in the future.[87]

On the one hand, some of this seems excessive if not a futile pursuit of redundancy. On the other, the commitment to minimalism—non-deployed posture, no first use, no testing—demonstrates adherence to an old policy of acquiring capability without exercising it fully. With successive governments doing little to move from the acquisition of capability to operationalization, it is not surprising that there has been little articulation of doctrine, which would express clearer preferences relating to targeting and the conditions under which nuclear weapons might be used. It can only be said in general that nuclear weapons have been viewed as countervalue weapons capable of cataclysmic destruction and hence not usable in any meaningful sense. Yet the very fact that the tests conducted in 1998 were of various yields leaves open the possibility that counterforce doctrine will be incorporated into India's nuclear posture.

The unhurried pace of operationalization reflects the relatively low priority given to nuclear weapons in the scheme of things. At the time of writing (early 2005), there has been some organizational development, but not such as to reflect a sense that nuclear weapons are a central or indeed a very significant component of national security strategy. The creation of a new tri-service Strategic Forces Command (SFC) directly under the Chairman, Chiefs of Staff Committee, was announced nearly five years after the 1998 tests in January 2003, and funds were allotted to it only some ten months later.[88] In mid-2004, the SFC still did not have adequate manpower or even a headquarters office of its own.[89] The creation of a Chief of Defence Staff (recommended by a ministerial committee), which could reduce endemic interservice rivalry, has been delayed by years. Instead, the government has been content to manage with an Integrated Defence Staff, which has been ineffective in integrating the services.[90] A nuclear command structure was announced—again late—in January 2003.[91] The Nuclear Command Authority consists of a Political Council and an Executive Council. The Political Council, chaired by the Prime Minister, is the sole body which can authorize the use of nuclear weapons, while the implementing body, the Executive Council, is headed by the National Security Advisor. While alternate command centers were announced in October 2003, a report cited officials as saying there were "only ad hoc systems in place."[92]

Non-official Preferences. Strategic experts have, by the very nature of their professional work, developed clear-cut preferences on the operational aspects of nuclear weapons. Their views and those of the strategic elite interviewed may be summarized as follows.

1. *Deployment*: Nair, Karnad, and Menon favor deployment. The DND, in distinguishing between "peacetime deployment" and "full employment" during a crisis, implies some form of predeployed posture during normal times. Kanwal, Singh, and Subrahmanyam prefer that weapons be kept in unassembled condition. Sundarji, in the work analyzed here, appears to favor deployment, but in a later recommendation allows that unassembled weapons will do, so long as they can be deployed within twenty-four hours.[93] Of the interviewees, a little over half favored deployment, while the rest preferred deterrence without deployment.

2. *Numbers*: How many are enough? If numbers are categorized into three ranges: less than 25, between 25 and 100, and over 100, Singh, Subrahmanyam, and Sundarji fall in the middle category. In a post-1998 opinion editorial, however, Subrahmanyam dramatically raises his requirement to 150.[94] Kanwal, Karnad, Menon, and Nair are placed in the third category, and the DND is noncommittal, though a close reading rules out the first option. It is worth noting that those in the middle category are widely labeled "hawks," as is Brahma Chellaney, who avers that less than 100 are enough.[95] Members of the strategic elite were evenly divided across the three categories.

3. *Platforms*: From among the three options—air-based, land-based, and sea-based—which are desirable? The DND, Kanwal, Karnad, Nair, Singh, and Sundarji want a triad, Subrahmanyam is not sure about the need for a sea-based deterrent, and Menon favors a single sea-based leg. The great majority of those interviewed advocated a triad.

4. *Targeting*: Menon favors a counterforce strategy. Karnad wants a secondary counterforce target list, while Sundarji dwells only briefly on counterforce targeting, implying that he does not consider it to be a serious option. The DND is not explicit. The remaining experts view nuclear weapons as countervalue weapons. Among those interviewed, about half said targets need not be specified, implying that the question is not significant. Very few favored counterforce (only one from among several military officers).

5. *Conditions under which nuclear weapons may be used*: Most of the experts believe nuclear weapons should only be used for a second strike. Only Karnad believes the concept is meaningless, since it cannot be taken for granted in actual war conditions.[96] Of those interviewed, only one favored a nuclear response to major losses in a conventional war (the loss of Kashmir was specified as an example). The rest felt a nuclear strike should only be a second strike.

A comparison of the official and nonofficial preference structures at the operational level shows some significant patterns. Some of these tend to erode minimum deterrence. While the official position eschews deployment, three of the eight expert analyses favor it, and the wider strategic elite is more inclined toward deployment. The growing support for deployment may pull the government from a primarily political understanding of nuclear weapons, as essentially nonusable devices, toward a more operational one in which there is a greater sense of these weapons being concrete, usable instruments of state power. The strength of support for relatively large numbers of weapons (in the over 100 range) supports this. The strong preference for a triad is consistent with relatively large numbers, since an element of redundancy in each leg of a triad is widely considered essential to minimize vulnerability. Thus, notwithstanding the lack of interest in competitive arms racing, the possibility of expanding numbers on the ground of vulnerability remains open.

On the other hand, there is little sentiment in favor of catching up in numbers or even in quality with China. This indicates a notable tolerance for apparent imbalances and a predisposition against arms racing. Also, there is no interest in nuclear warfighting. Nuclear weapons are generally regarded as countervalue weapons. There is a widely held understanding that the distinction between counterforce and countervalue targeting is not particularly useful since it is impossible to conceive of a clear threshold between the two. Finally, the consensus on nuclear use—that it should be for retaliation only—is consistent with the principles of true minimum deterrence.

The Structure of Indian Strategic Culture

The term "structure" is employed to stress the characteristics that set the parameters shaping a strategic culture's response to the environment. In the present formulation, it has three components: responses to changes in the strategic environment, tolerance of ambiguity, and disposition toward arms control.

Responses to Changes in the Strategic Environment (Restraint/Precipitateness). Clearly, there is a strong preference for nuclear restraint. Notwithstanding the periodic emergence of enhanced threat perceptions, shifts in nuclear policy have been incremental rather than sudden. The new Chinese threat in the 1960s and the dual Chinese and Pakistani threats in the 1980s and the 1990s did not result in dramatic departures. As has been shown, the BJP-led government's break with the past was not radical. All it did was to make overt and supplement through testing a nuclearization process set in motion much earlier. The slowness of the process is explained by the embeddedness of restraint in both the ideational and praxological components of strategic culture over several decades. The most recent and clear-cut evidence of restraint comes from India's reaction to the Kargil conflict, which involved the clandestine occupation of Indian-held territory by Pakistani forces in Kashmir in 1999. Despite being caught on the wrong foot and losing control over considerable territory; despite much anger at Pakistan's "betrayal" following the bonhomie generated by Prime Minister Vajpayee's February 1999 visit to Lahore; and in spite of the armed forces' demand for permission to open a new front and cross the Line of Control (LoC) in Kashmir, the government showed enormous restraint. Strict orders were given not to cross the LoC lest a low-intensity conflict be transformed into a conventional—and potentially a nuclear—war. The BJP's restrained response belied its long-standing tendency to adopt an aggressive posture toward external threats. Late in 2001, India did initiate a massive mobilization of conventional forces (see Chapter 4), but, though there was intense anger over continuing Pakistani support for terrorist activity in India, and strong pressures for at least limited military action, Indian forces remained on their side of the border. In the reverse direction, when Morarji Desai became prime minister in 1977, expectations of a dramatic departure in nuclear policy by means of the closing of the nuclear option were not realized. In every case, notwithstanding marked changes in the external and internal environments, nuclear policy was characterized by limited departures from the established posture.

Tolerance of Ambiguity (High/Low). Indian nuclear policy has displayed consistently high tolerance of ambiguity. The very fact that nuclear ambivalence (the open door, no deployment) has persisted attests to this. But a change is becoming apparent. Here, it is pertinent to reiterate the distinction between the coexisting political and operational components of deterrence. The former tends to view deterrence as existential and nuclear weapons as essentially unusable. The latter tends to conceive of nuclear weapons in usable terms, with characteristics (speed, accuracy, range, reliability, command and control, etc.) akin to those pertaining to conventional weapons. The former is not concerned with numbers and technological sophistication, the latter is. From the evidence presented above, it would seem fair to warn of a gradual but unmistakable shift in the structural frame of Indian strategic culture from a strongly political to a more operational character, from one highly tolerant of ambiguity to one with declining tolerance of ambiguity. This reflects both the technical imperative of weapons (they stimulate "practical" thinking) and the pressures of external circumstance (which induced the building of an arsenal). The transformation has been remarkably slow, from the first incremental steps of the 1960s to the building of a bare-bones infrastructure three decades later, but it is unquestionably there. While the risks of instability are reduced by a strong tradition of restraint in thought and practice, it is nevertheless true that the drift toward operationalization carries with it the possibility of diminished restraint as experts become more concerned with numbers, technological sophistication, and questions of credibility, vulnerability, and reliability. It is noteworthy that these issues occupy a prominent place in one major collective indicator of quasiofficial opinion, the DND.

Disposition toward Arms Control (Positive/Negative). Here, there is a reassuring continuity in Indian strategic culture. In the initial years, the entire focus was on global disarmament. By the late 1980s, with the steady transition from latent to actual capabilities, a new area was opened up in the form of nuclear-related arms control. The 1988 India-Pakistan agreement not to attack each other's nuclear facilities was its first manifestation. This was the natural consequence of a predisposition against large-scale destruction in war, a bias evident from the restrained conduct of all three wars between the two countries.[97] The Lahore Memorandum, signed by the foreign secretaries of the two countries in February 1999, confirms this preference. The thrust of the document is on ways and means to minimize nuclear risk. Moves to cultivate strategic stability between India and China were also initiated simultaneously. Following the India-Pakistan border confrontation of 2001–2, efforts to negotiate nuclear CBMs were revived in 2003. In light of this record, there is every reason to expect that Indian strategic culture will retain its propensity for negotiated solutions to adversarial nuclear-strategic relationships. At the same time, the long-standing preference for universal nondiscriminatory disarmament remains integral to this strategic culture. Though often derided by critics as unrealistic or even self-serving, India's unfailing advocacy of global solutions is consistent with the realist bottom line of its original open door policy on nuclear weapons: unless everyone closes the nuclear door, it is not in India's best interests to do so. The readiness to negotiate equitable arms control both bilaterally and multilaterally gives to Indian strategic culture a positive feature. In contrast to the constraining effects observed above, we find here an enabling effect: strategic culture facilitates arms control and hence the building of stable strategic relationships.

Strategic Culture and Change: Toward Operational Bias

The foregoing brings out significant gaps between the concept of minimum deterrence and Indian nuclear-strategic thinking and practice. A brief summation will make this clear. Major aspects that prioritize the political in conformity with the concept of minimum deterrence presented in Chapter 2 are: the lack of interest in nuclear balances, which encourages the belief that having a small number of weapons is enough and inhibits arms racing; abstention from deployment despite the experience of major crises with a nuclear adversary; related to the latter, the understanding that retaliation need not be immediate; rejection of counterforce targeting and nuclear warfighting; the belief that deterrence is in place and does not require further warhead testing; the languid pace of infrastructure building; and the strong preference for arms control. Against this, operational bias is evident in important respects: the persistent emphasis on credibility and survivability, both of which tend to encourage a focus on open-ended technological sophistication and larger numbers and types of weapons, including the preoccupation with obtaining a triad; and the elite preference for deployment. Another problematic aspect is the poor understanding of the relationship between nuclear and subnuclear conflict, which is examined at length in the next chapter. Finally, a neutral feature that is not intrinsic to minimum deterrence but is consistent with it is missile defense, which is discussed at length in Chapter 5.

What does this imply for the future of Indian strategic culture and nuclear strategy? Strategic cultures are normally like large ships. With few exceptions, as when they are subject to severe shocks, they change course very slowly.[98] There has been no dramatic shift in Indian strategic culture over the past several decades, though we find a steady drift toward nuclearization due in part to the impact of perceived threats from China and Pakistan, but also to the nonproliferation regime's pressure to close the nuclear option. Barring severe internal or external shocks, which cannot be foreseen, we may at best anticipate marginal change. However, the cumulative impact of the shift toward a more operational conception of nuclear weapons can be significant. As the tension between conflicting approaches to strategy grows, the uneasy balance between these approaches may shift as the weight of one increases relative to that of the other. It is possible, therefore, that over time the growing weight of the operational perspective may drag India's strategic culture away from a minimalist position toward a maximalist one, or to some sort of compromise position that detracts from the optimality of minimum deterrence.

The growth of operational pressures is natural when a nuclear infrastructure is built up, for that infrastructure must necessarily be in large part an operational one. Military officials charged with the practical nitty gritty of deterrence cannot but think of their weapons in operational terms. The persistence of external military threats tends to underscore the military perspective, thereby increasing the pressure to think in this way. If a strategic response to external pressure appears inadequate, the internal dissonance in a predominantly political approach to strategy may cause a "paradigmatic crisis" in the Kuhnian sense.[99] Alternatively, the transformation of strategic culture into one dominated by operational considerations may be cumulative and relatively smooth. Whichever form it takes, the shift to an operationally biased strategic culture can be prevented by reaffirming the fundamentals of minimum deterrence.[100] The militarization of strategy is discussed below, and a detailed critique of India's militarized response to severe external pressure presented in the next chapter.

The role of the military in Indian politics has been relatively small since Independence, but it has been increasing. This does not mean that the military is becoming politicized, but that politics is being militarized.[101] Manifestations of this since the 1980s are the frequent use of the army to quell insurgency and terrorism in Punjab, Kashmir, and the Northeast; and, externally, Indian military intervention in Sri Lanka (1987–90) and the Maldives (1988). Sunil Dasgupta notes that the militarization of Indian politics is civilian-led, or what is called "civilian militarism."[102] Dasgupta treats the advent of nuclear weapons as further evidence of militarization, but that is questionable. The acquisition of nuclear weapons in response to perceived nuclear threats does not constitute militarization, since the term implies a turn that is not necessary. A military response to a military threat cannot properly be viewed as a case of militarization. But the concept of civilian militarism does provide a useful insight into the dynamics of nuclear strategy. If strategic culture shifts from a preeminently political conception of nuclear weapons to a predominantly operational one, then we may say it has been militarized even if civilians remain in command.

There is some evidence for this in the context of Indian nuclear strategy. The Ministry of Defence, which is civilian-dominated, envisages a force of over 200 warheads in a triadic framework, which is considered a low figure necessary to avoid resistance from a government concerned about costs.[103] Since the 1980s, military war games have been fought in the nuclear context, and the idea of limited war has found strong support in both the civilian and military leaderships.[104] Thus, according to Michael Kraig, there are signs that "political leaders and analysts are buying into the reasoning of a new 'flexible response' doctrine that has been popular in some Indian military circles for some time now."[105] This militarization of Indian thinking and practice is attributable not simply to the armed forces' growing role in strategic politics, for the civilian government remains very much in command, but to the susceptibility of political leaders to conventional military solutions in a strategic environment (Pakistani support for terrorists in Kashmir) that they have been unable to tackle effectively. A detailed discussion follows in Chapter 4. Taken together with the inevitable operational pressures arising from the creation of a nuclear infrastructure (beginning with the inclusion of the three service chiefs in the Executive Council of the Nuclear Command Authority), this opens up additional space for India's nuclear minimalism to drift from its political moorings.

Conclusion

The foregoing analysis shows a significant degree of stability in India's nuclear posture. Critics have pointed to signs of instability in India-Pakistan relations in the form of an action-reaction process in nuclear and missile testing and the crises of 1999 and 2001–2. On the other hand, even in times of crisis, tit-for-tat missile testing has been preceded by observance of the terms of the Lahore Memorandum (February 1999), which requires each to inform the other in advance of impending tests. At the height of the confrontation that began in late 2001, India and Pakistan exchanged lists of their respective nuclear facilities as required by their 1988 agreement.[106] Above all, India has refrained from actively deploying its weapons despite a continuing environment of tension. But Indian strategic culture has not been static. Notwithstanding the strength derived from continuities in belief and practice, there have been signs of a shift in the balance between the political and the operational aspects of deterrence that make up the basic assumptions and practices of Indian strategic culture. The once-predominantly political understanding of nuclear weapons has slowly given way to a more operational conception of those weapons.

What are the implications of the diverging trajectories of the operational and political facets of deterrence? The risks associated with the operational aspect are related to the open-endedness of nuclear doctrine and posture. As shown in the preceding chapter, an operational view is inherently predisposed to conceiving of the credibility of deterrence in terms of the quantity and quality of weapons: the more and "better" the weapons, the greater the efficacy of one's arsenal. This accommodates arguments that stress the need for greater accuracy and reliability as well as conceptions of strategic balances that underline the need for qualitative and quantitative advantage. This is not to say that India is poised for arms racing. Not at all. But we do need to recognize that, as operational considerations assume greater salience, the tendency in this direction is likely to exercise a greater pull on nuclear decision making. The possibility that a predominantly restrained strategic culture will permit a shift from deterrence to warfighting must be anticipated. John Lewis and Xue Litai have shown how China's nuclear posture has shifted from a defensive-realist minimum deterrence to an operationally dominant one of decentralized decision making, limited war planning, and quick retaliation bordering on launch-on-warning.[107] Over time, if operational considerations are not restrained, the built-in propensity for expansion could prove to be costly as well as destabilizing. For the political leadership, it is imperative that this tendency be recognized and kept under control. A sound understanding of the fundamentals of minimum deterrence is an essential prerequisite for this.

At the same time, a largely political approach to nuclear weapons in decision-making circles is fraught with its own element of risk. If there is an inadequate appreciation of nuclear weapons as potentially usable instruments, and hence of the hazards associated with them, strategic risk-taking may come to be seen as more acceptable than otherwise. Indeed, calculated confrontation may not be viewed as risk-taking at all, but only as a strategic game to be played for political ends. India's proclivities in this respect are the subject of the next chapter.

4

Compellence in a Nuclear Environment

The terrorist attack on India's Parliament on December 13, 2001, marked a watershed in India's strategic doctrine. Operation Parakram (valor), the military buildup that India then initiated on its border with Pakistan, represented the emergence of a new dimension in its understanding of the role of nuclear weapons in shaping its conflict with that country.[1] Indian leaders' belief that nuclear weapons ruled out the use of military force was overridden by their determination to break out of the perceived strategic paralysis that this view was believed to have engendered. They now sought to project military force, backed by nuclear capabilities, toward an unambiguous political end: compelling Pakistan to drop its support to terrorist groups fighting the Indian government in the Kashmir valley. India's strategic doctrine was thus extended from a focus on deterrence alone to encompass compellence.[2] This was accomplished not by the posing of a direct nuclear threat, but by two other means: first, by asserting the military advantage India derived from a favorable nuclear-cum-conventional asymmetry; and second, by creating in a third party—the United States—sufficient fear of a nuclear war breaking out to induce it to intervene on behalf of Indian interests. In the process, India's somewhat indeterminate nuclear doctrine of "credible minimum deterrence" acquired a new and unexpected dimension that is strategically questionable and that threatens to undermine the essential stability of minimum deterrence. This chapter examines the evolution of India's strategic shift and the unfolding of its new strategy of compellence. It shows that strategy to be untenable because of its doubtful benefits and high potential costs.

Kargil, Terrorism, and the Search for Strategic Space

What is missing in both enunciations of Indian nuclear doctrine discussed earlier—the Draft Nuclear Doctrine (DND) and the Jaswant Singh interview—is a consideration of the relationship between nuclear weapons and the use of force at levels below the nuclear. The DND does note that "highly effective conventional military capabilities shall be maintained to raise the threshold of outbreak both of conventional military conflict as well as that of threat or use of nuclear weapons." This implies that conventional imbalance allows the possibility of conventional—and potentially, nuclear—war. But there is no mention of the accompanying problem of escalation. Singh does not raise the issue at all. Neither makes any reference to the possibility of low-intensity conflict in the context of mutual nuclear deterrence. The reason apparently lies in the leadership's thinking at the time that, once India and Pakistan had established mutual deterrence, prudence would be the order of the day. Pakistan would no longer risk a conflict in Kashmir, the strategic status quo would be permanently frozen, and India would be able to deal with its Kashmir insurgency as an internal problem.[3] This crucial error in Indian strategic thinking was exposed by the Kargil conflict of 1999. That event proved to be a turning point in Indian thinking about nuclear weapons and their utility. It is evident that before Kargil, India's strategic establishment did not give adequate thought to the possibility of subnuclear conflict in a nuclear environment.

According to the generally accepted wisdom on deterrence, nuclear weapons have overturned the relationship between politics and force: war is no longer a feasible option between nuclear powers. Confrontations between nuclear-armed states may be expected to result in two kinds of behavior. In the first, nuclear rivals may actively seek stability through arms control initiatives. This involves a mutual understanding that the destructive potential of nuclear weapons is sufficiently great to make strategic stability imperative. The actual realization may involve a learning process, as is evident in the case of the United States and the Soviet Union. In fact, the India-Pakistan relationship showed signs of a similar outcome very soon after the 1998 tests when their representatives signed the Lahore Memorandum in February 1999. The Memorandum mandated exchange of information on impending missile tests and anticipated a continuing dialogue on nuclear risk reduction. However, the expectations it generated were short-lived. Instead, the relationship degenerated into a second, very different kind of behavior pattern: sustained hostility under the "stability-instability paradox."[4] Since the advent of nuclear weapons appeared to rule out conventional war, India became vulnerable to subconventional pressures from Pakistan. These took the form of support for terrorist violence in Kashmir, and a covert campaign in the winter of 1998–99 to occupy strategic points in the Kargil region of Kashmir. For India, though frustrations began building soon after the 1998 test, the Kargil conflict was a distinct turning point. There certainly had been some recognition of the problem earlier. From at least as early as 1991, India's Joint Intelligence Committee repeatedly noted the Pakistani perception that low-intensity conflict was feasible against India because Pakistan's nuclear capability would deter India from escalating to conventional war.[5] However, the *Kargil Review Committee Report* merely drew the lesson that the tactic backfired in the case of Kargil, and did not make any recommendation as to an appropriate Indian response other than the need for more effective intelligence. The issue was clearly not thought through adequately. In any case, the political leadership appears not to have appreciated the working of the stability-instability paradox.

Kargil had a powerful impact on Indian thinking about the role of politics and force in the context of relations with Pakistan. Its foremost effect was a deep sense of betrayal over Pakistan's duplicity in welcoming Prime Minister Atal Behari Vajpayee to Lahore in February 1999, even as early Pakistani incursions into Kargil were under way. Vajpayee had invested considerable political capital in extending the olive branch to Prime Minister Nawaz Sharif, and Kargil came as a shock. The overwhelming Indian perception, in Vajpayee's words, was that "we were stabbed in the back."[6]

Still, Indian anger over Kargil did not immediately lead to the downgrading of diplomatic and political efforts to improve India-Pakistan relations. Though relations for about a year after Kargil remained embittered, a range of initiatives was subsequently undertaken to improve the political environment and push for negotiated solutions. In late 2000, a unilateral ceasefire was declared to facilitate talks between the Government of India and Kashmiri secessionists. At the same time, India and Pakistan agreed to revive the hot line between their respective Directors-General of Military Operations, which had become inoperative a year earlier. Subsequently, renewed diplomatic efforts led to the July 2001 Agra summit between Vajpayee and Pakistan's new military ruler, General Pervez Musharraf. In itself, therefore, Kargil was not a turning point. But, seen from the Indian perspective as the high point in a series of Pakistani actions representing a growing trend of interventionism and provocation over Kashmir, Kargil signifies a defining moment in India's recent strategic history. While political efforts failed repeatedly, the depth of Pakistani involvement in the insurgency in Kashmir remained unchanged. It was clear that Pakistan was using its nuclear capability as a cover for generating the stability-instability paradox to its advantage. While Indian and Pakistani nuclear weapons deterred each other, and India's conventional advantage was neutralized by the risk of escalation to nuclear conflict, Pakistan was able to put India under increasing pressure through covert intervention. Kargil was one form of this, with Pakistani troops in mufti accompanied by Pakistan-based secessionists. The more widely prevalent form was the abetting of terrorist violence, a strategy that went back to the 1980s—when India's Punjab state was troubled by a prolonged Pakistan-aided insurgency—and was now practiced in Kashmir.[7]

Following the nuclearization of the subcontinent in the late 1980s, support for cross-border terrorism had become a central feature of Pakistani strategy.[8] After 1998, the tide of terrorism swelled, adding to Indian frustrations. In December 1999, terrorists based in Pakistan hijacked an Indian Airlines aircraft to Kandahar in Afghanistan and forced the Indian government to release their jailed associates. To Indians, it seemed Pakistan was increasingly confident that their country was strategically paralyzed by Pakistan's nuclear capability. As the *Kargil Review Committee Report* expressed it, India's inability to respond to Pakistan's periodic assertion of its nuclear prowess against an Indian conventional threat strengthened Pakistani confidence: "It would not be unreasonable for Pakistan to have concluded by 1990 that it had achieved the nuclear deterrence it had set out to establish in 1980. Otherwise, it is inconceivable that it could sustain its proxy war against India, inflicting thousands of casualties, without being unduly concerned about India's 'conventional superiority.'"[9]

Indian policy makers struggled to develop a response that might enable them to break out of their strategic straitjacket. Convinced that a political approach was unworkable, they now sought ways in which they might project military force against an intransigent and malevolent Pakistan. The possibilities discussed included hot pursuit of terrorists into Pakistani territory, limited strikes or special operations missions against terrorist camps in Pakistan, and a vague and undefined conception of "limited war."[10] In January 2000, Defence Minister George Fernandes claimed that nuclear weapons "can deter only the use of nuclear weapons, but not all and any war," and that Kargil had demonstrated that Indian forces "can fight and win a limited war, at a time and place chosen by the aggressor."[11] Despite the acknowledgment that there were "definite limitations if escalation across the nuclear threshold was to be avoided," Fernandes asserted that conventional war "has not been made obsolete by nuclear weapons."[12]

In practice, this was easier said than done. Indian leaders were aware that any fighting between Indian and Pakistani forces could escalate into nuclear conflict. Besides, Kargil had underlined the sanctity of the Line of Control (LoC) in Kashmir and, by implication, the entire border. Indeed, India's restraint in not crossing the LoC at the time had earned it much international support, whereas Pakistan's infringement of the LoC had drawn global criticism. Under the circumstances, it was difficult to contemplate a serious breach of the LoC or the border without inviting similar opprobrium. Thus, India remained trapped between an intolerable strategic paralysis and the grave difficulties inherent in attempting to break out of it.

The terrorist attacks of September 11, 2001, dramatically altered the situation. The global horror they generated permitted Indian leaders to consider anew the proactive approach they had mulled earlier. Because of its emergence as a haven for Islamic radicals and its close links with the Taliban in Afghanistan, Pakistan was placed in a defensive position. The U.S. war in Afghanistan provided an added justification for Indian intervention, particularly after terrorists based in Pakistan attacked the Jammu and Kashmir Legislative Assembly on October 1 and the Indian Parliament on December 13. In the latter case, though they failed to do much damage, the terrorists came close to achieving spectacular success. At the time, there were some 200 Members of Parliament inside, including the Vice President, the Speaker of the Lok Sabha (the lower house), the Home Minister, the Defence Minister and other members of the cabinet. Besides, by attacking Parliament, the terrorists had struck at the heart of India's democracy and the primary symbol of its nationhood. As a result, India's commitment to retaliation was very strong.

Galvanized into action, India launched Operation Parakram on the India-Pakistan border shortly after the attack on Parliament. The mobilization embodied a major strategic shift that had been in the making since Kargil. As C. Raja Mohan, a former member of the group which had prepared the DND, observed, "there is a growing belief in New Delhi that the time has come to call Pakistan's nuclear bluff. If it does not, India places itself in permanent vulnerability to cross-border terrorism from Pakistan."[13]

Indian frustration was acute. To many, their country was like a helpless giant. As former Ambassador to the United States Naresh Chandra put it, "because of our softness, the feeling in Pakistan is that we will take it."[14] And as one perceptive commentator noted some months later, India too was a state dissatisfied with the status quo. It was now ready to play the stability-instability game as well, and would try to reshape the rules in its own favor.[15] The time appeared ripe for a radical break in the way Indian decision makers thought about the use of armed force in a nuclear-strategic environment.

December 13 and India's Strategic Shift

The ten-month-long military confrontation between India and Pakistan began late in December 2001 and concluded with India's decision to withdraw its forces in October 2002. The threat of war appeared to be high in the early stages (January–February 2002), subsided a little thereafter, and peaked again in the summer (May–June 2002). There followed another lull as the confrontation stretched out until elections were conducted in Jammu and Kashmir (September–October 2002). On October 16, India announced its decision to withdraw forces from the border—but not from the LoC—though the carefully used term was "redeployment."[16]

In broad terms, the reformulation of Indian strategy involved breaking out of the constriction of strategic uncertainty and the projection of armed force to turn the stability-instability paradox around and direct it at Pakistan.[17] While diplomacy remained an option, not much was expected of it, given the perception that Pakistan could not be trusted after Kargil. As one analyst put it, the Kargil experience bolstered an already existing view that "New Delhi cannot really 'do business' with Islamabad because it is essentially an untrustworthy partner."[18] It followed that power remained the only viable instrument for dealing with Pakistan. The sentiment was strengthened by the failure of the Agra summit and by the rising intensity of terrorist activity with support from across the border. The strategic shift from diplomacy and restraint to power projection involved three conceptual components: (1) the assertion, as noted above, of limited war as a viable option; (2) the reaffirmation of strategic asymmetry in a nuclear environment to deter subconventional threats; and (3) a two-pronged shift from deterrence to compellence to change Pakistani behavior through pressure imposed simultaneously in bilateral and trilateral frameworks. The use of a psychologically destabilizing strategy—"the threat that leaves something to chance"—underscored all three of the above.[19]

Limited War as Strategic Space

The first intimation of the view that "limited war" was feasible came in the closing moments of the Kargil conflict, when a large-scale buildup was initiated by India.[20] But the rapid winding down of the conflict altered the situation and the prospects of an intensified confrontation receded. Still, influential strategic analysts of moderate persuasion voiced support for the concept. For instance, Jasjit Singh, then Director of the Institute for Defence Studies and Analyses (IDSA), a government think tank (the country's largest for strategic issues), argued that "the most likely demand on our defence policy in future would be that posed by a local border war that our own interests may require to keep limited," and that "serious consideration must be given to planning for ways and means of winning such wars."[21] In the aftermath of the December 1999 Indian Airlines hijacking, Fernandes aired the idea of a limited war at an international conference in New Delhi. The Kargil conflict was presented as proof that a limited war was possible. Again, however, the pressure declined and, in the face of opposition from within the security establishment, official references to limited war decreased significantly.[22] But the concept continued to have adherents, and was once again brought to the forefront after September 11, 2001.

The terrorist attack on the Jammu and Kashmir legislature in October brought a strong reaction from the Indian government. In a statement obliquely backed by the Ministry of Defence as "theoretically correct," the commanding officer of the Indian Army's Northern Command, Lieutenant General R. K. Nanavatty, announced that notwithstanding the nuclearization of the subcontinent, "the stage exists for a limited conventional war."[23] Following the December 13 attack on the Indian Parliament, India's army chief, General S. Padmanabhan, similarly asserted that "there is scope for a limited war."[24] Exactly what "limited war" meant was not officially articulated. In informal conversations, officials indicated that such a war would not extend over the entire length of the India-Pakistan border and would not be aimed at capturing and holding territory, but would involve selective strikes on training camps and military facilities used by the terrorists.[25] The objective would be to convince Pakistan that its nuclear weapons would not deter India from military action, and that Pakistani support for terrorism in India would henceforth carry serious costs. The assertion that limited war is feasible represented the understanding that, in the words of an unidentified senior Indian official, "there is a lot of strategic space between a low-intensity war waged with Pakistan and the nuclear threshold," which permitted the utilization of a military option "without worrying about the nuclear threshold."[26]

What gave Indian leaders the confidence that such a war could be kept limited? In part, as we have seen in Chapter 3, the reason was that they had never treated nuclear weapons seriously as operational military instruments. In part, too, it is true that military confrontations on the India-Pakistan border were not new: they had occurred regularly over the past decade and a half, with regular shelling and firing on the border or LoC, and periodic crises in 1986–87, 1990, and 1999. The military struggle for control over the Siachen glacier in Kashmir, where there is neither a border nor an LoC, has been ongoing since 1984. A third reason is that, ironically, because neither side has actively deployed its nuclear weapons, the scope for military maneuvering at a lower level is that much greater. In terms of the theoretical framework developed in Chapter 1, the intensity of interaction between India and Pakistan has never been sufficiently high to override structural pressures inducing conflict behavior. But the strongest reason is that the physical presence of U.S. military forces in the region was seen as an effective firebreak against escalation: it made full-scale war very unlikely, and it was expected that if fighting did break out, the United States would immediately intervene and enforce a ceasefire.[27] The possibility of escalation to nuclear war was also discounted because, as one official put it, "we do not envision striking [Pakistan] in a way that would lead them to use their nuclear weapons."[28]

Strategic Asymmetry and Deterrence of Low Intensity Threats

Indian rethinking on the relationship between different levels of conflict sought to show that, in a limited war, the pre-Kargil notion that India would be deterred from a conventional military response by Pakistan's nuclear capability would no longer apply. On the contrary, India would have an advantage over Pakistan by virtue of its capacity to inflict much greater damage on that country than the other way around. Attention was repeatedly drawn to the asymmetry between them and Pakistan's consequent vulnerability. On December 25, 2001, Jana Krishnamurthy, the President of the Bharatiya Janata Party (BJP), the main party in India's ruling coalition, asserted that if Pakistan attempted to use nuclear weapons, "its existence itself would be wiped out of the world map."[29] On December 29, Defense Minister Fernandes warned: "Pakistan can't think of using nuclear weapons despite the fact that they are not committed to the doctrine of no first use like we are. We could take a strike, survive, and then hit back. Pakistan would be finished. I do not really fear that the nuclear issue would figure in a conflict."[30]

On January 11, a senior Indian official repeated the nuclear warning to a U.S. journalist: "They must be aware we could destroy their whole country."[31] On the same day, India's Army Chief, General S. Padmanabhan, reiterated the threat rather more graphically, saying: "If we have to go to war, jolly good." Asked specifically how India would respond to a Pakistani first strike, he declared that "the perpetrator of that particular outrage shall be punished so severely that their [sic] continuation thereafter in any form of fray will be doubtful."[32]

The chief point of the Indian threat was to show that relative capability does make a difference between nuclear powers. What matters is not simply the balance of nuclear power but *the combination of nuclear asymmetry and conventional asymmetry*. India's conventional advantage allowed it recourse to conventional war to the extent that Pakistan's vital interests were not sufficiently affected to warrant a resort to the use of nuclear weapons. Barring this, which India did not envisage, Pakistan had a strong disincentive to cross the nuclear threshold: if nuclear war did occur, it would bear a disproportionately high cost.[33] India's larger arsenal would inflict greater absolute damage, and its larger size would mean the damage it experienced would be much smaller in relative terms. India would survive, Pakistan would not. There was thus space for a limited war to inflict costs on an economically and politically unstable Pakistan. Behind this thinking, of course, lay a conception of nuclear weapons that was eminently political. As India's Navy Chief Admiral Sushil Kumar pointed out, "The nukes are for negotiations, they are not weapons of war."[34]

The implication of nuclear-cum-conventional asymmetry went still further. Because Pakistan was deterred by India's nuclear advantage and faced the prospect of conventional punishment, it could also be deterred from projecting subconventional threats toward India. Thus, Indian leaders sought to telescope the linkages between subconventional, conventional, and nuclear conflict and strategies. The logic was neat, and its import was clear. The stability-instability paradox now worked in India's favor. Pakistan was deterred, India was not.

From Deterrence to Compellence

The assertion of strategic asymmetry enabled the Indian leadership to go a step beyond deterring Pakistani interventionism to a strategy of compellence. It is important here to note the difference between deterrence and compellence. In deterrence, one threatens to punish the adversary when the latter initiates an action. In compellence, one initiates the action—of threatening to punish—oneself in order to change the adversary's behavior, and one continues to act until that behavior changes.[35] The Indians demanded that Pakistan not only roll back its support for terrorists operating in India, but also show evidence of a crackdown on extremist groups within its territory and hand over twenty persons wanted for criminal and subversive activities in India. Going well beyond the mere declaration of strategic asymmetry, India backed up its threat to punish Pakistan by mobilizing a massive military build-up along their mutual border—Operation Parakram—in December 2001.

The compellence threat was "decomposed" and projected in a calibrated series of actions accompanied by a parallel series of verbal statements designed to keep Pakistan off balance.[36] At the level of action, the first major move was made by India on December 22 when it recalled its ambassador to Islamabad and stopped bus and train services between the two countries. Two days later, it was announced that the Indian Army had "moved," but not "deployed," the nuclear-capable short-range Prithvi missile, normally stored far from the border at Secunderabad in the south, to the border region.[37] Another two days later, Defence Minister Fernandes said India had deployed fighter jets at bases along the border and that its missiles were "in position."[38] The following day, Pakistani civilian aircraft were prohibited from overflying India, and India ordered the strength of its mission in Islamabad, as well as that of the Pakistani mission in New Delhi, reduced by half. By this time, the Indian army was laying land mines, constructing bunkers, and positioning tanks and heavy field artillery—all signs of preparation for large-scale conventional conflict. Exchanges of fire were occurring regularly.[39] It was made known that the Army was preparing for its biggest exercise in fifteen years and would be testing its capacity to thwart a nuclear attack.[40] On the same day, it was reported that an Indian naval task force, consisting of India's sole aircraft carrier, six other ships, and two submarines had been deployed within striking distance of Karachi, Pakistan's largest port.[41] A day later, it was announced that India had moved three more divisions to the front. Nuclear signaling followed in nonverbal form: on January 25, 2002, India tested a Pakistan-specific (700–900 km range) version of the Agni missile.[42]

The mobilization was accompanied by strong rhetoric aimed at driving home the point that the advantage lay with India at both the nuclear and conventional levels of conflict. If Pakistan used nuclear weapons first, it would be annihilated by Indian retaliation. The nature of India's course of action was left unspecified but, given the extent of its deployment, conceivably included a major conventional thrust. On December 25, Prime Minister Vajpayee declared: "We do not want war, but war is being thrust on us, and we will have to face it."[43] The threat of nuclear devastation was accompanied by other threats. On December 26, an official let it be known that India had the option to open the gates of the Salal dam on the Chenab River, just 20 km upstream from the border, and flood vast swathes of Pakistani land.[44] Such threats were a psychological tactic, a form of "strategic acupuncture" designed to keep Pakistani leaders off balance and take the prospect of punishment seriously.[45]

Given the assumption that actual war was unlikely to break out, and that even if it did, would be quickly contained by the United States, this combination of actions and statements can only be interpreted as the calculated exercise of a compellence threat. There is evidence to show that it was in fact a bluff, and that war was never seriously intended. A report appearing a year after the event makes the plausible claim that the whole exercise was indeed a ruse and that "the Indian armed forces had neither effective plans, nor the wherewithal to punish Pakistan."[46] But at the time, given the scale of mobilization and the palpable anger behind it, the Indian threat to go to war was taken seriously by most. Inherent in the situation, whether intended or not, was the classic "threat that leaves something to chance."[47] The recipient of the threat could never be confident that the threatener had full control over events, which meant nuclear conflict might break out without it being intended. India was effectively able to convey the impression that it was a "contingently unsafe actor."[48]

Trilateral Compellence: The Role of the United States

Apart from posing a direct compellence threat to Pakistan, India also projected indirect pressure on it via the United States. The politics of nuclear weapons is generally understood in bilateral terms, involving either two nuclear states or one nuclear and one nonnuclear state. South Asia's nuclear rivals have added a new dimension by involving a third country.[49] Both have attempted with some success to induce other players—mainly the United States—to intervene in regional politics on their respective behalves by creating a general fear of approaching nuclear war. Pakistan did this by initiating the Kargil conflict in order to obtain U.S. support for its agenda on Kashmir. India used a similar trilateral stratagem by means of Operation Parakram, which aimed at putting Pakistan under intense U.S. pressure to desist from supporting cross-border terrorism. The results were mixed in both cases. The Kargil conflict rebounded immediately to Pakistan's discomfiture, forcing it to withdraw unconditionally, but the objective of placing the Kashmir dispute high on the global agenda was attained. India was unable to end cross-border terrorism permanently, but was able to put intense pressure on Pakistan via the United States to rethink its support for terrorist groups operating in Kashmir.

The two crises were not identical. In Kargil, Pakistan resorted to a covert approach. Pakistani decision makers calculated that, with mutual deterrence in place, India was no longer in a position to use its conventional advantage, and hence could be put under pressure by clandestine intrusion.[50] The forces which occupied territory on the Indian side of the LoC were mainly Pakistani troops in civilian garb, accompanied by insurgents. The aim was to create a crisis without officially crossing the LoC, i.e., to obtain a military advantage while retaining official deniability. This would precipitate a crisis and evoke a widespread fear of escalation from subconventional to conventional to nuclear conflict, thereby inducing international intervention. In the case of Operation Parakram, India made an overt threat to cross the LoC and the international border (i.e., in sectors other than Kashmir) without specifying the nature of the threatened intervention, but leaving open the possibility of escalation from limited conventional engagement to an unknown—conceivably nuclear—level. The possibility of such a process unfolding was enough to generate acute fear of nuclear conflict and thus invite U.S. involvement.

The Kargil crisis began as a success story for Pakistan, but ended as a military and diplomatic disaster. There were two reasons for this. A limited covert engagement was bound to fail because of the imbalance of commitment. Pakistan's involvement had to be restricted if it had to be covert, and would have been too dangerously provocative had it been overt. Since the fighting took place entirely on the Indian side of the LoC, India could, in contrast, throw in the full weight of its armed forces, so the advantage always lay on its side. Second, since there had been no particular provocation from India, Pakistan was perceived everywhere as the villain of the piece, the irresponsible nuclear power. India, by restraining its forces from crossing the LoC, appeared on the other hand to be a mature nuclear power. In retrospect, Pakistan was a victim of its own early success. Had the fighting been restricted to minor give-and-take skirmishes, it would have generated only sufficient concern to cause the United States and others to urge both countries to come to the negotiating table, which was the Pakistani objective in the first place. The unexpectedly large scale of the conflict raised much greater fears, and the extent of Pakistan's involvement, which could hardly be hidden for long, brought that country opprobrium instead of support. Still, Pakistan was able to achieve an important part of its objective, which was to place Kashmir firmly on the international agenda.

Operation Parakram was initially a more successful strategy for India. It had the advantage of moral outrage on its side because of the immediate provocation of the attack on the Indian Parliament and, earlier, on the Jammu and Kashmir Legislative Assembly. Since the United States and its allies had justified military intervention in Afghanistan as a war against terrorism, the Indian reaction was difficult to oppose. At the same time, Pakistan's record of support to the Taliban and to a number of terrorist groups was well known. The United States had little choice but to bring pressure to bear on it to curb its association with those whom it preferred to call "freedom fighters." Despite the presence of U.S. forces in Pakistan, the Indian military mobilization was sufficiently strong to evoke the fear of a conflict actually breaking out, and hence to compel the United States to demand that Pakistani support for terrorists based on its soil be reversed.

From the U.S. standpoint, South Asia is a difficult region to deal with. The United States has found itself in the thick of India-Pakistan crises since the mid-1980s.[51] It has not been inclined to help forge solutions to what appears to be an intractable problem, especially given India's insistence on resolving the Kashmir dispute bilaterally in accordance with the Indo-Pakistani Simla Agreement of 1972. But since the advent of nuclear weapons, the United States has felt compelled to intervene whenever the regional barometer has gone up. In the first two major crises after the steady covert nuclearization of the subcontinent—the Brasstacks crisis of 1986–87 and the Kashmir crisis of 1990—the United States became involved in peace-making.[52] In both cases, the United States was convinced that the risk of war was high, and that intervention was necessary for the revival of normalcy.[53] By intervening, it left itself open to future manipulation by the regional rivals. Kargil was the first result, the 2001–2 crisis the second. The latter was more problematic, since India's motivation was similar to that of the United States in Afghanistan.

The U.S. response was driven primarily by the fear of a regional war between the two nuclear antagonists. U.S. officials feared a "major miscalculation" by either side, particularly because neither side in their view "seems to have a great grasp of the other's doctrine or limits."[54] CIA Director George Tenet testified before the Senate Intelligence Committee to the Bush Administration's concern that "a conventional war, once begun, could escalate into a nuclear confrontation."[55] Even if there was a feeling that India was merely "huffing and bluffing," as one commentator put it, the risks were too great for the United States to ignore.[56] The United States sent a number of senior officials, including its Secretaries of State and Defense, to both countries, and President George W. Bush and other officials were frequently on the phone to the two South Asian leaders. The President's message to Pakistan's Musharraf was sharp, asking him to take "strong and decisive measures" to curb terrorism.[57] The United States itself formally declared two major Pakistan-based terrorist groups, the Lashkar-e-Taiba and the Jaish-e-Mohammed, as terrorist organizations.[58] Compelled to act, President Musharraf arrested about fifty members of two Muslim fundamentalist groups believed to have been responsible for the terrorist attack on the Indian Parliament.[59] As the crisis persisted, so did U.S. pressure.[60] It seemed to have an effect. In a major speech, Musharraf denounced terrorism and declared: "No organization will be allowed to indulge in terrorism in the name of Kashmir."[61]

U.S. hopes that the crisis would soon wind down were belied, as India insisted on seeing a sharp reduction in border crossing by terrorists. Despite Secretary of State Colin Powell's assertion that Musharraf had been true to his word, and that India should deescalate, Indian forces remained in place.[62] Following a prolonged lull, the strategic temperature rose again in the summer following the so-called "Kaluchak massacre" in Kashmir, in which thirty-two people, mostly wives and children of Indian soldiers, were killed by terrorists.[63] As terrorist attacks from groups based in Pakistan continued, Bush asked Musharraf in May to demonstrate "results in terms of stopping people from crossing the Line of Control."[64] In June, Powell admitted that the problem was persisting and that in spite of Musharraf's assurances, "we can still see evidence that it is continuing."[65] While urging calm on both sides, Bush, according to a White House official, used "very firm language" to insist that Pakistan cease support for terrorists active in Kashmir.[66] Deputy Secretary of State Richard Armitage also made it clear to Musharraf that Pakistan must ensure that infiltration into India by terrorist groups be halted.[67] Clearly, the Indian strategy had succeeded in inducing the United States, fearful of a potential nuclear conflagration in the subcontinent, to put considerable pressure on Pakistan to stop supporting cross-border terrorism.

Critical Assessment of the Strategic Shift

What were the dynamics underlying the strategic shift? The change in the environment has been highlighted. Who was ultimately responsible for the policy change? While hard evidence is difficult to come by, it appears that support for the tough stance toward Pakistan came from three main sources.[68] First, the armed forces pressed for a military response of some kind during and after the Kargil conflict. Second, there was similar pressure from the BJP, the main partner in the ruling coalition, and its associated organizations, the Rashtriya Swayamsevak Sangh (RSS) and the Vishwa Hindu Parishad (VHP). This was backed by a groundswell of public opinion, including sections within the wider strategic community (the media and think tanks). The ultimate decision lay with a small circle of policy makers, which included Prime Minister Vajpayee, Home Minister L. K. Advani, External Affairs Minister Jaswant Singh, Defence Minister George Fernandes, and National Security Advisor Brajesh Mishra. The shift seems to reflect not so much a reformulation of grand strategy or even a new operational strategy (recall the firm belief that a conflict would not actually occur), but a limited *political* response to a difficult, high-pressure situation. The decision was apparently an entirely political one. The service chiefs were not only not consulted in advance, but when given the order to mobilize, were not told what the objectives of the operation were.[69] Here, then, is a clear example of civilian-led militarization. The political leadership was influenced by the military's ideas about limited war, but not to the extent of letting the military conduct one.

This bears on the question of whether strategy—as the use of "military means to achieve political ends"—is meaningful or not.[70] Good strategy is difficult to devise, but not impossible. Notwithstanding the refrain that strategic thinking is largely absent in India, there is little doubt that the thinking behind India's military response to Pakistan-backed cross-border terrorism was "strategic."[71] Not only that, it was carefully calibrated too, encompassing step-by-step political and military escalation—accompanied by parallel rhetoric—to raise the stakes. Whether it was an *appropriate* strategy in the context of a nuclear environment is an altogether different question. It was not.

Indian leaders could claim some gains from Operation Parakram. At the political level, the Indian position on terrorism in Kashmir and Pakistan's role in it was effectively conveyed to the world; Islamabad was forced to make concessions on cross-border terrorism; and U.S. endorsement of the 2002 elections in the Indian-controlled portion of Jammu and Kashmir was obtained.[72] At the operational level, the armed forces were able to gain valuable experience in the organization and planning of a new kind of war.[73] But it would be hard to claim that the mobilization achieved a significant measure of success in relation to the political objective of transforming India's strategic position vis-à-vis Pakistan by the projection of a compellence threat. There are several reasons for this.

First, compellence is unlike deterrence in one important respect. In deterrence, the targeted state is required to refrain from a specific action or set of actions. In contrast, as Schelling points out, in compellence, "the very act of compliance—of doing what is demanded—is more conspicuously compliant, more recognizable as submission under duress, than when an act is merely withheld in the face of a deterrent threat."[74] While not doing something appears only to be an absence of gain, reversing an action under pain of punishment is more obviously a loss. As prospect theory tells us, loss aversion raises commitment to one's position and willingness to bear pain as well as take risks, and hence raises potential costs to one who is seeking gain.[75] Pakistan's deep commitment to its Kashmir policy made more than temporary reversal unlikely. Going back on the policy would have been tantamount to abandoning Kashmir, which was intolerable, even politically suicidal.

Second, between nuclear-weapon states, deterrence overrides compellence. A compellence threat can be "called," and a threatener required to follow up with action. In that case, when both have nuclear weapons, the state which has to act first and thereby bring both to the point of war is likely to find that act difficult in the extreme. As we have seen in Chapter 2, nuclear powers are compelled by the threat of devastation to stop two steps short of nuclear war, i.e., at some point *below* the threshold between skirmishing or subconventional conflict and conventional war. While there may be doubt as to what exactly constitutes the threshold, it seems fairly clear in the present case that the inviolability of the LoC (in terms of the movement of ground forces) and the international border had been tacitly agreed upon by India and Pakistan. This was in one sense violated when Pakistani forces crossed the LoC in 1999, but at the same time underscored because they felt the need to do so in civilian attire, and because the subsequent conduct of military engagements maintained the LoC's sanctity at considerable cost to both sides. Pakistan did not respond to the Indian assault on its forces with a counterattack across the line, and Indian forces refrained from crossing it, or the international border, during their campaign. During Operation Parakram, India was in the position of having to risk violating the LoC and the border and, in light of the size of its mobilization, risk launching a conventional war. That it did not do so was clearly because the potential cost was too great. Just as Pakistan was constrained in 1999, so was India in 2001–2. In effect, deterrence overrode compellence in both instances.

Pakistani actions reminded Indian leaders that they were confronting a nuclear power. Apart from responding with a matching large-scale troop buildup, Pakistan resorted to nuclear signaling, notably at the second peak point of the crisis in May. On May 20, word was unofficially given through the press that it had deployed the nuclear-capable Shaheen missile, which has a range of 750 km.[76] Shortly afterward, Pakistan conducted a series of missile tests, the first for the medium-range Ghauri missile, the remaining two for short-range missiles.[77] Prime Minister Vajpayee was conscious of the risk of escalation and the possibility of the crisis taking a nuclear turn.[78] After a point, then, with further escalation deterred, there was, as one analyst put it, "nowhere to go."[79] The stalemate persisted for a time. Eventually, with the Indian armed forces chiefs coming round to the view that Pakistan was no longer "responding," as one Ministry of Defence source expressed it, the whole exercise had to be called off.[80] Besides, as one observer has pointed out, an Indian march into Pakistani territory would have invited the same negative world reaction as Kargil did for Pakistan, because of the risk of crossing the threshold to full-scale war. Again, the game was not worth the candle.[81]

Third, compellence confronts a serious difficulty in the problem of reversibility. The Soviet-China border conflict is instructive in this respect. The situation preceding the Sino-Soviet border clashes of 1969 at Damansky island (or, as the Chinese call it, Zhenbao) on the Ussuri River bears a remarkable resemblance to the recent South Asian confrontation.[82] As with the Kashmir problem, the border dispute between China and the Soviet Union had its roots in the colonial era. Like Pakistan today, China was in a state of considerable internal instability as a result of the Cultural Revolution. Minor skirmishes had occurred at other places in the region before the first Damansky incident on March 1, 1969. At the time the March 1 fighting broke out, the Soviet Union had overwhelmingly superior conventional as well as nuclear forces. Following the first clash, it mounted a massive mobilization of conventional forces and resorted to coercive diplomacy through a series of threats as well as actual military engagements. A series of short encounters took place between March and August 1969. Unlike the South Asian case, the Soviet Union dropped hints of a nuclear first strike. Eventually, China reversed its earlier stand and agreed to come to the negotiating table, signed a one-year navigation agreement with respect to the disputed river, and dropped its insistence that the "unequalness" of the old treaties that had determined the Sino-Soviet border had rendered them worthless. The Soviet strategy seemed to have worked. But in the long run, it did not. Once the crisis had been resolved, the Chinese backed away from negotiations "they had no intention of carrying to conclusion on Soviet terms."[83]

While making concessions to Indian demands, Musharraf (or his successors) had the same option of reversing his pledge. He has already exercised it. In June 2002, he reverted to his old position by asserting that Kashmir was in the throes of a "freedom struggle," not "cross-border terrorism." He went on to say that while at the time "nothing is happening across the Line of Control," that was not a permanent state: "I'm not going to give you an assurance that for years nothing will happen."[84] In September, he equated his position to his survival, arguing that "no government of Pakistan can leave or abandon the issue of Kashmir" and that any leader who does so will be "eliminated."[85] This also underscores the matter of commitment. The effectiveness of a coercive strategy depends considerably on the balance of commitments on both sides, for the calculus of costs relates to commitment.[86] It is evident that Pakistani leaders have a high level of commitment to the cause of Kashmir as one vital to national identity, and hence would be willing to pay a high price to retain it, if for no other reason than for their own survival. In June, senior Pakistani military officers privately told the *Washington Post* that the militants fighting in Kashmir remained a vital component of Pakistan's strategy.[87] The reversibility problem, which can become manifest at a time of the coerced state's choosing, was already visible. Forethought would have shown that it was inherent in India's compellence strategy from the beginning.

A fourth difficulty is that the strategy of trilateral compellence is subject to the third party's interests being compatible with those of the state practicing it. When their interests diverge, the strategy may be adversely affected. In the present case, India had a common interest with the United States in curbing terrorism, but their priorities were different. India was concerned about terrorists operating in Kashmir, the United States primarily with destroying Al Qaeda and the Taliban, for which it needed Pakistani assistance. Hence, while the United States did put pressure on Pakistan to back off from its support for terrorists operating in Kashmir, it did not go beyond a point for fear of jeopardizing its joint antiterrorism campaign in that country. On the nuclear issue, U.S. interest lies in preventing a war and maintaining regional stability, but its view of regional stability does not necessarily coincide with India's. For the United States, a negotiated settlement to prevent war is the overriding concern; for India, an end to Pakistan's role in Kashmir comes first. U.S. involvement in both the Kargil conflict and the 2001–2 crisis has placed Pakistan on the defensive, but has also pushed the Pakistani agenda of negotiation on Kashmir forward.

A fifth problem for nuclear powers resorting to a coercive strategy is that of risk. As we have seen in Chapter 1, optimists tend to emphasize the rational consequence of nuclear possession, which is prudence and war avoidance. Critics tend to stress its nonrational elements, citing all that can go wrong. Even if both sides behave rationally, there may still be loss of control resulting in war.[88] A rational decision may be taken under a given set of circumstances, but that set may change—for one side in a conflict cannot control all that the other does—and bring about what appears to be an "irrational" outcome.[89] Thus, a crisis between nuclear-weapon states tends to contain both stable and unstable elements. The 2001–2 crisis is illustrative.

The overriding concern for any observer of—or participant in—the region's strategic politics is strategic stability, especially during a crisis. Nuclear stability has a number of requirements, notably that the participants in an adversarial relationship retain control of their actions and of the situation; and that the cost of launching a first strike be unacceptable.[90] There is no doubt that in the 2001–2 crisis, India and Pakistan would have considered the cost of initiating nuclear war intolerable. There were certainly strong elements of stability in the crisis. These included the non-centrality of nuclear weapons in the national security strategies of both countries, and the restraint they showed in not deploying nuclear weapons in spite of having obtained the capability to do so much earlier. In addition, the wars fought by them had all been limited in time and scope. Even after nuclearization (which preceded the 1998 tests by about a decade), India and Pakistan had engaged in constant border skirmishing without any serious risk of escalation to the level of conventional war. The Kargil conflict, which brought India closest to this, respected the two-steps-short rule, keeping fighting to a level two steps below the threshold of a nuclear conflict. India's goals in the 2001–2002 crisis were limited to stemming the terrorist tide, not to occupying territory or dismembering Pakistan. Indian forces were not in a position to launch a full-scale conventional war against that country, and Indian leaders were sensitive to the potential for a nuclear conflict if they did make such an attempt.[91] During Operation Parakram, action was taken against two top commanders who indirectly incurred risks. In January 2002, Lieutenant-General Kapil Vij, commander of India's 2 Corps, a strike corps, was abruptly removed from his post for positioning his forces too close to the border.[92] In March, Air Marshal V. K. Bhatia was transferred out of the LoC/border region after his aircraft strayed into Pakistani air space, was shot by Pakistani forces, and forced to make a distress landing at Leh.[93] Finally, as noted earlier, since U.S. forces were physically present in the region in large numbers, it was expected that the United States would prevent a conflict or intervene immediately in the event it did.

On the negative side, both the incidents cited above represent what can go wrong in a crisis. The problem with rational strategy is that it cannot guarantee rational outcomes. As Scott Sagan has shown, organizations associated with hazardous technologies are vulnerable to "normal accidents."[94] Such organizations are characterized by complexity of interaction and by lack of flexibility. The first tends to create unexpected problems because of unanticipated interaction between components; the second makes it difficult to improvise solutions. Besides, factors such as competing objectives and interests and the internal dynamics of organizations increase the probability of error and accident. Examples of high risk resulting from totally unexpected events abound. In 1962, as the Cuban Missile Crisis was winding down, the KGB apparently unknowingly activated a warning signal to the United States of an imminent Soviet attack (an arrested counterintelligence agent appears to have deceived them on the meaning of the signal).[95] The risks associated with war of any kind are indeterminate, and there is always the problem of losing control of events and succumbing to unintended escalation. As Paul Bracken has shown, there are four main paths to accidental nuclear disaster.[96] Of these, two are relevant to a crisis situation. A "pure" accident may be a tripwire, for instance a computer malfunction may cause a false warning of nuclear attack. Such an incident is unlikely in South Asia in the normal course if nuclear weapons remain in nondeployed status. But if weapons are deployed, a false alarm could trigger war, especially during a crisis. In a crisis, a second possibility comes up: that a conventional war will break out, which will increase the probability of an accident.

Loss of control over the escalatory process between any two levels of conflict may occur for a number of reasons.[97] There is no such thing as pure rationality. During a crisis, decision makers may be influenced by psychological factors, such as image biases, cognitive dissonance, and an inability to interpret subtle signals correctly, as well as by emotions. Too many things happen too quickly for decision makers to be adequately informed, and they may indeed be misinformed. They may not have full knowledge of and control over their own forces, and may also misinterpret the actions of the enemy's forces. During and after the crisis under discussion, besides the incidents involving senior military officers described above, there were several serious situations that could have gone out of control. Prolonged armed clashes took place in July and August 2002 when Pakistani forces occupied the Loonda Post on the Indian side of the LoC, and India reclaimed it with the use of 155 mm heavy artillery, Mirage 2000 aircraft, and helicopter gunships.[98] Indian forces also undertook unspecified "special missions" across the LoC during the crisis.[99] The deployment of India's western and eastern fleets in the Arabian Sea raised risks considerably. Maritime operations are particularly susceptible to escalation because of the absence of clear geographical "red lines" and the common use of tactics that cause opposing forces to come close and even mingle.[100] What would actually happen in a crisis if fighting were to break out? How would command and control function? No one can be really sure. Whether the United States would have been able to avert a war arising from loss of escalatory control is a matter of conjecture, not confidence.

In his comparative study of interstate crises, Russell Leng casts doubt on the widely held view that crises have the potential to spiral out of control.[101] Leng's study finds that national leaders tolerate high levels of escalation if they place a premium on avoiding war, and that hostilities even in most cases of conflict between nonnuclear states result from premeditation rather than loss of control. But the study is not comforting, since the number of cases is small (only four for nuclear dyads), and the possibility of war occurring despite high tolerance levels is too great to be ignored. We do know that the risk of an India-Pakistan war remains significant today because both are in their own respective ways deeply dissatisfied powers, and because armed clashes occur regularly along the border/LoC. Pakistani support for terrorists operating in India continues, LoC violations persist, and the Indian Army wants to create a Mountain Strike Corps to enhance its capacity to fight a limited war with Pakistan.[102]

In the end, the whole exercise in compellence did not yield the results it was expected to, and India's strategic situation vis-à-vis Pakistan remained largely unchanged. On balance, the risk was not worth it. Hindsight offers little comfort. It is not enough to look back and observe that war did not occur. The probability of war may never have been great; the consequences would.

Conclusion

The implications of Operation Parakram for India's nuclear future are uncertain. The exercise in compellence seems to have opened the door to an open-ended future in which a minimalist conception of deterrence will no longer be the solitary plank of nuclear policy. It is entirely possible that Indian thinking will move away from the highly restrained doctrinal position enunciated by Jaswant Singh toward an ill-understood process of expansion and risk-taking. Compellence directly contradicts minimum deterrence. If, as no less than its Defence Minister stressed, India enjoys the advantage of nuclear asymmetry, and that in turn can be the basis of coercive diplomacy, then the disadvantaged state has an inducement to catch up. In effect, Pakistan has an incentive to try and reach some sort of equivalence so as to be less susceptible to coercion. The same applies to India vis-à-vis China, which, after all, provided the raison d'être for India's official nuclearization. We have here the intellectual basis for a potential shift from minimum deterrence toward Cold War–type arms racing.

On the other hand, it is also possible that this was a one-of-a-kind crisis that will not be repeated. The peculiar concatenation of circumstances that created it—the backdrop of September 11 and the war in Afghanistan, the attack on India's Parliament, and the presence of U.S. forces in Pakistan—is unlikely to recur. Indian leaders seem to have been aware that the opportunity was a unique one. As one senior official told a U.S. correspondent, "this time we are determined to finish the problem one way or another."[103] Ultimately, nuclear posture is the creature of a wider politics of threat and counterthreat. The present period is profoundly important in a larger sense. It is a pivotal time in the historical trajectory of South Asia and the troubled relationship between India and Pakistan. A number of different outcomes are possible. Much depends on fundamental political decisions taken now. It may be of some comfort that continuing terrorist violence has not brought a fresh crisis, but instead the offer of an olive branch from Vajpayee to Musharraf (October 2003) and a period of patient negotiations. Possibly, this is a case of learning from experience.

The critical problem revealed by Indian strategy in the 2001–2 crisis is that the political understanding of nuclear weapons involves an inherent difficulty. While carrying the advantage of built-in restraint with respect to the direct role of nuclear weapons, it tends to permit a *politically instrumental* conception of nuclear weapons. Since the weapons are not viewed in operational terms, the risks associated with them as operational instruments may be underestimated. Political games may thus be the unfortunate consequence. A more balanced view of the operational and political characteristics of nuclear weapons would restrain decision makers from taking the risks we have examined in this chapter. There is a serious need, above all, to undertake a thorough examination of nuclear doctrine: of the role of force in a nuclear-strategic relationship, of the relationships between different levels of force—nuclear, conventional, and subconventional—and of the meaning of minimum deterrence.

5

Missile Defense

On May 1, 2001, President George W. Bush announced a strategic initiative that sought to effect a radical break with the past by supplementing offensive capability with missile defense as the centerpiece of U.S. national security strategy. The Government of India reacted with remarkable alacrity in shedding its earlier doubts and expressing its warm appreciation of the President's speech. The response surprised almost everyone, partly because it was a significant departure from the government's earlier misgivings about U.S. proposals for a national missile defense (NMD), and partly because of the rapidity with which it came. The public debate that followed was conducted with the vigor displayed earlier over important national security decisions on the Comprehensive Test Ban Treaty (CTBT) and over the nuclear tests of May 1998. Actually, the debate was a little late in coming. NMD had entered the U.S. strategic agenda much earlier during the Clinton Administration, but most Indians had given it little attention at the time. Besides, India's own interest in missile defense goes back several years. While much (though not all) of the current global attention has focused on U.S. NMD, India has for some years sought its own missile defense capability.

This chapter attempts to gauge the appropriate posture that India should take with respect to both kinds of missile defense.[1] The crucial question is whether missile defense has a destabilizing impact on deterrence relationships. Critics fear that a U.S. NMD will have a cascading effect—a new version of the old domino theory—on China, India, and Pakistan, in that order. As one state reduces its vulnerability, the next will feel threatened. This will lead to a missile defense race, or to an offensive missile race to reduce vulnerability, or to both. In this view, a state better able to defend itself will enjoy an advantage, and this will create incentives for the weaker side to initiate an arms race or contemplate an early first strike. The same argument in the context of Indian strategy holds that an Indian missile defense program will have similar effects on India's relations with China and Pakistan. Either way, missile defense can be seen as a destabilizing phenomenon. The argument here is that it is not. Because deterrence rests on the possibility of large-scale damage, it is not, and will not be, affected by anything other than perfect missile defense. Since missile defense cannot be perfect, and more importantly, cannot be *known* to be perfect, deterrence can never be weakened even by its most robust manifestation. But that does not mean that missile defense is useless. It is still valid because it is a state's only resort in the event of an unauthorized launch.

A brief description of missile defense as it has been conceived of in the United States is in order.[2] In U.S. parlance, NMD is designed to protect the homeland from long-range missile threats, while theater missile defense (TMD) defends against short-range missiles. The place of intermediate-range missile threats is somewhat ambiguous: they may be considered relevant to either form of missile defense, depending on which end of their ranges one is looking at. A missile has three phases in its path. The initial or boost phase lasts for no more than five minutes. In the second or mid-course phase, the missile is usually outside the earth's atmosphere. This phase may be subdivided into ascent and descent phases. This is the longest period of exposure to an antimissile weapon. The terminal phase consists of the last few minutes before the missile hits its target. NMD is applicable to all three phases, TMD only to the second and the third, since short-range missiles have very brief boost phases. Though a number of technologies are being developed, the most promising of them involve the use of airborne lasers and surface-launched projectiles to destroy a missile. The first phase of a U.S. NMD consisting of a land-based mid-course interceptor system was completed at Fort Greely in Alaska in late 2004. In all cases, there are significant difficulties associated with such factors as the short time available for response, the relative speeds and trajectories of missiles and interceptors, and the workability of advanced (X-band) radar systems for targeting missiles. Attackers also have a number of options for defeating missile defenses, such as special paints that reflect lasers, and decoys to confuse sensors.[3]

The concept of missile defense needs some clarification. In the U.S. strategic lexicon, NMD is generally understood as a response to the threat posed to the U.S. homeland by long-range missiles, while TMD is aimed at countering theater missile threats to U.S. interests overseas. The definition needs flexibility. For instance, if the continental United States were to be attacked by a ship-borne short-range missile, the appropriate defense would be from a so-called TMD system. In short, a TMD system may well play a role in

NMD. This is particularly true for India, which faces threats to its homeland from short- and intermediate-range missiles. Thus, the Indian interest in antimissile defensive systems is aimed at a limited *national* defense, even though the specific systems may be designated as TMD systems in the United States and elsewhere. To avoid confusion, the term "missile defense" is used in the Indian context, as is increasingly being done in the United States as well.

The chapter begins with a brief discussion of India's interest in missile defense. It then examines the official Indian response to the Bush initiative and explains the reasons for India's shift from doubtful distancing to politically astute applause. In the subsequent section, the response of the Indian strategic community to the Government of India's position is then analyzed. Thereafter, a case is presented in favor of missile defense on basic doctrinal grounds. Having demonstrated that missile defense does not affect minimum deterrence adversely, I extend the argument and call for a limited Indian missile defense for the purpose of protecting at least some Indian assets.

India's Interest in Missile Defense

Though India has sought to acquire missile defense capability for some time, strategic thinkers have paid relatively little attention to the issue.[4] Different countries have different reasons for an interest in missile defense. For the United States, defense against theater missile threats has been a long-standing concern, dating back to the late 1950s.[5] The extensive use of missiles by other states in strategically important areas, notably during the Iran-Iraq War and the Soviet war in Afghanistan, created a growing concern about a new "generic threat" to U.S. forces.[6] The most significant direct threat came during the Gulf War, in which the largest single instance of U.S. casualties resulted from an Iraqi Scud missile attack. The post–Cold War fear of "rogue states" gave rise to the call for NMD. Most recently, the terrorist acts of September 11, 2001, underscored the need for defenses against unexpected threats.[7] Missile defense became an "Asian issue" only after China's missile launches in the Taiwan Strait in 1995 and 1996, and the North Korean launch of a Taepodong missile in 1998. These events also created a serious interest in TMD among U.S. allies, notably Japan, South Korea, and Taiwan.[8]

While none of this impacted directly on India, it certainly enhanced awareness of the issue. Though less concerned about the ramifications of U.S. NMD, it had a more long-standing interest in missile defense because of its potential vulnerability to missile attacks.[9] Its attention to this was drawn from time to time by the Arab-Israeli War of 1973, the Iran-Iraq War, the Soviet war in Afghanistan, and Operation Desert Storm. The concern became more serious following reports about the transfer of Chinese M-11 missiles to Pakistan and the deployment of Chinese nuclear weapons in Tibet. American use of Tomahawk missiles in Afghanistan (1998) and Kosovo (1999) added to a general sense of unease. From the mid-1990s, the growth of Pakistani nuclear and missile capabilities has underlined the gravity of the problem. More recently, the prospect of Pakistani nuclear weapons falling into the hands of radical elements has created a new worry.[10]

The missile systems developed under the Integrated Guided Missile Development Program inaugurated by Prime Minister Indira Gandhi in 1983 include not only offensive missiles such as the nuclear-capable Prithvi and Agni, but also the Akash surface-to-air missile, which has TMD potential. Indian scientists have developed the Rajendra phased array radar and negotiated with Russia for its S-300V antitactical ballistic missile (ATBM) system, as also with Israel for the Arrow ATBM and the Phalcon airborne early warning (AEW) platform.[11] While the cost factor is a serious constraint (the S-300V is believed to cost from $55 million to $160 million, depending on the exact type), Indian interest has been sustained. India has been negotiating with Israel to integrate the technology of Akash and the Arrow-2, as also the Rajendra radar with the Arrow-2's Green Pine radar, which can track a missile from a distance of 300 km.[12] In April 2002, the Indian Parliament's Standing Committee on Defence demanded a time-bound schedule for the acquisition of missile defense capability.[13] The United States, wary of regional "destabilization" at a juncture when there was high tension between India and Pakistan (the 2001–2 crisis), applied the brakes on the transfer of Israeli technology to India.[14] But by June 2002, India had acquired from Israel two Green Pine radars for "advanced research" and aerostat balloons with a surveillance capability of 500 km.[15] Indian defense scientists have also begun working on indigenous missile defense technologies.[16] Russia has renewed its offer of the S-300V system, and has in addition mooted the sale of its short-range ToR-M1 and Buk-M1 systems.[17]

In October 2003, India finally acquired the Phalcon system in a trilateral deal with Israel, which supplied the radar, and Russia, which provided the Ilyushin-76 aircraft into which the radar would be fitted.[18] In the meantime, India had already requested the United States for "technical information" on its Patriot system, and the two had agreed on a missile defense workshop to be held in India.[19] By October 2004, according to U.S. Ambassador David Mulford, Indo-U.S. talks had progressed beyond the question of whether India needed missile defenses to discussions to "figure out" what is "needed where."[20] In India, missile defense is viewed from a limited perspective: Indian officials publicly justify it as an extension of air defense. Given this keen interest in obtaining missile defense systems, it is not surprising that, despite some concerns about the prospects for global arms control, India should have been comfortable with the U.S. missile defense program. Yet there has never been a clear articulation about what kind of missile defensive is sought, and why, nor any discussion about the relationship between missile defense and minimum deterrence.

India's Official Response to U.S. NMD

Much has been made of the remarkable Indian enthusiasm for the Bush initiative of May 2001. There had been some criticism of the U.S. interest in missile defense earlier, but it had been perfunctory and, considering India was pursuing similar capability, contradictory as well. In early July 2000, Defence Minister George Fernandes, when questioned about NMD, said that "the US should give up this whole exercise as it will lead to far too many problems than [sic] we can visualize now."[21] Less than a week later, Fernandes was ambivalent. While expressing some concern that U.S. NMD might alter the global nuclear balance and start a new arms race, he also noted that it would dismantle mutual assured destruction (MAD) and, more importantly, would not affect India's nuclear program.[22] Similarly, External Affairs Minister Jaswant Singh observed that India was against the militarization of outer space, but expressed his satisfaction with the talks he had held with his counterpart, Madeleine Albright, and her deputy, Strobe Talbott.[23] The mild and qualified criticisms expressed by senior members of the Indian cabinet may in part have been due to India's "reluctance to contradict its number one trading partner, its number one source of direct investment and technology, and its number one potential ally in its rivalry with China and Pakistan."[24] But it certainly was not the result of a lack of interest in missile defense as an issue.

Nevertheless, the Vajpayee government's warm reaction to Bush's May 2001 speech was unexpected. The Prime Minister lauded the United States for "moving away from the hair-trigger alerts associated with prevailing nuclear orthodoxies" by means of a shift which "seeks to transform the strategic parameters on which the Cold War security architecture was built."[25] The Ministry of External Affairs, in an official statement, applauded the President's effort to dismantle the "adversarial legacy of the Cold War" and his desire to "make a clean break from the past" by "stepping away from a world that is held hostage by the doctrine of MAD."[26] After the initial surprise, some commentators took a second look at the Indian position and discovered a nuance. Nicholas Berry pointed out that India had not endorsed NMD at all, but had only expressed enthusiasm for that portion of the Bush speech which underlined arms control.[27] The point was expressly conveyed by Indian officials to senior Russian and Chinese leaders, though not to the satisfaction of either.[28] Indian policy makers, caught between the United States on one hand and Russia and China on the other, had to engage in a fair bit of tightrope walking. The inducement held out by the Russians—transfer of missile defense technology (space-tracking radar and ATBM rockets) in addition to other military hardware—was considerable.[29] Still, as a senior Russian journalist observed, winning India over to the Russian point of view had "proven difficult."[30] At a joint press conference with visiting Russian Foreign Minister Igor Ivanov just three days after the Bush speech, Singh called on the United States not to abrogate the Antiballistic Missile (ABM) Treaty unilaterally, but to "engage Russia in dialogue," which was far from saying that the preservation of the treaty was a serious concern for India.[31] Singh also explicitly welcomed the Bush initiative, with the minor qualification that "[b]etween mutually agreed decisions and mutually assured destruction, the former is preferable."[32]

The new Congress Party–led coalition that came to power in 2004 with Manmohan Singh as Prime Minister was expected to be more critical of missile defense. Deputy National Security Advisor Satish Chandra expressed an old reservation in his apprehension that the United States "could consider resorting to the use of nuclear weapons in a pre-emptive mode."[33] But the definitive statement of continuity in policy came from Minister of State for External Affairs E. Ahamed, who told the Lok Sabha (the Lower House of India's Parliament) in August 2004 that "there is no change in the policy of the Government under which it has held preliminary discussions and dialogue with the U.S. on the subject of missile defence."[34]

Notwithstanding the careful choice of words, the fact remains that, on the whole, India's response to the Bush speech, and to U.S. policy generally, has been very favorable. What were India's motives in its early support for the U.S. missile defense program? Indian leaders were spurred by the prospect of a change in the old nuclear order, which they saw as discriminatory, the possibility of "complicating the nuclear calculus of both China and Pakistan," and developing a counter to the rising threat they perceived from extremist elements in their neighborhood, particularly in Pakistan.[35] According to one commentator, India wanted to obtain from the U.S. military and technical assistance as well as support for its drive for a permanent seat in the Security Council—"a good way to grease the wheel of India's rise to superpower status."[36] A more immediate objective may have been a desire to gain access to U.S. surveillance data, especially on Chinese and Pakistani missile sites.[37] A possible consideration was a strategic tie-up with the United States against China.[38] But these explanations are not enough. They do not tell us why an India long committed to global disarmament should have been willing to countenance so easily the abandonment of the ABM Treaty, to many the centerpiece of the existing structure of arms control. Furthermore, why, despite their constant concern with the Chinese threat, were Indian leaders unperturbed by the possibility of a Chinese buildup in response to the NMD? The answer lies in the character of Indian strategic culture.

As shown in Chapter 3, Indian thinking about nuclear weapons has always been a mix of power-oriented realism and idealistic restraint. While the realist element has been attracted to the possibilities offered by nuclear deterrence, the idealist element has found nuclear weapons morally abhorrent and hence sought to undo their potential effects through global disarmament. This latter component of Indian nuclear-strategic thought would find missile defense conceptually appealing. It is not surprising that the Indian response to the Bush initiative should have focused largely on the shift away from MAD and the space this creates for significant arms reductions. That the capacity to defend against missiles is taken seriously by the Government of India is evident from its long-standing interest, dating back to a time when the Bharatiya Janata Party (BJP) was not in power, in developing its missile defense capacity. Indian equanimity vis-à-vis the possible upgrading of China's arsenal is also explained by its nuclear-strategic culture. India has never been particularly anxious about vulnerability to a qualitative and quantitative gap between China's nuclear forces and its own. While some Indian strategists have been wont to focus on typically U.S. concerns like vulnerability to preemption, the fact that the pace of India's nuclearization has been leisurely at best is indicative of a distinct lack of enthusiasm for the operational minutiae of nuclear possession. Indian political leaders have often been accused of an overly political approach to nuclear weapons. In a way, this is one of their strengths. Theirs is an understanding that underlines their commitment to the fundamentals of minimum deterrence, to an insightful perception of the essentially political character of nuclear weapons, which explains their acceptance of the imbalances and anomalies that preoccupy professional deterrence theorists. In light of this, the BJP-led government's relaxed acceptance of missile defense, and its obvious intent—to extract the fullest advantage from a policy it is intrinsically comfortable with—is understandable.

Yet the absence of a well-reasoned justification for missile defense from the standpoint of minimum deterrence is potentially problematic. While Indian policy is intuitively in tune with the precepts of minimum deterrence, the lack of conceptual clarity may in the future jeopardize India's ability to sustain a posture that is consistent with the concept. There is a similar problem with much of the public discussion on the same issue.

The Indian Missile Defense Debate

The debate over missile defense was somewhat different from similar debates in the past. Earlier, public discussions on the CTBT (which India rejected in 1996) and on the 1998 nuclear tests demarcated fairly clearly the dividing line between those who thought nuclear weapons to be a boon and those who deemed them to be a curse. This time, however, opposition to the government's position came not only from the generally left-leaning peace constituency, but also from staunch nationalists on the other side of the ideological spectrum. Not only that, the new strategic bedfellows used the same language to oppose the government and its supporters, which is not a little ironic, since the left critics harbor a strong antipathy toward nuclear weapons, whereas the nationalists are comfortable with a nuclear option.

The chief objection of the critics was that U.S. NMD would have a destabilizing domino effect reaching all the way from the United States to South Asia.[39] The U.S. program would cause China to embark on a qualitative and quantitative buildup. This would likely entail an expanded arsenal, the deployment of multiple-warhead (MIRVed) missiles, and the adoption of an alert posture.[40] In India, the change would be perceived as threatening, the balance between moderates and hawks would tilt in favor of the latter, and a buildup would commence, followed by a like response from Pakistan. The result would be rising regional instability, raising the dire prospect of an already unstable India-Pakistan relationship sliding into war. U.S. critics, including former Secretary of State Madeleine Albright, echoed this view.[41] Indian detractors also feared that a China antagonized by U.S. missile defense might draw even closer to Pakistan and accelerate strategic cooperation with it.[42] This is an emotive issue. Indians have long complained about the China-Pakistan nuclear and missile nexus as the central component of China's efforts to "contain" and "encircle" India.

Another criticism was that NMD will have a disequilibriating effect on the global structure of arms control.[43] The U.S. rejection of the ABM Treaty was seen as the first step toward this.[44] It would not only present a difficult roadblock to further reductions, but also enhance tensions everywhere through the revival of arms racing. Ongoing efforts to agree on a Fissile Material Cutoff Treaty (FMCT) would be adversely affected, particularly if India and Pakistan were to seek to stockpile larger quantities of fissile materials in order to build more bombs. One critic observed that missile defense is not a truly defensive system, but is in fact a "means for bolstering offense" with no design for disarmament, and Indian interest in it shows that "[w]e have now deflected sharply from the elimination goalpost and are now adrift in the uncertain and dangerous course of a new weapon system."[45] The offensive implications of missile defense capability were a source of discomfort for several commentators. They were troubled by the prospect of a United States, made less vulnerable by NMD, becoming aggressively interventionist.[46] This brought to the fore an image that has not quite faded from the Indian strategic worldview: the fear of being pushed around by a hegemonic power.[47]

On the other side, a number of analysts found merit in India's stance. First, they rejected the domino theory. One argument, made before the Bush speech of May 2001, was that China will not react aggressively to a U.S. NMD because it will not need to: it will have adequate recourse to countermeasures, which are easier and cheaper to acquire than sophisticated weapons.[48] Another—also expressed early—conformed to the assumptions of minimum deterrence in holding that it does not really matter because India has long accepted an India-China disparity anyway: "What India is looking for is credible nuclear deterrence and not nuclear parity."[49] It was also argued that simple pragmatism backs the Indian position. Since the United States will go ahead with missile defense regardless of what others say, why not hop aboard the bandwagon and try to extract the maximum advantage?[50] Besides, as one observer noted, it was a "wily political decision" since it lauded the U.S. statement on arms cuts without supporting NMD directly.[51]

Another argument in favor of supporting the United States went a little further. It viewed the NMD issue as providing an opportunity for India to engineer a breakthrough in its relationship with the United States. The U.S. shift from established "nuclear theology" to missile defense had opened the door for a fruitful arms control dialogue between the two countries.[52] The result would be an improved strategic understanding between them. Finally, the Bush initiative was seen more broadly as heralding the "demise of the old nuclear order," which rested on the twin pillars of MAD and the NPT, both anathema to India's strategic thinking and interests.[53] It followed that India should be supportive of it.

The arguments outlined above are cast in military-strategic as well as political-strategic terms. Opposition to NMD and to India's stance on it rests fundamentally on the understanding that its military-strategic consequences are undesirable: NMD will alter the operational calculus of the nuclear players, and their resultant actions and reactions will have an adverse impact on global and Indian security. Supporters of the Indian position hold generally that operational effects do not matter or are of little consequence. The real significance of NMD is political: it provides the basis for a paradigm change, whether with regard to the global nuclear order and the prospects for arms control or, more narrowly, with respect to Indo-U.S. relations. The latter case is more persuasive. However, it needs to be argued at greater length since it is far from self-evident that the military implications of missile defense are not as undesirable as critics hold. Support for missile defense requires a more thorough consideration of the military and political aspects of missile defense from the minimum deterrence perspective than is evident in the debate.

There are some important difficulties in the opponents' position that need to be addressed. First, they take as axiomatic that any disequilibrium in military "balances" will lead to arms racing. This is based on an overly simplified understanding of the phenomenon of arms racing and the variable dynamics that underlie it. Not all changes in the balance of forces result in arms racing, and not all arms racing is the consequence of changes in the balance of forces. Mitigating factors and policy choices are important in determining the relationship between them. Critics are also off the mark when they express disappointment that the positive direction taken by developments in arms control after the end of the Cold War has been adversely affected by missile defense. The reality is that, after the flurry of arms control initiatives that marked the closing stages of the Cold War and its immediate aftermath, the momentum of arms control had actually slowed down well before missile defense became a major issue. The optimism of the early post–Cold War phase—the hope that nuclear weapons might at least be delegitimized, if not done away with—had already receded when President Bush made his May 2001 speech. Despite the absence of serious nuclear threats for a decade, the major nuclear powers had done little to retreat from their overkill postures. It is in this context that a paradigm shift in the fundamentals of doctrine can be seen as a small ray of hope.

Why Missile Defense Is Acceptable

The central issue about missile defense is whether it has a destabilizing effect on deterrence. In the United States, advocates of missile defense insist on the need to respond adequately to a wide range of threats, from Russia and China to rogue states.[54] It is also argued that missile defense need not fuel an arms race: after all, the Soviet Union had not responded to President Ronald Reagan's Strategic Defense Initiative (SDI) program with an arms buildup, and Russia did not do so either when missile defense was placed on the U.S. security agenda in the 1990s.[55] Critics argue that it is too expensive and technologically difficult, that missile defenses can easily be defeated by countermeasures, that the new threats are neither serious nor undeterrable, and that missile defense will result in arms racing, strategic instability, and the unraveling of painstakingly built arms control structures.[56] Gradually, there has emerged a middle position that calls for a limited missile defense that is cheaper and technologically more feasible. Its advocates believe that the United States can assuage the concerns of the Russian and the Chinese by deploying a defense that is too limited to threaten their retaliatory capabilities.[57] It would also be conducive to strategic stability and forward movement in arms control by marking a shift away from MAD, which sustains large arsenals.[58]

It does not appear likely that a reasonably effective missile defense will be produced in the foreseeable future. The technical and cost obstacles are extraordinarily high.[59] But the difficulty with missile defense goes much deeper. Even a very high level of missile defense capability is not enough to provide an effective missile shield. As the argument in Chapter 2 shows, nuclear threats are really not about weapons inventories and their operational capabilities. They are at heart about the possibility of immense damage to one's society. This is why it takes very few weapons to deter. Those who are even minimally threatened by the possibility of nuclear weapons being used against them are invariably compelled to restrain themselves. Unless missile defense is perfect, the risk of unacceptable damage will always be present. As McGeorge Bundy and his associates put it, even a "kill-rate" of 95 percent is not good enough where nuclear weapons are concerned.[60] Their argument is made in the U.S.-Soviet context and with an unconscious bias toward MAD thinking, assuming that the possibility of 150 warheads getting through is unacceptable. In reality, the prospect of a far smaller quantum of damage (the possibility of one nuclear weapon falling on one city) is sufficient to deter. A state which possesses an extensive missile defense capability will still be subject to the risk of nuclear retaliation because it can never be sure of preventing that single missile it fears from penetrating its shield. As James Lebovic has shown, even a highly effective missile defense is vulnerable to a very small arsenal: there is a significant risk (20 percent) that a strong missile defense with a kill ratio of 0.95 will be penetrated by a force of only four warheads.[61] In addition, it is often forgotten that missile defense is not designed to counter strategic bombers and cruise missiles.[62]

The belief that the introduction of missile capability alters deterrence equations is fallacious. But it is deeply embedded in MAD-oriented thinking. Thus, Charles Glaser argues that missile defense is inherently unstable because the prospect of imbalance in defensive capability creates incentives for coercion, arms racing, preemption, and war.[63] The untenable assumption here is that relative capabilities have an effect on deterrence, whereas we have seen that they do not. Similarly, Robert Powell claims that rising missile defense capability will increase the United States' confidence in its ability to intervene against a small nuclear power and thereby provoke a war.[64] It is difficult to conceive of a U.S. political leader allowing such paper probabilities to allow the fear of large-scale destruction to be overridden in making policy. The possessor of a robust NMD will always be vulnerable to some unknown quantum of risk from an adversary's first or second strike. That being the case, even the best of NMD systems cannot guarantee a total defense, not even from an adversary who possesses a handful of weapons. This means that the possessor of a highly developed NMD cannot use it as a cover to launch a first strike in the anticipation that there will be no counterstrike. At least a small risk with very large potential consequences will remain. What possible objective can justify the taking of such a risk? Once an adversary has nuclear weapons, it has deterrent capability, and one's possession of missile defenses has only a notional—not a real—effect on that deterrence capability. In effect, a small nuclear power has no good reason to be afraid of an adversary, large or small, possessing NMD. From the standpoint of the possessor of NMD, its defensive capability will not be a disincentive to proliferation. Nor will NMD give it an "edge" in its relationship with a small nuclear power.

This, however, does not mean missile defense is without value. It does have one indisputable merit: it can limit damage to one in the event deterrence fails (or, if you prefer, does not work). There are three ways in which deterrence might not work: if there is an accidental launch, if there is an unauthorized "renegade" launch, and if an undeterrable adversary engages in a suicidal launch. Given the extensive precautions and safety measures surrounding nuclear weapons, and the marginal likelihood of an irrational launch, the probability of any of these events occurring is extremely low.[65] Before September 11, the last would not even have been considered by most of us, prone as we are to clothe deterrence in a narrowly conceived "rationality" that sees strategic suicide as unthinkable. Today, it cannot entirely be ruled out. It follows that, notwithstanding all the perfectly sensible objections to missile defense—that it is technologically questionable, that it is too expensive, and that it is unlikely to work very well—its legitimacy lies in its capacity, regardless of the level of its sophistication and its operational effectiveness, to enable a significant number of people to survive an intended or unintended nuclear strike. To put it differently, the weight of risk works the other way here: the small risk that remains has to be countered to the extent possible. It may be viewed as a form of "catastrophe insurance."[66] There is a moral obligation on the part of the state to protect its citizens. There can in principle be no argument against saving *some* lives in the event of a nuclear strike. How an actual system of defense is conceived of is a matter of the tradeoff between costs and risks.

The argument against missile defense is couched in quite different terms. It is an argument that leans on numerical balances and on the understanding that the certainty of very large-scale destruction underpins deterrence. But, in practice, it is not one's certainty of raining untold destruction upon the other that deters. Rather, it is the other's *uncertainty* about *preventing* such destruction that deters. The argument against missile defense, then, reveals a logic resting on weak foundations. Missile defense has no fundamental effect on nuclear deterrence. For this reason, the possession of some degree of missile defense capability is not destabilizing at all.

But there is still a major difficulty. In the anarchic system that is international politics, the mere possession of significant military capability by a state tends to be a source of some discomfort to other states. The extent of that discomfort varies with the overall character of relationships: the greater the level of cooperation, the less the discomfort. In relationships characterized by uncertainty or tension, the numbers game starts to assume significance. Thus, even as the United States and China move toward greater cooperation through steadily increasing trade and investment relations, the politics of relative military capability is reduced, but not eliminated. This is particularly true of the politics relating to nuclear weapons since the potential consequences of their use, however unlikely, are so great. In consequence, such relationships function at two levels. At the primary level, there is mutually reinforcing economic cooperation and interdependence, which raises the cost of any form of conflict. At the secondary level, there is a game of move and countermove dictated in large part by the distribution of notional rather than meaningful capability (such as the possession of weapons beyond the basic requirements of deterrence), and by changes in that distribution.

If one does not make this distinction, it is arguable that belief in the potential effects of missile defense is sufficient to generate behavior that is self-fulfilling: the belief that missile defense is dangerous might be sufficient to create the adverse reaction of arms racing and set in motion a destabilizing process. But once a more discriminating view is taken, different outcomes are possible. Since the dangers associated with missile defense are not primary, it becomes possible to mitigate the perceptions that make it appear as an object of fear and tension. This can be accomplished by means of a strategy of reassurance.[67] That missile defense need not be destabilizing has been evident for some time, though in a limited way, in the perceptible shift in Russia's response to U.S. NMD plans, from outright rejection to a willingness to listen, discuss, and negotiate. That President Vladimir Putin should have departed significantly from his position on NATO expansion, to which Russian opposition has been even stronger than to NMD, is indicative of the possibilities. U.S.-Russian cooperation over the past decade has occurred at the primary level, involving a sharp decline in mutual threat perceptions, collaboration on major military-strategic issues (notably Russian nuclear safety), and growing levels of economic interaction. Hiccups on issues where their views have been divergent, such as U.S. interventions in Bosnia and Kosovo, or Russia's handling of the Chechen rebellion, have been secondary. Differences over NMD and the Bush Administration's stated objective of dismantling the ABM Treaty fall in the latter category. The divergence over this issue has appeared significant because of the extent of the Bush program's departure from established consensus between the two countries. Should the gulf be narrowed, the problem will become less serious. There are already signs that this may happen. Despite their disagreement on the ABM Treaty, the United States and Russia remain committed to arms control and, more important, to a closer Russian relationship with NATO. The same applies to the U.S.-China relationship. The United States has conveyed its acceptance of Chinese strategic modernization and shown an interest in engaging China on missile defense. One must also bear in mind that an arms race is precisely what both Russian and China do *not* want at a time when their preoccupations revolve more around economic growth and stability than anything else. Not surprisingly, neither Russia nor China has responded strongly to the U.S. rejection of the ABM Treaty. Nor has either of them reacted piquantly to the decision to begin deployment of the first phase of NMD by 2004.[68]

A U.S.-China arms race is certainly not inevitable. In this connection, Bruno Tertrais's distinction between two types of arms race is useful.[69] Type-I arms races are strategically rational races, whereas Type-II arms races are driven by symbols and politics. Drawing from Tertrais, I develop my own formulation. Where arms races are related to actual capabilities on the field of battle, such that they would affect actual outcomes, they may be classified as Type-I or strategic arms races. Where arms races have little relevance to actual outcomes on the battlefield or to the employment of capabilities, they may be characterized as Type-II or symbolic arms races. Further, the two types of arms races relate differently to the types of political relationship described above. In a relationship of hostility at the primary level, an arms race may be either Type-I or Type-II when nuclear weapons are not in the picture. Where nuclear weapons states are concerned, all arms races are symbolic or Type-II races, for once minimum deterrence has been obtained, the enhancement of capability becomes meaningless. Where the relationship between nuclear powers is one of cooperation at the primary level and tension is restricted to the secondary level, the arms race must by definition be Type-II or symbolic.

The significance of this typology relates to the possibility of reducing risk through arms control. While symbolic politics may in a sense be as "real" as strategic politics—the eye of the beholder being a major determinant—it is nonetheless far more amenable to reassurance than is strategic politics. If changes in "balances" cannot make any fundamental strategic difference, arms control is viable. As such, notwithstanding the many differences between them, it is well within the realm of possibility that the United States and China could come to an understanding that prevents an arms race resulting from the deployment of a U.S. NMD. Some of the possibilities for reassurance that the United States can offer include a very limited and nonthreatening NMD deployment, enhanced political and economic cooperation on a range of issues, and prudence on Taiwan. Again, it is worth pointing out that an expansionary response is not the most cost-effective one for China, which would prefer not to divert precious funds from its main goal of economic development.[70]

Even if a U.S.-China arms race does occur, a Chinese move to expand offensive capability will not affect India directly. To target the United States more "effectively," China would need to augment its long-range missile capability, whereas China targets India with intermediate-range missiles.[71] Thus, it is unlikely that there would be cause for anxiety in India about China's reaction to a U.S. NMD. Besides, such nuclear expansion as it does undertake will not reduce India's deterrence capacity. India has long accepted the nuclear "gap" between itself and China. The widening of the "gap" will not make much difference to a minimum deterrence strategy. The number and relative sophistication of Chinese forces do not matter. Once Chinese targets (not necessarily Beijing) are targeted by even a small number of Indian missiles, it is immaterial whether China has a hundred or two hundred weapons targeting India. No Chinese leader can risk even a single Indian missile hitting a Chinese city. There is no rationally conceivable objective that China can hope to attain that would justify such a risk. It need scarcely be added that, with China very unlikely to respond in a big way to a US NMD, and with India equally unlikely to expand its capabilities, Pakistan too will not be affected by the putative domino effect of missile defense.

Might a U.S. NMD pose a more direct political threat to India? It bears repetition that some critics have found discomfiting the prospect of an already unilateralist United States emboldened by missile defense to intervene globally at will. From a hard realist perspective, a robust U.S. NMD could be conceived of as directly threatening Indian deterrence capability. However, capabilities in themselves do not constitute threats. If they did, the United States would find the French nuclear arsenal threatening, and the French would find the U.S. one even more so. It may be that there are situations when a friendly relationship does turn sour—as, admittedly, it did in the case of Kuwait and Iraq in 1990—but threat perceptions must be based on conflicts of interest that are basically political in nature. Whatever the balance of capabilities in a given relationship might encourage us to think, it means little in the absence of a threat perception. In the case of India and the United States, the mutual misgivings of the Cold War era are history. Their specific interests may diverge at times, but as capitalist democracies they are fundamentally in accord as never before. Given the strong expectation of continuity in their relationship because of this essential congruence, it is difficult to think of a U.S. missile defense capability as a direct strategic threat to India.

Once the alleged adverse effects of missile defense are disposed of, it makes sense to support missile defense because it attempts, to whatever degree, to save human lives. Indeed, this is a moral imperative. Moreover, the argument that missile defense has intrinsic merit because it marks a radical departure from a static nuclear order also carries considerable weight. The Reaganite view that nuclear weapons are inherently evil, which underlay SDI and propels the present missile defense program, strikes a powerful chord in Indian thinking, which has always rejected the idea that the security of nations can be maximized by an unbridled threat to destroy one another. The rejection of the moral validity of nuclear weapons provides a much sounder basis for arms control than does the Cold War conception of stability based on assured destruction. Indeed, the disembedding of MAD and the consequent fillip to arms reduction may turn out to be the primary contribution of the U.S. missile defense program.[72]

The Case for Limited Missile Defense

If missile defense does not have a destabilizing effect on deterrence, it is a desirable acquisition to the extent that it is affordable. It will be readily evident that a cost-benefit calculation in the Indian context would not encourage an ambitious defensive system against missile strikes. There are too many potential targets to be defended, too few resources to defend them. In a way, this should mitigate the unrealistic fears of those who worry about India's missile defense program. How have India's nuclear adversaries reacted to it? China does not consider India a serious nuclear threat because of the limited reach of Indian weapons, though this is changing. There is some concern about Indo-Russian and Indo-Israeli cooperation and where it might lead in the long run.[73] But the Chinese approach to missile defense has been more political than military, as David Finkelstein has shown.[74] Notwithstanding the tension arising from the border dispute and the Sino-Pakistani nuclear and missile nexus, the China-India relationship remains stable. Trade is on the rise and there is a tacit understanding that differences should not stand in the way of cooperation.

The same is not the case with the India-Pakistan relationship. Military tensions have been high. The Pakistani response to U.S. NMD and to the Indian interest in missile defense has been negative. At the UN Conference on Disarmament in Geneva, Foreign Secretary Inamul Haq argued that the creation of "shields" would cause others to improve their "lances," which could "heighten tensions between major powers, jeopardize the global strategic balance and turn back the disarmament clock."[75] Shortly after Bush's May 2001 speech, Pakistan's Chief Executive, General Pervez Musharraf, criticized the NMD program, averring that it could "jeopardize international stability, trigger a new arms race and undermine international efforts aimed at arms control and disarmament."[76] The Pakistani view is in accord with the domino theory on NMD, which springs from a MAD-based perception that one man's missile defense is another's first-strike vulnerability. That, as we have seen, is of dubious merit.

For Pakistan, an Indian missile defense would appear to be more worrying still.[77] Seen from the MAD perspective, Indian missile defense creates a problem of vulnerability and credibility for Pakistan's nuclear deterrent. It nevertheless does not necessarily require an arms racing response. As one Pakistani analyst sees it, an arm race is unaffordable. It would be more appropriate to counter an Indian missile defense with hardened and mobile basing, countermeasures, and a small numerical preponderance in relation to Indian defense capability.[78] A South Asian ABM Treaty is also desirable.[79] This viewpoint is based on the flawed assumptions criticized above. The doctrinal case for a limited Indian missile defense is basically the same as that for U.S. NMD, which is that it neither reduces nor augments deterrence; that it is consequently not inherently destabilizing; and that it has the merit of promising some damage limitation in the event, unlikely though that may be, of deterrence failing. It is also worth stating the obvious: that India can scarcely afford an extensive missile defense system sufficient to shield the dozens of cities that are within range of Pakistani missiles and bombers carrying nuclear weapons. To deter India, Pakistan does not need to target New Delhi or Mumbai.

From India's perspective, deterrence failure cannot be ruled out in either of its adversarial nuclear-strategic relationships. But Indian strategic planners have particular reason to be concerned about the relationship with Pakistan. Deterrence may not work in two ways: as a result of command and control errors arising from short reaction time, resulting in accidental launches, or if Pakistani nuclear weapons fall into the wrong hands. (From their point of view, Pakistani strategists would worry about the same things in reverse.) Strategic defense makes sense if it is not intrinsically destabilizing. Realistically, no matter how strong its missile defense capabilities—and these are bound to be very limited because of the sheer magnitude of the task of defending more than a few of its strategic assets—India cannot be certain of defending adequately against a Pakistani strike. To reiterate, Pakistan will not be rendered vulnerable by Indian missile defense because India will still be deterred. No Indian decision maker can possibly consider acceptable even a small risk of a single Pakistani bomb detonating over any Indian city. By adding more weapons to its inventory, Pakistan will not alter India's strategic calculus. There will be no need to. The purpose of an Indian missile defense can at best be to try to minimize damage after deterrence has failed, which is very different from saying that it will give an Indian leader the confidence to strike first.

The existing India-Pakistan agreement not to attack each other's nuclear facilities carries a fundamental underlying assumption that is congruent with missile defense. The very notion that nuclear facilities should not be attacked implies that they are not acceptable targets. In that case, the idea of defending them cannot be termed unacceptable. Thus, it is reasonable for India and Pakistan to come to an understanding that extends the agreement and permits the defense of nuclear facilities. This might later be extended to other targets.

The process of coming to such an agreement would obviously involve much discussion and negotiation. The important point is to come to an understanding that, by its very nature, minimum deterrence, to which both countries adhere, does not require the principles of assured destruction to underpin it. Missile defense does not undermine stability, for each understands that the other is easily deterred by a small risk of large-scale damage. On the contrary, minimum deterrence doctrine facilitates missile defense, in itself a moral obligation for governments, by accepting that a less than absolute capacity to defend against missiles leaves deterrence intact. At the political level, India needs to assuage Pakistani concerns with reassurance initiatives. While the Kargil episode was a setback, there is still a need—and scope for—reassurance-based efforts toward strategic stability, whether through bilateral or unilateral efforts. These may take the form of nuclear confidence building measures (NCBMs), regular discussions aimed at building doctrinal bridges, and perhaps a mutual commitment, tacit or formal, to eschew deployment.

There have been reports that Pakistan has also decided to acquire missile defense technology from the United States. A Pakistani program is of no strategic import for India for the same reasons an Indian one will not affect Pakistan. To reiterate, missile defense does not alter strategic equations. On the contrary, if both countries feel some confidence that missile defense capability, howsoever limited, is a useful hedge against the improbable, this can only be a source of regional stability.

Conclusion

Missile defense has been much misunderstood. Its efficacy is limited. It does not meaningfully alter the fundamentals of deterrence, not even in so-called "asymmetric" nuclear relationships. The preoccupation of established deterrence thinking with numbers and vulnerability is off the mark. Numbers are not important; risk is. Even a small possibility of nuclear damage overrides the possible objectives to be attained by initiating nuclear conflict. In effect, the only utility of missile defense is the extent, always limited, to which it can restrict damage after deterrence has failed. The benefits of missile defense being narrow, its fate will eventually be decided by politics and by the cost factor. The more extreme U.S. NMD ambitions will be moderated by both. The likelihood of a domino effect on China, India, and in turn Pakistan is very low. Such secondary fears as are evoked by missile defense can be assuaged by active reassurance strategies. The argument that an India-Pakistan agreement on "balanced" missile defense deployments with U.S. assistance would have a stabilizing effect is an interesting one.[80] But, given the irrelevance of missile defense to the working of deterrence, it does not amount to much.

Despite its obvious merits, India cannot pursue missile defense in a big way. It is simply unaffordable. It is also a technically daunting task, though a facilitating factor would be collaboration with the United States, Israel, and Russia. Whatever the difficulties, it is incumbent upon the Indian government to take at least some steps to protect its citizens against the small risk of deterrence failure by error, accident, or twisted design. On the other hand, a government that is fully cognizant of the fundamentals of minimum deterrence will not allow missile defenses to take on unnecessarily large proportions. Such an eventuality would only be to the advantage of bureaucratic and business interests.[81]

The primary contribution of missile defense to a better world may be doctrinal. The disembedding of MAD and its associated baggage—the requirement of large, sophisticated, and diverse arsenals assuredly capable of inflicting monumental damage—may eventually generate a new momentum for arms control by facilitating deep cuts. That would be a welcome development for all states, nuclear and nonnuclear. From the Indian perspective, as official statements have already acknowledged, the expanded potential for arms reduction offered by missile defense is in accord with India's sustained commitment to reducing the global threat of nuclear weapons. Even if it does not happen, missile defense will do no harm.

Finally, a collaborative approach to missile defense can be a solid basis for strengthening Indo-U.S. relations. Nonalignment was a strategy born of weakness and fear. A stronger and more confident India can afford to move closer to the United States, as indeed it has begun to do. For all its periodic proneness to unilateralism, the United States, as a hegemonic power, needs to work with existing allies and to build coalitions. It has shown this in the Gulf, in the Balkans, in Afghanistan, and even in Iraq. As an "emerging power," India can offer it useful economic, political, and military cooperation.[82] India has much to gain from a stronger relationship with the United States, not least the possibility of augmenting its small missile defense capability. Cooperation on missile defense can be one pillar—an important one—to buttress this growing relationship while simultaneously enhancing India's security.

6

Nuclear Terrorism

Following the terrorist attacks of September 11, 2001, terrorism has come to occupy front stage in global strategic politics.[1] Given the scale of those attacks, the possibility of terrorist acts using weapons of mass destruction (WMD)—involving biological organisms, chemicals, and nuclear materials—has also been given considerable attention.[2] This chapter focuses on the specific area that is loosely known as "nuclear terrorism," which encompasses the possibility of terrorists exploding a nuclear bomb as well as radiological terrorism or the release of radiation without a nuclear explosion.[3] Given that there has never been a serious threat, let alone an actual incident, of nuclear terrorism, how seriously should we take the possibility? The view that it is an "overrated nightmare" stems from numerous factors, notably the technical difficulties involved and the availability to terrorists of alternatives offering higher returns on investment.[4] But as in everything about nuclear weapons, the risk—even a small one—of a nuclear catastrophe cannot be ignored. After September 11, the global awareness of this risk has increased sharply, amplified by evidence that terrorists have actually shown considerable interest in acquiring nuclear capability.

Most definitions of terrorism specify the use of physical acts of violence, whether actual or threatened. But terror is in itself a form of violence, and because terror may result from the use of unconventional "weapons" (notably, the Internet) or from the mere conveying of a false threat, it is important to define it more generally. H. H. A. Cooper provides a useful definition: "Terrorism is the intentional generation of massive fear by human beings for the purpose of securing or maintaining control over other human beings."[5] Below, this definition provides the basis for analyzing the threats India faces from terrorists using nuclear instruments of destruction. These instruments may be in their possession in the form of nuclear bombs or materials. They may also be nuclear targets not in their possession, such as nuclear warheads or plants, which could be attacked by terrorists.

While much attention has been paid to the threat of nuclear catastrophe being unleashed by terrorists, little has been said about the relationship between nuclear strategy and nuclear terrorism. This is surprising. The number, quality, and deployment posture of armed force is determined by threat perception (though group interests do play a role). In all nuclear-weapon countries today, this involves relationships between the state, its external adversaries, and foreign and domestic terrorist groups. This chapter will attempt a comprehensive understanding of these relationships. Nuclear terrorism has two distinct components. First, it poses a direct threat to a state's citizens by causing blast and radiation damage. Second, it poses an indirect threat by way of its potential to trigger war between hostile nuclear-armed states. In both cases, there is a significant link between the threat and the state's nuclear posture. The thrust of the argument here is that a true minimum deterrence posture based on the assumptions discussed in Chapter 2 minimizes the threat posed by nuclear terrorism.

In the broadest sense, as Thomas Schelling has observed, *any* use or potential use of nuclear force may be described as "terrorist," a definition that encompasses the arsenals of states with nuclear weapon and the concept of deterrence (in which the root word "terror" is embedded).[6] After all, the idea of a "balance of terror" is part of the lexicon of nuclear politics. From this standpoint, the specter of nuclear terrorism can only be eradicated by the elimination of nuclear weapons. This book has a more limited perspective. It focuses on the use of terror by nonstate actors—mainly, terrorist groups, but conceivably also individuals—through their attainment of some level of nuclear capability. Nuclear terrorism encompasses the acquisition, use, and threatened use of nuclear materials, as well as the resort to false threats or hoaxes which, to the extent they are convincing, would have similar effects.[7] The materials that could conceivably be used encompass manufactured or stolen nuclear weapons (whether crude or sophisticated), fissile materials like highly enriched uranium and plutonium, and radioactive materials such as nuclear waste, natural uranium, and radionuclides used for medical and industrial purposes. The last two involve radiological terrorism, a subcategory of nuclear terrorism, in which fissile and radioactive materials may be utilized—perhaps in conjunction with regular explosives—to disperse radiation in order to contaminate the human environment. Conceivable acts of nuclear terrorism range from a hoax threatening a nuclear explosion or radiological attack to an actual nuclear blast in a densely populated area. The physical damage caused may range from the marginal to the catastrophic, but in every case intense fear will be generated in the minds of policy makers and the public.

Nuclear strategy is normally conceived of as a set of ideas and practices that defines the security relationship between states. That is not entirely the case. Today, there is considerable evidence that terrorists have an interest in developing nuclear capabilities. As nonstate actors, they are not amenable to strategies of deterrence because they do not have a clear and separate geographical location, and because they do not have a population or other assets which can be meaningfully threatened with nuclear weapons. In addition, they may not be psychologically suitable targets for deterrence. This seems particularly true of those whose mindset shows an inclination to use these weapons as coercive instruments to advance their goals. On the other hand, terrorists might use nuclear capability to exercise deterrence against states. The pages that follow will discuss the ways in which the threat of nuclear terrorism might affect national security, the sources of the threat, and its relationship with minimum deterrence. The intimate relationship between strategy and terrorism will become clear.

The Nature of the Threat

The nuclear-terrorist threat spans the spectrum of nuclear materials found in a society. Much of the threat lies in the realm of civilian rather than military activity. For instance, radioactive materials such as natural uranium and an array of radionuclides are widely used in power generation, for medical research and treatment, for scientific research, and for a variety of industrial purposes ranging from oil exploration to the manufacture of smoke detectors. Beyond lies the dual-use nuclear infrastructure, which includes the nuclear plants that generate power as well as fissile materials utilized for making weapons, the surrounding complex in which materials and weapons are produced and wastes stored, and research facilities. Finally, there is the military end, which encompasses the manufacture, assembly, and stockpiling of warheads, and if deployment occurs, transportation systems, facilities for mating warheads with delivery vehicles, and those positions where deployed forces are based, whether in stationary or mobile mode. Each point along the spectrum is vulnerable to terrorist attack. In every case, there is a risk of war when nuclear terrorism is linked to an external source. In such a setting, minimum deterrence as envisaged here plays a significant role in keeping to a low level the risk of calamity.

There are three main ways in which nuclear terrorism could raise such risks:

1. Terrorists could target a public building with a radiological dispersion device (RDD) or "dirty bomb," which involves the use of a conventional explosive in conjunction with radiological materials commonly found in industry (e.g., gamma radiography cameras containing Iridium-192 for oil exploration) and medical establishments (e.g., brachytherapy units containing Cobalt-60, Cesium-137, and Iridium-192).[8] At worst, a nuclear detonation could be triggered in an urban population center.

2. Terrorists could directly attack facilities, such as hospitals, research reactors, and power plants using radiological and nuclear materials. Here, terrorists need not possess the means for spreading radiation in advance, but could use devices, systems, and materials already existing and designed for other purposes as "weapons."[9]

3. Finally, terrorists could target a state's military forces, including its nuclear forces, either with their own weapons, or using the forces' weapons as targets, to produce an RDD effect, or, in a worst case, a nuclear detonation.

In each of these cases, if there is a link between terrorism and an adversary state, even if that adversary state does not expressly initiate or even desire a nuclear-terrorist event, the act could trigger a crisis and war. If the states involved are nuclear powers, the war may cross the nuclear threshold. As Chapter 4 shows, a serious act of terrorism raises the risk of nuclear war between nuclear-armed states. Because a nuclear/radiological terrorist attack creates a qualitatively high level of terror, it multiplies the risk of war, and makes adherence to a minimum deterrence posture critical. An act of nuclear terrorism against a state's military forces, and especially deployed nuclear forces, would raise the risk of war sharply, especially if it occurs during a crisis. That risk is kept to a relatively low level by a minimum deterrence posture based on a small, nondeployed arsenal.

How serious is the threat? So far, there has been no reason to fear an imminent act of nuclear terrorism. But the potential consequences can be so devastating that they merit close attention. While terrorists may be unlikely to manufacture or steal a usable bomb, the possibility has to be taken into account. A nuclear explosion in a large Indian city such as Mumbai (Bombay) would have catastrophic effects. One study on wartime use of nuclear weapons has estimated that a 20-kiloton detonation targeting the Western Naval Command at the southern tip of the city would cause 113,000 fatalities.[10] Another calculates that a 15-kiloton explosion in Mumbai would result in somewhere between 160,000 and 866,000 deaths.[11] A third estimates about 95,000 immediate deaths and a total of 800,000 casualties from a 5-kiloton explosion.[12] A smaller explosion would cause much less harm, but would still have the potential to kill thousands and create panic and chaos. Another possibility, perhaps a little less unlikely, is a terrorist attack on an installation where nuclear warheads are kept. The plutonium released by causing the surrounding high explosive of a small nuclear warhead to detonate could have serious effects. If a large city like Delhi or Mumbai is downwind of the detonation, the result would be from 5,000 to 20,000 cancer deaths over some decades.[13] Terrorists might launch an assault on a nuclear plant. A small, well-armed team of terrorists dressed in military uniform could force their way through security barriers and, perhaps with the help of an insider, gain access to a reactor or to a spent fuel storage area. A powerful conventional explosion might then directly release radiation, or cause a meltdown by damaging the containment system of a reactor. In effect, the terrorists would have detonated a powerful RDD. Even a relatively small RDD could have grave consequences. A report produced by the Federation of American Scientists undertook three hypothetical case studies of RDDs being exploded over urban concentrations (in the United Sates) using cesium, cobalt, and americium. The study found that, while immediate casualties would be few, there would be a significant number of cancer deaths, high levels of cancer risk over fairly large areas, and the need to evacuate and decontaminate or rebuild much of the contaminated area. For instance, if a typical quantity of americium used for oil well surveys were to be blown up with one pound of TNT, an area covering twenty city blocks would have to be evacuated within half an hour, and, if an area of sixty city blocks had to be rebuilt, the cost could run to more than $50 billion.[14] A similar study on New Delhi estimates that as little as nine grams of Cobalt-60 (which could be taken from a single cancer teletherapy unit) dispersed with five pounds of TNT would probably require cleanup covering an area of about two square km.[15] The most powerful effects would be in the form of panic, social tension, and the undermining of societal stability.

In light of this, it is not unreasonable to infer that a nuclear-terrorist incident in a major Indian city could have severe physical and social effects. If a nuclear device or RDD were to be exploded in the city of Mumbai—or, perhaps, a number of RDDs in a nuclear version of the multiple bomb blasts of 1993—the following sequence of events are likely to occur. The immediate result would be widespread panic. People would attempt to flee from the scene of devastation as quickly as possible. The streets would be clogged with vehicles and people, trains and buses jammed with a populace desperately seeking escape from the unseen hazards of radiation. Violence would likely result, perhaps on a mass scale, against those perceived to be "responsible" for the disaster, as was the case in Delhi and other places in 1984, when thousands of Sikhs were killed in reaction to Prime Minister Indira Gandhi's assassination by her Sikh bodyguards. The incident would also generate immediate and intense hostility toward Pakistan as happened in December 2001 following the terrorist attack on India's Parliament. This in turn would very likely bring about an India-Pakistan crisis and raise the specter of war. Terrorist attacks on India's armed forces, particularly on its nuclear forces, have the highest probability of generating war, particularly in a crisis, since it may be difficult to know where the attack came from, and Pakistan might be held directly responsible.

The Sources of Threat

There are numerous sources of threat that, taken together, call for a high level of preparedness in countering the possibility of nuclear terrorism in India. These are sufficiently serious to necessitate a thorough evaluation.

Technology

Basic bomb designs are not hard to obtain or develop, since the technical knowledge has now been publicly available for many years. More difficult is the task of obtaining fissile material and, still more, of employing the techniques that go into the actual fabrication of a nuclear bomb. But the possibility of a workable nuclear weapon being put together by a terrorist group cannot be ignored.[16] A relatively simple gun-type nuclear weapon design (such as that used for the Hiroshima bomb) involves the firing of a subcritical highly enriched uranium (HEU) projectile into a subcritical HEU target to achieve a nuclear chain reaction. A more difficult implosion type design of the kind used over Nagasaki requires a near-critical piece of fissile material (uranium or plutonium, possibly uranium oxide or plutonium oxide) to be compressed by the detonation of a surrounding high explosive in order to achieve supercriticality. The minimum quantity of material required for the least sophisticated bomb would be 45–60 kg of HEU for the first type, and, for the latter, 5–6 kg of plutonium, or 20–25 kg of HEU, or about 55 kg of uranium oxide, or about 17.5 kg of plutonium oxide.[17] A more sophisticated type with a reflector would reduce the quantity of fissile material required by a factor of two (for a natural uranium, iron, or tungsten reflector) or three (for a beryllium reflector). Not only would the amount of material required be large, the making of a bomb would take considerable time (weeks, and probably months, at best), and require at least three or four experts—probably more—with different specializations in metallurgy, neutronics, radiation effects, high explosives, hydrodynamics, and electronics. The end product in the case of a simple design would be a large and unwieldy bomb, weighing over a ton. More manageable sizes would involve more difficult processes.

Still, very crude devices, sometimes with very limited effects, could be built. Reactor-grade plutonium from a commercial light water reactor could be used to develop a bomb with a minimum yield of one or a few kilotons. Even if this does not work very well, because reactor-grade plutonium tends to "preinitiate" on account of spontaneous fission of some of its components, the resultant "fizzle yield" would still produce a small and devastating blast.[18] The simplest devices could involve bringing uranium parts together without explosives. It is known, for example, that a 100-pound mass of uranium dropped on another 100-pound uranium mass from a height of six feet could produce a blast of 5–10 kilotons.[19] On the whole, it would seem that the obstacles in the path of nuclear bomb–making are sufficiently difficult in terms of availability of knowledge and materials to make the prospect appear very low. Nevertheless, the possibility has to be taken seriously, for the low level of probability is offset by the high level of risk. Another possibility is that a bomb or its components might be stolen or taken by force from a storage site, during transportation, or from the place of deployment.

Fissile material from bombs, nuclear plants, and other sources could be used in conjunction with conventional explosives to produce an RDD. Unlike an actual nuclear weapon, an RDD does not presume technical sophistication. Its effects would be variable, depending on the size of the conventional explosive used (which would determine the extent of dispersion of radioactivity) and the quantity and quality of the radioactive material (which would determine its lethality).

Nuclear plants are subject to a set of potential threats. These are captured by the concept of Design Basis Threat (DBT), which anticipates direct attacks from the ground, air, and water.[20] DBTs may not take into account some worst-case scenarios that are hard to ignore after September 11. The destruction of the World Trade Center has brought particular attention to the potential effects of a large passenger plane crashing into a nuclear reactor. Such a threat was actually made in the United States in 1972, when hijackers warned they would crash a Southern Airways jetliner into the Oak Ridge nuclear weapons complex, but was not carried out.[21] Experts believe that most nuclear plants were not built to withstand the impact of a direct hit from a large passenger aircraft of today.[22] Its engines, which are its most rigid parts, would probably penetrate the containment structure and cause a major fire or explosion, releasing radioactivity on a massive scale.[23] Most nuclear plants are also ill equipped to counter a serious and sophisticated armed attack. A large, well-placed truck bomb could have a similar effect as above, destroying a plant's cooling systems and breaching the containment structure of a reactor, causing a meltdown and possible dispersal of radiation.[24] Armed ground assaults might also be launched to take over plants temporarily and indulge in sabotage, perhaps by destroying safety systems. Spent fuel pools often contain more hazardous material than reactors and are less well protected than reactor buildings. While most spent fuel pools are underground, they are extremely vulnerable: should the cooling system be damaged, or should a crack allow the water used to cool them to escape, the spent fuel will either melt or burn, causing radiation to spread.[25] In the case of dry storage, spent fuel casks can be penetrated by armor or blown up.[26] The effects of the kind of sabotage described above would not be as severe as a nuclear bomb explosion, but would nevertheless have the potential to cause significant radiation damage.

Storage locations for fissile material, unassembled or partially assembled bomb components, and assembled weapons are also vulnerable for similar reasons. Conventional explosions could convert them into RDDs. This applies to fully prepared warheads as well, whether mated or not. Nuclear materials are particularly vulnerable to sabotage during transportation.[27] This includes the transportation of nuclear materials within a nuclear power complex. Methods of attack may include using armor-piercing shells to penetrate storage casks; capturing and blowing up casks; destroying transportation infrastructure, such as a bridge or tunnel during movement of nuclear material; and causing high-speed derailment. Nuclear weapons or their components (separated cores, unmated warheads) during transportation may also be subject to attack. The relationship between nuclear weapons and terrorist threats in this context is direct: the more the number of weapons (or components), the more the number of targets for terrorists.

Materials

Terrorists might obtain nuclear materials from diverse sources, both from outside India and within it. William Potter has identified seven cases of diversion of significant quantities of nuclear material, and four other possible cases.[28] A recent report reveals that equipment and materials for nuclear bomb-making have vanished without a trace from Iraq.[29] Though there are many sources of inadequately secured material, the biggest is Russia, which has experienced in recent years a combination of terrorist violence, the growth of organized crime, and an abundance of poorly guarded nuclear facilities.[30] A February 2002 assessment by the U.S. National Intelligence Council states that undetected diversion of weapons-grade and weapons-usable materials has taken place from several Russian institutions, but "we do not know the extent or magnitude of such thefts."[31] Russia is estimated to possess 150 tons of weapons-grade plutonium, 1,000 tons of enriched uranium, and, at the Chelyabinsk complex alone, 685,000 cubic meters of radioactive waste.[32] Given the reality of poor accounting, organizational deterioration on account of adverse economic conditions, and inadequate physical controls, it is not surprising that there are numerous examples of material diversion, more often than not by insiders.[33] In December 2004, President Vladimir Putin acknowledged that Russia was sitting on as much as seventy million tons of radioactive waste, and that the infrastructure for processing the waste was "extremely inadequately" developed.[34] Moreover, projections of Russian weapons inventories show that, over the next decade, about 3,500 warheads containing about 84,000 kg of fissile material will be removed from deployment.[35] Despite assistance from the United States and from other countries, the potential for leakage remains considerable.

Pakistan too is a significant potential source.[36] Though its overall nuclear infrastructure is relatively small, the possibility of leakage is widely feared because of the general sense of the country as a weak if not failing state, and extensive evidence of nuclear proliferation emanating from the highest levels of the nuclear etsablishment.[37] Pakistan's main uranium enrichment facility is at Kahuta (Khan Research Laboratories). Smaller uranium enrichment facilities exist at Sihala and Golra and possibly at Gadwal. Plutonium extraction work is done at the New Lab, Nilhore, and at Khushab in central Punjab. Pakistan has two nuclear power plants, one located at Karachi, the other at Chasma. Its nuclear weapons are believed to be in an unassembled state, with fissile cores kept separate from bomb assemblies. The bomb components and the wider infrastructure are under military control. In February 2000, a National Command Authority was established. In January 2001, the Pakistan Nuclear Regulatory Authority (PNRA) was created to regulate the civilian infrastructure. Still, given Pakistan's deteriorating law and order environment and its involvement in proliferation to a number of countries, concerns about leakage remain.

India's nuclear establishment, most of it civilian, is much larger.[38] Its Atomic Energy Commission (AEC) stands at the apex of an extensive infrastructure that incorporates warhead manufacture, electrical power production (fourteen reactors, with six more under construction), fuel fabrication and reprocessing, waste management, mining, research, and medical and industrial applications. The physical security of nuclear installations is managed by an independent security organization, the Central Industrial Security Force (CISF), a paramilitary force under the Ministry of Home Affairs. The CISF is also responsible for the protection of other high-risk facilities such as defense production units, space installations, oil refineries, airports, and major ports. But little is known about how it actually organizes the security of nuclear facilities.[39] Personal conversations with former officials indicate that security is tight, enhanced by the fact that the CISF does not fall under the purview of the Department of Atomic Energy. The Atomic Energy Regulatory Board (AERB) is empowered to regulate all civilian facilities, while the Bhabha Atomic Research Centre (BARC) has an internal review mechanism for military-related facilities. Though much of the AERB's function is related to preventing and responding to accidents, part of the counterterrorism function of controlling nuclear plants and other facilities and responding to emergencies would be covered by the same systems.[40] BARC, located at the edge of Mumbai city, is designated a nuclear-weapons laboratory, and warhead components are stored there in an unassembled state.[41] According to informed sources, the nuclear warheads located at BARC facilities are under military security. A study by P. R. Chari notes that air defense cover is provided by the Indian Army, security is strict, and access control is maintained by physical barriers and electronic systems.[42]

Indian nuclear plants are characterized by a high level of built-in safety, which indirectly makes them relatively less vulnerable to sabotage. Several of the accident-related safety features of the Canada Deuterium Uranium (CANDU) reactor design widely used in India are also relevant to security from terrorist acts.[43] For instance, the subdivision of the core into two thermal hydraulic loops in most CANDU designs and into hundreds of individual pressure tubes within each loop localizes a loss-of-coolant incident. The risk of a fuel meltdown is kept low by the large-volume, low-pressure, low-temperature moderator surrounding the pressure tubes. The steam generators are positioned well above the core, which promotes natural thermosyphoning (heat movement) in case shut-down cooling is lost. In addition, CANDU plants are enclosed by heavy concrete walls, including a reactor vault with a minimum four-foot thickness surrounding the nuclear core itself. Hence, it is unlikely that a large passenger aircraft crashing into the vault could cause a major disaster.[44] However, it is not known what effect an aircraft loaded with high explosives might have if it crashes into a typical Indian reactor building. The two VVER-1000 type plants being built by Russia at Koodankulam in the southern Indian state of Tamil Nadu may be inherently vulnerable to an airliner crash. Weaknesses of existing plants of this type include the inadequate strength of walls and roof, the location of the control room at the lower levels of the reactor building (necessitating early evacuation in case of melt-through of the containment), and close proximity of steam lines and isolation valves (hence, vulnerability to a single blast).[45]

Small but sometimes powerful sources of radioactive material are comparatively poorly guarded, and numerous occasions of theft are known to have occurred. For instance, in July 1998, police recovered more than 8 kg of natural uranium stolen from the Indira Gandhi Centre for Atomic Research in Chennai.[46] In July 2002, a gamma radiography camera containing a powerful source of Iridium-192 was stolen from the luggage compartment of a public bus in the terrorist-infested state of Assam.[47] In August 2003, three sources of Cobalt-60 used for metal testing were stolen from a large steel plant in Jamshedpur.[48]

Organizational Sources

Organizational vulnerabilities are of two kinds: internal and external. A serious potential threat to nuclear facilities, whether military or civilian, comes from insiders. The range of possible threats includes theft of materials; support to outsiders by disruption of alarm systems; sabotage of facilities or specific processes (such as cooling systems); and simple acts of assistance, such as providing building layouts or access codes to terrorists.[49] Most acts of sabotage have been attributed to disgruntled employees expressing their anger by, among other things, cutting electrical cables, setting fires, and destroying security cameras.[50] But that does not rule out political motivations. Most nuclear-related organizations are also vulnerable to cyber-security threats. Information on any aspect of a nuclear facility from bomb design to security measures can be misappropriated by an insider.[51] A major security breach in this regard occurred in October 2003 when between eighteen and twenty computers containing highly classified data, including communication codes vital for ensuring secrecy of intragovernmental communications, were stolen from a Delhi office of the Defence Research and Development Organization (DRDO), an integral part of the nuclear-weapons establishment.[52] To compound the failure, the codes remained unchanged for nearly nine months. In September 2004, a senior scientist at the Remote Sensing Applications Centre in Lucknow in northern India was arrested along with his wife, a former employee at the Centre, for selling classified satellite pictures and data.[53]

The insider threat applies to military facilities too. Herbert Abrams has highlighted the seriousness of the problem by recording significant levels of psychiatric disorders and drug and alcohol abuse, as well as of actual violent acts, by military personnel cleared through personnel reliability screening programs.[54] While this study applies to the U.S. armed forces, there is no reason to believe that military and paramilitary personnel in India are significantly different in their behavior patterns. A major security failure involving one or more insiders was the theft of as many as twenty-nine aluminum alloy titanium rings (used in rocket engines) from the high-security Indian Space Research Organisation's Liquid Propulsion Systems Centre in Bangalore in February 2004.[55] The CISF, which was in charge of security at the site, had left the rings in the open. The CISF is known to have experienced major problems with its personnel, including, in 2003 alone, several suicides, the killing of a superior officer, and the taking of hostages.[56] Available information on personnel reliability is scanty. The potential for serious damage is evident from a parallel case: the killing of Prime Minister Indira Gandhi by her bodyguards in 1984.

Externally oriented security encompasses the intelligence network and asset protection. In one sense, there is ground for reassurance, since there are no known cases of significant security failure involving the Indian nuclear infrastructure. But this may be the result of a lack of interest and effort thus far on the part of terrorists. Again, a look at the general security environment and repeated organizational problems is instructive. Terrorists have periodically penetrated zones of high-level military security. In mid-July 2001, five army men were killed in an attack on a military camp in the Indian state of Jammu and Kashmir.[57] In early November 2001, a similar attack killed four soldiers, and two of the three terrorists involved escaped.[58] Two weeks later, ten soldiers and three civilians died in an assault by two terrorists.[59] In May 2002, three terrorists dressed in army uniforms stormed an army camp at Kaluchak near Jammu city and killed five soldiers and twenty-five civilians before being killed themselves.[60] A repetition of the "Kaluchak massacre" was narrowly prevented in August 2002 when militants entered a high-security zone housing senior police and civilian officials and their families before being intercepted.[61] In February 2003, five policemen guarding a vital bridge in Kashmir were divested of their rifles and ammunition by militants.[62] In July, a terrorist attack led to the death of a brigadier and eight soldiers, and injuries to the camp commandant and to Lieutenant General Hari Prasad, chief of the Army's Northern Command.[63] Such incidents illustrate the relative ease with which areas under high levels of security cover are penetrated by small numbers of determined terrorists. Between July 2001 and June 2002, as many as 635 army personnel were killed by terrorists.[64] The assault on India's Parliament by a small team of heavily armed terrorists in a car loaded with explosives on December 13, 2001, was a shocking security breach.[65]

To take a related aspect, between April 2000 and May 2001, as many as six major fires occurred at army ammunition dumps, some of them very large ones, such as the enormous fire that destroyed some 10,000 tons of ammunition in Bharatpur on April 28, 2000.[66] While army officials variously attributed the disasters to local geography, the malfunctioning of electrical equipment and, in one instance, to an "act of God," intelligence officials disclosed that at least three of the fires were caused by sabotage.[67] The fact that no nuclear facilities have so far been penetrated is not in itself reassuring in this respect. In a telling security lapse, when India's nuclear tests were being carried out in 1998, an unauthorized individual—an army washerman who had jumped into a military truck with other soldiers because he wanted to help—was discovered at the test site, that too by accident because he had been bitten by a scorpion.[68] All of this shows that however robust nuclear security may be, the possibility of failure, with its immense potential for disaster, must be accepted as real.

The Motivations of Terrorist Groups

Politics provides the key to gauging the scale of risk accurately, for ultimately, human motivation is the driving factor. A world in the process of globalization—the worldwide transformation of patterns of production and communication, and the uncertainties it has engendered—is fertile soil for the terrorist. The erosion of traditional identities, combined with the disparities and insecurities produced by economic change, has given rise to growing anger and frustration, and "selective technopolitical rage."[69] Terrorists are driven both by strategic goals and by deep psychological motivations. As rational calculators, they may resort to violence because they lack adequate mass support, because they are subject to severe repression, or perhaps out of a need to seize quickly upon a critical moment of government weakness or the infusion of new resources.[70] At the same time, terrorists are also creatures of a "special psycho-logic": often propelled by a pattern of educational and vocational failure and a sense of social rejection, they are aggressive, stimulus-hungry, and prone to violence against those in whom they seek to project their own failures.[71] Group pressures tend to propel individuals across the threshold of violence and sometimes to encourage a rising graph of bloodshed.

What might motivate a terrorist to "go nuclear"? The history of terrorist mass destruction is a relatively sketchy and short one.[72] The resort to nuclear terrorism, with its potential for mass annihilation, appears to have inherent constraints from the rational standpoint. Indeed, there are very few examples of mass killing by terrorists over the past hundred years or so.[73] Terrorists have numerous reasons for eschewing a strategy of mass casualty attacks.[74] They usually want to create fear, not revulsion. As Brian Jenkins puts it, "terrorists want a lot of people *watching*, not a lot of people *dead*."[75] Resort to mass killing can alienate not only the public, but members of a terrorist organization as well. Terrorists have numerous alternatives that can accomplish the objective of creating widespread fear with less difficulty, such as hijackings, bomb blasts, and kidnappings. For those who want to exterminate large numbers, as in the "ethnic cleansing" that has occurred in recent times in Rwanda and Bosnia, simple weapons may be sufficient. Besides, most terrorist groups wish to displace governments, and hence to behave—at least to some extent—like governments themselves, which places a constraint on unrestrained and indiscriminate violence.[76]

Nuclear-terrorist threats have been rare, and have never actually been carried out. In 1985, for instance, the Armenian Scientific Group threatened to destroy Turkey's major cities by exploding three nuclear devices, but nothing came of it.[77] In 1995, evidently on information provided by a rebel Chechen leader, a Russian television crew found a small quantity of Cesium-137 in a Moscow park.[78] Again, nothing happened. However, there is no minimizing the threat from at least two groups that have actually carried out acts of mass terrorist violence. Aum Shinrikyo, the Japanese cult group which carried out a chemical weapons attack in the Tokyo subway in 1995, is known to have attempted unsuccessfully to acquire nuclear capability.[79] More recently, Osama bin Laden's Al Qaeda is also known to have tried (with no more success so far as we know) to obtain nuclear material and technology.[80] History may not be an adequate guide to the future. Indicators of a new trend toward mass killing warn of an increased risk of nuclear terrorism in times to come.[81] The steady diffusion of technical knowledge means there is an ever-growing pool of capable individuals from which terrorist groups can draw. Nuclear materials are widely distributed around the world, and are often inadequately guarded. Above all, the rise of religion-based terrorism and of doomsday cults has been accompanied by ever-higher levels of violence, most recently manifested in the September 11 attacks in the United States. Religious terrorists are less inhibited in their destructiveness because their ultimate audience is not the government or the public, but their god. For them, violence becomes "a sacramental act, dictated and legitimized by theology."[82] The biggest threats come from "megalomaniacal hyperterrorists," individuals who dream of altering the trajectory of history through great acts of destructive transformation.[83] Though they may act alone (as did Timothy McVeigh, the Oklahoma bomber), they often show a capacity to organize and lead terrorist groups (bin Laden of Al Qaeda, Shoko Asahara of Aum Shinrikyo, Ramsey Yusuf, who masterminded the World Trade Center bombing of 1993). Hence, bin Laden's exhortation to Muslims in "The Nuclear Bomb of Islam" to do their "duty" and "prepare as much force as possible to terrorize the enemies of God" has to be taken very seriously.[84]

India has a long history of terrorist activity.[85] The northeastern states have witnessed continual secessionist violence since the 1950s. During the 1980s, the chief center of terrorist activity was the state of Punjab, where Sikh extremists engaged in a secessionist movement that took a heavy toll in lives, including that of Prime Minister Indira Gandhi.[86] From the 1990s, the focus has shifted to Jammu and Kashmir, especially the Kashmir Valley, and to groups such as the Harkat-ul-Muahideen (HuM) and the Jaish-e-Mohammed (JeM). Less well known are groups active in other parts of the country, such as the Tamil Nadu Liberation Army (TNLA) in the south, the Akhil Bharatiya Nepali Ekta Samaj (ABNES) in the north, and the Hindu Army in the northeast. The genesis of most current terrorist movements has been internal, their motivations diverse. The rise of left-wing extremist organizations like the People's War Group (PWG) has been fueled by deprivation and by the exploitation of the poor by upper caste landowners. Over the past decade, these groups have been prominent in the eastern states of Bihar and Jharkhand, and the central states of Andhra Pradesh and Maharashtra. From both of these focal regions, they have begun to spread outward.[87] Ethnic movements seeking autonomy or independence employ terror strategies in the northeastern states, especially Assam, Nagaland, and Tripura. Religion has been the basis of major terrorist movements in Punjab and Kashmir. In the latter case, the tendency of observers to focus solely on Islamic separatism is misleading. The movement arose in pursuit of the regional identity of "Kashmiriyat," which accounts for the public sympathy it has evoked. The rise of "jihadi" groups espousing militant Islam is a more recent phenomenon, drawing its power from bases in other countries, mainly Pakistan and Afghanistan.[88] All the domestically based movements have been relatively local in their focus and have shown no inclination toward mass killing. However, the jihadi groups are of a different character.

Islamic extremists have steadily increased their presence in Kashmir, as statistics show. The number of foreign militants killed by Indian security forces grew from 30 in 1991 to 194 in 1996, and 541 in 2001.[89] These groups, which have their bases mainly in Pakistan, are driven by a Pan-Islamist agenda that seeks to transform the world order through a "war of a thousand cuts."[90] Not all Muslim terrorist groups active in India are connected to this larger enterprise, as one intelligence expert has pointed out.[91] But the potential to drive them to it is there. Discussions of terrorism in India pay insufficient attention to the widespread acts of terror—usually described as "communal violence"—to which right-wing elements of the Hindu majority resort against other communities.[92] But it is precisely these that are likely to push locally oriented groups into the wider network of terrorists that we call "jihadis."[93] Perhaps the first terrorist group with an Islamic orientation, the

Tanzim Islah-ul-Mumineen, was formed in Mumbai (then Bombay) in 1985. This group was responsible for a series of bomb blasts in Mumbai and Hyderabad (Andhra Pradesh state) on December 6, 1993, the first anniversary of the destruction of the Babri Masjid by Hindu extremists.[94] Earlier, in March that year, a series of bomb blasts in Mumbai killed some 250 people in what was one of the worst cases worldwide of mass attacks by terrorists.[95] The attacks were apparently designed to avenge the large-scale killing of Muslims by Hindu extremists in Mumbai in December 1992 and January 1993. Events like the anti-Muslim pogrom in Gujarat in 2002 could give rise to social polarization and terrorism.[96] Already there is evidence of Gujarati Muslim extremists traveling to Kashmir to acquire arms and ammunition.[97] The threat, direct or indirect, of nuclear terrorism from such groups cannot be ruled out if they become further radicalized.

External Motivations: Jihadis and States in South Asia

India is located in a region of political turbulence and militancy characterized by the ubiquitous presence of terrorism and porous borders. In recent years, radical and terrorist movements have flourished in neighboring Afghanistan, Bangladesh, Bhutan, Myanmar, Nepal, Pakistan, and Sri Lanka. Of these, only two sources of terrorism have shown the potential to engage in mass killing. The Liberation Tigers of Tamil Eelam (LTTE) in Sri Lanka is one. The LTTE has resources, organizing capability, and a capacity for suicide attacks, which would allow the handling of radiological materials without much care for self-preservation. However, it seems to have learned from the Rajiv Gandhi assassination that there are political limits to the use of violence. That single act deeply alienated the Indian public, including sympathetic Indian Tamils.[98] Besides, though the possibility of a reversal remains at the time of writing (early 2005), the LTTE has shifted from the path of unremitting violence to negotiation, not least because the global "war on terrorism" has diminished its financial inflows.[99] In any case, the LTTE has not shown a commitment to revolutionary transformation comparable to the jihadis. Its goal remains at most the establishment of a Tamil state.

The main source of a nuclear-terrorist threat, therefore, stems from the jihadi groups that have taken up arms in Kashmir, such as the HuM, the JeM, the Hizb-ul-Mujahideen (HM), and the Lashkar-e-Taiba (LeT). Of these, only HM has some Kashmiri membership, but like the others, it is based in Pakistan. Though their major membership is Pakistani, their fighters are drawn from a wide catchment area and include Middle Eastern Arabs, Chechens, and Afghans.[100] All of them have a commitment to jihad as well as links to Al Qaeda, and all except HM are ideologically and operationally intertwined with Al Qaeda.[101] The latter has explicitly declared that India is a target. In December 1999, a fax message to the Voice of America in Washington on behalf of Nazeer Ahmed Mujjaid, military advisor to Al Qaeda, proclaimed the goal of these groups: to fight against "Americans, Russians and Indians," and ensure that "Islam will spread over the entire world."[102] Militant leaders have proclaimed Kashmir as a "gateway to India" and established links with fundamentalist and terrorist organizations in different parts of the country, notably in southern India.[103]

The politics of the region is conducive to a sustained threat from Al Qaeda and its affiliates. Muslim fundamentalism and the instruments of violence became a powerful combination with massive U.S. funding of the Afghan resistance to Soviet occupation in the 1980s.[104] A regular flow of funds from Saudi Arabia led to the proliferation of *madrasas* (religious educational institutions) that spawned radical militancy throughout Pakistan, Afghanistan, and Central Asia.[105] Afghanistan remained turbulent after the Soviet withdrawal and eventually fell under the control of the Pakistan-sponsored Taliban. Al Qaeda found a safe base there until the United States launched Operation Enduring Freedom in response to the September 11 attacks. Three years later, at the time of writing (early 2005), remnants of Al Qaeda and the Taliban continue to fight from the region along the Pakistan-Afghanistan border. There are indications that Al Qaeda's organization is recovering, with training camps drawing fresh volunteers.[106] Afghanistan itself remains troubled by violence and internecine warfare among numerous tribal groups. The production of opium has risen dramatically.[107] A third of it is expected to go through India.[108] This increases the scope for terrorist activity in the region as there is a close linkage between organized crime, especially the drug trade, and terrorist groups.[109]

Pakistan's links to terrorism and Islamic radicalism are well known.[110] Support for terrorists operating in India has been a useful, low-cost instrument to put India under constant pressure.[111] After September 11, 2001, when it turned against the radicals it had formerly sponsored in Afghanistan and Kashmir, Pakistan has had to contend with a rising incidence of internally oriented terrorism. Its political and economic condition is vulnerable. Military rule has not sufficed to bring about fundamental reforms relating to corruption, tax restructuring, bonded labor, and the deweaponization of society.[112] Radical Islam is on the rise, carrying with it a "jihadi culture" of violence.[113] There are believed to be as many as 18 million illegal weapons in the country.[114] Notwithstanding President Musharraf's proclaimed commitment to crushing terrorism, terrorist groups have flourished.[115] In the 2002 elections, the Muttahida Majlis-e-Amal (MMA), an alliance of six religious parties, came to power in the North West Frontier Province (NWFP) and Baluchistan (through a coalition in the latter case). A few weeks later, the new Chief Minister of Baluchistan ordered the release of all militants in the province.[116] As a result of these developments, the region bordering Afghanistan, never much under control, became a base for former Taliban members.[117] Al Qaeda was believed by U.S. and Pakistani intelligence services to have set up base in Pakistan.[118] By early 2003, most arrested terrorists had been released and the cross-border flow of jihadis into Kashmir was on the rise again.[119] Under pressure from the religious right, Musharraf had allowed the resumption of cross-border terrorism, in part to safeguard his own regime, and in part because the jihadis were now the only dependable instrument for sustaining Pakistani pressure on India.[120] Though the joint U.S.-Pakistani hunt for members of Al Qaeda and the Taliban continues, its success has been limited.[121]

The general threat environment for India is aggravated by evidence of the presence of Al Qaeda in Bangladesh.[122] For instance, the Harkat-ul-Jihad-al-Islami (HUJI) is an offshoot of the Pakistan-based HuM when it was known as the Harkat-ul-Ansar. Its leader, Abdul Salam Muhammad, also known as Fazlur Rahman, was one of the six constituents of the World Islamic Front for the Jihad against the Jews and the Crusaders announced in 1998.[123] Strongly influenced by the Taliban, HUJI is a militant advocate of Islamic orthodoxy and of a future in which Bangladesh "will become Afghanistan."[124] The Indian government in early 2003 identified as many as ninety-nine terrorist camps in Bangladesh.[125] The problem has been exacerbated by the regular flow of illegal migrants from Bangladesh into India, which is estimated to have been as much as fifteen million between 1981 and 1991 alone, and still continues.[126]

Given the widespread evidence of Islamic extremists in South Asia, the cause for anxiety is strong. In the immediate aftermath of the September 11 attacks, terrorists operating in Kashmir vowed catastrophic damage to sensitive installations in India. Sheikh Jamilur Rehman, leader of the Tehrik-ul-Mujahideen, explicitly threatened to target Indian nuclear facilities.[127] While this may have been mere rhetoric, there is a real fear arising from Al Qaeda's known interest in acquiring nuclear capability.[128] An investigation by the television channel Al-Jazeera revealed in June 2002 that the original plan for September 11, 2001, was to crash hijacked jets into nuclear plants, but that the plan was changed.[129] Qualified personnel are also available in the region. At least one Pakistani and two Afghan nuclear scientists have been approached by Osama bin Laden for help in making a bomb.[130] Late in 2002, it was reported that nine Pakistani nuclear scientists had "disappeared."[131] The unraveling of the proliferation network presided over by A. Q. Khan, the "father of the Pakistani bomb," has revealed the transfer of nuclear expertise, including complete bomb designs, to a number of countries.[132] Though there is no evidence of this so far, the possibility that some transfer to Islamic radicals may have occurred remains. While none of these reports is individually a strong piece of evidence indicating the advent of nuclear terrorism to South Asia, they together paint a disturbing picture of a potential threat that cannot be ignored, especially in light of the political conditions outlined earlier. After September 11, 2001, the realm of the possible has been greatly expanded.

The Benefits of Minimum Deterrence

Perhaps the least explored aspect of nuclear terrorism is the relationship between terrorism and national strategic postures. From the standpoint of strategic stability, the minimum deterrence doctrine espoused by both India and Pakistan—especially their nondeployed postures—minimizes the risk of war. The greater the strategic distance between them, the lower the probability of nuclear conflict. However, there are still a number of vulnerabilities vis-à-vis the terrorist threat. Some of the possibilities may be viewed as unlikely, but they cannot be discounted, and adequate thought needs to be given to preventing them. Minimum deterrence as understood in this book is particularly valuable in three respects.

Numbers

A strategy of minimum deterrence has a built-in advantage if an arsenal is kept down to small numbers. The smaller the number of weapons, the fewer the targets for terrorists. As argued earlier, the question of sufficiency in numbers is not so much one of certainty of success in causing damage, but of the level of risk associated with the potential use of nuclear weapons. Since the overwhelming preference is that nuclear weapons not be used, their very existence is associated with a significant level of risk. This applies to the relationship between weapons and terrorists as well. If the meaning of what constitutes sufficiency is ambiguous, then the possibility of an expanding arsenal is significant. This may be driven by changing perceptions of threat, by bureaucratic interests, or merely by inertia of motion. Furthermore, if the trend toward greater diversity—by means of the development of a triad, for instance—is sustained, numbers will almost certainly go up, since there will be pressure to ensure that each leg has a "sufficient" number of weapons. The questionable notion that there must be "enough" weapons to make a second strike capability "credible" will inevitably apply to each leg, and the number of weapons—and targets for terrorists—will expand accordingly. Whatever the reason, growth in numbers will increase vulnerability to terrorists. The risks related to the former Soviet Union's large arsenal are well known. On a smaller but still significant scale, particularly in light of the numerous organizational vulnerabilities observed earlier, the same risks apply to India.

Deployment

In the event that weapons are assembled, mated to warheads, and deployed, the problem assumes substantial proportions. While at the time of writing deployment is not considered a serious issue, it may occur in two kinds of circumstances. Nuclear weapons may be deployed in normal conditions, as is the case with the five major nuclear powers. This may happen over time if the emphasis on "credibility" remains as uninformed by adequate understanding of the concept of minimum deterrence as is the case now and a decision to deploy is made in order to convince adversaries of Indian capabilities. Upon deployment, the level of exposure to terrorism will be increased. While numbers make for more targets, deployment makes for easier ones. Assuming the number of weapons to be constant, their vulnerability will increase with deployment because their distribution will create more opportunities for terrorists.

Deployment during a crisis would have the advantage of giving little time for terrorists to target weapons. Against this, when times are not normal, the probability of security failure is higher. In case of predelegation of launch authority, or the adoption of alert and perhaps even launch-on-warning postures, the linkage between an act of terrorism and nuclear posture is tightened. A terrorist attack might be misconstrued as an attack by enemy forces. This could happen in varying circumstances. In the worst case, if a nuclear device explodes—say, in an urban area—it could be interpreted as a Pakistani strike, and a military response would be difficult to resist. Second, a similar attack on military forces would likely be perceived as a first strike, and a forceful response would be almost inevitable. Third, a terrorist attack with an RDD or conventional explosives on deployed nuclear forces could be viewed as an act of war by the enemy state, which again would evoke a military response. Fourth, the same would apply to a terrorist attack on the nuclear command and control structure. In the last case, admittedly unlikely, terrorists might be able to disrupt a command and control system not only by physical attacks, but electronically. Following India's nuclear tests, Internet hackers attacked web sites of the Indian nuclear establishment.[133] It is not inconceivable that terrorists could penetrate the Indian nuclear command and control structure and create havoc, possibly sparking off war. Given all these possibilities, political leaders need to appreciate that deployment, by exacerbating the "never" side of the so-called always/never problem, carries needlessly high costs.

Weapons or their components are most vulnerable during transportation prior to mating with warheads, or after mating, when they are in the process of being moved to active deployment locations. Stationary targets are easier to secure, moving ones far harder to protect because they will likely have to traverse numerous points of vulnerability. Against this, interdiction of weapons during transportation is made more difficult by the lack of time for preparing an attack. In all cases, deployment during crisis will increase risks because of the tension and speed that are likely to be part of the process.

If the weapons are assembled but not actively deployed, they could still be taken by force or stolen. If terrorists were to obtain Indian weapons in this manner, even if they were safeguarded by electronic safety locks (PALs, or permissive action links), they could be used as RDDs. Alternatively, terrorists could merely threaten to use them in some unspecified way. Such a threat would be "credible" in the same way as an untested weapon is. Indian leaders would scarcely want to risk finding out the hard way whether they are or not. Finally, terrorists could attack and blow up deployed weapons with conventional explosives and release radiation.

Even in disaggregated condition, India's nuclear weapons are subject to the designs of terrorists in at least two ways. First, like nuclear plants and materials, they are potential targets. They could be targeted at the place of storage. As noted above, even high levels of security alertness can be—and have been—penetrated by small numbers of terrorists. It is conceivable that an unassembled weapon could be blown up with conventional explosives. Alternately, admittedly a more difficult task, a nuclear core or other components could be stolen or removed by force. This could be done with or without the assistance of an insider. If a nuclear core is removed, then it is potentially usable as a weapon. In the most extreme case, it could be used to manufacture a nuclear weapon, even if only a crude one. Or it could be used as an RDD at a time and place of the terrorists' choosing. To be sure, there is a trade-off between the risk to assembled weapons and that to unassembled ones. The former would be easier to protect with sophisticated electronic locks. A stolen weapon fitted with such locks—that is, a fully assembled one—would nevertheless be usable as an RDD, though almost certainly not as a nuclear weapon.

Compellence

Finally, as Chapter 4 has made clear, the use of a compellence strategy is fraught with risk. In addition to the risk of escalation, compellence raises the strategic temperature and may tempt India and Pakistan to shift from nondeployment to deployment. This applies to all the forms of compellence attempted in South Asia since the advent of nuclear weapons in the 1990s: covert border transgression, support for terrorists, and mobilization for a possible limited war. Each raises tensions and provides opportunities for terrorists to engage in acts of nuclear terrorism. To reduce the probability of this happening, India and Pakistan need to disengage operationally and engage politically.

Terrorists as Deterrers

Most writings on nuclear terrorism assume that terrorists who manage to acquire some level of nuclear capability (including radiological capability) will actually use that capability to wreak havoc on their targets. That need not be so. Like states, terrorists may well find it more useful to use their capability to deter adversary states by threatening to retaliate against the superior "conventional" military and paramilitary forces of the state. Given the existential basis of minimum deterrence, a terrorist group would not have to do a great deal to be credible. A stolen bomb or stolen radioactive material would have a deterrent effect. If it felt the need, the group might give a small demonstration of its capability, say, in an unpopulated area.

Moreover, just as states do, terrorists may obtain the benefits of minimum deterrence. Having acquired nuclear or radiological weapons, they could threaten to use them unless the government exercised restraint. Indeed, they would find it expedient to use nuclear capability for compellence. In pursuing a compellence strategy backed by deterrence, they will not face the same constraints that states do. In almost no case can they be deterred by the state's nuclear capabilities, for states cannot conceive of using a first or even retaliatory strike against amorphous, nonterritorial adversaries.[134] Furthermore, as Schelling points out, unlike in the taking of hostages or the hijacking of ships or aircraft, "there is no inherent limitation on how long a nuclear threat can last and no necessity for surrender of the weapon at the end of a successful negotiation."[135]

The combination of deterrence and compellence capability would permit terrorists to coerce a state in several ways. They might demand the release of prisoners, the initiation of negotiations, specific concessions to their political agenda such as changes in law or government, the withdrawal of military or paramilitary forces, the vacation of territory, and so on. How would the Indian government respond to a demand backed by nuclear or radiological threats that its forces withdraw from Kashmir, or even a part of it? A government confronted with such demands would find it very difficult to accommodate them, but just as hard to reject them. In short, states facing the challenge of terrorist nuclear capability would find themselves in an intrinsically weak position. Hence the need to ensure that terrorists do not obtain the capability to unleash nuclear/radiological damage.

Conclusion: Combating the Threat

Whether nuclear terrorism is a likely prospect is a matter of debate. For most terrorists, an act of nuclear terror would be politically inexpedient as well as morally unacceptable. Building a nuclear bomb is a very difficult task, as several states with considerable resources at their command have found. Even a dirty bomb may be hard to make, as the handling of radioactive materials is a difficult enterprise.[136] Other means of mass destruction—chemical, biological, and even effectively placed high explosives—are more easily available.[137] From a terrorist's standpoint, these alternatives may be more cost-effective, spreading fear at relatively low levels of technology and effort. On the other hand, nuclear technology offers terrorists the same attraction it does to states: the enormous political power that goes with a qualitatively unmatched instrument of destruction. Besides, extreme radicals, unlike states, may be less concerned about the risks associated with handling nuclear materials, and satisfied with attaining crude capability. While no incident of nuclear terrorism has occurred as yet, there is clear evidence of interest in it on the part of terrorist organizations such as Aum Shinrikyo and Al Qaeda. A nuclear bomb may be hard to make, but not impossible; and a dirty bomb is well within the capacity of many. So long as there is will, opportunities and capabilities will always be sought. Combating the threat will require both domestic and international efforts.

Domestic Measures

At the domestic level, a comprehensive strategy to counter the threat of nuclear terrorism is imperative.[138] Such a strategy should revolve around the following elements:

Technology: Counterterrorism requires technical sophistication for the physical security of nuclear weapons components and nuclear materials and installations, and considerable investment in order to achieve that. Particular attention also needs to be given to the monitoring and safety of transportation of nuclear weapons and materials. The role of technology encompasses anticipation, detection, delay, and rapid response.

Organization and Training: The ramifications of nuclear terrorism bring numerous organizations into contact with one another for detection, prevention, and emergency response. These include the atomic energy establishment, the intelligence community, civilian authorities associated with command and control, and military, paramilitary, and police forces. Control and supervision of the security of materials across organizations requires comprehensive planning, coordination, and oversight. A beginning has been made with the establishment of a Disaster Management Division in India's Ministry of Home Affairs.[139] The ministry has authorized the establishment of a National Emergency Response Force of paramilitary personnel drawn from the CISF and three other organizations, and a training infrastructure at the central and state levels. Seventy-two teams from four paramilitary battalions are being trained to respond to nuclear, chemical, and biological emergencies. This may not be enough. The protection of nuclear assets requires a high level of specialized training, for which an integrated force of scientific and other specialists as well as paramilitary personnel, such as the Nuclear Emergency Search Teams (NEST) in the United States, needs to be organized for prevention as well as quick response to an alarm or attack.[140] Wider arrangements will involve the military, the civilian administrative apparatus, the police, hospitals, the fire brigade, public health services, transportation systems, and the like for tackling a nuclear emergency; and arrangements for the dissemination of information and confidence to the public through government and private media. The reluctance to allocate adequate resources to what is viewed as an unlikely event can have horrendous consequences, as the disastrous effects of the tsunami that hit the eastern coast of India in December 2004 revealed.[141] Even more telling is the slow response by the government to warning of the impending event.[142] Care in organization is essential. Simply adding more security personnel (or devices) may be counterproductive since it may actually increase the probability of failure in a complex system.[143] A well-designed personnel reliability program that includes psychological testing is also essential. While little information is available on personnel reliability policy in India, the system of intelligence vetting is not believed to be complemented by regular psychological testing, behavior analysis, or a reporting system such as the Continuous Behavior Observation Program in the United States.

Accountability: Independent monitoring of organizations that comprise the nuclear-weapons infrastructure is important to ensure accountability. The role of an independently appointed executive body comprised of both government and independent experts, or of a legislative committee (assisted by experts) analogous to Parliament's Public Accounts Committee, is crucial in this respect. There is no such accountability system in the Indian nuclear infrastructure. Problems arising from this lacuna are discussed in the next chapter.

Strategic Doctrine: Nuclear doctrine must include a full consideration of the threat of terrorism, and especially nuclear terrorism. The discussion in this chapter makes it abundantly clear that a minimalist posture of small, nondeployed forces is best suited not only to counter nuclear threats from states, but to reduce the threat posed by nuclear terrorism as well.

International Cooperation

Multilateral: Domestic endeavors to strengthen the security of nuclear assets can be supplemented by cooperative efforts at the international level. All countries, and especially those menaced by radical groups capable of catastrophic acts, have a common interest in tackling the threat of nuclear terrorism. Nuclear capability obtained from one country could be used anywhere. Besides, the risk of a nuclear catastrophe in the region is a matter of concern around the world. At the global level, the Proliferation Security Initiative (PSI) launched by eleven states (Australia, France, Germany, Italy, Japan, the Netherlands, Poland, Portugal, Spain, the United Kingdom, and the United States) in May 2003 offers the possibility of a multilateral framework to combat the nuclear-terrorist threat.[144] The PSI envisages the employment of legal, diplomatic, economic, military, and other means to interdict shipments of WMD and missile-related equipment and technologies that threaten global security. Doubtless there is good reason for states to be cautious, particularly since the PSI is directed not only against terrorists, but also against states. This involves tricky issues about identifying the states that are threats to global security. Besides, there are numerous legal obstacles stemming from the rights of states, notably the right to freedom of the high seas, and potential political problems in overcoming them.[145] The Indian establishment has indicated as much in showing reluctance to accept the PSI.[146] Nevertheless, a multilateral program to curb the risks of nuclear (and other WMD) terrorism is a necessary response to what is indubitably a global problem of serious dimensions.

Bilateral: At the bilateral level, the United States and other countries could provide invaluable assistance by making available modern technologies and equipment in radiological detection, remote sensing, video monitoring, alarms, and tamper-indicating seals. They could also provide valuable guidance on the organization of security and disaster management. These are politically sensitive issues. Policy makers in other countries are constantly under pressure not to "reward" proliferation. Indians, on the other hand, are concerned that the United States and its allies may have a hidden nonproliferation agenda that seeks to penetrate and tighten controls over India's nuclear program.[147] Nevertheless, since both sides have an overriding interest in minimizing the dangers posed by nuclear terrorism, a beginning can be made on a mutually agreed and nonintrusive basis to transfer at least some technologies and best practices to India.[148]

Notwithstanding their history of mutual suspicion, long-standing tension, and recurring crises, India and Pakistan have a shared interest in thwarting nuclear terrorism. The same applies to China. It is not in the interests of any of them to allow terrorist groups to obtain nuclear capability. First, a nuclear-terrorist threat is an equally important concern for all. Despite Pakistan's tendency to use terrorists as its instruments to put India on the defensive, it cannot countenance nuclear capability in the hands of these groups as they could pose a serious threat to Pakistan itself. Groups with nuclear-terrorism potential which have attacked Indian targets from bases in Pakistan—such as the JeM and the al-Alami group, an offshoot of HuM—have also targeted the Pakistani leadership.[149] As states, both countries have a stake in preserving their monopoly over weapons of mass destruction. Second, acts of nuclear terrorism may well bring about a war in the subcontinent, an eventuality that neither India nor Pakistan desires. These are common interests that provide the basis for them to develop at least a modicum of cooperation. It is important to recall that in the past, India and Pakistan have been able to cooperate on nuclear-strategic matters even during times of high tension. In December 1988, they signed an agreement to avoid attacking each other's nuclear facilities, the terms of which they have adhered to by exchanging lists of their respective facilities even at the height of confrontation. Similarly, both have consistently informed each other of impending missile tests in accordance with the Memorandum of Understanding signed at Lahore in 1999.

Future cooperation between India and Pakistan, and between India and China, might include joint commitments on rejecting all forms of nuclear terrorism, sharing of information on nuclear-terrorist threats, and early communication at the highest level in case a nuclear-terrorist incident occurs. The Lahore Memorandum envisaged discussions on nuclear doctrine and concepts. The tacit India-Pakistan understanding on nondeployment, critical to minimizing the nuclear terrorism threat, could be strengthened by such discussions and possibly an agreement not to deploy, barring extreme exigencies. Because Pakistan's nuclear posture tends to respond to India's, it behooves India to take the lead in circumscribing the scope for nuclear terrorism. India's affirmation of minimum deterrence, based on a better understanding of its underlying assumptions and restraint with respect to the quantity, quality, and deployment of forces, will help loosen the link between nuclear terrorism and interstate war.

7

Minimum Deterrence and Democracy

Most discussions on India's nuclear posture focus on the external dimension of national security policy. In fact, nuclear weapons also have a bearing on pivotal aspects of domestic political life. The adoption of a strategy of nuclear deterrence carries not only the security dilemma with respect to the state's external sphere, but equally serious domestic dilemmas for democracies. These dilemmas involve three major contradictions:

The immorality of threatening indiscriminate destruction versus the moral imperative of securing the survival of the state and its citizens: Nuclear weapons pose for democratic societies an extraordinarily difficult moral problem. How can we reconcile the moral responsibility of the state to protect its citizens from external threats and our perception of ourselves as a good society with the threat to destroy other human beings indiscriminately?

The high degree of centralized control that nuclear weapons require versus the obligation of democracies to disperse authority: Whereas democracy is at its core a decentralized system built on the idea that the people are the ultimate arbiters of their own fate, nuclear weapons directly contravene this axiom and tend to maximize centralized power and decision making.

The need for secrecy that surrounds nuclear weapons versus accountability and the rule of law, which are vital pillars of democracy: Nuclear weapons breed a secretiveness that evades accountability and which, if unchecked, allows the subversion of basic democratic norms.

As in the case of the external security dilemma, none of these domestic dilemmas can be resolved fully. They can at best be reduced to the lowest possible level by means of a strict adherence to minimum deterrence. This requires that minimum deterrence be understood in the broadest sense: that nuclear weapons are not assigned the predominant place in national security arrangements; and that states acknowledge the ways in which nuclear weapons violate democratic norms and seek to contain as far as possible the moral and political inroads they make into the democratic good society. True minimum deterrence refuses to privilege nuclear weapons and treats them as political rather than operational instruments of security. Consequently, it keeps under control the tension between nuclear weapons and democracy. The smaller the weapons infrastructure, the less the vulnerability of democratic society to erosion by the accoutrements of deterrence.

Even a cursory reading of the history of nuclear weapons in India leaves us troubled about its propensity to undermine democracy. Nuclear India has for the most part been secretive, statist, and undemocratic in its workings.[1] Ironically, the much-criticized tests of 1998 did democracy a service in at least one respect. They removed the shroud of secrecy from nuclear policy and brought it into the public eye, thus creating an environment for accountability that had been lacking in the past. But the future remains unsure, for it is by no means certain that this "democratization" of nuclear policy will be sustained. It is the argument here that while the contradiction between nuclear weapons and democracy cannot be resolved so long as nuclear weapons are not eliminated—a dim prospect, as we have seen in Chapter 1—minimum deterrence offers the optimal "solution." It minimizes the domestic political costs of possessing nuclear weapons and thereby offers the best possible balance between the requirements of external security and those of democracy. This chapter examines first the troubling dilemma of targeting innocents with nuclear weapons. Then follows a discussion on the ways in which nuclear weapons detract from a cornerstone of democracy: the right of citizens to determine their own fate. Finally, the chapter focuses on the accumulation of state power under the guise of national security and the erosion of public accountability and the rule of law.

The Moral Dimension

Indians tend often to bask in the virtues of Gandhian nonviolence. In reality, an elementary acquaintance with India's history and social-political life reveals a story similar to that of any other society, one that is replete with power and violence. Gandhi's antipathy toward nuclear weapons was strong: he found them morally repugnant and unacceptable.[2] But we have seen in Chapter 3 that he was ambivalent about the use of armed force against external enemies. Antinuclear activists often fail to acknowledge his ambivalence.[3] Nor do they concede that this ambivalence pervades Indian thinking about the ethics of war. The ancient scriptures of Hinduism, to which the great majority of Indians adhere, reflect the ethical tension between *samanya dharma* (the common virtues), which gives primacy to *ahimsa* (nonviolence), and *visesa dharma* (particular duties), which, among other things, makes killing a duty for warriors.[4] Still, there was a deep-seated moral distaste attached to nuclear weapons during the early years after Independence. The need to respond to growing threats was reined in by a revulsion against the indiscriminate and apocalyptic character of nuclear weapons. Indian policy drifted in an uncertain sea. A succession of leaders felt compelled, however reluctantly, to at minimum keep the nuclear option open and simultaneously to resist the demand for the acquisition of a nuclear arsenal. Even Morarji Desai, as stubbornly hostile to nuclear weapons as Gandhi, could not bring himself to close the option. This reflects the contradiction between the political reality of the world around us and the moral sensitivities that we aspire to be true to.

Democracy is at heart an ethical system centered upon, among other things, respect for the life and liberty of one's fellow human beings and upon moral choice and the individual and collective responsibility of making it. From this perspective, nuclear weapons pose grave difficulties for democratic society. Is deterrence morally defensible? Many Indians assert that it is not.[5] But this is an absolute position. The real world is complex, requiring us to grapple with its contradictory elements. Appreciation of this complexity is embedded in Hindu thinking about mass destruction.[6] On one hand, the scriptures and epics proscribe indiscriminate killing and insist on the principle of proportionality, which demands that the use of violence be proportional to objectives. On the other, they allow for setting these moral considerations aside in exceptional circumstances and as a last resort, both of which are implicit arguments in favor of nuclear weapons.[7] If we regard it as a moral right to defend ourselves by the use of force, then it may be argued that nuclear deterrence is acceptable as an extension of this.

But there must be limits on the means we use to achieve desirable ends. This brings us to the question of targeting. The strategy of massive retaliation declared by India involves the threat to annihilate large numbers of noncombatants. How, it may be asked, can we justify the attainment of peace by targeting innocents and threatening them with indiscriminate destruction? Paul Ramsey, who rejects countervalue targeting, argues: "It is never right to do wrong that good may come out of it. . . . Neither is it right to *intend* to do wrong that good may come out of it. If deterrence rests upon genuinely intending massive retaliation, it is clearly wrong no matter how much peace results."[8]

Ramsey invokes the distinction between *jus ad bellum* (just cause) and *jus in bello* (just means) in war.[9] The former, involving the right to make war, differentiates between legitimate and illegitimate grounds for waging war. The latter rests on two principles: discrimination, or the minimization of harm (particularly to noncombatants), and proportionality. By the standard of just means, deterrence based on countervalue strategy, which targets cities and makes no distinction between combatants and noncombatants, appears to be morally reprehensible. In comparison, a warfighting or counterforce strategy, which targets the adversary's military forces, may be considered acceptable. But this is not a satisfactory argument, for the distinction between countervalue and counterforce strategies is notional. In practice, many so-called "counterforce" targets are located in or near large population centers: airfields, cantonments, military command centers, and so on. Thus, for instance, one study shows that total fatalities from twenty kiloton counterforce attacks on Pakistani military targets could be extremely high: 173,925 in the case of the 12 Army Corps stationed at Quetta, and 321,864 if the 11 Army Corps at Peshawar is targeted.[10] Ramsey's argument holds that the inadvertent "collateral damage" from counterforce warfare is acceptable, since it is unintended.[11] But at this level of destruction, such a moral distinction is meaningless, the more so since simulation studies enable us to anticipate what is likely to happen. Collateral damage in such cases is no more than a euphemism for an impact not qualitatively different from that caused by countervalue targeting.

There are three serious objections to counterforce strategy. First, while it is extremely difficult to contemplate the extinction of cities, a strategy of attacking the adversary's forces, because it seems less objectionable, is more doable, especially when the use of low-yield nuclear weapons is envisaged. Second, a strategy which allows the probability of collateral damage that could affect very large numbers is hard to justify as morally sound. Third, the distinction between the two strategies is not really meaningful if we take into account the problem of escalation. Given the high degree of uncertainty associated with the concept of limited nuclear war, it is not improper to argue that "the strength with which the conviction, that war will be limited, is expressed, is matched only by the weakness of the politico-strategic theory which accompanies it."[12] Because both strategies are just as likely to lead to large-scale nuclear conflict, they are equally immoral. The advantage of minimum deterrence is that, while undeniably immoral in an absolute sense, it accomplishes its purpose of obtaining security at minimum actual risk to innocents, and hence is relatively more acceptable from a moral as well as a practical standpoint. India's rejection of tactical weapons for nuclear warfighting and commitment to minimum deterrence is thus ethically tolerable.

Some critics are so morally outraged that they will not allow the very existence of nuclear weapons. In her passionate response to the Indian tests of 1998, the writer Arundhati Roy decries "the end of imagination" and writes of nuclear weapons: "The fact that they exist at all, their very presence in our lives, will wreak more havoc than we can begin to fathom. Nuclear weapons pervade our thinking. Control our behavior. Administer our societies. Inform our dreams. They bury themselves like meat hooks deep in the base of our brains. They are purveyors of madness."[13]

Similarly, Ashis Nandy is critical of the "genocidal mentality" and "psychic numbing" characteristic of what he calls "nuclearism," which "so numbs one's sensitivities that normal emotions and moral considerations cannot penetrate one any more."[14] These are powerful criticisms indeed. But they lack an appreciation of the security dilemma. How do we disentangle ourselves from the horror that cannot be disinvented? The central difficulty is that there is no escape from the moral dilemma which parallels the security dilemma. No one recognizes the moral dilemma better than Reinhold Niebuhr. In *Moral Man and Immoral Society*, Niebuhr explains the dialectical relationship between realism and morality.[15] Realist politics carries with it the seeds of its own destruction, whereas pure moralism, emphasizing love, does not recognize the contradictions of existence. There can be no absolute distinction between violence and nonviolence. Nonviolence too can be coercive, as it was in Gandhi's methods, while at times, violence may be "the servant of moral goodwill."[16]

A state has a moral obligation to defend the lives of its citizens. If it is faced with a security dilemma that compels it to obtain nuclear deterrence, then there is little point raising absolutist objections. Roy underscores the dreadfulness of nuclear destruction: "Our cities and our forests, our fields and villages will burn for days. Rivers will turn to poison. The air will become fire. . . . What shall we do, then, those of us who are still alive? Burned and blind and bald and ill, carrying the cancerous carcasses of our children in our arms, where shall we go?"[17]

The horrific portrait of civilization devastated by nuclear war cannot be wished away. The realist's dilemma is that *the same picture might be painted of a nonnuclear country subject to nuclear attack.* The undeniable historical reality—one that requires no imagination—is that of Hiroshima and Nagasaki. The realist could well ask: What might have prevented those catastrophes? A sense of moral aversion might have restrained President Truman from unleashing the atom bomb on noncombatants in his determination to obtain an unconditional surrender from Japan. But the end was allowed to justify the means, and it never occurred to Truman that "Americans owed the Japanese *people* an experiment in negotiation."[18] The other possibility was that if Japan had been in possession of the bomb, U.S. restraint would have been unavoidable. The question facing an Indian citizen is: To prevent the possibility of a nuclear attack, even an unlikely one, do I rely on deterrence or on the moral compunctions of others? The answer is obvious.

The reality of existence qualifies our notions of morality. For this reason, the International Court of Justice, while opining on the legitimacy of nuclear weapons, has held that "the Court cannot conclude definitively whether the threat or use of nuclear weapons would be lawful or unlawful in the extreme circumstance of self-defence, in which the very survival of a State would be at stake."[19] The judgment captures the essence of the moral dilemma associated with nuclear weapons: they are terrible things, but we may need them. The fundamental contradiction between the realist logic of an anarchic world and the sense of goodness and justice that underlie human morality appears impossible to resolve. As Geoffrey Goodwin points out, moral outrage is not good enough. "A responsible attitude is not helped by indulging in idealistic prescriptions which ignore the realities of power in simplistic notions of international right and wrong. . . . In short, what is needed is a concern not only with what states *ought* to do, but also for what they *can* do."[20]

Ultimately, the preservation of society requires us to take recourse to "immoral" means. There is no way out of the moral dilemma. This may be rejected as a consequentialist position which undervalues people as human beings. John Finnis and his colleagues argue that the killing of innocents is not justified because "the dignity of human persons is protected by moral absolutes," one of which "forbids choices to destroy human lives."[21] There are two objections to this. First, the choice involved in deterrence is not one of killing innocents for some political end, but rather that of targeting them in order, paradoxically, to protect their lives by avoiding war. Second, surely it is at least as immoral to not use deterrence to protect one's own citizens from the prospect of mass destruction. The human rights argument fails to acknowledge that while it is perfectly legitimate to speak of people in universal terms, the reality is that they are divided into communities organized into states. If the state has to choose between one immorality and another—between targeting the people of adversary states and not defending its own citizens from those who would target them—the former choice is morally troubling, but one that is still legitimate.

Is existential or virtual deterrence a way out? It might be argued that the mere possession of nuclear weapons or even capability alone is moral, for it achieves the effect of deterrence without directly threatening an adversary. Not quite, for this would be no more than ethical sleight of hand, a pretence still based on "moral approval of the function of deterrence."[22] The only viable way of limiting—but not eliminating—one's moral culpability is to minimize the possibility of the potential outcome: the decimation of millions in a nuclear war. For that, a minimum deterrence posture based on defensive realism and a predominantly political conception of nuclear weapons is desirable. In every respect, therefore, the democratic principles on which society is built must underpin the way we think about nuclear weapons and the way we organize them toward our collective ends.

Reducing to a minimum the possibility of war also entails an abiding commitment to arms control, whether tacit or formal. Fortunately, as we have seen in Chapter 3, Indian strategic culture with respect to nuclear weapons is imbued with a strong predisposition toward arms control. Contrary to the widespread perception that India's nuclearization is reflective of a new aggressiveness, interest in arms control has remained strong. The initiative that led to the Lahore Declaration in 1999 was in conformity with the preference for arms control exhibited in the pre-1998 period through a series of agreements and confidence-building measures (CBMs) signed with China and Pakistan.[23] Despite the high tension of the 2001–2 crisis, India and Pakistan continued to observe the 1988 agreement not to attack each other's nuclear facilities and to exchange lists of their respective facilities. There is scope for more, but conditions may be more favorable for tacit rather than formal arms control. Aspects of this will be discussed in the concluding chapter.

Nuclear Weapons, State Power, and the Citizen

The argument of this book is that minimum deterrence is a rational strategic response to the security dilemma of states confronted by a threat to their survival. In practice, strategic rationality may become intertwined with a symbolic communitarian agenda concerned with national identity. The relationship between state power and the citizen has been problematic for all societies, and for developing countries in particular. After Independence, India adopted a constitutional framework that was underlined by a respect for democratic controls over executive action. But it was also recognized that the state had to be the locus of enormous power in order to foster economic growth, protect the country from external threats, and tackle fissiparous movements that had the potential to unravel the fragile fabric of national identity. Over the half century and more of its history, independent India's legitimacy has been challenged by numerous secessionist movements as well as radical class-based movements. Periodically, the Indian state has sought to redefine itself in response. Jawaharlal Nehru regarded the liberal democratic state as the dominant focal point of the economic and political life of the new India. During her first tenure as prime minister (1966–77), Indira Gandhi attempted first to give it a populist face, then to rule under a constitutional dictatorship (1973–75). The failed effort to foster political stability and state-led economic growth led ultimately to the Bharatiya Janata Party's (BJP) attempt to redefine Indian society and the state through the concept of *Hindutva*, or "Hindu-ness" (for want of a better word).[24]

Critics often assert that the BJP's communitarian extremism is the driving force behind India's nuclearization. There is certainly a good case for the view that the political Hinduism of the BJP and its allies has married the concept of *Hindutva* with state power, and by extension, nuclear weapons.[25] However, it would be simplistic to equate the party's ideology directly with India's acquisition of nuclear weapons. As the overview of India's nuclear history in Chapter 3 shows, diverse groups and personalities contributed to the nuclearization process. Indeed, the bomb was built long before the BJP assumed power. For the same reason, it is not an entirely acceptable claim that the 1998 tests were a symbolic act of national redefinition.[26] All the same, it is not without significance that, in conducting the tests, the BJP should have dared to tread where others did not wish to or perhaps quite have the gumption to. The tests may not in themselves have represented the BJP's ideology, but they were certainly in congruence with the party's attempt to refashion a national identity being buffeted by the intrusion of globalization processes from "above" and by the intensifying rejection of the nation—the Punjab, Kashmir, and other insurrections—from "below." Whether intentionally or not, the BJP has associated nuclear weapons with its conception of a centralized and "Hinduized" state.[27] Its readiness, moreover, to engage in the kind of risk-taking discussed in Chapter 4 indicates an instrumental view of nuclear weapons that goes well beyond the parameters of minimum deterrence. In both its external and internal facets, the party's nuclear politics have tended to undermine security.

There are signs that, under the BJP, nuclear weapons have become an integral component of the apparatus of a "national security state." One should not underestimate the threat. The crystallization of the national security state into a rigid and oppressive instrument with which to beat the citizenry into submission is a well-known phenomenon.[28] The condemnation of those opposed to nuclear policy as "unpatriotic" reveals how easily the values placed on nuclear weapons can become antidemocratic.[29] The harassment of T. K. Jayaraman, a scientist at the Indian Institute of Mathematical Sciences, Chennai, which is funded by the Department of Atomic Energy, is a case in point.[30] Such sentiment manifests itself in other unpleasant ways, such as censorship. The film *War and Peace*, directed by Anand Patwardhan, was subjected to extensive cuts by the Indian Censor Board because of its explicit criticism of the Indian nuclear tests and policy.[31] The image of unquestionable power attached to nuclear policy thus undercuts the basic value of freedom of expression in democracy. If not restrained, the national security state that possesses nuclear weapons may become one in which "a permanent state of war, not by the nature of political will or the character of international antagonisms, but as a structural reflection of the nature of modern weaponry, casts a dark shadow across the very possibility of a democratic polity."[32] In this context, the emergence of a "peace constituency" critical of India's nuclearization is a welcome corrective development.[33]

A deeper understanding of deterrence should also include the awareness that nuclear weapons inescapably detract from democratic decision making by privileging centralization over decentralization. Where do nuclear weapons stand in the relationship between state and society? There is a tension between the need for control over the weapons (centralization) and the imperative of democracy (decentralization). Recall from Chapter 2 Harknett's point that nuclear weapons are unique: their combination of speed and massive destruction does not allow us to respond to their use in any way that is meaningful. This necessitates tight control over them so as to reduce the possibility of an erroneous or renegade decision to initiate nuclear use. Against this, it is axiomatic that, in a democratic social order, decisions about the future of society should eventually lie with the people. The more a society allows its fate out of the hands of its people, the less democratic it is. With nuclear weapons, this is carried to the extreme: the individual with his or her finger on the nuclear button can in a few moments inflict incalculable devastation on an adversary, and in so doing invite a like outcome for his or her own people. As Richard Falk so aptly puts it, "authority and power to inflict such results by a single process of decision suggest the extent to which the citizenry is inevitably and permanently excluded from determinations that decisively shape societal destiny."[34] From the perspective of the average Indian, nuclear weapons disempower the citizen. The risk-taking that occurred during Operation Parakram was a manifestation of the public's loss of control over "societal destiny." While the public may in such instances be largely unconscious of this, it is undeniable that the end result is a permanent and deeply troubling one: the threat posed by nuclear weapons becomes "the context of our lives, a shadow that persistently intrudes upon our mental ecology."[35]

Who, indeed, does have some control over nuclear India's collective fate? Once an operational system is in place, the meaning of choice may be so eroded as to make informed decision making practically impossible. In managerial terms, there is a command and control system in place, with the prime minister heading the Nuclear Command Authority. A two-key system prevents unauthorized launch.[36] But in the India-Pakistan case, the time available for response to a perceived threat is very short. On what basis can a decision be made in the event of an alarm indicating an incoming nuclear missile? Or if a war breaks out, and there is a warning that the other side has decided to escalate to the use of nuclear weapons, how will the executive decision be made? In the words of an American Defense Department official, a president's "decision" to launch nuclear weapons during the Cold War would have had to be made with very little scope for informed choice: "It is no use to give him a room full of status boards and say, 'Here it is, boss, make a decision.' It has to be boiled down to a scale—for example, green, yellow and red."[37]

We cannot expect the situation to be different in the Indian context. While it may be true that in principle there is no need for a nuclear response to be immediate, in practice it would be difficult to prevent a rapid reaction, for instance if the command and control system is thrown out of gear, or if a local commander is too quick to make the wrong decision. During the Cuban Missile Crisis, despite express orders not to fire unless directly attacked, local Soviet commanders—after failing to contact their superiors—shot down an unarmed U.S. U-2 surveillance aircraft. At that point, believing this to be a premeditated act with authorization from the top, U.S. decision makers came to believe that war was inevitable. That it did not actually happen was fortuitous.[38] Minimum deterrence, with weapons systems undeployed, reduces the urgency of this problem, though it does not eliminate it.

Democracy requires the citizen's participation in society's political processes. In practice, since the citizen has neither the time nor the competence for actual participation in day-to-day policy making and governance, power is delegated. In the case of many subjects, and especially technically complex subjects like nuclear weapons and strategy, decisions are made by experts. Whether explicitly or otherwise, these experts act as "guardians" in the Platonic sense of specialists best qualified to make social decisions. Robert Dahl's discussion of the contradiction between democracy and guardianship draws our attention to a central problem associated with nuclear weapons.[39] More than anything else, they seem to permit—indeed, necessitate—guardianship: the idea of "a well-qualified minority, who rule over the rest, governing in the best interests of all, fully respecting the principle of equal consideration, indeed perhaps upholding it far better than would the people if they were to govern themselves."[40] Yet, as Dahl observes, there are several reasons why the claims of experts to exercise guardianship may be questioned.

First, while a decision to go to war must perforce be a centralized decision, the policies guiding such a decision need not and should not be, for the basic choices are moral choices. Questions about targeting and about the circumstances under which nuclear weapons may be used, and indeed, whether nuclear deterrence is acceptable or not, are moral questions. There is "not the slightest reason for supposing that the small circle of policy makers who have established our nuclear policies are particularly well qualified in their moral understanding."[41] Second, specialists are inherently incapable of a holistic instrumental understanding of nuclear weapons because specialization by definition gives each only partial knowledge. Third, experts do not necessarily have the capacity to make judgments relating to risks, uncertainty, and trade-offs, all of which are so much a part of nuclear strategy. An additional problem is that specialists, by the very nature of their expertise, are hard to contradict, which makes it possible for them to advocate policies that benefit their own sectional interests rather than the national interest.[42]

As Dahl recognizes, we are ultimately left with a crucial dilemma. On the one hand, instrumental elites do not possess the moral capacity to claim exclusive control over nuclear weapons. On the other, ordinary people lack the instrumental capacity to exercise meaningful control.[43] How do we overcome this basic difficulty? The obvious answer is that the citizen must be more competent and better able to exercise control over policy. Dahl himself is not satisfied with general exhortations in this respect. He argues instead for the wide availability of information, the provision of facilities for interactive dialogue between citizen and state, and the creation of institutions of professionals that can act as bridges between the people and decision makers. Finally, Dahl recommends the creation of the *minipopulus*, a body of responsible citizens with both an interest in and knowledge of a specialized subject such as nuclear weapons.[44] Spread across the land, such bodies could invigorate democratic life by bringing the ultimate power of decision making closer to those who are also the holders of ultimate authority: the people.

The idea is attractive, though it is a moot point whether many citizens might be sufficiently familiar with as well as interested in the arcane world of nuclear strategy to become active in this respect. If the *minipopulus* is as yet a distant achievement, there is undoubtedly movement in the right direction. From the 1990s, there has been a significant increase in the public debate in India on nuclear issues, some portions of which have been alluded to in these pages. Newspapers and popular magazines pay considerable attention to issues of nuclear strategy and arms control. Think tanks engaged in the diffusion of information and policy advocacy are far more active today than a couple of decades ago. A peace movement has emerged to educate Indians on its side of the nuclear debate. These are welcome developments. It is worth bearing in mind that in a democracy, when the citizen feels helpless and unable to influence the course of his or her life, or to shape the social environment, it is a short step to the abdication of responsibility in order to escape the heavy burden of freedom.[45]

For democratic society, the security dilemma carries a moral ancillary. On one hand, nuclear weapons take away from us our capacity to shape our future and that of our children. On the other, we cannot ignore the threats that cause us to possess nuclear weapons in the first place. The only reasonably satisfactory solution lies in minimum deterrence based on the principles delineated in Chapter 2. The more defensive the posture, the less likely the prospect of crisis and, possibly, war. The more prudent the behavior, especially in showing awareness of the risks related to escalation, the less likely that the weapons, by their innate characteristics, will become the arbiters of societal destiny. Society's loss of control may be offset by the gain from deterrence, but unless the associated risks are minimized by means of informed public participation and control, the benefits of deterrence may prove to be ephemeral.

Minimum deterrence is also relevant to economic development. A common objection is that nuclear weapons entail immense waste, and that the funds might better be used for economic growth and welfare.[46] But it is not particularly useful to present to one's interlocutors a straightforward choice between guns and butter, as it were. A society must have both. The meaningful question is how much relative weight it should give to the two. With regard to the cost of nuclear weapons, it is hard to assess costs in one sense: we do not know the possible costs that might be incurred if a nuclear attack were to take place. They would undoubtedly be extraordinarily high. Critics often lament the costs of possessing nuclear weapons without paying any attention to the costs of not having them.[47] The cost of deterrence is a form of societal investment: large though it may be, it is small considering the value of the loss that is envisaged if the investment is not made. It is not helpful to assert that a nuclear attack will not happen. There is no guarantee that it will not.

That having been said, the relevant question appears to be: How much is enough? But in terms of the requirements of minimum deterrence, the appropriate question is: How *little* is enough? For if the cost of deterrence can be kept to a minimum, the guns-butter tradeoff can be made less painful. It is far from clear how accurate most estimates for India are, since most discussions are very general in nature.[48] One detailed study of the United States— an "atomic audit" for the period 1940–96—shows the cost can be extraordinarily high.[49] The relevant finding is not the aggregate cost of the U.S. nuclear weapons program, since India's will be far smaller, but the high relative cost: at $5.481 billion, it is the third-highest amount spent in a list of nineteen categories of expenditure.[50] Moreover, U.S. spending on nuclear weapons accounts for as much as 29 percent of all military spending, and 11 percent of all government expenditures.[51] The price paid by society for such levels of spending can be high. Estimates for a full-fledged Indian arsenal vary from $5 billion to $15 billion.[52] From another perspective, taking defense expenditure at 3 percent of gross domestic product and an annual rate of economic growth of 7 percent, the cost of the arsenal would decline steadily over a thirty-year period from 3 percent of defense spending today to 0.03 percent in the year 2030.[53]

But there are other less direct costs. Though it is often said that military expenditure brings valuable benefits (stimulating demand, providing jobs, and so on), the apparent economic advantages of government spending on nuclear infrastructure are deceptive.[54] Unlike civilian economic investment, much military investment is not self-generating: it does not create a significant number of additional or second-level goods or jobs. Second, nuclear facilities are often established in relatively isolated, low-wage areas. The wage scale at nuclear facilities tends to be relatively high, with the result that nonnuclear firms are driven out of the area, resulting in job loss. On the whole, nondefense spending produces more jobs than defense spending. Third, nuclear research and development (R&D) tends to consume a disproportionately high level of resources. Studies also show that, contrary to commonly made claims, defense R&D does not generate valuable spin-offs. This is not an argument against the possession of a nuclear arsenal. It is only an argument against unrealistic expectations about the advantages of building one and against spending too much in the process. On the face of it, a nuclear posture of minimum deterrence should by definition be relatively inexpensive, since it does not regard nuclear weapons as a central pillar of national security. Nonetheless, given the potential for an uncritical operational view of nuclear weapons (see Chapter 3), we should not lose sight of the possibility of spiraling expenditures. Excess spending on the nuclear infrastructure is a denial of social spending to a society that is acutely short of resources. A democratic society must ensure that minimum deterrence is truly kept to a minimum.

Minimum deterrence is also relevant to civil-military relations, which are a major concern in discussions on the organization of nuclear weapons.[55] In Chapter 3, we have seen that the military in India has not been as cut off from nuclear policy as is sometimes believed. However, it is also true that the involvement of the military in the operationalization of India's nuclear capability has been a slow and carefully regulated process. The late General Krishnaswamy Sundarji, who played a prominent role in encouraging Indians, and military personnel in particular, to think about nuclear weapons, was so exercised over the Indian political leadership's reluctance to translate technology into practical capability that he wrote a thinly disguised critique of official policy in the form of a novel.[56] At the present juncture, as India's operational nuclear capability is being streamlined, it is essential that political control be carefully maintained. This is not to say that India's armed forces are a threat to the government. Far from it. But the loss of political control of a different kind is still possible. Lack of strong political leadership may allow the military an unnecessarily prominent role in the making of nuclear strategy.

As the Indian deterrent develops, those who control its instruments will demand increasing attention. At present, they do not control the weapons entirely, since warheads are in civilian custody. But they do control the delivery vehicles, which drive the readiness posture to a significant degree. They also have a voice in the organization of the command and control system.[57] The armed forces will seek to shape the development of the arsenal, and their perspective will be operational. In their quest for more, they will have ready support from the scientific bureaucracy, which has a built-in interest in developing new weapon systems. The expansion of the "strategic enclave" by the incorporation of the armed forces would make it potentially very powerful. Policy makers need to have a clear understanding of the true requirements of minimum deterrence. They must ensure that operational considerations do not override political ones in shaping nuclear strategy. That would undermine democracy.

Nuclear Secrecy, Accountability, and the Rule of Law

A doctrine of minimum deterrence must recognize the need for a balance between the secrecy requirements of nuclear weapons and democratic openness. By placing a premium on secrecy, nuclear weapons pose a grave threat to democracy, which in turn erodes public accountability and the rule of law. From the beginning, India's entire nuclear program was characterized by concealment. In part, this was inevitable because of the dual-use character of nuclear energy. Touted for its civilian benefits, it was curtained from public view because of its covertly developed military application. Besides, like any bureaucracy, the scientific establishment found secrecy a useful device to insulate itself from criticism and public accountability.[58] In the 1950s, Meghnad Saha, a nuclear physicist who had been elected to Parliament, attempted to make the Indian nuclear program more accountable to the public. But the

Atomic Energy Commission, led by Homi Bhabha, and backed by Jawaharlal Nehru, succeeded in shielding nuclear policy from public criticism. As a result, the nuclear establishment was able to build a powerful technocratic empire largely unaccountable to the public.[59]

This secrecy and concentration of power in the hands of a small number of individuals have undermined Indian democracy in important ways. The case of B. Subbarao, a naval scientist falsely accused of spying, shows how secrecy and the stamp of "national security" can easily be harnessed by vested interests to violate the rule of law and subvert democracy.[60] As an independent expert, Subbarao had thrice pointed out major flaws in designs developed by the Bhabha Atomic Research Centre (BARC) for an indigenous nuclear-powered submarine. Subsequently, he was himself asked to prepare a design. The design was rejected by BARC without giving reasons. Subsequently, Subbarao's work was accepted by the Indian Institute of Technology in Bombay for the award of a doctoral degree. In 1988, at Prime Minister Rajiv Gandhi's behest, he was asked to take over the nuclear submarine project. At this juncture, on the verge of a professional trip abroad, he was arrested on charges of espionage and violation of the Official Secrets Act. Though accused of carrying classified material, Subbarao in fact had with him only publicly available material, including his doctoral thesis. A review of the case reveals a story of manipulation and falsehoods perpetrated by the police and by prosecutors in what can only be called sustained abuse of the due process of law. The judiciary too came under a cloud. As a former justice of the Supreme Court pointed out, the trial and prosecution of Subbarao was reminiscent of the infamous Dreyfus case. Only three of the numerous judges who heard the case even tried to ascertain whether the "evidence" was genuine.[61] The trial of Subbarao took place over a period of five years, despite the complete absence of any evidence, until he was eventually acquitted by the Supreme Court on technical grounds.

The Subbarao case illustrates the ease with which a democratic system can be subverted on grounds of national security. While this may occur in respect of any aspect of security, nuclear policy, owing to its highly secretive and sensitive nature, is particularly susceptible to this kind of abuse.[62] The fallout from such events can be harmful in other ways. Subbarao's painful example may well deter others, whether inside the system or outside it, from challenging authority and drawing attention to the failings of the establishment. This in turn opens up the possibility of entrenched insiders wasting immense resources and foisting substandard products upon the country's security apparatus. One can scarcely imagine the enormous wastage that would have ensued had Subbarao not rejected BARC's flawed designs. It is also impossible to estimate the loss to the exchequer from the rejection of his own design and the resultant delay of the nuclear submarine project. The misuse of "national security" may thus contribute to the very real impairment of national security. In contrast, an open and properly functioning democratic system, in which the nuclear establishment is held accountable to the public, will contribute more effectively to the nation's security.

In a similar case, six persons, including two scientists of the Indian Space Research Organization (ISRO), which is linked to the nuclear program, were arrested in 1994 on charges of espionage. In 1996, the case was dismissed after the investigating agency, the Central Bureau of Investigation (CBI) assessed the case not merely to be lacking in evidence, but to be "false." There was nevertheless an attempt by the government of the state of Kerala (where the ISRO is headquartered) to revive prosecution, until the Supreme Court intervened in April 1998 and quashed the case, holding the order to revive it a *"mala fide* exercise of power" that "does not comport with the known pattern of a responsible government bound by a rule of law."[63] At least two of the accused, a senior ISRO scientist, S. Nambinarayan, and a citizen of the Maldives, Mariam Rasheeda, were subject to physical and mental torture. In March 2001, the National Human Rights Commission ordered the Kerala government to pay Nambinarayan compensation to the value of one million rupees (approximately $20,000) for the gross infringement of his human rights.[64]

These egregious violations of the rule of law raise troublesome questions about the nature of the state, the conception of national security, and the roots of democratic processes. Certainly, there are similar cases to be found in other countries.[65] But that is hardly consolation for those who suffer from the use of "national security" to club the innocent into submission. As a senior Indian newspaper editor has observed, it is alarmingly easy to subvert democracy on national security grounds, for few dare to question such accusations, and even worse, the perpetrators of such injustices are almost never brought to book, which means there is little risk attached to the deliberate miscarriage of justice.[66] Unfortunately, there is little sign that the state is seriously concerned about its erosion as a democratic entity as a result of such cases. The problem has serious potential in the era of terrorism. Because of the constant terrorist threat that has prevailed in parts of the country since Independence and in large areas since the early 1980s, the rule of law has always been under pressure. Law enforcement by police, paramilitaries, and the army has tended frequently to deteriorate into virtual civil war, in which the "enemy" is disposed off by the quickest method available: fake armed "encounters." The law itself is rewritten in repressive format to override due process.

The most recent manifestation of this in the aftermath of the December 2001 attack on India's Parliament was the Prevention of Terrorism Act (2002). The law curtailed the rights of accused persons in numerous ways, notably by overriding the presumption of innocence and making bail difficult to obtain. Its initial introduction as a presidential ordinance was denounced as "draconian" by the National Human Rights Commission, but the law was nevertheless retained with some amendments in January 2002.[67] The government's position was disturbing. Union Minister for Rural Development M. Venkaiah Naidu maintained that only "human beings," not terrorists, were entitled to human rights.[68] For critics, however, the government was agglomerating power in a way that gave it the characteristics of a police state.[69] The act was repealed in December 2004, only to be replaced by another draconian law. In the present context, the nuclear-armed state subject to nuclear-terrorist threats is even more susceptible to the violation of democratic norms and the erosion of human rights. The overall environment—the prevailing high-level terrorist threat, the singularly apocalyptic nature of the threat to the nuclear infrastructure, the pervasive secrecy and lack of accountability of the nuclear establishment, and the antidemocratic bent of the state and its agencies in matters of security—all combine to create a troubling potential for abuse of power and the steam-rolling of democracy should the threat be realized in some dramatic and painful way, say in a manner comparable to the December 13 attack on Parliament. In particular, a nuclear-terrorist incident is likely to have adverse effects in the extreme.

Once again, the democratic dilemma is present here. There is no denying the threat to democracy posed by the linkage between terrorism and nuclear weapons and facilities. Equally, the sensitive and dangerous character of nuclear technology makes a high level of secrecy and tight, centralized control inevitable. It has to be acknowledged that if we are always to keep in sight the state's ultimate responsibility toward its citizens, which is, after all, their security, then some latitude has to be allowed the state in its efforts to fulfill this task. But there should be a constant awareness of the state's need to balance its responsibility for the public's security with its responsibility to protect the democratic rights and way of life of the selfsame public. If this balance is to be ensured, the accountability of agencies of the state is essential. This applies at once to security agencies and to agencies which constitute the nuclear infrastructure. In respect of both, it is vital that there be adequate independent oversight. In both cases, the picture is not encouraging.

The position regarding the law and its enforcement has been discussed above. The monitoring of India's nuclear infrastructure is equally problematic.[70] The Atomic Energy Regulatory Board (AERB), which is charged with regulating the nuclear establishment, comes under the supervision of the Atomic Energy Commission (AEC), whose chairman is also the secretary of the Department of Atomic Energy (DAE), which the AERB is supposed to supervise. The AERB is overwhelmingly staffed by personnel drawn from the DAE, and hence lacks real autonomy.[71] Furthermore, on grounds of maintaining a higher level of secrecy for security purposes, the AERB has been divested of some of its power—that relating to the military application of nuclear power—which has reverted to BARC's internal review mechanism. In comparison, the Defense Nuclear Facilities Safety Board (DNFSB), which regulates the defense facilities of the Department of Energy (DOE) in the United States, has a majority of independent experts who are not part of the nuclear establishment. Furthermore, the DNFSB holds a number of public hearings and makes many of its activities open to public appraisal via the Internet. In contrast, BARC's "Internal Safety Committee Structure" has no independent experts and is sheltered from the public eye. Thus, the emphasis on secrecy for the sake of "national security," by not allowing for a system of autonomous oversight, tends actually to undercut security by retaining a regulatory mechanism that is inherently faulty.

Also a matter of grave concern is the internal security of the nuclear infrastructure with respect to personnel reliability. In the United States, the DOE has a well-organized Personnel Assurance Program designed to ensure that all personnel are regularly certified in order to meet standards relating to mental and physical stability. These standards may be inadequately met, for instance because of drug or alcohol abuse, or psychiatric problems, or simply the assessment that an individual does not measure up to the high standards required by the job. The demands of work are particularly severe for military personnel under whom weapons are placed. These individuals have to remain on high alert at all times, are often subject to high levels of stress because of the nature of their work, and frequently suffer from physical and psychological complaints.[72] Personnel reliability is conceptually designed to ensure that all those who are connected with nuclear weapons are competent, alert, and dependable. Yet, as reports show, the system does not always work very well.[73] For instance, in 1981, a U.S. navy jet crashed into the flight deck of the nuclear-powered aircraft carrier, *Nimitz*, killing fourteen men. It was found that six of the men were habitual marijuana users, that at least three of them had smoked the drug heavily that day or just before the crash, and that the pilot of the jet had consumed antihistamines six to eleven times above the recommended level.[74] Without doubt, the sensitivity of nuclear weapons is so great as to necessitate a high level of centralized control and intrusive monitoring of personnel. The individual's right to privacy will inevitably be far more restricted than in most other occupations, even security-related ones.

A related problem is that of accidents associated with nuclear materials and weapons. This affects sophisticated systems with high levels of technology and risk management too. In the United States, for example, one report shows that between 1950 and 1968, as many as 1,250 nuclear weapon accidents of varying degrees of severity took place, of which 272 (approximately 22 percent) involved severe impacts, some resulting in the detonation of surrounding conventional explosives. Of the total, 39 percent were bombs or rockets dropped during storage, assembly, or loading, 18 percent warheads mated to missiles or reentry vehicles at the time of being dropped, 15 percent occurred aboard aircraft that crashed, 10 percent were bombs in containers involved in accidents during storage, assembly, or loading, 9 percent were accidentally lost from aboard ships and aircraft, 8 percent were involved in ground transportation crashes, and 1.5 percent were accidentally crushed or punctured.[75] Such accidents, reflecting the organizational problem of "normal accidents" discussed earlier, are a vital public concern. The establishment of adequate mechanisms of supervision is an imperative that no democratic society can afford to neglect.

In India, accidents have been a periodic feature in matters relating to hazardous materials, most notably the great Bhopal gas disaster of 1984. India's AEC Chairman, R. Chidambaram, claimed in 2000 that, with 150 reactor years of safe operation, "there is no possibility of any nuclear accident in the near or distant future in India." But, as M. V. Ramana has pointed out, at the time of the Chernobyl accident, the Soviet Union had had over one thousand years of reactor experience.[76] Besides, India *has* experienced numerous major accidents in its nuclear plants, though none so far has gone out of control.[77] The armed forces too have seen their share of major calamities. Between April 1991 and March 1997, the Indian Air Force (IAF) lost as many as 147 aircraft and 63 pilots in accidents.[78] In February 2003, Defence Minister George Fernandes told Parliament that thirty-one IAF pilots had been killed and sixty-eight aircraft lost in air crashes during the preceding three years.[79] In February 2004, an underwater rocket exploded on a naval warship off the Mumbai coast.[80] In a serious accident at the Bharat Dynamics Limited premises in Kanchanbagh in the state of Andhra Pradesh in January 2001, the accidental launch of an antitank missile killed one person.[81] The nuclear establishment has not been immune to accidents. In February 2004, a major explosion at ISRO's Solid Propellant Booster Plant on Sriharikota Island off India's east coast killed six people.[82] Numerous other security failures have been mentioned earlier in the chapter on nuclear terrorism. The prospect of nuclear accidents raises concerns about the organizational responsibilities of a democracy. These responsibilities cannot be ignored.

In all of the above discussion, there is an underlying thread. Nuclear policy is not only concerned with securing the nation from external threats, but equally with ensuring societal safety and security from internal threats. These threats are in part directly the result of the physical existence of nuclear materials and weapons and their vulnerability to accidents and to the malign intentions of the disaffected. They are also an indirect outcome of the aura of secrecy and unquestioned authority and power that surrounds nuclear matters, thereby enabling vested interests to commandeer them for their own purposes. There is, to be sure, a tension between the need for secrecy in the interests of security and the need to establish public control and accountability, also in the interests of security. While maintaining a balance between the two will always be difficult, a minimum deterrence posture based on the principles discussed earlier will make it less problematic in three ways. First, it will reduce the exposure of the infrastructure to mishap by accident or design. The smaller the network, the less the points of vulnerability. Second, it will constrain external tension and hence ensure a smaller degree of threat and tension between India and its adversaries. In doing so, it will minimize domestic tensions and restrain the common tendency of state power and organizational interests to resist public control under the banner of national security. Third, the combination of the first two will make it that much easier for democratic political life to function normally and hence for the citizen to have that vague but indispensable sense of being in control of his or her destiny which is so important for the vitality of a democratic society.

Conclusion

The relationship between nuclear weapons and democracy is a complex one. It is often forgotten by critics that nuclear weapons are—to most of us, at any rate—defensive weapons, and, therefore, considered to be unusable for any purpose other than deterrence of threats to national survival. In an inherently insecure world, nuclear weapons have some role to play in defending democracy. Ideally, they should be done away with altogether. Short of that, prudence may require their possession. For if some who come to possess them have no compunctions about using them for political ends, the one thing certain to prevent them from carrying out their designs will be the threat of punishment at the hands of nuclear weapons possessed by others. Nuclear weapons are closely linked to the preservation of society and democracy, for it is the moral obligation of the state to be accountable to the people for their security, and nuclear weapons may be a necessary means for fulfilling that obligation. Against this, possession of these weapons does present an inescapable moral dilemma. Threatening the extinction of countless lives is not a comfortable ethical position. Minimum deterrence cannot provide a way out of the dilemma, but can keep it to a tolerable level.

The question of morality also has a bearing on the state and its legitimacy. The security dilemma requires the state to navigate a hazardous course between the Scylla of nuclear abstinence and the Charybdis of nuclear possession. The moral dilemma is no less problematic. Even as it struggles with the security dilemma and the moral paradox of nuclear weapons, the state must be aware of the difficult balance it must try to maintain between the morality of deterring war and the immorality of increasing its probability by its own lack of discipline, accountability, or recklessness. If the state violates its responsibility to secure the citizen from mass annihilation, whether by eschewing nuclear weapons or by acquiring them, it risks losing the allegiance of the citizen.[83] It is thus incumbent on the state in any democratic conception of political organization to ensure that its people are the beneficiaries of prudent protection. This is an irrefutable argument for making minimum deterrence the cornerstone of nuclear security in a democratic society.

8

Conclusion: Shaping the Uncertain Future

The preceding pages have sketched the outlines of India's nuclear strategy in light of the fundamentals of minimum deterrence. Chapter 1 assesses the place of nuclear weapons in a complex world of conflict and interdependence and argues that minimum deterrence is the optimal position for a state faced with a serious security threat. Not having nuclear weapons would leave India vulnerable to the nuclear threats of those whose motives are suspect. Assuming a posture like most other nuclear powers would create new insecurities, bringing risks of war as a result of error, misperception, or accident. Chapter 2 shows why minimum deterrence is the most cost-effective strategy. Given the revolutionary character of nuclear weapons—their incontestable capacity to wreak colossal damage within a very short time—the central concept that shapes strategic behavior is risk. No decision maker can afford to treat as acceptable even a small risk of a single nuclear weapon exploding over his or her country. The key issue is not the deterrer's certainty of retaliation but the deterree's uncertainty about preventing it.

From this are deduced other principles of minimum deterrence. Credibility and survivability are not serious concerns. A small arsenal with a limited range of weapons of relatively low technical sophistication suffices to deter even large and technically advanced systems. Nuclear warfighting and counterforce targeting are risky and unnecessary. The possibility of inadvertent escalation rules out conventional war and makes the concept of limited conventional war hazardous. Deployment is not required: it raises tensions, facilitates loss of control, and invites rapid escalation. Command and control is something of a misnomer. Command, which focuses on the assurance that one's weapons will be effectively used if need arises, does not impinge upon the adversary's view of risk. Control, which has to do with the assurance that one's weapons will not be used unless desired, directly impacts the deterrer's risk and is of far greater importance. Above all, since it takes little to deter, a nonthreatening minimum deterrence posture, based on a political rather than an operational conception of deterrence, can best obtain the benefits of deterrence while keeping the strategic and economic costs down.

Principles and Reality

How has India fared with respect to these basic principles? Chapters 2 and 3 reveal that Indian thinking and practice have in many ways been able to articulate a minimum deterrence position fairly well. First, despite the ongoing quest for capabilities beyond the requirements of minimum deterrence, there is no serious push for developing a large and sophisticated nuclear inventory. Second, Indian strategy is not preoccupied with nuclear balances. Hardly anyone has shown an interest in attaining parity with China. Thus, there is no proclivity for arms racing. Third, the almost universal rejection of counterforce doctrine and nuclear warfighting recognizes the risks involved in escalation. Fourth, the widespread belief expressed both in official policy and nonofficial discourse that more nuclear tests are not necessary reflects an understanding that higher levels of technological sophistication are not required for deterrence to be effective. Fifth, India's consistent interest in arms control acknowledges the high element of risk inherent in nuclear confrontations and displays an abiding preference for strategic stability. Sixth, the retention of a nondeployed posture despite a recent history of recurrent crises under the nuclear shadow shows strong commitment to a nonthreatening posture with a low potential for escalation. The last is examined in Chapter 4, which also reveals a seventh way in which Indian policy adheres to the canons of minimum deterrence. During both the Kargil conflict and Operation Parakram, Indian forces refrained from violating the two-steps-short rule that makes it imperative for nuclear powers not to cross the threshold to conventional war.

Indian strategy is in harmony with the principles of minimum deterrence in three other somewhat inchoate ways. Interest in missile defense, appraised in Chapter 5, is compatible with minimum deterrence, which holds that a missile shield will have no bearing on nuclear equations, though there does not appear to be a sound appreciation of the relationship between the two. India's nondeployed posture reflects the advantages of minimum deterrence in the context of the threat posed by nuclear terrorism, which was discussed in Chapter 6, but again there is no evidence that decision makers are aware of this. Finally, the public declaration of India's nuclear status in 1998 unwittingly reduces the acuteness of India's domestic security dilemma, which was the focus of Chapter 7. It acknowledges the reality of nuclear threats and simultaneously creates conditions for greater public participation in and accountability from a nuclear-strategic apparatus that has been secretive and prone to violate the rule of law.

On the negative side, there are several features of Indian nuclear thinking and practice that do not fit well with the requirements of minimum deterrence. First, the ubiquitous emphasis on credibility and survivability, evident from Chapters 2 and 3, is deeply problematic. Under pressure of adverse circumstances, it could encourage an open-ended expansion of India's arsenal and bring about a shift to deployment, both of which would raise tensions with its nuclear adversaries and thereby reduce security. Second, Chapter 3 reveals a significant preference for deployment, so far not reflected in top policy-making circles, among many of India's nuclear specialists and the wider strategic elite. This shows a scant appreciation of the dangers of shifting from a nonthreatening to a threatening posture among those who are likely to influence policy makers. Third, as Chapter 4 shows, the practice of compellence and the belief that limited conventional war is feasible in a nuclear environment, together with the view that India's ability to inflict greater nuclear damage on Pakistan than vice versa gives it an advantage, undercut the essence of minimum deterrence. Limited conventional operations border dangerously on violation of the two-steps-short rule, while the notion of Indian advantage labors under the misperception that relative and not absolute damage matters. Fourth, Chapter 7 exposes relatively low tolerance of dissent and the lack of an adequate accountability mechanism, thereby exacerbating the domestic security dilemma of a democracy with nuclear arms. Above all, a deficient understanding of the fundamentals of minimum deterrence makes India vulnerable to operational pressures of the kind that have driven the other major nuclear powers toward strategies that are not in accord with minimum deterrence, even if their behavior has been reflective of it.

Potential Change: Alternative Deterrence Models

At present, India's nuclear posture is still uncertain, its doctrine yet to be fully and clearly articulated. What direction will it take in the future? Table 1 presents four ideal-type models to which it may approximate. The models are devised so as to reflect likely futures in terms of four criteria: conceptions of deterrence, the size and sophistication of the arsenal, the relationship between levels of armed conflict, and the status of arms control.

TABLE 1

Deterrence Models

	Conception of Deterrence	Size and Range of Arsenal	Relationship between Levels of Conflict	Arms Control Status
True Minimum Deterrence Model	Minimalist; risk-based; no deployment	>25; one leg (land-based missiles only)	Only sub-conventional conflict possible	Stable; tacit and limited formal agreements; reassurance
Static Model	Minimalist, but unclear; certainty-based; no deployment	50–100; 2 ½ legs (air, land, and surface-sea); slow development of subsurface sea leg	Limited conventional conflict possible	Uneven, crisis-driven; formal and tacit agreements
Creeping Growth Model	Interest in limited deterrence, including counterforce weapons; limited deployment	100–250; growing push for a full-fledged triad	Limited conventional conflict possible	Uncertain; interest in arms control, but with growing emphasis on verification
Robust Expansion Model	MAD-oriented limited deterrence; full deployment, possibly on alert status	Over 250; open-ended; triad; MIRV-ed weapons	Full-scale conventional war and limited nuclear war possible	Uncertain; interest in arms control, but only with high certainty based on verification

The *true minimum deterrence model* provides an optimal strategy in concurrence with the principles outlined in Chapter 2. In this, the posing of a small risk of nuclear retaliation to the adversary is sufficient to deter it. Deployment is not only unnecessary but undesirable because of the escalation risks associated with it. The model regards a small arsenal of up to twenty-five nuclear warheads on a single type of delivery vehicle (land-based missiles) as sufficient to deter any adversary within range in the twenty-first century.[1] Because an adversary cannot be confident of preempting or defending against all of them (the one-bomb-on-one-city problem), the risk posed to that adversary is too great for it not to be deterred. More weapons (other than a handful required to deter China) would be wasteful, even counterproductive, because they would increase the risk of inadvertent deterrence failure. Under the two-steps-short rule, only subconventional conflict is possible. Limited conventional war is sufficiently close to violating the rule to warrant rejection. Arms control is an article of faith, backed by political initiatives aimed at reassurance of adversaries (elaborated on below), but is likely to be confined to confidence-building measures (CBMs) and tacit agreements.

The *static model*, which reflects continuity along the lines of current thinking and practice, is minimalist and yet conceptually unclear because of its reliance on certainty, credibility, and nonvulnerability for assured deterrence. It envisions a period of modest growth until operational capabilities, mainly with respect to deterring China, are sufficient to convince political decision makers that no more expansion is necessary. Some fifty to one hundred weapons are considered sufficient for deterrence. The arsenal remains relatively limited in range and sophistication, with air-deliverable warheads (gravity bombs and air-launched missiles), land-based missiles, and surface sea-based systems. Limited conventional war is considered feasible, while at the same time a stable framework of arms control, again restricted to CBMs and tacit understandings, is in place. Because of its internal inconsistency, it is open to replacement under stress by the next model.

In the *creeping growth model*, at least partial deployment is seen as necessary because credibility is equated with visibility. Minimum deterrence is conceived of in larger numbers, say, 100–250 air-, land-, and surface–sea-based weapons (with perhaps a concerted push for subsurface naval capability), on the basis of some notion of redundancy against the event of an enemy first strike. There is a growing interest in limited deterrence concepts and counterforce targeting, acquisition of a greater variety of capabilities, and attainment of high levels of technical sophistication. As in the previous model, limited conventional war is thought possible. There is interest in arms control, but with a growing emphasis on verification. Both the static and creeping growth models are not far removed from the current trend, but the trajectories they represent diverge significantly over time.

Finally, the *robust expansion model* represents a shift to mutual assured destruction (MAD)-oriented thinking and a more ambitious conception of limited deterrence—a smaller arsenal cast in the image of the U.S. and Russian ones. This will be fully deployed, possibly on alert status, accompanied by a vigorous and open-ended acquisition and development process aimed at high levels of technical sophistication (such as multiple-warhead [MIRVed] missiles), and going beyond 250 warheads. It is conceived that full-scale conventional war and perhaps limited nuclear war are possible. In this model, there is still interest in arms control, but with an insistence on high levels of verification.

Which model will India choose to pursue? Prediction in international politics is difficult at the best of times. The construction of alternative futures is fraught with uncertainty because of the sheer complexity of the task: the variables that come into play are numerous, and these in turn interact with one another to produce a wide variety of possible outcomes.[2] Some of the main variables that will affect India's nuclear future are examined below.[3] It is not proposed to present an exhaustive list of variables that might lead India to adopt one or the other of these models. A few examples will suffice to show the range of possibilities.

The India-Pakistan Relationship

Since the advent of nuclear capability to South Asia in 1974, India and Pakistan have not fought wars (though the Kargil conflict came close), but tensions and crises have been endemic, particularly from the mid-1980s. These could get worse. If the secessionist problem in Kashmir is exacerbated, domestic pressures may impel the Indian government to retaliate, perhaps by quick strikes against terrorist bases in Pakistan, or by a tit-for-tat game of fomenting trouble in the Pushtun community that straddles the Pakistan-Afghan border. The continuing deterioration of Pakistan's fragile political system may bring to power more radical elements bent on stirring up trouble with India. The result could be the ratcheting up of tensions and the beginnings of a nuclear arms race as hardliners on both sides garner support and press for stronger forces to counter the growing threat from the other.

On the other hand, it is equally likely that, learning from the risks their confrontations expose them to, Indian and Pakistani leaders will bridge the gulf that prevented a détente at the Agra summit of 2001. Though there has been an increase in the number of crises and subwar conflicts, regular high-level negotiations have also taken place, reflecting the awareness among Indian and Pakistani leaders that South Asia needs a "peace process." While both countries seem to be driven by a fear of losing that is greater than their desire to win, there is also an appreciation in them that their hostility over Kashmir is dangerous and damaging to their respective national interests. Thus, a negotiated settlement cannot be ruled out, even if it is limited to an agreement to disagree. This would lower tensions, reduce the impetus for the expansion of capability, and facilitate arms control. Finally, a serious nuclear crisis, which is not inconceivable, would compel the two countries to seek a more stable relationship.

The India-China Relationship

India and China have of late been able to shed much of their old rancor and distrust, but the relationship is not entirely predictable in the long term. For a pessimist, there is good reason to expect its deterioration. Their border dispute lingers and is complicated by China's refusal to recognize India's sovereignty over its northeastern state of Arunachal Pradesh and by the fact that Pakistan has allowed a substantial part of Kashmir, where the Karakoram highway has been constructed, to come under Chinese control. China's propensity to use force in resolving a number of its international disputes (for instance, with Vietnam and Taiwan, and over the Spratly Islands) might still come into play. Both China and India have the potential to fall under the control of more aggressive regimes in the event of domestic turbulence. Unexpected events could also aggravate the tension between them. If Tibet were to be inflamed by a burst of secessionism, a rightist Indian regime, irked by the sustained China-Pakistan nuclear-missile nexus, might be tempted to exploit the situation to enhance its bargaining power, provoking an angry Chinese response. An India-China confrontation would likely have a nuclear dimension, and India would be motivated to seek a higher level of deterrent capability than the static model envisages. An unstable successor regime in China might be tempted to consolidate its position by intervening in insurgency-ridden northeastern India or by assuming a hawkish posture in an India-Pakistan crisis, thereby precipitating the same result.

From an optimist's perspective, the long-term trend in Sino-Indian relations is distinctly encouraging and unlikely to be reversed. It will probably be reinforced through a mutually beneficial positive-sum game. The two countries have over the years agreed not to allow their border dispute to prevent steadily growing cooperation on trade. Prodded by concerns about terrorism and the growing presence of an interventionist United States in its neighborhood, China may prefer to assuage India's anxieties by gradually reducing its support for Pakistan, pushing for a quick resolution of the border dispute, and, reversing its current stand on India's nuclearization, launching arms control talks. At a minimum, the rising graph of India-China economic cooperation would be sustained, perhaps assuming a steeper incline. Nuclear hawks would have one less argument for a more robust posture.

The Global Strategic Environment

The post–Cold War global environment has been in flux, with conflict and cooperation coexisting. Different scenarios are conceivable that could impact significantly on India's nuclear posture. One negative scenario for India involves growing U.S.-China rivalry and tension. Chinese leaders have shown a willingness to extend limited cooperation to the West on specific issues such as the campaign against the Taliban. But China's overall objective is to become one of the world's independent power centers, to which end it is engaged in a major program of military modernization. There are important divergences of strategic interest between China and the United States over Taiwan, and over the U.S. missile defense program. A crisis over Taiwan may bring a Sino-American confrontation. In such a deteriorating situation, China may expand its arsenal rapidly and assume a more aggressive nuclear posture. China's response—an increase in its inventory of intercontinental ballistic missiles (ICBMs), many or all with multiple warheads—may not directly threaten India, but the overall threat environment would encourage India to move toward a more robust posture, particularly if India-China relations are vitiated by continuing Chinese nuclear and missile assistance to Pakistan. A Chinese perception that India is part of a U.S. strategy to contain China would raise Sino-Indian tensions several notches. A more tense and unstable nuclear relationship may emerge as a result. A strong Indian nuclear response to adverse changes in its relationship with China would tend to raise the strategic temperature between India and Pakistan.

On the positive side, world politics is characterized by an accelerating integrative process of globalization that has brought more and more nations into a seamless web of information flows, investment, production, and trade. The winding down of the Cold War has simultaneously reduced great power tensions and the threat of a global nuclear holocaust. The cooperative global trend might be reinforced. The present U.S. tendency toward intervention may diminish over time as the United States adopts a multilateralist strategy, perhaps as a result of postintervention problems in Afghanistan and Iraq. Growing costs and financial difficulties, coupled with domestic opposition, could well bring about a moderation of U.S. objectives. The United States, Europe, Russia, and China may draw closer together and pay more attention to economic issues while cooperating on the common threat of terrorism. A renewed interest in arms control could bring a new agreement on cuts, the beginnings of a multilateral framework on arms control, and a new era of strategic stability. In that case, India's own strategic environment would become generally more stable, even if regional conditions were not entirely congenial.

Surprises

The terrorist attacks of September 11 were in many ways a watershed: they showed how a single incident can transform the perceptions and behavior of many states. A nuclear incident such as an accidental detonation or a nuclear-terrorist attack in South Asia will almost certainly have a comparable impact on Indian and Pakistani behavior. On one hand, it may cause a severe crisis; on the other, it may generate greater cooperation by way of efforts to prevent a recurrence. A nuclear incident elsewhere in the world might also cause regional planners to rethink their nuclear strategies and capabilities. Other surprises can be envisaged. There might, for all we know, emerge a South Asian Gorbachev willing to take the kind of risk that can dramatically transform strategic relations. It is a sobering reminder that many of the most startling turns in global politics, such as Ayatollah Khomeini's revolution, the end of the Cold War, and the events of September 11, have caught the world napping. Prudence requires us to expect the unexpected.

Domestic Preferences

Indian strategic culture has been remarkably resistant to significant changes in the preferences of domestic policy makers, as we have seen in Chapter 3. The possibility of a shift away from minimum deterrence arises not so much from leadership inclinations as from other factors. One is shock. The occurrence of an unexpected nuclear event, such as an inadvertent launch or an act of nuclear terrorism, could precipitate a policy change toward, conceivably, rapid stabilization in the former case or toward spiraling tensions and rethinking on strategy in the latter. A second possibility is related to the ability of policy makers to come to grips with the basic principles of minimum deterrence. Continuing lack of clarity will allow operational preferences to accumulate and carry strategy in the direction of operational dominance. How far this will take nuclear strategy will depend on the impact of external events. At best this could mean a change from the static model to the creeping growth model. At worst, it could bring on a galloping pace toward the robust expansion model. A lucid understanding of what minimum deterrence really means will facilitate adoption of the true minimum deterrence model and render strategy highly resistant to negatively oriented change. Regardless of external events, a leadership that comprehends the essence of minimum deterrence as delineated in this book will hold fast to a strategy that at once maximizes security and minimizes its external and domestic costs.

Implications for Stability: Reassurance and Arms Control

The picture that emerges is one of uncertainty as to the trajectory of India's nuclear-strategic future. What can be done? The purpose of this book has been to set a standard with which to judge policy. That standard—true minimum deterrence—requires a clear understanding that nuclear weapons confer power, by which is meant the power to deter, in an absolute rather than in a relative sense. Once a certain minimum level of capability has been reached (and here, again, the question must be: how little—and not how much—is enough?), reaching for "better" deterrence capability is a futile and wasteful exercise. Minimum deterrence provides the platform from which India can attempt to optimize its external environment and get on with the difficult task of developing the social, economic, and political environment of the citizen. While it may not be possible to control the strategic context entirely, India's own strategic posture and behavior will certainly have a role to play in shaping its security milieu.

Specific policy recommendations, especially on arms control, are not attempted here. These have been presented at length elsewhere.[4] But it is necessary to emphasize the close linkage between the principles underlying minimum deterrence enunciated in Chapter 2 and the prospects for stability, peace, and arms control. There are three basic requirements for maximizing the prospects for a stable nuclear posture. First, it is essential to obtain a clear understanding of the political and the operational aspects of nuclear weapons and of the concomitant need to prioritize the political. Second, a strategy of reassurance that underscores the commitment to defensive realism and non-offensive defense would help to promote strategic stability. And third, the basic concepts of minimum deterrence must provide the conceptual foundation for arms control, whether tacit or formal.

The core of a proper understanding of nuclear weapons lies in the distinction between their political and military facets. To recapitulate, the political aspect lies in the nonusable character of nuclear weapons as the most devastating instruments of mass destruction. Their unique combination of speed and large-scale destructiveness makes those who possess them and those confronting the prospect of nuclear war behave with great prudence. Yet the same weapons have qualities they share with all weapons: they are usable instruments of military power that have to be built and maintained according to operational criteria such as accuracy, firepower, speed, and reliability, and, in the extreme, deployed for action. If they possessed no military value whatsoever, they would have no political meaning, and if they were to be treated merely as freely usable extensions of national military power, they would be dangerous political absurdities. We would rather they did not exist at all, but they do, and we cannot wish them away. The only way to minimize the danger they pose to civilization is to agree to marginalize them. Negotiated strategic stability offers the only course of action that approaches a solution. The basis for stability lies in privileging the political over the military characteristics of these weapons. Further, political initiative must be at the forefront of stabilization initiatives. Reassurance underscores such an approach.

Reassurance

An important question is whether Indian leaders have learned from the failure of Operation Parakram. There is reason to believe that they have. Terrorist violence in Kashmir had increased significantly a year after India called off its massive deployment, but Indian leaders did not respond with a renewed compellence threat, or even talk of limited war.[5] Instead, Prime Minister Vajpayee sprang a surprise in October 2003 by proffering an olive branch with a proposal to revive transportation links and sporting ties, thus setting in motion a series of talks during 2004–5. Clearly, this is a case of learning from experience.[6] But it is one thing to learn *that* a policy does not work, quite another to learn *how* to tackle a problem better.[7] The latter requires a clear conception of what can and cannot be done, and a preliminary approach that facilitates the maximization of the doable. Here, the concept of "reassurance" is useful.[8] Reassurance attempts to stabilize a strategic relationship among adversaries by reducing the risk of provocation and encouraging the use of diplomacy rather than force for the attainment of political objectives. It overlaps considerably with confidence building, but is aimed not so much at specific agreements as at reducing deep mistrust among antagonistic states. There are five main forms of reassurance:[9]

Reassurance through restraint: The immediate objective is to reduce provocation or military tension, as was accomplished by the withdrawal of substantial numbers of troops by India and Pakistan to end the Brasstacks crisis in 1987. This case was one of a specific action relating to a specific issue, but we may also include in this category tacit or formal agreements to refrain from provocative action. India and Pakistan so far have a tacit understanding not to place their respective nuclear warheads in active deployment. Given the close relationship between nuclear and subnuclear conflict, a similar understanding on offensive conventional forces would also be mutually beneficial.

Reassurance through the establishment of norms of competition: There also appears to be, at least to some degree, an understanding between India and Pakistan, and perhaps between India and China, that nuclear arms racing should be abjured. In effect, interstate arms competition has been restricted. An area in which India and Pakistan have yet to reach an understanding is that of refraining from intervention in each other's political difficulties. Pakistan's encouragement of secessionism in Kashmir is, in fact, a central problem between the two countries.

Reassurance through irrevocable commitment: A powerful incentive to stabilization can be provided by a unilateral commitment to peace and stability. A classic example was President Anwar Sadat's ground-breaking visit to Israel in 1977 to demonstrate his commitment to peace. His initiative in traveling to Israel and addressing the Knesset was successful because, among other things, it was irreversible, involved considerable political risk to him, shattered the stereotype of the unyielding Arab, and went over the heads of Israeli leaders to appeal directly to the public.[10] Prime Minister Atal Behari Vajpayee's bus ride to Lahore was a similar attempt to achieve a dramatic breakthrough in India-Pakistan relations, but the Kargil conflict nearly destroyed any hope of a transformation in India-Pakistan relations. Given the disillusionment that Kargil left in its wake, this particular tack might be difficult to take in the near future. The failure of the Agra summit in 2001 was not surprising. A more incremental approach of the kind envisaged in Vajpayee's October 2003 proposal may arouse fewer expectations and be more rewarding over time.

Reassurance through limited security regimes: This overlaps with confidence building and envisages at least some formal arms control, such as limits on deployment or the implementation of a military "no fly zone" along the border. Some significant achievements have been made in this category, such as the India-Pakistan agreement not to attack each other's nuclear facilities (1988), the semiformal understanding under the Lahore Memorandum (1999) to inform each other of impending missile tests, and above all, the tacit agreement not to deploy. Incremental progress on these pragmatic lines offers more room for optimism than exaggerated expectations of a grand turnaround.

Reassurance through reciprocity: Ultimately, this is the most vital prerequisite to achieving progress in strategic stability. It may be attained by way of a sweeping change, or more modestly through a focused process of gradual reciprocation in tension reduction (GRIT).[11] Reassurance, it must be stressed, has to be mutual to be meaningful. This is where the difference between the India-China and the India-Pakistan relationships is most striking. In the former case, notwithstanding continuing conflicts of interest, a measure of stability has been possible because of a reciprocal commitment to reassurance. In the latter, this is strikingly absent. The Lahore summit seemed to augur a new era, but the fallout of Kargil and Operation Parakram left mutual distrust in its wake. Yet, strategic stability demands persistent efforts, and the 2004–5 round of negotiations provides a basis for optimism.

Arms Control

Arms control and disarmament are integral to Indian strategic culture. Because India has a strongly political view of nuclear weapons, it is easier to agree to arms control than it would be if operational considerations were predominant. The latter would create immense obstacles because an arsenal that is still developing would be resistant to constraints. Arms control that involves purely political commitments (such as the agreement not to attack each other's nuclear facilities) rather than bargaining at the operational level is more apt to be acceptable to Indian leaders. For the foreseeable future, India is also likely to be amenable to the primary level of arms control—transparency measures (as with hot lines or notification of tests)—but not to the advanced level of arms control involving constraints on specific weapons systems.[12]

The temptation to present a blueprint for arms control has been resisted here because the prerequisites for arms control are as yet not present in India's strategic relationships with its nuclear adversaries. It is not that there are no prospects for stability. Stability based on political understanding and tacit agreements is possible without detailed formal agreements. The latter are difficult because they would require substantial changes in India's relationships with China and Pakistan. With China, the problem is its insistence on clinging to the legalistic Nuclear Nonproliferation Treaty (NPT)-based status quo, which assumes that any agreement with India would mean "recognizing" its nuclear status. So long as this persists, India would find it difficult to negotiate seriously with Pakistan. This is not because of the so-called two-front nuclear security problem, which a strategy of minimum deterrence rejects, but because, beyond a point, unidirectional arms control would be politically difficult to sell at home. More important, Pakistan's reluctance to separate nuclear-strategic issues from the "core issue" of Kashmir and its continuing commitment to extracting advantage out of the stability-instability paradox block the possibility of serious negotiations on nuclear arms control with that country. That formal arms control is *not* a prerequisite for strategic stability is illustrated by the steady improvement in the India-China relationship despite a history of border problems, war, and confrontation not dissimilar to the India-Pakistan one.[13]

Another reason why arms control is not a likely prospect is the sheer absence of pressure for it. While South Asia's recurrent crises are generally viewed with alarm, the fact remains that these have been "nuclear" crises only in an indirect sense. The actual threat of a nuclear conflict has never been direct (i.e., by way of a confrontation between the nuclear weapons of the two sides), let alone imminent. In consequence, the pressure to institutionalize nuclear stability has been limited. Most conventional CBMs between India and Pakistan were agreed on in the wake of actual conventional wars or imminent conventional conflicts.[14] The agreement not to attack each other's nuclear facilities (1988) was the result of Pakistan's strong fear in the mid-1980s of a preemptive strike against its nuclear facilities. The fact that the proposed CBM on notification of missile tests (1999) took six years to formalize partly reflects the mutual hostility generated by the Kargil conflict, but also the reality that the need for an agreement has never been pressing. A glance at U.S.-Soviet agreements is also instructive. Major arms control initiatives came at junctures where the direct threat of nuclear conflict was strong.[15] There is no comparable situation in South Asia. In theoretical terms, the intensity of nuclear-strategic interaction has not been sufficiently high to induce serious efforts at deterrence management through arms control. In all likelihood, India-Pakistan agreements will for some time remain restricted to nuclear CBMs involving improved communication for risk reduction.

While formal agreements are unlikely, tacit agreements can play an important role in inducing stability. This is particularly relevant to the troubled India-Pakistan relationship. Most analysts have tended to focus on its unstable elements. Few have noticed its stable aspects: the mutual recognition that deterrence exists; the common espousal of minimum deterrence; the relative caution shown during military confrontations (as Chapter 4 shows, even during the forward deployment of Operation Parakram); the absence of nuclear deployment, even at the height of tension in 1999 and 2001–2; and the tacit acknowledgment of the Line of Control (LoC) and the border as "red lines" not to be overtly transgressed by conventional forces. Thus, a kind of "nontraditional" deterrence has been in place for some time, starting with the "opaque" years of the 1980s and continuing today.[16] Building on this requires reassurance before the expectation of arms control can be considered realistic.

The need for an integrated framework of defensive realism, nonoffensive defense, a balanced conception of minimum deterrence, and a commitment to reassurance is undeniable. Tacit agreements with Pakistan are not only feasible on nondeployment, communication, types of weapons, and the like, but would in themselves be a form of reassurance to China and an encouragement to the latter to follow suit. Similarly, informal understandings with China would send a strong signal to Pakistan and encourage it to come to terms with India on the issue of nuclear weapons. Ultimately, a minimum deterrence doctrine and posture recognize that nuclear weapons are no more than a necessary evil. They have a place in the scheme of national security. But that place, though not insignificant, is a small one, and must be kept that way, with a permanent commitment to diminish their malevolent presence. Not only does India's desire for peace and security in the comity of nations require it; its future as a democratic society demands it.

Notes

Notes

1. Introduction: Nuclear Weapons in World Politics

1. Scott Sagan, "Why Do States Build Nuclear Weapons? Three Models in Search of a Bomb," *International Security*, 21, 3 (Winter 1996–97), pp. 54–86. For a range of discussions on the Indian decision to go nuclear, see Stephen P. Cohen, "Why Did India 'Go Nuclear'?" in Raju G. C. Thomas and Amit Gupta, eds., *India's Nuclear Security* (New Delhi: Vistaar Publications, 2000); Sumit Ganguly, "Explaining the Indian Nuclear Tests of 1998," in Thomas and Gupta, eds., *India's Nuclear Security*; Devin T. Hagerty, "South Asia's Big Bangs: Causes, Consequences, Prospects," *Australian Journal of International Affairs*, 53, 1 (April 1999), pp. 19–29; Prem Shanker Jha, "Why India Went Nuclear," *World Affairs*, 2, 3 (July–September 1998), pp. 80–96; Pratap Bhanu Mehta, "India: The Nuclear Politics of Self-Esteem," *Current History*, 97, 623 (December 1998), pp. 403–6; Deepa Ollapally, "Mixed Motives in India's Search for Nuclear Status," *Asian Survey*, 41, 6 (November–December 2001), pp. 925–42; and K. Subrahmanyam, "Nuclear India in Global Politics," *World Affairs*, 2, 3 (July-September 1998), pp. 12–40.

2. For the view that doctrines have scarcely mattered in the U.S. context, see Desmond Ball, "The Role of Concepts and Doctrine in U.S. Strategic Nuclear Force Development," in Bernard Brodie, Michael D. Intrilligator, and Roman Kolkowicz, eds., *National Security and International Stability* (Cambridge, MA: Oelgeschlager, Gunn & Hain, 1983).

3. Francis Fukuyama, *The End of History and the Last Man* (New York: Free Press; Toronto: Maxwell Macmillan Canada, 1992).

4. Samuel P. Huntington, *The Clash of Civilizations and the Remaking of World Order* (New York: Simon & Schuster, 1996).

5. Ralph A. Cossa, "Toward a Post-post-Cold War World," *Policy Forum Online*, Nautilus Institute, October 18, 2001 <http://www.nautilus.org/fora/Special-Policy-Forum/30_Cossa.html#sect1>.

6. Mikhail Gorbachev, *Perestroika: New Thinking for Our Country and the World* (New York: Harper & Row, 1987).

7. A seminal publication that received widespread attention was Jessica Tuchman Mathews, "Redefining Security," *Foreign Affairs*, 68, 2 (Spring 1989), pp. 162–77,

though it was preceded by a less-appreciated work of the Cold War era: Richard H. Ullman, "Redefining Security," *International Security*, 8, 1 (Summer 1983), pp. 129–53. For Indian perspectives, see Rajesh M. Basrur, ed., *Security in the New Millennium: Views from South Asia* (New Delhi: India Research Press, 2001); and Navnita Chadha Behera, ed., *The State, People and Security* (New Delhi: Har-Anand, 2002). For the extensive debate over the definition of security in the post-Cold War world, see David A. Baldwin, "Security Studies and the End of the Cold War," *World Politics*, 48, 1 (October 1995), pp. 117–41; Barry Buzan, Ole Waever, and Jaap de Wilde, *Security: A Framework for Analysis* (Boulder, CO and London: Lynne Rienner, 1998); Keith Krause and Michael C. Williams, eds., *Critical Security Studies: Concepts and Cases* (London: UCL Press, 1997); and Stephen M. Walt, "The Renaissance of Security Studies," *International Studies Quarterly*, 35, 2 (June 1991), pp. 211–39.

8. Robert Jervis, *System Effects: Complexity in Political and Social Life* (Princeton, NJ: Princeton University Press, 1997).

9. K. J. Holsti, *The State, War and the State of War* (Cambridge [England] and New York: Cambridge University Press, 1996).

10. Stephanie G. Neuman, "International Relations Theory and the Third World: An Oxymoron?" in Stephanie G. Neuman, ed., *International Relations Theory and the Third World* (Basingstoke and London: Macmillan, 1998), p. 2.

11. K. J. Holsti, "International Relations Theory and Domestic War in the Third World," in Neuman, ed., *International Relations Theory and the Third World*.

12. Max Singer and Aaron Wildavsky, *The Real World Order: Zones of Peace, Zones of Turmoil* (Chatham, NJ: Chatham House Publishers, 1993).

13. David Thomson, *Europe since Napoleon*, 2nd ed. (London: Longmans Green, 1962).

14. Rajesh M. Basrur, *India's External Relations: A Theoretical Analysis* (New Delhi: Commonwealth Publishers, 2000).

15. K. J. Holsti, *The Dividing Discipline* (Boston: Allen & Unwin, 1985).

16. Ken Booth and Steve Smith, eds., *International Relations Theory Today* (University Park, PA: Pennsylvania State University Press, 1995); Scott Burchill and Andrew Linklater, *Theories of International Relations* (Basingstoke: Macmillan, 1996); Holsti, *Dividing Discipline*; Charles W. Kegley, Jr., ed., *Controversies in International Relations Theory* (New York: St. Martin's Press, 1995); A. P. Rana, "Restructuring International Relations as a Field in India: A Programme for the Disciplinary Development of International Relations Studies," *Studying International Relations: The Baroda Perspective, Occasional Review*, I, 1 (March 1988), pp. 17–26.

17. Holsti, *Dividing Discipline*, pp. 75–77. A prominent work on Marxist theory of international relations devotes barely half a dozen pages to the issue of war. See V. Kubalkova and A. A. Cruickshank, *Marxism-Leninism and Theory of International Relations* (London: Routledge & Kegan Paul, 1980).

18. The preeminent constructivist treatise is Alexander Wendt, *Social Theory of International Politics* (Cambridge: Cambridge University Press, 1999).

19. Jennifer Sterling-Folker, "Competing Paradigms or Birds of a Feather? Constructivism and Neoliberal Institutionalism Compared," *International Studies Quarterly*, 44, 1 (March 2000), pp. 97–119. As Robert Jervis points out, constructivism, in stressing the role of identities in inducing cooperation, "mistakes effect for cause: its description is correct, but the identities, images, and self-images are superstructure"

and "what is crucial is not people's thinking, but the factors that drive it." "Theories of War in an Era of Peace," Presidential Address, American Political Science Association Annual Conference, 2001, *American Political Science Review*, 96, 1 (March 2002), p. 4.

20. B. B. Naik, *Ideals of Ancient Hindu Politics and the Arthashastra of Kautilya* (Dharwar: B. B. Naik, 1932); Thucydides, *History of the Peloponnesian War*, transl. Rex Warner (Harmondsworth: Penguin, 1954); N. Machiavelli, *The Prince*, transl. W. K. Marriott (London: J. M. Dent & Son, 1908).

21. This view lay at the heart of the writings of Hans Morgenthau, indisputably the most influential post-Second World War thinker on international politics in the English language. See Hans J. Morgenthau, *Politics among Nations: The Struggle for Power and Peace*, 3rd ed. (New York: Alfred A. Knopf, 1960).

22. Kenneth N. Waltz, *Theory of International Politics* (Reading, MA: Addison-Wesley, 1979). See also his "Structural Realism after the Cold War," *International Security*, 25, 1 (Summer 2000), pp. 5–41; and Joseph M. Grieco, "Realist International Theory and the Study of World Politics," in Michael M. Doyle and G. John Ikenberry, eds., *New Thinking in International Relations Theory* (Boulder, CO: Westview Press, 1997). For a sympathetic review, see Barry Buzan, "The Timeless Wisdom of Realism?" in Steve Smith, Ken Booth, and Marysia Zalewski, eds., *International Theory: Positivism and Beyond* (Cambridge: Cambridge University Press, 1996).

23. Jean Jacques Rousseau, "The State of War," in M. G. Forsyth, H. M. A. Keens-Soper, and P. A. Savigear, eds., *The Theory of International Relations: Selected Texts from Gentili to Trietschke* (New Delhi: S. Chand & Co., 1970), pp. 172–73. For a discussion on Rousseau, including a comparison with Thomas Hobbes, who regarded recurrent war as stemming from human nature, see Ian Clark, *Reform and Resistance in the International Order* (Cambridge: Cambridge University Press, 1980).

24. Stanley Hoffmann, *The State of War: Essays in the Theory and Practice of International Politics* (London: Pall Mall Press, 1965), pp. 62–63. See also Holsti, *Dividing Discipline*, pp. 18–19.

25. See, for example, Hedley Bull, *The Anarchical Society: A Study of Order in World Politics* (London and Basingstoke: Macmillan, 1977); Robert O. Keohane, *After Hegemony: Cooperation and Discord in the World Political Economy* (Princeton, NJ: Princeton University Press, 1984); Robert O. Keohane and Joseph S. Nye, Jr., *Power and Interdependence: World Politics in Transition* (Boston: Little Brown, 1978); and Stephen D. Krasner, ed., *International Regimes* (Ithaca, NY: Cornell University Press, 1983). For an overview, see Richard Little, "The Growing Relevance of Pluralism?" in Smith, Booth, and Zalewski, eds., *International Theory*.

26. F. H. Hinsley, *Power and the Pursuit of Peace: Theory and Practice in the Relations between States* (Cambridge: Cambridge University Press, 1963), pp. 81–91; Holsti, *Dividing Discipline*, pp. 27–30.

27. Joseph S. Nye, Jr., "Neorealism and Neoliberalism," *World Politics*, 40, 2 (January 1988), p. 83. For a more recent effort to build a "scientific" liberal theory, see Andrew Moravcsik, "Taking Preferences Seriously: A Liberal Theory of International Politics," *International Organization*, 51, 4 (Autumn 1997), pp. 513–53.

28. On globalization, see Ian Clark, *Globalization and Fragmentation* (Oxford: Oxford University Press, 1997); David Held, Anthony McGrew, David Goldblatt, and Jonathan Perraton, *Global Transformations: Politics, Economics and Culture* (Cam-

bridge: Polity Press, 1999); and Ankie Hoogvelt, *Globalisation and the Postcolonial World* (Basingstoke: Macmillan, 1997); For the view that globalization is rendering the state dysfunctional and in decline, see Kenichi Ohmae, *The Borderless World* (London: HarperCollins, 1990); and Peter F. Drucker, *The New Realities* (New York: HarperCollins, 1993). For the contrary view, which holds that the state is still a powerful actor, see Robert J. Holton, *Globalisation and the Nation-State* (Basingstoke and London: Macmillan; and New York: St. Martin's Press, 1998); and Janice E. Thomson, "State Sovereignty in International Relations: Bridging the Gap between Theory and Empirical Research," *International Studies Quarterly*, 39, 2 (June 1995), pp. 213–33.

29. Robert Jervis, "Realism, Neoliberalism and Cooperation: Understanding the Debate," *International Security*, 31, 4 (Summer 1999), pp. 42–63.

30. For the view that globalization involves new means for the exercise of power, whether by states or nonstate actors, see Sean Kay, "Globalization, Power and Security," *Security Dialogue*, 35, 1 (March 2004), pp. 9–25.

31. David von Drehle, "World War, Cold War Won. Now the Gray War," *Washington Post*, September 12, 2001, p. A9.

32. Ulrich Beck, "The Silence of Words: Terror and War," *Security Dialogue*, 34, 3 (September 2003), p. 259. For his seminal work on the subject, see Ulrich Beck, *Risk Society: Towards a New Modernity*, translated from the German by Mark Ritter (London: Sage Publications, 1992).

33. John Pomfret, "China Sees Interests Tied to US," *Washington Post*, February 2, 2002, p. A1.

34. T. V. Paul, *Power versus Prudence: Why Nations Forgo Nuclear Weapons* (Montreal, Kingston, London, and Ithaca: McGill-Queen's University Press, 2000). For the realist argument that states act in specific ways in accordance with the level of threat experienced by them, see Stephen M. Walt, *The Origin of Alliances* (Ithaca and London: Cornell University Press, 1987).

35. Ariel E. Levite, "Never Say Never Again: Nuclear Reversal Revisited," *International Security*, 27, 3 (Winter 2002–3), pp. 59–88.

36. Kenneth N. Waltz, "The Emerging Structure of International Politics," *International Security*, 18, 2 (Fall 1993), pp. 44–79.

37. Lawrence Freedman, *The Evolution of Nuclear Strategy*, 3rd ed. (Basingstoke and New York: Palgrave Macmillan, 2003), pp. 424–28.

38. Michael Quinlan, "The Future of Nuclear Weapons: Policy for Western Possessors," *International Affairs*, 69, 3 (July 1993), pp. 485–96.

39. Ibid., p. 487. For a similar view, see McGeorge Bundy, William J. Crowe, Jr., and Sidney Drell, *Reducing Nuclear Danger: The Road Away from the Brink* (New York: Council on Foreign Relations Pres, 1993), pp. 32–33.

40. Keith B. Payne, *Deterrence in the Second Nuclear Age* (Lexington: University Press of Kentucky, 1996); Brad Roberts, *Nuclear Multipolarity and Stability* (Alexandria, VA: Institute for Defense Analyses, and Washington, DC: Defense Threat Reduction Agency, November 2000) <http://www.dtra.mil/about/organization/d2539dtra.doc>.

41. Rajesh M. Basrur, "US Nuclear Policy after the Cold War," in A. A. Mutalik-Desai, V. K. Malhotra, T. S. Anand, and Prashant K. Sinha eds., *A Mosaic of Encounters—India & USA: Literature, Society and Politics* (New Delhi: Creative Books, 1999).

42. Philip C. Bleek, "Nuclear Posture Review Released, Stresses Flexible Force Planning," *Arms Control Today*, 32, 1 (January–February 2002) <http://www.armscontrol.org/act/2002_01-02/nprjanfeb02.asp>.

43. Neil Joeck, "Nuclear Developments in India and Pakistan," *Access Asia Review*, National Bureau of Asian Research, 2, 2 (July 1999) <http://www.nbr.org/publications/review/vol2no2/essay.html>; Haider Nizamani, *The Roots of Rhetoric: Politics of Nuclear Weapons in India and Pakistan* (Westport, CT and London: Praeger, 2000); George Perkovich, *India's Nuclear Bomb: The Impact on Global Proliferation* (Berkeley, Los Angeles, and London: University of California Press, 1999); Sagan, "Why Do States Build Nuclear Weapons?"; Kalpana Sharma, "The Hindu Bomb," *Bulletin of the Atomic Scientists*, 54, 4 (July–August 1998), pp. 30–33.

44. For useful histories of the process, see Raj Chengappa, *Weapons of Peace* (New Delhi: HarperCollins, 2000); Stephen P. Cohen, *India: Emerging Power* (Washington, DC: Brookings Institution Press, 2001), pp. 157–97; Sumit Ganguly, "India's Pathway to Pokhran II: The Prospects and Sources of New Delhi's Nuclear Program," *International Security*, 23, 4 (Spring 1999), pp. 148–77; Perkovich, *India's Nuclear Bomb*; and K. Subrahmanyam, "Indian Nuclear Policy, 1964–98 (A Personal Recollection)," in Jasjit Singh, ed., *Nuclear India* (New Delhi: Knowledge World, 1998).

45. K. Subrahmanyam, "Politics of Shakti: New Whine in an Old Bomb," *Times of India*, May 26, 1998, p. 12.

46. William M. Arkin, "New Nukes," *Washington Post*, April 23, 2001 <http://www.washingtonpost.com/wp-dyn/articles/A48726-2001Apr22.html>; "Nuclear Weapons Action Alert: Stop Mini-Nuke Development Now!" International Physicians for the Prevention of Nuclear War, Cambridge, MA, April 30, 2001 <http://www.ippnw.org/>. For more extensive discussions, see Center for Counterproliferation Research, National Defense University, *U.S. Nuclear Policy in the 21st Century*, Washington, DC, 1998; and Robert Manning, "The Ultimate Weapon Redux? US Nuclear Weapon Policy in a New Era," in Burkard Schmitt ed., *Nuclear Weapons: A New Great Debate*, Chaillot Papers, 48 (Paris: Institute for Security Studies of Western European Union, July 2001).

47. Pavel Podvig, *Russian Strategic Nuclear Forces* (Cambridge, MA and London: MIT Press, 2001); and Nikolai Sokov, *Russian Strategic Modernization: Past and Future* (Lanham, MD: Rowman & Littlefield, 2000).

48. On Iran and Iraq, see Gitty M. Amini, *Weapons of Mass Destruction in the Middle East* (Washington, DC: Nuclear Threat Initiative, February 1, 2003) <http://nti.org/e_research/e3_24b.html>. On North Korea, see "North Korea's Nuclear Program, 2003," *Bulletin of the Atomic Scientists* (March–April 2003) <http://www.thebulletin.org/issues/nukenotes/ma03nukenote.html>.

49. Ramesh Thakur, "Envisioning Nuclear Futures," *Security Dialogue*, 31, 1 (March 2000), p. 33. For the internal debate on Japan's nuclearization, see Brad Roberts and Shen Dingli, "The Nuclear Equation in Asia," in Schmitt, ed., *Nuclear Weapons: A New Great Debate*, pp. 136–38.

50. On the India-China nuclear relationship, see George Perkovich, "The Nuclear and Security Balance," in Francine R. Frankel and Harry Harding, eds., *The India-China Relationship: Rivalry and Engagement* (Oxford: Oxford University Press, 2004). Surprisingly, there are no comprehensive works on the India-Pakistan nuclear relationship. But see Sumit Ganguly, *Conflict Unending: India-Pakistan Tensions since*

1947 (Oxford: Oxford University Press, 2002); and Michael Krepon, Rodney W. Jones, and Ziad Haider, eds., *Escalation Control and the Nuclear Option in South Asia* (Washington, DC: Henry L. Stimson Center, 2004).

51. Bates Gill and James Mulvenon, "The Chinese Strategic Rocket Forces: Transition to Credible Deterrence," in *China and Weapons of Mass Destruction: Implications for the United States* (Washington, DC: National Intelligence Council, November 5, 1999) <http://www.cia.gov/nic/pubs/conference_reports/weapons_mass_destruction.html>; Robert A. Manning, Ronald Montaperto, and Brad Roberts, *China, Nuclear Weapons, and Arms Control: A Preliminary Assessment* (New York: Council on Foreign Relations, 2000).

52. Michael D. Swaine and Ashley J. Tellis, *Interpreting China's Grand Strategy* (Santa Monica, CA and Washington, DC: RAND, 2000). On China's future superpower status, see Emilio Casetti, "Power Shifts and Economic Development: When Will China Overtake the USA?" *Journal of Peace Research*, 40, 6 (November 2003), pp. 661–75.

53. Farhan Bokhari, "Pakistan-Chinese Missile Proliferation," *Japan Times*, September 17, 2001, Nuclear Control Institute <http://www.nci.org/01/09/17-5.htm>; Sridhar Krishnaswamy, "China Supplied Missile Technology to Pak: CIA," *Hindu*, September 9, 2001 <http://www.hinduonnet.com/thehindu/2001/09/09/stories/030390006.htm>; T. V. Paul, "Chinese-Pakistani Missile Ties and the Balance of Power, *Nonproliferation Review*, 10, 2 (Summer 2003), pp. 1–9.

54. There are relatively few unclassified sources of Pakistani nuclear thinking. The best available are: Paolo Cotta-Ramusino and Maurizio Martellini, "Nuclear Safety, Nuclear Stability and Nuclear Strategy in Pakistan," *A Concise Report of a Visit by Landau Network—Centro Volta* (Como, Italy: January 2002) <http://lxmi.mi.infn.it/~landnet/>; Mahmud Ali Durrani, *Pakistan's Strategic Thinking and the Role of Nuclear Weapons*, Occasional Paper 37, Cooperative Monitoring Center, Sandia National Laboratories, Albuquerque, NM, July 2004; and Zafar Iqbal Cheema, "Pakistan's Nuclear Use Doctrine and Command and Control," in Peter R. Lavoy, Scott D. Sagan, and James J. Wirtz, eds., *Planning the Unthinkable: How New Powers Will Use Nuclear, Biological, and Chemical Weapons* (Ithaca, NY and London: Cornell University Press, 2000).

55. Kanti Bajpai, "The Fallacy of an Indian Deterrent," in Amitabh Mattoo, ed., *India's Nuclear Deterrent: Pokhran II and Beyond* (New Delhi: Har-Anand, 1999), pp. 152–59.

56. Praful Bidwai and Achin Vanaik, *South Asia on a Short Fuse: Nuclear Politics and the Future of Global Disarmament* (New Delhi: Oxford University Press, 1999), pp. 89–91.

57. Achin Vanaik, "India's Draft Nuclear Doctrine: A Critique," in Smitu Kothari and Zia Mian, eds., *Out of the Nuclear Shadow* (Delhi: Lokayan and Rainbow Publishers; London: Zed Books, 2001), pp. 292–93.

58. "The Bigger Bombs in Our Backyard," Special Report, *Sunday Times of India*, May 24, 1998, p. 15; and Kuldip Nayar, "Between Welfare and Weapons," *Indian Express*, August 31, 1999, p. 8.

59. Aijaz Ahmad, "The Hindutva Weapon," in Kothari and Mian, eds., *Out of the Nuclear Shadow*; Praful Bidwai, "Dangerous Descent: Flawed Logic of Nuclear Tests," *Times of India*, May 5, 1998, p. 12; and Nayar, "Between Welfare and Weapons."

60. The seminal debate, recently updated, is in Scott D. Sagan and Kenneth N. Waltz, *The Spread of Nuclear Weapons: A Debate Renewed* (New York and London: W. W. Norton, 2003). This includes a chapter on the India-Pakistan relationship (pp. 88–124). For a recent review of the literature, see Jeffrey W. Knopf, "Recasting the Proliferation Optimism-Pessimism Debate," *Security Studies*, 12, 1 (Autumn 2002), pp. 41–96. In the South Asian context, see Devin T. Hagerty, *The Consequences of Nuclear Proliferation: Lessons from South Asia* (Cambridge, MA and London, MIT Press,1998).

61. Lewis A. Dunn, *Controlling the Bomb* (New Haven, CT: Yale University Press, 1982); and Kathleen C. Bailey, *Doomsday Weapons in the Hands of Many: The Arms Control Challenge of the 1990s* (Urbana, IL: University of Illinois Press, 1991).

62. Michael Krepon, *The Stability-Instability Paradox, Misperception, and Escalation Control in South Asia* (Washington, DC: Henry L. Stimson Center, May 2003), p. 8.

63. Amartya Sen, "India and the Bomb," in Kothari and Mian, eds., *Out of the Nuclear Shadow*, p. 127.

64. Michael Ryan Kraig, "The Political and Strategic Imperatives of Nuclear Deterrence in South Asia," *India Review*, 2, 1 (January 2003), pp. 15–17.

65. Peter D. Feaver, "Proliferation Optimism and Theories of Nuclear Operations," *Security Studies*, 2, 3–4 (Spring–Summer 1993), p. 162.

66. Bernard Brodie, "Implications for Military Policy," in Bernard Brodie, ed., *The Absolute Weapon* (New York: Harcourt, Brace, 1946), p. 76.

67. Robert Jervis, "Cooperation under the Security Dilemma," *World Politics*, 30, 2 (January 1978), pp. 1167–214. For reviews of the subsequent literature, see Allan Collins, "State-Induced Security Dilemma: Maintaining the Tragedy," *Cooperation and Conflict*, 39, 1 (March 2004), pp. 27–44; and Charles L. Glaser, "The Security Dilemma Revisited," *World Politics*, 50, 1 (October 1997), pp. 171–201.

68. The theoretical relationship between structure and interaction is developed at length in Basrur, *India's External Relations*, pp. 46–79.

69. Hoffmann, *State of War*, p. 61.

70. Immanuel Kant, "Idea for a Universal History from a Cosmo-Political Point of View," in Forsyth et al., eds., *Theory of International Relations*, p. 183.

71. David Hamilton, *Evolutionary Economics: A Study of Change in Economic Thought* (Albuquerque, NM: University of New Mexico Press, 1970), p. 88.

72. William Walker, "Nuclear Order and Disorder," *International Affairs*, 76, 4 (October 2000), pp. 703–24.

73. Hoffmann, *State of War*, pp. 77–82.

74. Ibid., p. 82.

75. Jeffrey W. Taliaferro, "Security Seeking under Anarchy: Defensive Realism Revisited," *International Security*, 25, 3 (Winter 2000–1), pp. 128–61. See also Stephen G. Brooks, "Dueling Realisms," *International Organization*, 51, 3 (Summer 1997), pp. 445–77. Major offensive realists include John J. Mearsheimer, *The Tragedy of Great Power Politics* (New York: W. W. Norton, 2001); and Randall L. Schweller, *Deadly Imbalances: Tripolarity and Hitler's Strategy of World Conquest* (New York: Columbia University Press, 1997). Defensive realists include Walt, *Origin of Alliances*; and Robert Jervis, *The Meaning of the Nuclear Revolution* (Ithaca, NY: Cornell University Press, 1989).

76. Paul, *Power versus Prudence: Why Nations Forgo Nuclear Weapons*, pp. 148–

49. Paul's conception of "prudential realism" is essentially the same as defensive realism.

77. Andrew Butfoy, *Common Security and Strategic Reform* (Basingstoke and London: Macmillan; New York: St. Martin's Press, 1997), pp. 38–67; Bjørn Møller, *Common Security and Nonoffensive Defense: A Neorealist Perspective* (Boulder, CO: Lynne Rienner, 1992); and United Nations Institute for Disarmament Research, *Nonoffensive Defense: A Global Perspective* (New York: Taylor & Francis, 1990).

78. Quincy Wright, *A Study of War*, 2nd ed. (Chicago and London: University of Chicago Press, 1965), p. 1242.

Chapter 2. The Essentials of Minimum Deterrence

1. Peter Gizewski, *Minimum Nuclear Deterrence in a New World Order*, Aurora Papers, 24, Canadian Centre for Global Security, Ottawa, March 1994, p. 2.

2. For a review of the main forms of nuclear doctrine and posture (though not all those which have been identified here), see Freedman, *Evolution of Nuclear Strategy*; and Philip Windsor, *Strategic Thinking: An Introduction and Farewell* (Boulder, CO: Lynne Rienner, 2002).

3. On American nuclear thinking, see John Lewis Gaddis, *Strategies of Containment: A Critical Appraisal of Postwar American National Security Policy* (Oxford: Oxford University Press, 1982); and Charles L. Glaser, *Analyzing Strategic Nuclear Policy* (Princeton, NJ: Princeton University Press, 1990). On Soviet thinking, see Stephen J. Cimbala, *Nuclear War and Nuclear Strategy: Unfinished Business* (New York, Westport, CT, and London: Greenwood Press, 1987), pp. 67–97; and Andrei A. Kokoshin, *Soviet Strategic Thought* (Cambridge, MA and London: MIT Press, 1998). On Russia, see Nikolai Sokov, "Russian Ministry of Defense's New Policy Paper: The Nuclear Angle," *CNS Reports*, Center for Nonproliferation Studies, Monterey Institute of International Studies, Monterey, CA, n.d. <http://cns.miis.edu/pubs/reports/sok1003.htm> (accessed October 26, 2003).

4. The United States has shown considerable interest in small nuclear weapons, while Russia continues to develop large ones. See Christopher Paine, "The Party of Preemption," *Bulletin of the Atomic Scientists*, 60, 1 (January–February 2004), pp. 75–76; and Vladimir Radyuhin, "New Nuclear Missile System Has No Parallel: Russia," *Hindu*, November 19, 2004 <http://www.thehindu.com/2004/11/19/stories/2004111902911300.htm>.

5. On China, see Gill and Mulvenon, "The Chinese Strategic Rocket Forces"; Avery Goldstein, *Deterrence and Security in the 21st Century: China, Britain, France, and the Enduring Legacy of the Nuclear Revolution* (Stanford, CA: Stanford University Press, 2000), pp. 62–138; and Litai Xue, "Evolution of China's Nuclear Strategy," in John C. Hopkins and Weixing Hu, eds., *Strategic Views from the Second Tier: The Nuclear Weapons Policies of France, Britain, and China* (New Brunswick, NJ and London: Transaction Publishers, 1995).

6. Gill and Mulvenon, "Chinese Strategic Rocket Forces," p. 7.

7. Alastair Iain Johnston, "China's New 'Old Thinking': The Concept of Limited Deterrence," *International Security*, 20, 3 (Winter 1995–96), pp. 5–42.

8. John L. Lumpkin, "China Launches New Class of Nuclear Sub," *Washington Post*, December 4, 2004 <http://www.washingtonpost.com/wp-dyn/articles/A34249-2004Dec4.html>.

9. On British nuclear policy, see Goldstein, *Deterrence and Security in the 21st Century*, pp. 139–80; and Michael Quinlan, "British Nuclear Weapons Policy: Past, Present, and Future," in Hopkins and Hu, eds., *Strategic Views from the Second Tier*. On France, see Goldstein, *Deterrence and Security in the 21st Century*, pp. 181–216; Bruno Tertrais, "Nuclear Policy: France Stands Alone," *Bulletin of the Atomic Scientists*, 60, 4 (July–August 2004), pp. 48–55; and David S. Yost, "Nuclear Weapons Issues in France," in Hopkins and Hu, eds., *Strategic Views from the Second Tier*. On India, see Kanti Bajpai, "India's Nuclear Posture after Pokhran II," *International Studies*, 37, 4 (October–December 2000), pp. 267–301; Waheguru Pal Singh Sidhu, "India's Nuclear Use Doctrine," in Lavoy, Sagan, and Wirtz, eds., *Planning the Unthinkable*; and Ashley J. Tellis, *India's Emerging Nuclear Posture* (Santa Monica, CA: RAND, 2001). On Pakistan, see Cheema, "Pakistan's Nuclear Use Doctrine and Command and Control"; Durrani, *Pakistan's Strategic Thinking and the Role of Nuclear Weapons*; Timothy D. Hoyt, "Pakistani Nuclear Doctrine and the Dangers of Strategic Myopia," *Asian Survey*, 41, 6 (November–December 2001), pp. 956–77; and Smruti S. Pattanaik, "Pakistan's Nuclear Strategy," *Strategic Analysis*, 27, 1 (January–March 2003), pp. 94–114. On South Asia as a whole, see Rodney W. Jones, *Minimum Nuclear Deterrence Postures in South Asia: An Overview* (Washington, DC: Defense Threat Reduction Agency, October 1, 2001).

10. Avner Cohen and Benjamin Frankel, "Opaque Nuclear Proliferation," *Journal of Strategic Studies* 13, 3 (September 1990), pp. 14–44. In the South Asian context, see Hagerty, *Consequences of Nuclear Proliferation*, pp. 39–62. Both works refer to opaque "proliferation," but the concept is essentially the same as opaque deterrence. On Israel, see Avner Cohen, *Israel and the Bomb* (New York: Columbia University Press, 1998); and Warner D. Farr, *The Third Temple's Holy of Holies: Israel's Nuclear Weapons*, Counterproliferation Papers, Future Warfare Series, 2, USAF Counterproliferation Center, Air War College, Air University, Maxwell Air Force Base, Alabama, September 1999; and Zeev Maoz, "The Mixed Blessing of Israel's Nuclear Policy," *International Security*, 28, 2 (Fall 2003), pp. 44–77.

11. Hagerty, *Consequences of Nuclear Proliferation*, pp. 40–43.

12. "North Korea's Nuclear Program, 2003," *Bulletin of the Atomic Scientists*, 59, 2 (March–April 2003), pp. 74–77.

13. The possibilities for virtual deterrence are discussed in the literature on "virtual nuclear arsenals." See, for example, Michael J. Mazarr, ed., *Nuclear Weapons in a Transformed World: The Challenge of Virtual Nuclear Arsenals* (New York: St. Martin's Press, 1997); and Michael J. Mazarr, *Virtual Nuclear Arsenals: A Second Look* (Washington, DC: Center for Strategic and International Studies, January 1999). For a skeptical assessment, see Kenneth N. Waltz, "Thoughts about Virtual Nuclear Arsenals," *Washington Quarterly*, 20, 3 (Summer 1997), pp. 153–61. A narrowly focused conception of this from a nonproliferation standpoint has been articulated by George Perkovich as "nonweaponized deterrence." See his "A Nuclear Third Way in South Asia," *Foreign Policy*, 91 (Summer 1992), pp. 85–104.

14. See "Japan: Special Weapons Guide. Nuclear Weapons Program," Federation of American Scientists, Washington, DC, n.d., (accessed February 18, 2003) <http://www.fas.org/nuke/guide/japan/nuke/>.

15. Karl-Inge Åhäll, Marianne Lindström, Olov Holmstrand, Björn Helander, and Miles Goldstick, "Nuclear Waste in Sweden: The Problem Is Not Solved," Peo-

ples' Movement against Nuclear Power and Weapons ("Folkkampanjen mot kärnkraft och kärnvapen"), Stockholm, June 1988 <http://www.folkkampanjen.se/nwchap2.html>; Mark N. Gose, "The New Germany and Nuclear Weapons Options for the Future," *Airpower Journal*, Special Edition, 1996, pp. 67–78.

16. Chapter 3 provides greater detail.

17. On the recently observed phenomenon of collaboration between new and potential nuclear powers, see Chaim Braun and Christopher S. Chyba, "Proliferation Rings: New Challenges to the Nuclear Nonproliferation Regime," *International Security*, 29, 2 (Fall 2004), pp. 5–49. The technology disseminated by Pakistani scientists at least partly originated in China, which had provided nuclear assistance to Pakistan earlier. Bomb designs and other papers made public by Libya are partly in the Chinese language. Joby Warrick and Peter Slevin, "Libyan Arms Designs Traced Back to China," *Washington Post*, February 15, 2004 <http://www.washingtonpost.com/wp-dyn/articles/A42692-2004Feb14.html>. Notwithstanding Chinese denials, there have been reports of continuing Chinese nuclear aid to Pakistan. Vice Admiral Lowell E. Jacoby, Director of the U.S. Defense Intelligence Agency, told the Senate Select Committee on Intelligence in February 2004 that "Chinese companies remain involved with nuclear and missile programmes in Pakistan and Iran." See "Pak Capable of Producing Plutonium: US Official," *Times of India*, February 26, 2004 <http://timesofindia.indiatimes.com/articleshow/519721.cms>.

18. Comparable cases are those of China and Pakistan, which are equally secretive about their nuclear weapons programs and thinking.

19. The estimated warhead potential, measured as "nuclear weapon equivalents" (NWEs) is believed to have been over 100 in 2000. Jones, *Minimum Nuclear Deterrence Postures in South Asia*, p. 36.

20. For details on warheads and delivery vehicles, see Center for Defense Information, *World Nuclear Arsenals*, Washington, DC, July 8, 2004 <http://www.cdi.org/program/document.cfm?DocumentID=2187&StartRow=1&ListRows=10&appendURL=&Orderby=D.DateLastUpdated&ProgramID=32&from_page=index.cfm>. Remarkably, interest in developing a sea-based deterrent as well as a land-based ICBM dates back to as early as 1970, when Mrs. Gandhi initiated preparations for India's solitary 1974 nuclear test. Project Valiant was a feasibility study for a long-range missile, while Project 937 aimed to build an indigenous nuclear-powered submarine (SSBN). Chengappa, *Weapons of Peace*, pp. 130–31. Though rumors persist, intent to build an ICBM has been consistently denied. One reason for a lack of serious interest is that there is no real need for it at the present time. Another reason may be the calculation that the time is not opportune, and would needlessly invite U.S. displeasure. See Bharat Karnad, *Nuclear Weapons and Indian Security: The Realist Foundations of Strategy* (Delhi: Macmillan, 2002), p. 531. On the ongoing quest for an indigenously designed SSBN, see ibid., pp. 646–59.

21. "NCA Councils Review Nuclear Deterrence," *Indian Express*, September 2, 2003 <http://www.indianexpress.com/full_story.php?content_id=30765>.

22. Government of India, Ministry of External Affairs, "The Cabinet Committee on Security Reviews Operationalization of India's Nuclear Doctrine," Press Release, January 4, 2003 <http://meadev.nic.in/news/official/20030104/official.htm>.

23. Government of India, Ministry of External Affairs, *Draft Report of National*

Security Advisory Board on Indian Nuclear Doctrine, August 17, 1999 <http://meadev.nic.in/govt/indnucld.htm>.

24. Karnad, *Nuclear Weapons and Indian Security*, p. 616. For a review of the debate between maximalists and minimalists, see Kanti Bajpai, "The Great Indian Nuclear Debate," in Anindyo J. Majumdar, ed., *Nuclear India into the New Millennium* (New Delhi: Lancer's Books, 2000). Bajpai identifies three schools: rejectionists, pragmatists, and maximalists. The first two are in practice minimalists, with the rejectionists distinguishable as reluctant ones.

25. K. Sundarji, "Nuclear Deterrence: Doctrine for India—I & II," *Trishul*, December 1992 and July 1993 (advance copy; hereafter referred to as "Doctrine-I" and "Doctrine-II"); K. Sundarji, "India's Nuclear Weapons Policy," in Jørn Gelstad and Olav Njølstad, eds., *Nuclear Rivalry and International Order* (Oslo: PRIO; and London, Thousand Oaks, and New Delhi: Sage, 1996); and K. Sundarji, *Blind Men of Hindoostan: Indo-Pak Nuclear War* (New Delhi: UBS Publishers' Distributors, 1993). The last is a work of fiction, but is also an exposition of strategic concepts, including an affirmation of minimum deterrence.

26. Sundarji, *Blind Men of Hindoostan*, p. 150.
27. Sundarji, "Doctrine-II," pp. 12–13.
28. Sundarji, "Doctrine-I," p. 3.
29. Sundarji, "India's Nuclear Weapons Policy," p. 177.
30. Sundarji, "Doctrine-I," p. 13.
31. Sundarji, "India's Nuclear Weapons Policy," p. 177.
32. Sundarji, "Doctrine-I," pp. 10–13. To be fair, this in part reflects his felt need for deception to ensure survivability, but Sundarji does offer arguments typical of assured destruction theorists when he expresses his doubts about the survivability of silo-based missiles and his preference for SLBMs. I expand on this aspect in the critique below.

33. Gizewski, *Minimum Nuclear Deterrence in a New World Order*, pp. 2–3.
34. Karnad comes closest, though still distant, with his requirement of an arsenal of 408 warheads. Karnad, *Nuclear Weapons and Indian Security*, p. 617.
35. George H. Quester, "The Continuing Debate on Minimum Deterrence," in T. V. Paul, Richard J. Harknett, and James J. Wirtz, eds., *The Absolute Weapon Revisited: Nuclear Arms and the Emerging International Order* (Ann Arbor: University of Michigan Press, 1998), pp. 177–78.
36. Charles L. Glaser, *Analyzing Strategic Nuclear Policy* (Princeton, NJ: Princeton University Press, 1990), pp. 49–60.
37. Bernard Brodie, *Strategy in the Missile Age* (Princeton, NJ: Princeton University Press, 1965), p. 277.
38. Scott Sagan, "More Will Be Worse," in Sagan and Waltz, *The Spread of Nuclear Weapons*, p. 63.
39. Krepon, *The Stability-Instability Paradox*, p. 7 (emphasis added).
40. Ashley J. Tellis, "Toward a 'Force-in-Being': The Logic, Structure and Utility of India's Nuclear Posture," in Sumit Ganguly, ed., *India as an Emerging Power* (London and Portland, OR: Frank Cass, 2003), pp. 76, 82.
41. Tellis, *India's Emerging Nuclear Posture*, pp. 671–724.
42. Goldstein, *Deterrence and Security in the 21st Century*, pp. 174–75.

43. Yost, "Nuclear Weapons Issues in France."
44. Xue, "Evolution of China's Nuclear Strategy," pp. 173–77.
45. Morton H. Halperin, *Nuclear Fallacy: Dispelling the Myth of Nuclear Strategy* (Cambridge, MA: Ballinger, 1987), pp. 49–60.
46. On the nuclear taboo, see Nina Tannenwald, "The Nuclear Taboo: The United States and the Normative Basis of Nuclear Non-Use," *International Organization*, 53, 3 (Summer 1999), pp. 433–68.
47. Lawrence Freedman, *Deterrence* (Cambridge, England, and Malden, MA: Polity Press, 2004), p. 10.
48. Brodie, *Strategy in the Missile Age*, pp. 147–72.
49. P. M. S. Blackett, *Fear, War and the Bomb* (New York and Toronto: Whittlesey House, 1948), p. 5.
50. For concise descriptions of the effects of nuclear weapons, see Steve Fetter, "The Effects of Nuclear Detonations and Nuclear War," in Graham T. Alison, Jr., Robert D. Blackwill, Albert Carnesdale, Joseph S. Nye, Jr., and Robert B. Beschel, Jr., eds., *A Primer for the Nuclear Age* (Lanham, MD: University Press of America, 1990); and United Nations, Department of Disarmament Affairs, Report of the Secretary-General, *Study on the Climatic and Other Global Effects of Nuclear Weapons*, Document no. A/43/351, New York, 1989.
51. For a detailed discussion, see Jervis, *Meaning of the Nuclear Revolution*.
52. Richard J. Harknett, "State Preferences, Systemic Constraints and the Absolute Weapon," in Paul, Harknett, and Wirtz, eds., *Absolute Weapon Revisited*, p. 50.
53. Cited in Freedman, *Evolution of Nuclear Strategy*, p. 49.
54. Cited in Gaddis, *Strategies of Containment*, p. 135n.
55. McGeorge Bundy, "Existential Deterrence and Its Consequences," in Douglas MacLean, ed., *The Security Gamble* (Totowa, NJ: Rowman & Allanheld, 1984).
56. Ibid., pp. 9, 10.
57. Donald M. Snow, "Stability and Soviet-American Relations: The Influence of Nuclear Weapons," in Donald M. Snow, ed., *Soviet-American Relations in the 1990s* (Lexington, MA and Toronto: Lexington Books, 1989).
58. Kenneth N. Waltz, "Nuclear Myths and Political Realities," *American Political Science Review*, 84, 3 (September 1990), pp. 735–36.
59. Rajesh M. Basrur, "Nuclear Confidence-Building in the Post-Kargil Scenario," in Moonis Ahmar, ed., *The Challenge of Confidence-Building in South Asia* (New Delhi: Har-Anand, 2001).
60. On the last, for a prolonged 1986–87 border confrontation which has received scant attention, see V. Natarajan, "The Sumdorong Chu Incident," *Bharat Rakshak Monitor*, 3, 3 (November–December 2000) <http://www.bharat-rakshak.com/MONITOR/ISSUE3-3/natarajan.html>.
61. Bundy, "Existential Deterrence and Its Consequences," p. 8.
62. Ibid., p. 10 (italics original).
63. K. Subrahmanyam, "Not a Numbers Game: Minimum Cost of N-Deterrence," *Times of India*, December 7, 1998, p. 10. See also K. Subrahmanyam, "Nuclear Force Design and Minimum Deterrence Strategy for India," in Bharat Karnad, ed., *Future Imperilled* (New Delhi: Viking, 1994), p. 188.

64. K. Subrahmanyam, "A Credible Deterrent: Logic of the Nuclear Doctrine," *Times of India*, October 4, 1999, p. 10.

65. Aniruddha Bahal and Krishna Prasad, "A Ghauri Sight," *Outlook*, May 25, 1998, pp. 52–53; Robert T. Batcher, "The Consequences of an Indo-Pakistani Nuclear War," *Review of International Studies*, 6, 4 (December 2004), pp. 135–62; S. Rashid Naim, "Aadhi Raat Ke Baad (After Midnight)," in Stephen Philip Cohen, ed., *Nuclear Proliferation in South Asia* (New Delhi: Lancer International, 1991); and M. V. Ramana, "Bombing Bombay? Effects of Nuclear Weapons and a Case Study of a Hypothetical Explosion," *IPPNW Global Health Watch Report No. 3* (Cambridge, MA: International Physicians for the Prevention of Nuclear War, 1999).

66. Subrahmanyam, "Not a Numbers Game."

67. Rajesh Rajagopalan, "Deterrence and Nuclear Confrontations: The Cuban Missile Crisis and the Sino-Soviet Border War," *Strategic Analysis*, 24, 3 (June 2000), pp. 441–57.

68. Sundarji, "Doctrine-I," p. 8.

69. Gurmeet Kanwal, *Nuclear Defence: Shaping the Arsenal* (New Delhi: Knowledge World, 2001), pp. 76, 110.

70. Karnad, for instance, acknowledges the common abhorrence of mass civilian damage by India and Pakistan in their wars, which implies that both are easily deterred. Karnad, *Nuclear Weapons and Indian Security*, pp. 561–66.

71. Jervis, *Meaning of the Nuclear Revolution*, pp. 193–214; Vijai K. Nair, "The Structure of an Indian Nuclear Deterrent," in Mattoo, ed., *India's Nuclear Deterrent*, pp. 84–85; Thomas C. Schelling, *Arms and Influence* (New Haven and London: Yale University Press, 1966), pp. 36–43.

72. Government of India, Ministry of External Affairs, *Draft Report of National Security Advisory Board on Indian Nuclear Doctrine*.

73. Kanwal, *Nuclear Defence*, p. 133.

74. Sundarji, "India's Nuclear Weapons Policy," p. 176.

75. Subrahmanyam, "A Credible Deterrent."

76. Kanti Bajpai, "India's Diplomacy and Defence after Pokhran-II," in *Post-Pokhran II: The Way Ahead* (New Delhi: India Habitat Centre, 1999), pp. 32–36, 39–42; and Jasjit Singh, "A Nuclear Strategy for India," in Jasjit Singh, ed., *Nuclear India* (New Delhi: Knowledge World, 1998), pp. 321–23.

77. Kapil Kak, "Command and Control of Small Nuclear Arsenals," in Singh, ed., *Nuclear India*, p. 270; Raja Menon, *A Nuclear Strategy for India* (New Delhi, Thousand Oaks, and London: Sage, 2000), pp. 204, 220–24; and Nair, "Structure of an Indian Nuclear Deterrent," p. 101.

78. C. Uday Bhaskar, "Staying on Course: Subs Have Vital Role in Deterrence," *Times of India*, August 31, 2000, p. 10; Kanwal, *Nuclear Defence*, pp. 131–33; Karnad, *Nuclear Weapons and Indian Security*, pp. 585–91; and Menon, *Nuclear Strategy for India*, pp. 224–27.

79. Waltz, "Nuclear Myths and Political Realities," p. 734 (emphasis added).

80. Naim, "Aadhi Raat Ke Baad (After Midnight)," p. 48, Table 2.1.

81. Schelling, *Arms and Influence*, p. 98.

82. Goldstein, *Deterrence and Security in the 21st Century*, pp. 46–52.

83. Karnad, *Nuclear Weapons and Indian Security*, pp. 620–21; Mani Shankar Aiyar, "By Washington's Grace," *Indian Express*, June 12, 2001, p. 6.

84. M. R. Srinivasan, "Pakistani Nuclear Weapons," *Hindu*, May 4, 2003 <http://www.thehindu.com/2003/05/04/stories/2003050400521000.htm>.

85. Bajpai, "India's Diplomacy and Defence after Pokhran-II," p. 45; and Kapil Sibal, "Toy Gun Security: Flaws in India's Nuclear Deterrence," *Times of India*, January 13, 1999, p. 12.

86. Kanwal, *Nuclear Defence*, pp. 207, 213; Karnad, *Nuclear Weapons and Indian Security*, p. 625; and Nair, "Structure of an Indian Nuclear Deterrent," pp. 102–4.

87. Brahma Chellaney, "After the Tests: India's Options," *Survival*, 40, 4 (Winter 1998–99), p. 107; Sundarji, "Doctrine-I," pp. 13–14; and Sundarji, "India's Nuclear Weapons Policy," pp. 176–77.

88. Srinivas Laxman, "'India Should Retain Option to Carry Out More Tests,'" *Times of India*, January 11, 2000, p. 3; and P. K. Iyengar, "Nuclear Nuances: Credible Deterrent through Testing," *Times of India*, August 22, 2000, p. 10.

89. For extensive discussions on targeting, see Desmond Ball and Jeffrey Richelson, eds., *Strategic Nuclear Targeting* (Ithaca and London: Cornell University Press, 1986); Ian Clark, *Limited Nuclear War* (Oxford: Oxford University Press, 1982); and Glaser, *Analyzing Strategic Nuclear Policy*, pp. 207–56. On India, see Kanwal, *Nuclear Defence*, pp. 75–89; and Sundarji, "Doctrine-II," pp. 12–18. For exceptions, see Arvind Kumar, "Need to Consider Tactical Nuke Option," *Deccan Herald*, September 30, 2002 <http://www.deccanherald.com/deccanherald/sep30/edst.htm>; and Nair, "Structure of an Indian Nuclear Deterrent."

90. Kanwal, *Nuclear Defence*, pp. 76–77; Sundarji, "Doctrine-I," p. 3.

91. Kanwal, *Nuclear Defence*, p. 69; Sundarji, "Doctrine-II," pp. 1–2.

92. Prakash Nanda, "PM Unveils Doctrine of Minimum Credible Deterrent," *Times of India*, August 5, 1998, p. 1.

93. Chellaney, "After the Tests," p. 107; Subrahmanyam, "Nuclear Force Design and Minimum Deterrence Strategy for India," p. 192; Sundarji, "Doctrine-I," p. 11; and Sundarji, "India's Nuclear Weapons Policy," p. 177.

94. Sumit Ganguly and R. Harrison Wagner, "India and Pakistan: Bargaining in the Shadow of Nuclear War," *Journal of Strategic Studies*, 27, 3 (September 2004), pp. 479–507.

95. Russell Leng, "Escalation: Competing Perspectives and Empirical Evidence," *Review of International Studies*, 6, 4 (December 2004), pp. 51–64.

96. For a contrary view, which regards the conventional imbalance between India and Pakistan as a source of instability, see Rodney W. Jones, "Nuclear Stability and Escalation Control in South Asia," in Krepon, Jones, and Haider, eds., *Escalation Control and the Nuclear Option in South Asia*.

97. On compellence in South Asia, see Verghese R. Koithara, "Coercion and Risk-Taking in Nuclear South Asia," CISAC Working Paper, Center for International Security and Cooperation, Stanford University, Stanford, CA, March 2003. The issue is discussed at length in Chapter 4.

98. Sundarji, "Doctrine-II," pp. 16–17; and Waltz, "Nuclear Myths and Political Realities," p. 734. Menon, however, argues that India is vulnerable to a decapitation threat from China. Menon, *Nuclear Strategy for India*, pp. 254–56.

99. Knopf, "Recasting the Proliferation Optimism-Pessimism Debate," p. 61.

100. Sumit Ganguly and Kent L. Biringer, "Nuclear Crisis Stability in South Asia," *Asian Survey*, 41, 6 (November–December 2001), p. 909.

101. Cited in Jervis, *Meaning of the Nuclear Revolution*, p. 136, note 1.

102. P. R. Chari, "Nuclear Crisis, Escalation Control, and Deterrence in South Asia," Working Paper, Henry L. Stimson Center, Washington, DC, August 2003, p. 24.

103. The term is attributed to Jasjit Singh. See Singh, "A Nuclear Strategy for India." For the view that nondeployment is a source of vulnerability, see Karnad, *Nuclear Weapons and Indian Security*, pp. 593–94.

104. Humphrey Hawksley, "India's Nuclear Muscle," *BBC News*, January 13, 2003 <http://news.bbc.co.uk/1/hi/world/south_asia/2646979.stm>.

105. Sundarji, "India's Nuclear Weapons Policy," p. 178.

106. I am indebted to an anonymous reviewer for drawing my attention to this point.

107. The point about the sharp postdeployment increase in risk is made in Kraig, "The Political and Strategic Imperatives of Nuclear Deterrence in South Asia," p. 6.

108. On command and control in general, see Paul Bracken, *The Command and Control of Nuclear Forces* (New Haven: Yale University Press, 1983); and Ashton B. Carter, "Assessing Command System Vulnerability," in Ashton B. Carter, John D. Steinbruner, and Charles A. Zraket, eds., *Managing Nuclear Operations* (Washington, DC: Brookings Institution, 1985). On India, see Sanjay Dasgupta, "Command and Control in the Nuclear Era," in Maroof Raza, ed., *Generals and Governments in India and Pakistan* (New Delhi: Har-Anand, 2001); Kak, "Command and Control of Small Nuclear Arsenals"; and Kanwal, *Nuclear Defence*, pp. 143–69.

109. Peter Douglas Feaver, *Guarding the Guardians: Civilian Control of Nuclear Weapons in the United States* (Ithaca and London: Cornell University Press, 1992), pp. 3–28.

110. Lee Clarke, *Mission Improbable: Using Fantasy Documents to Tame Disaster* (Chicago and London: University of Chicago Press, 1999). Clarke's focus is on the management of disaster, but his analysis applies equally to the planning of nuclear war.

111. Ibid., p. 16.

112. Ibid., p. 41.

Chapter 3. Strategic Culture

1. Nanda, "PM Unveils Doctrine of Minimum Credible Deterrence."

2. Government of India, Ministry of External Affairs, *Draft Report of National Security Advisory Board on Indian Nuclear Doctrine*.

3. Rajesh M. Basrur, "Enduring Contradictions: Deterrence Theory and the Draft Nuclear Doctrine," *Economic and Political Weekly*, 35, 8–9 (September 26, 2000), pp. 610–13; and P. R. Chari, "India's Nuclear Doctrine: Confused Ambitions," *Nonproliferation Review*, 7, 3 (Fall–Winter 2000), pp. 123–35.

4. "India Not to Engage in a Nuclear Arms Race: Jaswant," (Interview), *Hindu*, November 29, 1999, p. 14.

5. "Cabinet Committee on Security Reviews Operationalization of India's Nuclear Doctrine."

6. Michael W. Desch, "Culture Clash: Assessing the Importance of Ideas in Security Studies," *International Security*, 23, 1 (Summer 1998), pp. 141–70. For a wider appraisal of culture in social science, see Richard J. Ellis and Michael Thompson, eds., *Culture Matters* (Boulder, CO and Oxford: Westview Press, 1997).

7. This section and the next draw extensively from Rajesh M. Basrur, "Nuclear Weapons and Indian Strategic Culture," *Journal of Peace Research*, 38, 2 (March 2001), pp. 181–98.

8. Colin S. Gray, *Modern Strategy* (Oxford: Oxford University Press, 1999), p. 28.

9. Colin S. Gray, "In Praise of Strategy," *Review of International Studies*, 29, 2 (April 2003), p. 292. There has, however, been a methodological debate as to whether it is possible to isolate and measure cultural variables. Gray, a realist, is skeptical, while Iain Johnston, a culturalist, is not. See Colin S. Gray, "Strategic Culture as Context: The First Generation of Theory Strikes Back," *Review of International Studies*, 25, 1 (January 1999), pp. 49–69; Alastair Iain Johnston, "Strategic Cultures Revisited: Reply to Colin Gray," *Review of International Studies*, 25, 3 (July 1999), pp. 519–23; Stuart Poore, "What Is the Context? A Reply to the Gray-Johnston Debate on Strategic Culture," *Review of International Studies*, 29, 2 (April 2003), pp. 279–84; and Gray, "In Praise of Strategy."

10. Jack Snyder, "Anarchy and Culture: Insights from the Anthropology of War," *International Organization*, 56, 1 (Winter 2002), pp. 7–45.

11. Muthiah Alagappa, ed., *Asian Security Practice: Material and Ideational Influences* (Stanford, CA: Stanford University Press, 1998).

12. Alastair Iain Johnston, *Cultural Realism: Culture and Grand Strategy in Chinese History* (Princeton, NJ: Princeton University Press, 1995). See also Jeffrey S. Lantis, "Strategic Culture and National Security Policy," *International Studies Review*, 4, 3 (Fall 2002), pp. 87–113.

13. Desch, "Culture Clash," pp. 146–47.

14. Ken Booth, *Strategy and Ethnocentrism* (New York: Holmes & Meier, 1979).

15. Gregory D. Foster, "A Conceptual Foundation for the Development of Strategy," in James C. Gaston, ed., *Grand Strategy and the Decisionmaking Process* (Washington, DC: National Defense University Press, 1992), p. 74.

16. Elizabeth Kier, "Culture and Military Doctrine: France between the Wars," *International Security*, 19, 4 (Spring 1995), pp. 65–93.

17. Beatrice Heuser, *Nuclear Mentalities? Strategies and Beliefs in Britain, France and the FRG* (Basingstoke and London: Macmillan; New York: St. Martin's Press, 1998), pp. 260–68.

18. Peter J. Katzenstein, ed., *The Culture of National Security* (New York: Columbia University Press, 1996).

19. Miriam D. Becker, "Strategic Culture and Ballistic Missile Defense: Russia and the United States," *Air Power Journal*, 8, Special Issue (1994), pp. 57–68; Johnston, *Cultural Realism*. For a contrary view emphasizing the defensive nature of Chinese strategy, see Tiejun Zhang, "Chinese Strategic Culture: Traditional and Present Features," *Comparative Strategy*, 21, 2 (July–September 2002), pp. 73–90.

20. Hans Binnendijk, ed., *National Negotiating Styles* (Washington, DC: Center for the Study of Foreign Affairs, Foreign Service Institute, U.S. Department of State, 1987).

21. Michael Haas, "Asian Culture and International Relations," in Jongsuk Chay, ed., *Culture and International Relations* (New York, Westport, CT and London: Praeger, 1990).

22. George K. Tanham, *Indian Strategic Thought: An Interpretive Essay* (Santa Monica, CA: Rand, 1992), p. 17.

23. Andrew Latham, "The Role of Culture and Identity in Indian Arms Control and Disarmament Policy," in Keith Krause, ed., *Cross-Cultural Dimensions of Multilateral Nonproliferation and Arms Control Dialogue* (Ottawa: Nonproliferation, Arms Control and Disarmament Division, Department of Foreign Affairs and International Trade, 1997), p. 120.

24. Michael Krepon, Khurshid Khoja, Michael Newbill, and Jenny S. Drezin, eds., *A Handbook of Confidence Building Measures for Regional Security*, 3rd ed. (Washington, DC: Henry L. Stimson Center, 1998), pp. 189–210.

25. Jaswant Singh, *Defending India* (Basingstoke: Macmillan, 1999), pp. 13, 16.

26. Sandy Gordon, *India's Rise to Power* (Basingstoke and London: Macmillan, 1995), p. 7.

27. Kanti Bajpai, "Indian Strategic Culture," in Michael R. Chambers, ed., *South Asia in 2020: Future Strategic Balances and Alliances*(Carlisle, PA: Strategic Studies Institute, U.S. Army War College, November 2002).

28. The same methodological problem is present in Andrew Scobell's otherwise excellent essay, "'Cult of Defense' and 'Great Power Dreams': The Influence of Strategic Culture on China's Relationship with India," in Chambers, ed., *South Asia in 2020*. For a more balanced approach analyzing both thought and practice, see Hasan-Askari Rizvi, "Pakistan's Strategic Culture," in the same volume.

29. Bajpai, "Indian Strategic Culture," p. 250. Bajpai is referring to Johnston's detailed study of Chinese strategic culture in *Cultural Realism*.

30. True, there may persist preferences that incongruously hark back to an earlier era, such as strategies for conventional war in a nuclear context. The problem is touched on in Chapter 4.

31. Mary Jo Hatch, *Organization Theory: Modern, Symbolic and Postmodern Perspectives* (Oxford: Oxford University Press, 1997), p. 205.

32. Peter Lasuutari, *Researching Culture* (London, Thousand Oaks, and New Delhi: Sage, 1995), p. 25.

33. Yosef Lapid, "Culture's Ship: Returns and Departures in International Relations Theory," in Yosef Lapid and Friedrich Kratochwil, eds., *The Return of Culture and Identity in International Relations Theory* (Boulder, CO and London: Lynne Rienner, 1996), p. 7. For a dynamic, historical perspective in a related area—changing popular culture with respect to atomic weapons in the United States—see Scott C. Zeman and Michael A. Amundson, eds., *Atomic Culture: How We Learned to Stop Worrying and Love the Bomb* (Boulder, CO: University Press of Colorado, 2004).

34. For a discussion of change, including the possibility of abrupt change, see Lantis, "Strategic Culture and National Security Policy," pp. 109–13.

35. Critics often confuse the Indo-Pakistani tit-for-tat testing of missiles with arms racing. This is more profitably viewed as a form of rhetoric which, along with verbal battles, is a powerful element in the strategic rivalry between India and Pakistan. The Indian quest for improved capability (intermediate-range missiles, deep strike bombers, SLBMs) is aimed at acquiring what is believed to be a minimal capability against China.

36. M. N. Panini and Veena R. Kumar, "Sociology of Strategic Decision-Making on National Security Issues in India," *Journal of Peace Studies*, 5, 2 (1998), pp. 7–28.

37. Karnad, *Nuclear Weapons and Indian Security*, pp. 3–20. Karnad makes an inter-

esting case (pp. 14–20) for the ancients' familiarity with at least the concept, if not the technology, of weapons of mass destruction, including chemical and biological warfare.

38. Jayantanuja Bandyopadhyaya, *The Making of India's Foreign Policy*, revised ed. (New Delhi: Allied Publishers, 1979), pp. 286–321.

39. Karnad, *Nuclear Weapons and Indian Security*, pp. 30–65.

40. Cited in Y. P. Anand, *What Mahatma Gandhi Said about the Bomb* (New Delhi: National Gandhi Museum, 1998), pp. 15–16.

41. Karnad, *Nuclear Weapons and Indian Security*, p. 32.

42. For the view that Nehru failed to understand the centrality of power in international relations, see Gopal Krishna, "India and the International Order: Retreat from Idealism," in Hedley Bull and Adam Watson, eds., *The Expansion of International Society* (Oxford: Clarendon Press, 1984), esp. p. 286.

43. Kanti Bajpai, "Nehru and Disarmament," in M. V. Kamath, ed., *Nehru Revisited* (Mumbai: Nehru Centre, 2003). As Bajpai points out, Nehru was no dreamer. His vision of universal disarmament was tempered by an awareness that measured arm control agreements were valuable steps toward that goal. Ibid., p. 372.

44. Michael Brecher, *India and World Politics: Krishna Menon's View of the World* (London: Oxford University Press, 1968), pp. 231–32, 312–14.

45. Cited in B. N. Mullick, *My Years with Nehru* (Bombay: Allied Publishers, 1972), p. 161.

46. N. M. Ghatate, "Disarmament Logic: Learning from Nehru's Nuclear Vision," *Times of India*, September 18, 1998, p. 12.

47. Cited in Ashok Kapur, *Pokhran and Beyond: India's Nuclear Behavior* (New Delhi: Oxford University Press, 2001), p. 54.

48. Ashok Kapur, *India's Nuclear Option* (New York: Praeger, 1976), pp. 193–94.

49. Subrahmanyam, "India's Nuclear Policy," p. 27.

50. B. N. Pande, *Indira Gandhi* (New Delhi: Publications Division, Ministry of Information and Broadcasting, Government of India, 1989), p. 363.

51. Cited in Perkovich, *India's Nuclear Bomb*, p. 201.

52. R. R. Subramanian, "The Janata Government's Nuclear Policy," in Surendra Chopra, ed., *Studies in India's Foreign Policy* (Amritsar: Department of Political Science, Guru Nanak Dev University, n.d. [1980]), p. 44.

53. "Vajpayee Opposed Move to Resume Nuclear Programme in 1979: Congress," *Hindu*, April 3, 2004 <http://www.thehindu.com/2004/04/03/stories/2004040304631100.htm>. Desai was personally opposed to restarting the program, but accepted a 3:2 vote in favor of resumption.

54. Cited in Chengappa, *Weapons of Peace*, p. 304.

55. Ibid., p. 330.

56. Ibid., pp. 331–32; Subrahmanyam, "India's Nuclear Policy," p. 44.

57. Chengappa, *Weapons of Peace*, pp. 384–87; Raj Chengappa, "Boom for Boom," *India Today*, April 23, 1999, pp. 54–56.

58. C. Raja Mohan, "Portrait of Rao as N-architect," *Indian Express*, December 7, 2004 <http://www.indianexpress.com/full_story.php?content_id=61667>.

59. Chengappa, *Weapons of Peace*, pp. 332–33.

60. "Credit Rao for Pokhran-II: Atal," *Times of India*, December 27, 2004 <http://timesofindia.indiatimes.com/articleshow/971809.cms>.

61. Cited in "Impact of a Nuclear Strike," *BBC News*, May 29, 2002 <http://www.bbc.co.uk/1/hi/world/south_asia/2012543.stm>.

62. K. Subrahmanyam, "Politics of Security: When Vajpayee Said 'No' to Going Nuclear," *Times of India*, April 10, 2004 <http://timesofindia.indiatimes.com/articleshow/608713.cms>. Vajpayee's objection did not amount to rejection of nuclear deterrence, but was prompted by the desire not to provoke Pakistan.

63. Amit Baruah, "UPA Continuing NDA Policy on Missile Defence," *Hindu*, August 20, 2004 <http://www.thehindu.com/2004/08/20/stories/2004082013951100.htm>.

64. Vinod Sharma and Saurabh Shukla, "Common N-doctrine Needed: Natwar," *Hindustan Times*, June 2, 2004 <http://www.hindustantimes.com/news/181_827979,001301080000.htm>.

65. Ganguly, "India's Pathway to Pokhran II," 162–63.

66. Cited in Chengappa, *Weapons of Peace*, p. 260.

67. Perkovich, *India's Nuclear Bomb*, pp. 450–51.

68. Chengappa, *Weapons of Peace*, pp. 253–55, 260, 294–95, 297–98, 301.

69. Shrikant Paranjpe, *Parliament and the Making of Indian Foreign Policy* (New Delhi: Radiant, 1997).

70. Itty Abraham, *The Making of the Indian Atomic Bomb* (New Delhi: Orient Longman, 1998); Perkovich, *India's Nuclear Bomb*.

71. Chengappa, *Weapons of Peace*, pp. 88–89.

72. Ibid., pp. 260–61.

73. Ibid., p. 393.

74. Ibid., p. 397.

75. David Cortright and Amitabh Mattoo, eds., *India and the Bomb* (Notre Dame, IN: University of Notre Dame Press, 1996), p. 117.

76. Ibid., p. 118.

77. Heuser, *Nuclear Mentalities?*

78. Kanwal, *Nuclear Defence*; Karnad, *Nuclear Weapons and Indian Security*; Raja Menon, *A Nuclear Strategy for India* (New Delhi, Thousand Oaks, and London: Sage, 2000); Vijai K. Nair, "The Structure of An Indian Nuclear Deterrent," in Mattoo, ed., *India's Nuclear Deterrent*; Jasjit Singh, "A Nuclear Strategy for India," in Jasjit Singh, ed., *Nuclear India* (New Delhi: Knowledge World, 1998); K. Subrahmanyam, "Nuclear Force Design and Minimum Deterrence Strategy for India," in Bharat Karnad, ed., *Future Imperilled* (New Delhi: Viking, 1994); and K. Sundarji, "Doctrine—I & II."

79. Menon, *Nuclear Strategy for India*, p. 298.

80. For a recent review, see *The World's Nuclear Arsenals*, Center for Defense Information, Washington, DC, July 8, 2004 <http://www.cdi.org/program/document.cfm?DocumentID=2187&StartRow=1&ListRows=10&appendURL=&Orderby=D.DateLastUpdated&ProgramID=32&from_page=index.cfm>.

81. The estimate of warheads is taken from *World's Nuclear Arsenals*.

82. Chengappa, *Weapons of Peace*, p. 129.

83. The handing over of the Agni missiles to the Army was announced by Defence Minister Fernandes in October 2003. Arun Dhar and Sujit Chatterjee, "India's Nuke Command Chain in Place: Fernandes," *Rediff.com*, October 5, 2003 <http://in.rediff.com/news/2003/oct/05fer.htm>.

84. Vladimir Radyuhin, "Russia Building Nuclear Submarines for India," *Hindu*, October 14, 2004 <http://www.thehindu.com/2004/10/14/stories/2004101406141200.htm>.

85. See "India Special Weapons Guide: Submarines," Federation of American Scientists, Washington, DC <http://216.239.57.100/search?q=cache:SV1X4BKT01IC: www.fas.org/nuke/guide/india/sub/+sagarika,+cruise+missile&hl=en&ie=UTF-8 (accessed February 19, 2003>. For a detailed description of the latter, see Karnad, *Nuclear Weapons and India's Security*, pp. 646–59. However, very little progress appears to have been made. See Praveen Swami, "Nuclear Submarine Project May Get a Kick–Start," *Hindu*, May 27, 2004 <http://www.thehindu.com/2004/05/27/stories/2004052705480100.htm>.

86. "Dhanush Missile Successfully Test–fired," *Hindu*, November 8, 2004 <http://www.thehindu.com/2004/11/08/stories/2004110806870100.htm>.

86. T. S. Subramanian, "Brahmos–II Bang on Target," *Hindu*, December 22, 2004 <http://www.thehindu.com/2004/12/22/stories/2004122202981200.htm>. The missile, which is supersonic, officially has a range of 290 km. It has been successfully tested from sea and land platforms, and an air–launched version is on the cards.

88. Josy Joseph, "India's nuclear infrastructure nearly ready," *Rediff.com*, October 10, 2003 <http://us.rediff.com/news/2003/oct/10spec.htm>.

89. Rajat Pandit, "Nuclear Force Chief Set to Retire," *Times of India*, June 1, 2004 <http://timesofindia.indiatimes.com/articleshow/711515.cms>.

90. Rahul Bedi, "A Credible Nuclear Deterrent?" *Frontline*, March 29–April 11, 2003 <http://www.frontlineonnet.com/fl2007/stories/20030411003009700.htm>. This was admitted as much by the Chief of Integrated Defence Staff, Lieutenant General P. S. Joshi. R. H. Tahiliani, "Calling for the Tri–Shakti Spirit," *Indian Express*, October 28, 2004 <http://www.indianexpress.com/full_story.php?content_id=57794>.

91. "Cabinet Committee on Security Reviews Operationalization of India's Nuclear Doctrine."

92. Joseph, "India's Nuclear Infrastructure Nearly Ready."

93. Gregory F. Giles and James E. Doyle, "Indian and Pakistani Views on Nuclear Deterrence," *Comparative Strategy*, 15, 2 (April–June 1996), p. 143.

94. Subrahmanyam, "A Credible Deterrent."

95. Chellaney, "After the Tests," p. 107.

96. Karnad, "A Thermonuclear Deterrent," in Mattoo, ed., *India's Nuclear Deterrent*, pp. 120–21.

97. Kotera M. Bhimaya, "Nuclear Deterrence in South Asia: Civil-Military Relations in Decision-Making," *Asian Survey*, 34, 7 (July 1994), pp. 644–45; Brahma Chellaney, "Nuclear-Deterrent Posture," in Brahma Chellaney, ed., *Securing India's Future in the New Millennium* (Hyderabad: Orient Longman, 1999), pp. 211–12.

98. Lantis, "Strategic Culture and National Security Policy." For a study of sudden change from an offensive realist to a defensive realist strategic culture, see Henrikki Heikka, *Beyond the Cult of the Offensive: The Evolution of Soviet/Russian Strategic Culture and Its Implication for the Nordic-Baltic Region* (Helsinki: Ulkopoliittinen Instituuttti & Institut für Europäische Politik, 2000).

99. Here, the term "paradigm" is used differently from Chapter 1 to denote established ways of doing things based on consensual rules and standards. Thomas S. Kuhn, *The Structure of Scientific Revolutions*, 2nd ed. (Chicago and London: University of Chicago Press, 1970). Strategic culture as a "standardized" set of beliefs and practices is analogous to Kuhn's conception of paradigms in science. A strategic culture,

like a Kuhnian paradigm, may experience a sense of increasing anomalies in response to internal and external pressures, which may result in a "crisis" that leads to its transformation. For Kuhn's discussion of paradigmatic crisis, see *Structure of Scientific Revolutions*, pp. 66–91.

100. Obviously, the Kuhnian analogy stops here. Unlike the crises that bring about scientific revolutions, the crisis of Indian strategic culture is in large measure due to a failure to fully comprehend and adhere to the fundamentals of minimum deterrence.

101. Sumona Dasgupta, "Militarization of the Indian State since the 1980's," in Raza, ed., *Generals and Governments in India and Pakistan*.

102. Sunil Dasgupta, "India: The New Militaries," in Muthiah Alagappa, ed., *Coercion and Governance: The Declining Political Role of the Military in Asia* (Stanford, CA: Stanford University Press, 2001).

103. Karnad, *Nuclear Weapons and Indian Security*, p. 616.

104. Kraig, "The Political and Strategic Imperatives of Nuclear Deterrence in South Asia," pp. 24–30.

105. Ibid., p. 30. Kraig adds a qualification (ibid.): this is based not on the U.S. Cold War approach of keeping open a variety of *nuclear* options, but on the U.S. goal during the Cold War of "creating uncertainties for the Soviets about the consequences of aggressive *conventional* moves" (emphasis added).

106. "India, Pak Renew Nuclear Pact Despite Tension," *Times of India*, January 1, 2002 <http://timesofindia.indiatimes.com/articleshow.asp?art_id=963168785>.

107. John Wilson Lewis and Xue Litai, "China's Search for a Modern Air Force," *International Security*, 24, 1 (Summer 1999), pp. 76–82.

Chapter 4. Compellence in a Nuclear Environment

1. For an earlier version of this chapter, see Rajesh M. Basrur, "Coercive Diplomacy in a Nuclear Environment: The December 13 Crisis," in Rafiq Dossani and Henry S. Rowen, eds., *Prospects for Peace in South Asia* (Stanford, CA: Stanford University Press, 2005).

2. For general discussions on compellence, or coercive diplomacy, embracing both conventional and nuclear weapons, see David Baldwin, "Thinking about Threats," *Journal of Conflict Resolution*, 15, 1 (March 1971), pp. 71–78; Daniel Byman and Matthew Waxman, *The Dynamics of Coercion: American Foreign Policy and the Limits of Military Might* (Cambridge: Cambridge University Press, 2002); Gordon A. Craig and Alexander L. George, *Force and Statecraft: Diplomatic Problems of Our Time* (New York and Oxford: Oxford University Press, 1983), pp. 189–204; Alexander L. George, *Forceful Persuasion: Coercive Diplomacy as an Alternative to War* (Washington, DC: U.S. Institute of Peace Press, 1991); and Walter J. Petersen, "Deterrence and Compellence: A Critical Assessment of Conventional Wisdom," *International Studies Quarterly*, 30, 3 (September 1986), pp. 269–94. For specifically nuclear contexts, see Desmond Ball, Hans A. Bethe, Bruce G. Blair, Paul Bracken, Ashton B. Carter, Hillman Dickinson, Richard L Garwin, Kurt Gottfried, David Holloway, Henry W. Kendall, Lloyd R. Leavitt, Jr., Richard Ned Lebow, Condoleezza Rice, Peter C. Stein, John D. Steinbruner, Lucja U. Swiatkowski, and Paul D. Tomb, *Crisis Stability and Nuclear War* (Ithaca, NY: Peace Studies Program, Cornell University, 1987); Richard K. Betts, *Nuclear Blackmail and Nuclear Balance* (Washington, DC: Brookings

Institution, 1987); Daniel S. Geller, "Nuclear Weapons, Deterrence, and Crisis Escalation," *Journal of Conflict Resolution*, 34, 2 (June 1990), pp. 291–310; Paul Huth and Bruce Russett, "Testing Deterrence Theory: Rigor Makes a Difference," *World Politics*, 42, 4 (July 1990), pp. 466–501; Edward Rhodes, *Power and MADness: The Logic of Nuclear Coercion* (New York: Columbia University Press, 1989); Thomas C. Schelling, *Strategy of Conflict* (Cambridge, MA and London: Harvard University Press, 1960); and Schelling, *Arms and Influence*. On South Asia, see Chari, "Nuclear Crisis, Escalation Control, and Deterrence in South Asia"; and Koithara, "Coercion and Risk-Taking in Nuclear South Asia."

3. Sabina Inderjit, "Advani Tells Pakistan to Roll Back Its Anti-India Policy," *Times of India*, May 19, 1998, p. 7.

4. Michael Krepon and Chris Gagné, eds., *The Stability-Instability Paradox: Nuclear Weapons and Brinkmanship in South Asia* (Washington, DC: Henry L. Stimson Center, June 2001). For the original formulation of the concept, see Glen Snyder, "The Balance of Power and the Balance of Terror," in Paul Seabury, ed., *The Balance of Power* (San Francisco: Chandler, 1965), pp. 194–201.

5. *From Surprise to Reckoning: The Kargil Review Committee Report* (New Delhi: Sage, 2000), pp. 197–99.

6. Cited in Harjinder Sidhu, "Ansari Arrest Proves Pak Hand: PM," *Hindustan Times*, February 11, 2002 <http://www.hindustantimes.com/nonfram/110202/detNAT01.asp>. The widespread Indian perception of betrayal tended initially to be directed at the Pakistani military, but later became less discriminating. The point became moot after General Musharraf's coup soon after Kargil.

7. Stephen Philip Cohen, *The Idea of Pakistan* (New Delhi: Oxford University Press, 2004), pp. 77, 105; and Sumit Ganguly, "Conflict and Crisis in South and Southwest Asia," in Michael E. Brown, ed., *The International Dimensions of Internal Conflict* (Cambridge, MA and London: MIT Press, 1996), p. 157.

8. Peter Chalk, "Pakistan's Role in the Kashmir Insurgency," *Jane's Intelligence Review*, September 1, 2001, reproduced on the website of the RAND Corporation: <http://www.rand.org/hot/op-eds/090101JIR.html> (accessed February 14, 2003).

9. *From Surprise to Reckoning*, p. 241.

10. Kraig, "The Political and Strategic Imperatives of Nuclear Deterrence in South Asia," pp. 24–30. See also "Hot Pursuit Option Still Open: Advani," *Hindu*, October 25, 2001 <http://www.hinduonnet.com/thehindu/2001/10/25/stories/01250001.htm>.

11. Cited in C. Raja Mohan, "Fernandes Unveils 'Limited War' Doctrine," *Hindu*, January 25, 2000 <http://www.the-hindu.com/stories01250001.htm>.

12. Ibid.

13. C. Raja Mohan, "Between War and Peace," *Hindu*, December 20, 2001 <http://www.hinduonnet.com/thehindu/2001/12/20/stories/2001122001231000.htm>.

14. Cited in Celia W. Dugger, "In Kashmir Sequel, Seeking a New Ending," *New York Times*, January 2, 2002 <http://www.nytimes.com/2002/01/02/international/asia/02INDI.html>.

15. Michael Krepon, "Last-Minute Diplomacy," *Outlook*, April 29, 2002, p. 24.

16. Sandeep Dikshit, "Govt Orders Withdrawal of Troops from IB," *Hindu*, October 17, 2002 <http://www.thehindu.com/2002/10/17/stories/2002101707350100.htm>.

17. Rajesh M. Basrur, "Kargil, Terrorism, and India's Strategic Shift," *India Review*, 1, 4 (October 2002), pp. 39–56.

18. Ashley J. Tellis, C. Christine Fair, and Jamison Jo Medby, *Limited Conflicts under the Nuclear Umbrella: Indian and Pakistani Lessons from the Kargil Crisis* (Santa Monica, CA: RAND, 2001), p. 16.

19. Schelling, *Strategy of Conflict*, pp. 187–203.

20. V. R. Raghavan, "Limited War and Nuclear Escalation in South Asia," *Nonproliferation Review*, 8, 3 (Fall–Winter 2001), p. 89.

21. Singh, "Beyond Kargil," p. 226.

22. For a trenchant critique from a leading analyst and former Director General of Military Operations in the Indian Army, see V. R. Raghavan, "Limited War and Strategic Liability," *Hindu*, February 2, 2000 <http://www.the-hindu.com/stories/05022523.htm>. Raghavan makes the plausible case that Kargil was not a limited war, but "a series of local military actions . . . to clear Indian territory of intruders."

23. "Indian Army General Warns Pak," *Times of India*, October 31, 2001 <http://www.timesofindia.com/articleshow.asp?art_id=534060591>.

24. Rajiv Chandrasekaran, "For India, Deterrence May Not Prevent War," *Washington Post*, January 17, 2002 <http://www.washingtonpost.com/wp-dyn/articles/A58170-2002Jan16.html>.

25. Ibid.

26. Cited in Seymour M. Hersh, "The Getaway," *New Yorker*, January 28, 2002 <http:www.newyorker.com/FACT/?020128fa_FACT>.

27. This point, though never officially articulated, was made twice in quick succession by K. Subrahmanyam, the influential strategic analyst and former Convenor of the NSAB. See K. Subrahmanyam, "Containing Pakistan," *Times of India*, December 31, 2001 <http://timesofindia.indiatimes.com/articleshow.asp?art_id=53929403>; and K. Subrahmanyam, "Indo-Pak Nuclear Conflict Unlikely," *Times of India*, January 2, 2002 <http://timesofindia.indiatimes.com/articleshow.asp?art_id=1674711498>.

28. Cited in Chandrasekaran, "For India, Deterrence May Not Prevent War."

29. "Pak Would Be Wiped Out if It Uses Nuclear Bomb: BJP" *Hindustan Times*, December 26, 2001 <http://www.hindustantimes.com/nonfram/251201/dLNAT03.asp>.

30. Cited in "We Could Take a Strike and Survive. Pakistan Won't: Fernandes," *Hindustan Times*, December 30, 2001 <http://www.hindustantimes.com/nonfram/301201/detfea06.asp>.

31. Cited in Celia Dugger, "Following India's Brinkmanship, Ominous Preparations to Follow Through," *New York Times*, January 12, 2002 <http://www.nytimes.com/2002/01/12/international/asia/12DELH.html>.

32. Cited in Celia W. Dugger, "Indian General Talks Bluntly of War and a Nuclear Threat," *New York Times*, January 12, 2002 <http://www.nytimes.com/2002/01/12/international/asia/12INDI.html>. While an official hastened to say that the General's remarks had not been cleared by the Prime Minister's Office, that would have pertained to the actual form and style rather than the substance of what he said. In the context of civil-military relations in India, it is inconceivable that an Army Chief would have broached the subject of potential nuclear conflict without clearance from the political leadership.

33. This logic was stated to a newsman by C. Uday Bhaskar, Deputy Director of the IDSA. Chandrasekaran, "For India, Deterrence May Not Prevent War."

34. Cited in Gaurav C. Sawant, "'Nuclear Wars Are Not Meant to Be Fought, Especially between Nuclear Powers,'" (Interview), *Indian Express*, January 6, 2002 <http://www.indian-express.com/ie20020106/cent1.html>.

35. Schelling, *Arms and Influence*, pp. 69–78.

36. On the decomposition of threats for greater effectiveness, see Schelling, *Strategy of Conflict*, pp. 41–43.

37. Vishal Thapar, "Prithvi Missiles Moved Near Border in Punjab," *Hindustan Times*, December 25, 2001 <http://www.hindustantimes.com/nonfram/arcscript/htarchive.asp>.

38. Terrey Friel and Jane Macartney, "India Deploys Planes as Tensions with Pakistan Rise," *Washington Post*, December 26, 2001 <ttp://www.nytimes.com/2001/12/28/international/asia/28INDI.html >.

39. Celia W. Dugger, "India and Pakistan Add to War Footing," *New York Times*, December 28, 2001 <http://www.washingtonpost.com/wp-dyn/articles/A25643-2001Dec26.html>.

40. "Army Prepares for Exercise along Border," *Times of India*, December 29, 2001 <http://timesofindia.indiatimes.com/articleshow.asp?art_id=1155620316>.

41. John F. Burns, "Pakistan Appeals to US as India Continues Border Buildup," *New York Times*, December 30, 2001 <http://www.nytimes.com/2001/12/30/international/asia/30INDI.html>.

42. Celia W. Dugger, "India Test-Fires Intermediate-Range Missile," *New York Times*, January 25, 2002 <http://www.nytimes.com/2002/01/25/international/asia/25INDI.html>.

43. John F. Burns, "Pakistan Leader in Sharp Rebuke to Indian Threat," *New York Times*, December 26, 2001 <http://www.nytimes.com/2001/12/26/international/asia/26STAN.html>.

44. Parul Chandra, "India Can Breach Indus Waters Treaty to Flood Pakistan," *Times of India*, December 27, 2001 <http://timesofindia.indiatimes.com/articleshow.asp?art_id=1522637704>.

45. Michael Pillsbury, "Strategic Acupuncture," *Foreign Policy*, 41 (Winter 1980–81), pp. 44–61.

46. Manoj Joshi, "Modernizing the Military: More Bark and More Bite," *Times of India*, November 15, 2003 <http://www.timesofindia.indiatimes.com/cms.dll/xml/uncomp/articleshow?msid=283543>.

47. Schelling, *Strategy of Conflict*, pp. 187–203.

48. Goldstein, *Deterrence and Security in the 21st Century*, pp. 46–52.

49. The relevance of a third party does, however, apply to extended deterrence (the protection of allies), which is not germane here. For an interesting discussion on how a small power may deter and coerce a large one by threatening its ally, see Robert E. Harkavy, "Triangular or Indirect Deterrence/Compellence: Something New in Deterrence Theory?" *Comparative Strategy*, 17, 1 (January–March 1998), pp. 63–81.

50. Shaukat Qadir, "An Analysis of the Kargil Conflict 1999," *Journal of the Royal United Services Institution*, 147, 2 (April 2002), pp. 24–30; Ayesha Siddiqa-Agha, *Pakistan's Arms Procurement and Military Buildup, 1979–99* (Basingstoke and New York: Palgrave, 2001), pp. 178–83.

51. The United States did get politically involved in the 1971 war to the extent of tilting toward Pakistan at the time, but only from afar. U.S. officials were not engaged in active diplomacy in the region at the time.

52. For case studies of the two crises, see Sumit Ganguly and Devin T. Hagerty, *Fearful Symmetry: India-Pakistan Crises in the Shadow of Nuclear Weapons* (New Delhi: Oxford University Press, 2005), pp. 68–115; and Hagerty, *Consequences of Nuclear Proliferation*, pp. 91–116, 133–70.

53. Interestingly, U.S. perceptions about the high risk of nuclear war in 1990 contrasted significantly with those of Indians and Pakistanis, who thought the risk was low. P. R. Chari, Pervaiz Iqbal Cheema, and Stephen Philip Cohen, *Perception, Politics and Security in South Asia: The Compound Crisis of 1990* (London and New York: RoutledgeCurzon, 2003), pp. 134–35.

54. David E. Sanger with Judith Miller, "Bush Meets India's Envoy; Fears of Pakistan War Deepen," *New York Times*, January 11, 2002 <http:www.nytimes.com/2002/01/11/international/asia/11PREX.html>. See also Michael R. Gordon, "As Threat Eases, U.S. Still Sees Peril in India-Pakistan Buildup," *New York Times*, January 20, 2002 <http:www.nytimes.com/2002/01/20/international/asia/20STRA.html>.

55. Cited in S. Rajagopalan, "Risk of Indo-Pak War Highest since 1971," *Hindustan Times*, February 2, 2002 <http://www.hindustantimes.com/nonfram/arcscript/htarchive.asp>.

56. Nicholas D. Kristof, "This Is Not a Test," *New York Times*, December 28, 2001 <http:www.nytimes.com/2001/12/28/opinion/28KRIS.html>.

57. "Bush Leans on Pakistan's President," *New York Times*, December 29, 2001 <http://www.nytimes.com/aponline/national/AP-Bush-India-Pakistan.html>.

58. Peter Slevin, "Pakistan Groups Called Terrorist Organizations," *Washington Post*, December 27, 2001 <http://www.washingtonpost.com/wp-dyn/articles/A28185-2001Dec26.html>.

59. John F. Burns, "Pakistan Moves against Groups Named by India," *New York Times*, December 29, 2001 <http://www.nytimes.com/2001/12/29/international/asia/29STAN.html>.

60. Alan Sipress, "Musharraf Urged to Calm S. Asia," *Washington Post*, January 12, 2002 <http://www.washingtonpost.com/wp-dyn/articles/A34181-2002Jan11.html>.

61. Cited in "In Musharraf's Words, a Day of Reckoning," *New York Times*, January 12, 2002 <http://www.nytimes.com/2002/01/12/international/12WIRETEXT.html>.

62. Chidanand Rajghatta, "Burden of De-escalation Now on India: Powell," *Times of India*, January 15, 2002 <http//:www.timesofindia.indiatimes.com/Articleshow.asp?art_id=1995028370>.

63. "Morning Terror in Jammu Casts Shadow on Days Ahead," *Indian Express*, May 15, 2002 <http://www.indianexpress.com/archive_frame.php>.

64. "Show Results, Bush Tells Musharraf," *Hindu*, May 27, 2002. <http:www.hinduonnet.com/thehindu/2002/06/01/stories/2002050704360100.htm>.

65. Sridhar Krishnaswami, "Infiltration Still On: Powell," *Hindu*, June 1, 2002 <http:www.hinduonnet.com/thehindu/2002/06/01/stories/2002060106880100.htm>.

66. David E. Sanger and Celia W. Dugger, "Bush Intervenes in Effort to Stop

Kashmir War," *New York Times*, June 6, 2002 <http://www.nytimes.com/2002//06/06/international/asia06PREX.html>.

67. Dirk Beveridge, "U.S. Envoy Says Tension Easing in South Asia," *Washington Post*, June 7, 2002 <http:www.washingtonpost.com/wp-dyn/articles/A11874-2002Jun.html>.

68. On this aspect, I rely on personal conversations with senior officials who have requested anonymity.

69. V. K. Sood and Pravin Sawhney, *Operation Parakram: The War Unfinished* (New Delhi, Thousand Oaks and London: Sage, 2003), pp. 62–63.

70. Richard K. Betts, "Is Strategy an Illusion?" *International Security*, 25, 2 (Fall 2000), pp. 5–50.

71. On the alleged absence of a culture of strategic thinking, see K. Subrahmanyam, "A Stillborn NSC: No Culture of Strategic Thinking," *Times of India*, October 30, 2000, p. 10.

72. C. Raja Mohan, *Crossing the Rubicon: The Shaping of India's New Foreign Policy* (New Delhi: Viking, 2003), p. 199.

73. Sood and Sawhney, *Operation Parakram*, pp. 178–79.

74. Schelling, *Arms and Influence*, p. 82.

75. Ross McDermott, *Risk-Taking in International Politics: Prospect Theory in American Foreign Policy* (Ann Arbor, MI: University of Michigan Press, 1998).

76. "Pak Deploys Shaheen," *Hindu*, May 21, 2002 <http://www.hinduonnet.com/thehindu/2002/05/21/stories/2002052106580100.htm>.

77. "Pakistan Test Fires Nuclear-Capable Missile," *Hindustan Times*, May 25, 2002 <http://www.hindustantimes.com/nonfram/arcscript/htarchive.asp>; "Pakistan Test Fires Second Missile," *Hindustan Times*, May 26, 2002 <http://www.hindustantimes.com/nonfram/arcscript/htarchive.asp>; "Pakistan Test Fires Third Missile," *Hindustan Times*, May 28, 2002 <http://www.hindustantimes.com/nonfram/arcscript/htarchive.asp>.

78. Sood and Sawhney, *Operation Parakram*, pp. 70–71.

79. C. Raja Mohan, cited in Vishal Thapar, "Troop Build-Up Marks a First in Military History," *Hindustan Times*, October 18, 2002 <http://www.hindustantimes.com/news/printedition/181002/detNAT02.shtml>.

80. Ibid.

81. Premvir Das, "The War that Never Was," *Indian Express*, November 18, 2002 <http://www.indianexpress.com/full_story.php?content_id=13210>.

82. Thomas W. Robinson, "The Sino-Soviet Border Conflict," in Stephen S. Kaplan, ed., *Diplomacy and Power: Soviet Armed Forces as a Political Instrument* (Washington, DC: Brookings Institution, 1981); Thomas Robinson, "The Sino-Soviet Border Conflict of 1969: New Evidence Three Decades Later," in Mark A. Ryan, David Michael Finkelstein, and Michael A. McDevitt, eds., *Chinese Warfighting: The PLA Experience since 1949* (Armonk, NY: M. E. Sharpe, 2003).

83. Robinson, "The Sino-Soviet Border Conflict," p. 283.

84. "Musharraf: Here's What I'll Do" (Interview), *Washington Post*, June 23, 2002 <http://www.washingtonpost.com/wp-dyn/articles/A26486-2002Jun21.html>.

85. "No Pak Leader Can Abandon Kashmir: Musharraf," *Hindu*, September 15, 2002 <http://www.thehindu.com/2002/09/15/stories/2002091504580100.htm>.

86. See George, *Forceful Persuasion*, pp. 77–78, for a discussion on this. "Asym-

metry of motivation," which George identifies as a key ingredient of success for a state attempting coercion, is the same as a favorable balance of commitment.

87. Karl Vick and Kamran Khan, "Pakistani Ambivalence Frustrates Hope for Kashmir Peace," *Washington Post*, June 29, 2002 <http://www.washingtonpost.com/wp-dyn/articles/A63680-2002Jun28.html>.

88. Paul Bracken, "Accidental Nuclear War," in Graham T. Allison, Albert Carnsdale, and Joseph S. Nye, Jr., eds., *Hawks, Doves and Owls* (New York and London: W. W. Norton, 1985); Jervis, *Meaning of the Nuclear Revolution*, pp. 87–94; Richard Ned Lebow, *Nuclear Crisis Management: A Dangerous Illusion* (Ithaca, NY and London: Cornell University Press, 1987); Jeffrey W. Legro, "Military Culture and Inadvertent Escalation in World War II," *International Security*, 18, 4 (Spring 1994), pp. 108–42; Rhodes, *Power and MADness*; Scott D. Sagan, *The Limits of Safety: Organizations, Accidents, and Nuclear Weapons* (Princeton, NJ: Princeton University Press, 1993); and Hakan Wiberg, Ib Damgaard Petersen, and Paul Smoker, eds., *Inadvertent Nuclear War: The Implications of the Changing Global Order* (Oxford: Pergamon Press, 1993).

89. Robert Powell, "The Theoretical Foundations of Deterrence," *Political Science Quarterly*, 100, 1 (Spring 1985), pp. 75–96.

90. Robert Powell, *Nuclear Deterrence Theory: The Search for Credibility* (Cambridge: Cambridge University Press, 1990), pp. 124–30.

91. Gaurav Kampani, "Placing the Indo-Pakistani Standoff in Perspective," *CNS Web Reports*, Center for Nonproliferation Studies, Monterey Institute of International Studies, Monterey, CA, April 8, 2002 <http://cns.miis.edu/pubs/reports/pdfs/indo-pak.pdf>.

92. "Lt-Gen Vij Moved Forces 'Too Close' to Border," *Times of India*, January 21, 2002 <http://timesofindia.indiatimes.com/articleshow.asp?art_id=1970101322>.

93. R. Prasannan, "Fall of a Star," *The Week*, March 17, 2002 <http:www.theweek.com/22mar17/events2.htm>; Sandeep Dikshit, "Air Marshal Bhatia Shifted," *Hindu*, April 25, 2002 <http://www.hinduonnet.com/thehindu/2002/04/25/stories/2002042508830100.htm>.

94. Sagan, *Limits of Safety*, pp. 28–45.

95. Ibid., pp. 146–50.

96. Bracken, "Accidental Nuclear War."

97. Jervis, *Meaning of the Nuclear Revolution*, pp. 87–94.

98. Praveen Swami, "When Pakistan Took Loonda Post," *Frontline,* August 31–September 13, 2002 <http://www.frontlineonnet.com/fl1918/19180220.htm>.

99. "War-Time Awards Conferred for 'Special Missions,'" *Hindu*, November 3, 2002. <http://www.hinduonnet.com/thehindu/2002/11/03/stories/2002110305071100.htm>.

100. Ball et al., *Crisis Stability and Nuclear War*, pp. 64–65.

101. Russell J. Leng, *Bargaining and Learning in Recurring Crises: Soviet-American, Egyptian-Israeli, and Indo-Pakistani Rivalries* (Ann Arbor: University of Michigan Press, 2000), esp. p. 278.

102. "Cross-Border Terrorism Still Continuing: Saxena," *Times of India*, October 21, 2002 <http://timesofindia.indiatimes.com/cms.dll/articleshow?artid=25860391>; Amit Baruah, "Pak. Not Honouring Commitment, India Tells Japan," *Hindu*, October 23, 2002 <http://www.thehindu.com/2002/10/23/stories/2002102306451100.

htm>; "Pak Troops Raid Indian Post," *Times of India*, October 9, 2003 <http://timesofindia.indiatimes.com/cms.dll/xml/uncomp/articleshow?msid=222109>; Saikat Datta, "Pak Thinks We Can't Attack, Use that to Advantage," *Indian Express*, June 8, 2003, p. 1.

103. Cited in Celia Dugger, "Following India's Brinkmanship, Ominous Preparations to Follow Through," *New York Times*, January 12, 2002 <http://www.nytimes.com/2002/01/12/international/asia/12DELH.html>.

Chapter 5. Missile Defense

1. The chapter draws extensively on Rajesh M. Basrur, "Missile Defense: An Indian Perspective," in Chris Gagné and Michael Krepon, eds., *The Impact of Missile Defenses on Southern Asia* (Washington, DC: Henry L. Stimson Center, 2002); reprinted in Michael Krepon and Chris Gagné, eds., *Nuclear Risk Reduction in South Asia* (New Delhi: Vision Books, 2003).

2. Tim Folger, "Shield of Dreams," *Discover*, 22, 11 (November 2001) <http://www.discover.com/current_issue/index.html>; James M. Lindsay and Michael O'Hanlon, *Defending America: The Case for Limited National Defense* (Washington, DC: Brookings Institution Press, 2001), pp. 29–49; *National Missile Defense: What Does It All Mean?* (Washington, DC: Center for Defense Information, September 2000).

3. In addition to the references in note 2, see Andrew M. Sessler, John M. Cornwall, Bob Dietz, Steve Fetter, Sherman Frankel, Richard L. Garwin, Kurt Gottfried, Lisbeth Gronlund, George N. Lewis, Theodore A. Postol, and David C. Wright, *Countermeasures: A Technical Evaluation of the Effectiveness of the Planned US National Missile Defense System* (Cambridge, MA: Union of Concerned Scientists and MIT Security Program, April 2000).

4. None of the Indian writings reviewed in Chapter 3 discusses the issue at length.

5. Daniel Smith, "A Brief History of 'Missiles' and Ballistic Missile Defense," in *National Missile Defense: What Does It All Mean?*

6. David M. Finkelstein, "Theater Missile Defense in Asia," paper presented at the Second Collaborative Workshop on East Asia Regional Security Futures, Nautilus Institute and Center for American Studies, Fudan University, at Shanghai, March 3–4, 2001 <http://www.nautilus.org/nukepolicy/workshops/shanghai-01/finkelsteinpaper.html>.

7. Dennis M. Gromley, "Enriching Expectations: 11 September's Lessons for Missile Defence," *Survival*, 44, 2 (Summer 2002), pp. 19–35.

8. Berry, "US National Missile Defense."

9. Waheguru Pal Singh Sidhu, "Regional Perspective: South Asia," in *International Perspectives on Missile Proliferation and Defenses*, Occasional Paper No. 5, Center for Nonproliferation Studies, Monterey, CA, March 2001.

10. C. Raja Mohan, "Countering Pak.'s Nuclear Blackmail," *Hindu*, January 1, 2003 <http://thehindu.com/2003/01/01/stories/2003010102021200.htm>.

11. Gregory Koblentz, "Theater Missile Defense and South Asia: A Volatile Mix," *Nonproliferation Review*, 4, 3 (Spring–Summer 1997), pp. 54–62.

12. Atul Aneja, "Indo-Israeli Partnership for a Missile Shield," *Hindu*, September 6, 2001 <http://www.hinduonnet.com/stories/0206000h.htm>.

13. "Time Bound Schedule Demanded for Developing Missile Shield," *Hindus-*

tan Times, April 23, 2002 <http://www.hindustantimes.com/nonfram/230402/dLNAT47.asp>.

14. "Washington Mulls Arrows to India," Missile Defense Briefing Report No. 69, American Foreign Policy Council, Washington, DC, September 4, 2002 <http://www.afpc.org/mdbr/mdbr69.htm>.

15. "Talks On with U.S. to Acquire Missile Shield," Hindu, June 29, 2002 <http://www.hinduonnet.com/stories/2002062902891100.htm>.

16. "'India Developing Ballistic Missiles to Counter Threats,'" Hindu, February 10, 2003 <http://thehindu.com/2003/02/10/stories/2003021001420800.htm>.

17. Rajat Pandit, "Russia Missile Offer Again," Times of India, December 1, 2002 <http://www.timesofindia.indiatimescom/cms/dll/xml/comp/articleshow?artid=2982177>.

18. "India Signs Radar Deal," BBC News, October 10, 2003 <http://news.bbc.o.uk/go/pr/fr/-/2/hi/south_asia/3180114.stm>.

19. Rajat Pandit, "India Wants Info on Patriot Missile System," Times of India, August 14, 2003 <http://www.timesofindia.indiatimes.com/cms/cms.dll/html/uncomp/articleshow?msid=129320>.

20. Amit Baruah, "'U.S., India Have Gone beyond Talking about Ballistic Missile Defences,'" Hindu, October 9, 2004 <http://www.thehindu.com/2004/10/09/stories/2004100912031200.htm>.

21. "India Asks US to Give Up Missile Testing," Hindu, July 4, 2000, cited in Michael J. Green and Toby F. Dalton, "Asian Reactions to US Missile Defense," NBR Analysis, 11, 3 (November 2000), p. 35.

22. "US Missile Test Won't Affect Indian Nuclear Plans," Hindu, July 10, 2000 <http://www.hinduonnet.com/thehindu/2000/07/10/stories/01100007.htm>.

23. "Talks with Albright, Talbott Fruitful, Says Jaswant," Hindu, July 30, 2000 <http://www.indiaserver.com/thehindu/2000/07/30/stories/01300003.htm>.

24. Berry, "US National Missile Defense," p. 28.

25. Cited in "India Welcomes Bush's NMD Plans," Times of India, May 3, 2001, p. 8.

26. C. Raja Mohan, "India Welcomes Bush Plan for Cuts in N-Arsenals," Hindu, May 3, 2001 <http://www.the-hindu.com/stories/010300001.htm>; Pramit Pal Chaudhuri, "India Endorses Nuke Strategy Shift," Hindustan Times, May 3, 2001 <http://www.hindustantimes.com/nonfram/030501/detfr002.asp>.

27. Nicholas Berry, "Did India Endorse Missile Defense? Not Exactly," Center for Defense Information Asia Forum, May 29, 2001 <http://www.cdi.org/asia/fa052901.html>.

28. J. N. Dixit, "'India's Response to NMD Was Hasty,'" Indiaabroaddaily.com, May 19, 2001 <http://www.indiaabroaddaily.com/2001/05/19/19hasty.html>.

29. Fred Weir, "Russia Offers NMD System to India," Hindustan Times, June 7, 2001 <http://www.hindustantimes.com/nonfram/070601/detFOR06.asp>.

30. Ibid.

31. C. Raja Mohan, "Indian Support to NMD Not at Russian Cost," Hindu, May 5, 2001 <http://www.the-hindu.com/stories/01050002.htm>.

32. "USA, Russia Should Discus NMD: India," Statesman, May 5, 2001 <http://www.thestatesman.net/page.news.php3?id=13454&type=Pageone7theme=A>.

33. Cited in Siddharth Varadarajan, "India Signals Wariness on Missile Defence,"

Hindu, September 6, 2004 <http://www.thehindu.com/2004/09/06/stories/2004090603261200.htm>.

34. Cited in Amit Baruah, "UPA Continuing NDA Policy on Missile Defence," *Hindu*, August 20, 2004 <http://www.thehindu.com/2004/08/20/stories/2004082013951100.htm>.

35. Raja Mohan, *Crossing the Rubicon*, pp. 20–24.

36. Steve LaMontagne, "NMD Will Slow India's Rise," *Hindu*, June 14, 2001 <http://www.the-hindu.com/stories/05141341.htm>.

37. Atul Aneja, "Defense Ministry Debating Deal with US over NMD," *Hindu*, May 13, 2001 <http://w.the-hindu.com/stories/0113000c.htm>.

38. View expressed by Bharat Karnad in Ramananda Sengupta, "Why India Embraced NMD," *Rediff.com*, May 10, 2001 <http://www.rediff.com/news/2001/may/10nmd.htm>.

39. Deepanshu Bagchee and Mathew C. J. Rudolph, "Misguided Missiles," *Hindu*, May 5, 2001 <http://www.the-hindu.com/stories/05051340.htm>; Muchkund Dubey, "Missile Defence and India," *Hindu*, May 9, 2001 <http://www.the-hindu.com/stories/05092523.htm>; Gaurav Kampani, "How a US National Missile Defence Will Affect South Asia," *CNS Reports*, May 2000 <http://cns.miis.edu/pubs/reports/usmlsa.htm>; Mandavi Mehta, "Looking beyond the Subcontinent," *Newspaper Today*, May 14, 2001 <http://www.thenewspapertoday.com/editor/?>; Arpit Rajain, "The US National Missile Defense and South Asia," Article No. 395, Institute for Peace and Conflict Studies, July 30, 2000 <http://www.ipcs.org/issues/articles/395-ndi-arpit.html>; and Achin Vanaik, "Ballistic Missile Defense: Consequences for South Asia," Nuclear Age Peace Foundation, 2002 <http://www.wagingpeace.org/articles/bmd/vanaik_consequences_for_south_asia.html>. In fairness, I must acknowledge this was my initial view as well. See Rajesh M. Basrur, "Missile Defense: An Indian Perspective," in David Krieger and Carah Ong, eds., *A Maginot Line in the Sky: International Perspectives on Ballistic Missile Defense* (Santa Barbara, CA: Nuclear Age Peace Foundation, 2001). However, as is evident from my argument here, I have revised my opinion on this specific point. Note: The reference in note 1 of this chapter was inadvertently given the same title by editors as the paper cited here, but is different in content.

40. To a limited extent, reflecting thought rather than action, this view is confirmed by the prevailing sentiment in the Chinese strategic community. See Joanne Tompkins, "How U.S. Strategic Policy Is Changing China's Nuclear Plans," *Arms Control Today*, 3, 1 (January–February 2003) <http://www.armscontrol.org/act/2003_01-02/tompkins_janfeb03.asp>.

41. "'Bush's Security Team Can Destabilize South Asia,'" *Hindustan Times*, January 12, 2001 <http:www.hindustantimes.com/nonfram/120101/detFOR05.asp>. For a more qualified assessment, see Timothy D. Hoyt, "South Asia," in James J. Wirtz and Jeffrey A. Larsen, eds., *Rockets' Red Glare: Missile Defenses and the Future of World Politics* (Boulder, CO: Westview Press, 2001). See also Brad Roberts, "US Ballistic Missile Defenses: Implications for Asia," paper presented at the Second Collaborative Workshop on East Asia Regional Security Futures, Nautilus Institute and Center for American Studies, Fudan University, at Shanghai, March 3–4, 2001 <http://www.nautilus.org/nukepolicy/workshops/shanghai%2D01/robertspaper.txt>; and Green and Dalton, "Asian Reactions to US Missile Defense."

42. Bagchee and Rudolph, "Misguided Missiles"; and Kampani, "How a U.S. National Missile Defense Will Affect South Asia." See also the views of the opposition Congress Party in C. Raja Mohan, "Cong. Against Antagonizing China on NMD," *Hindu*, May 8, 2001 <http://www.the-hindo.com/stories/0108004.htm>.

43. Bagchee and Rudolph, "Misguided Missiles"; Vanaik, "Ballistic Missile Defense"; Rajain, "The US National Missile Defense and South Asia"; Kampani, "How a US National Missile Defense Will Affect South Asia"; and V. R. Raghavan, "Missile Defense and Strategic Stability," *Hindu*, May 17, 2001 <http://www.the-hindu.com/stories/05172523.htm>.

44. "A New Arms Race?" (editorial) *Hindustan Times*, December 12, 2001. <http://www.hindustantimes.com/nonfram/151201/detedio2.asp>; "Offensive Defence," (editorial), *Times of India*, December 18, 2001 <http://timeofindia.indiatimes.com/articleshow.asp?art_id=451216166>; and Manpreet Sethi, "A Goodbye to Global Security?" *Indian Express*, December 19, 2001 <http://www.indian-express.com/ie20011219/ed4.html>.

45. Dubey, "Missile Defence and India."

46. Achin Vanaik, "India's Response to the NMD," *Hindu*, May 25, 2001 <http://www.the-hindu.com/stories/05252524.htm>; Amulya Ganguli, "America Rules, Okay?" *Hindustan Times*, May 14, 2001 <http://www.hindustantimes.com/nonfram/140501/bigidea.asp>; Inder Malhotra, "Long on Flowery Rhetoric, Short on Realism," *Hindu*, May 10, 2001 <http://www.the-hindu.com/storie/0510134a.htm>; and Dubey, "Missile Defense and India."

47. "Offensive Defence."

48. C. Raja Mohan, "Indo-US Dialogue on NMD?" *Hindu*, March 14, 2001 <http://www.hinduonnet.com/thehindu/2001/03/14/stories/05142523.htm>.

49. S. Chandrasekharan, "NMD, TMD and India: Let Not Our Imagination Run Riot," Paper no. 140, South Asia Analysis Group, August 30, 2000 <http://www.saag.org/papers2/paper140.html>. This view has also found support in the United States. See Lindsay and O'Hanlon, *Defending America*, pp. 137–39.

50. Raja Menon (Interview), *Newspaper Today*, August 7, 2001 <http://www.thenewspapertoday.com/interview/index.phtml?INTERVIEW=INT_RAJA>. See also "Shield for a Sword," (editorial), *Telegraph*, May 7, 2001 <http://www.telegraphindia.com/>; and K. Subrahmanyam, "India Should Bargain for Support to NMD," *Times of India*, May 11, 2001, p. 11. For the contrary view that India has little strategic bargaining power and would do better to focus on economics, see Manoj Joshi, "Irrational Exuberance: No Brownie Points for Welcoming NMD," *Times of India*, May 11, 2001, p. 10.

51. P. R. Chari, "Posers on the NMD," *Hindu*, June 6, 2001 <http://www.the-hindu.com/stoies/05071348.htm>.

52. Raja Mohan, "Indo-US Dialogue on NMD?"

53. C. Raja Mohan, "In Praise of Diplomatic Exuberance," *Hindu*, May 7, 2001 <http://www.the-hindu.com/stories/05071348.htm>.

54. See, e.g., Mark. T. Clark and Brian T. Kennedy, "Why Nuclear War Is Possible: The Common Sense Case for a National Missile Defense," Claremont Institute, Claremont, CA, July 1999; *Defending America: A Plan to Meet the Urgent Missile Threat: Report by the Heritage Foundation's Commission on Missile Defense* (Washington, DC: Heritage Foundation, March 1999).

55. Keith B. Payne, "Action-Reaction Metaphysics and Negligence," *Washington Quarterly*, 24, 4 (Autumn 2001), pp. 115–17.

56. Donald E. Mosher, "Understanding the Extraordinary Cost of Missile Defense," *Arms Control Today*, 30, 10 (December 2000), pp. 9–15; Steven E. Miller, "The Flawed Case for Missile Defense," *Survival*, 43, 3 (Autumn 2001), pp. 95–109; and Sessler et al., *Countermeasures*.

57. Leon Fuerth, "Return of the Nuclear Debate," *Washington Quarterly*, 24, 4 (Autumn 2001), pp. 97–108; Charles L. Glaser and Steve Fetter, "National Missile Defense and the Future of US Nuclear Weapons Policy," *International Security*, 26, 1 (Summer 2001), pp. 40–92; Lindsay and O'Hanlon, *Defending America*; and Tom Sauer, "Beyond the ABM Treaty: A Plea for a Limited National Missile Defense System," BCSIA Discussion Paper, 2002–3, Belfer Center for Science and International Affairs, John F. Kennedy School of Government, Harvard University, Cambridge, MA, March 2002.

58. Michael Krepon, "Moving Away from MAD," *Survival*, 43, 2 (Summer 2001), pp. 81–95.

59. Philip E. Coyle, "Is Missile Defense on Target?" *Arms Control Today*, 33, 8 (October 2003), pp. 7–14.

60. McGeorge Bundy, William J. Crowe, Jr., and Sidney Drell, "Reducing Nuclear Danger," *Foreign Affairs*, 72, 2 (Spring 1993), pp. 140–55.

61. James H. Lebovic, "The Law of Small Numbers: Deterrence and National Missile Defence," *Journal of Conflict Resolution*, 46, 4 (August 2002), pp. 455–83.

62. Glaser, *Analyzing Strategic Nuclear Policy*, pp. 104–5.

63. Ibid., pp. 103–32.

64. Robert Powell, "Nuclear Deterrence Theory, Nuclear Proliferation, and National Missile Defense," *International Security*, 27, 4 (Spring 2003), pp. 86–118.

65. Lebovic, "The Law of Small Numbers," pp. 458–64.

66. William J. Perry, "Preparing for the Next Attack," *Foreign Affairs*, 80, 6 (November–December 2001), pp. 31–45.

67. For a discussion on reassurance, see Chapter 8.

68. Susan B. Glasser, "Russia Has Warning, and Overture, on Missile Plan," *Washington Post*, December 19, 2002 <http://www.washingtonpost.com/wp-dyn/articles/A8996-2002Dec18.html>; and Michael Wines, "Moscow Miffed over Missile Shield, But Others Merely Shrug," *New York Times*, December 19, 2002 <http://www.nytimes.com/2002/12/19/international/europe/19MISS.html>.

69. Bruno Tertrais, "Do Arms Races Matter?" *Washington Quarterly*, 24, 4 (Autumn 2001), pp. 123–33.

70. On Chinese nuclear policy and options, see Robert A. Manning, Ronald Montaperto, and Brad Roberts, *China, Nuclear Weapons and Arms Control: A Preliminary Assessment* (New York: Council on Foreign Relations, 2000); Philip C. Saunders and Jing-dong Yuan, "China's Strategic Force Modernization: Issues and Implications for the United States," in Michael Barletta, ed., *Proliferation Challenges and Nonproliferation Opportunities for New Administrations* (Monterey, CA: Center for Nonproliferation Studies, Monterey Institute of International Studies, September 2000); and Li Bin, "The Impact of US NMD on Chinese Nuclear Modernization," *Pugwash Online*, April 2001 <http://pugwash.or/reports/rc/rc8e.htm>.

71. K. Subrahmanyam, "Son of Star Wars: US Aims to Degrade China's Deterrent," *Times of India*, February 12, 2001, p. 10.

72. On the significance and desirability of a shift from MAD, see Krepon, "Moving Away from MAD."

73. Roberts, "US Ballistic Missile Defenses," p. 5.

74. Finkelstein, "Theater Missile Defense in Asia," pp. 7–9.

75. Cited in Stephanie Nebehay, "Pakistan Warns on Dangers of US Missile Shield," Campaign for the Accountability of American Bases, Otley, W. Yorkshire, UK, January 5, 2001 <http://cndyorks.gn.apc.org/caab/articles/pakistan.htm>.

76. Cited in B. Murlidhara Reddy, "Musharraf opposes NMD," *Hindu*, May 13, 2001 <http://www.the-hindu.com/stories/01130003.htm>. See also Celia W. Dugger, "US Nurtures Growing Defense Bond with India," *New York Times*, May 13, 2001 <http://www.nytimes.com/2001/05/13/world/13INDI.html>.

77. Mutahir Ahmed, "Missile Defense and South Asia," in Michael Krepon and Chris Gagné, eds., *The Impact of US Ballistic Missile Defense on Southern Asia* (Washington, DC: Henry L. Stimson Center, July 2002); Shaukat Qadir, "Deterrence and ABMs," *Daily Times*, January 30, 2003 <http://www.dailytimes.com.pk/default.asp?page=story_11-1-2003_pg3_4>; and Zafar Nawaz Jaspal, "India's Endorsement of the US BMD: Challenges for Regional Stability," *IPRI Journal*, 1, 1 (Summer 2001), pp. 28–43.

78. Jaspal, "India's Endorsement of the US BMD," pp. 41–42.

79. Ibid., pp. 40–41.

80. Andreas Katsouris and Daniel Gouré, "Strategic Crossroads in South Asia," *Comparative Strategy*, 18, 2 (April–June 1999), pp. 173–89.

81. Gerson da Costa, *Nuclear Politics: Destruction and Disarmament in A Dangerous World* (New Delhi: Kanishka, 2000), pp. 212–15.

82. On India as an "emerging power," see Stephen Philip Cohen, *India: Emerging Power* (Washington, DC: Brookings Institution Press, 2001).

Chapter 6. Nuclear Terrorism

1. The burgeoning literature on the subject includes Yonah Alexander, ed., *Combating Terrorism: Strategies of Ten Countries* (Ann Arbor, MI: University of Michigan Press, 2002); Bruce Hoffman, *Inside Terrorism* (London: Victor Gollancz, 1998); Charles W. Kegley, Jr., *The New Global Terrorism: Characteristics, Causes, Controls* (Upper Saddle River, NJ: Prentice-Hall, 2003); Harvey W. Kushner, ed., *Essential Readings on Political Terrorism: Analyses of Problems and Prospects for the Twenty First Century* (New York: Gordian Knot Books, 2002); and Jessica Stern, *The Ultimate Terrorists* (Cambridge, MA: Harvard University Press, 1999).

2. Academic interest predates the September 11 attacks. See, e.g., Yonah Alexander and Milton Hoenig, eds., *Super Terrorism: Biological, Chemical and Nuclear* (Ardsley, NY: Transnational Publishers, 2001); Richard A. Falkenrath, Robert D. Newman, and Bradley A. Thayer, *America's Achilles' Heel: Nuclear, Biological, and Chemical Terrorism and Covert Attack* (Cambridge, MA and London: MIT Press, 1998); and Brad Roberts, ed., *Hype or Reality? The "New Terrorism" and Mass Casualty Attacks* (Alexandria, VA: Chemical and Biological Arms Control Institute, 2000).

3. On this narrow area, see Graham Allison, *Nuclear Terrorism: The Ultimate Preventable Catastrophe* (New York: Times Books, 2004); Gavin Cameron, *Nuclear Terror-*

ism: A Threat Assessment for the 21st Century (Basingstoke and London: Macmillan; New York: St. Martin's Press, 1999); Matthew Bunn and Anthony Wier, *Securing the Bomb: An Agenda for Action* (Cambridge, MA: Belfer Center for Science and International Affairs, John F. Kennedy School of Government, Harvard University, May 2004); Charles D. Ferguson and William C. Potter, with Amy Sands, Leonard S. Spector, and Fred L. Wehling, *The Four Faces of Nuclear Terrorism* (Monterey, CA: Center for Nonproliferation Studies, Monterey Institute of International Studies, 2004); Frank von Hippel, "Recommendations for Preventing Nuclear Terrorism," *FAS Public Interest Report*, 54, 6 (November–December 2001) <http://www.fas.org/faspir/2001/v54n6/prevent.htm>; Paul Leventhal and Yonah Alexander, eds., *Nuclear Terrorism: Defining the Threat* (McLean, VA: Pergamon-Brassey's International Defense Publishers, 1986); *Report of the International Task Force on Prevention of Nuclear Terrorism* (Washington, DC: Nuclear Control Institute, 1986); and *Wild Atom: Nuclear Terrorism* (Washington, DC: Center for Strategic and International Studies, 1998). Detailed day-to-day coverage can be found on the Nuclear Control Institute's website: <http://www.nci.org>. For studies covering India, see Kishore Kuchibhotla and Matthew McKinzie, "Nuclear Terrorism and Nuclear Accidents in South Asia," in Michael Krepon and Ziad Haider, eds., *Reducing Nuclear Dangers in South Asia* (Washington, DC: Henry L. Stimson Center, January 2004); and Paul Leventhal and Brahma Chellaney, *Nuclear Terrorism: Threat, Perception and Response in South Asia* (Washington, DC: Nuclear Control Institute, October 10, 1988). See also Rajesh M. Basrur and Hasan-Askari Rizvi, "Nuclear Terrorism and South Asia," Occasional Paper, 25, Cooperative Monitoring Center, Sandia National Laboratories, Albuquerque, NM, February 2003; and Rajesh M. Basrur and Friedrich Steinhausler, "Nuclear and Radiological Threats for India: Risk Potential and Countermeasures," *Journal of Physical Security*, 1, 1 (2004) <http://jps.lanl.gov/vol1_iss1/3-Threats_for_India.pdf>, from which portions of this chapter are drawn.

4. Karl-Heinz Kamp, "An Overrated Nightmare," *Bulletin of the Atomic Scientists*, 52, 4 (July–August 1996), pp. 30–34.

5. H. H. A. Cooper, "Terrorism: The Problem of Definition Revisited," in Kushner, ed., *Essential Readings on Political Terrorism*, p. 7. Although in the study of global politics today the spotlight has fallen on nonstate actors (terrorist groups), state terrorism is very much a part of this definition.

6. Thomas C. Schelling, "Thinking about Nuclear Terrorism," *International Security*, 6, 4 (Spring 1982), pp. 61–77.

7. For a chronology of WMD terrorism incidents, see Wayne Turnbull and Praveen Abhayaratne, *2002 WMD Chronology: Incidents Involving Sub-national Actors and Chemical, Biological, Radiological, or Nuclear Materials* (Monterey, CA: Center for Nonproliferation Studies, Monterey Institute of International Studies, 2003) <http://cns.miis.edu/pubs/reports/pdfs/cbrn2k2.pdf>.

8. An RDD need not involve a detonation with conventional explosives. Radiation could be spread merely by placing or scattering radiological material at fixed points, but the use of conventional explosives, which are easily available to terrorists, would have a greater psychological impact.

9. Bennett Ramberg, *Nuclear Power Plants as Weapons for the Enemy: An Unrecognized Peril* (Berkeley, CA: University of California Press, 1980), highlights this point

from the perspective of interstate war, in which nuclear plants could be an enemy's weapons.

10. Batcher, "Consequences of an Indo-Pakistani Nuclear War," Table 6, p. 154.

11. Ramana, "Bombing Bombay?" The study focuses on accidents, but the effects of sabotage would be similar.

12. Kuchibhotla and McKinzie, "Nuclear Terrorism and Nuclear Accidents in South Asia," pp. 34–35.

13. Zia Mian, M. V. Ramana, and R. Rajaraman, "Plutonium Dispersal and Health Hazards from Nuclear Weapon Accidents," *Current Science*, 80, 10 (May 25, 2001), pp. 1275–84.

14. Federation of American Scientists, "Dirty Bombs: Response to a Threat," *Public Interest Report*, 55, 2 (March–April 2002), pp. 2, 6–10. For a similar study on London, see "What if a Dirty Bomb Hit London?" *BBC News*, January 30, 2003 <http://www.bbc.co.uk/1/hi/uk/2708635.stm>.

15. Kuchibhotla and McKinzie, "Nuclear Terrorism and Nuclear Accidents in South Asia," pp. 27–28.

16. J. Carson Mark, Theodore Taylor, Eugene Eyster, William Maraman, and Jacob Wechsler, "Can Terrorists Build Nuclear Weapons?" Nuclear Control Institute, Washington, DC, n.d. <http://www.nci.org/k-m/makeab.htm> (accessed February 15, 2003); Milton Hoenig, "Terrorists Going Nuclear," in Alexander and Hoenig, eds., *Super Terrorism*; Falkenrath, Newman, and Thayer, *America's Achilles' Heel*, pp. 126–36.

17. Falkenrath, Newman, and Thayer, *America's Achilles' Heel*, p. 131; See also Hoenig, "Terrorists Going Nuclear," p. 34; and Mark et al., "Can Terrorists Build Nuclear Weapons?"

18. Hoenig, "Terrorists Going Nuclear," pp. 35–36.

19. Matthew L. Wald, "Suicidal Nuclear Threat Is Seen at Weapons Plants," *New York Times*, January 23, 2002, p. A9.

20. For a discussion of Design Basis Threats, see *U. S. Nuclear Weapons Complex: Security at Risk* (Washington, DC: Project on Government Oversight, October 2001), pp. 9–11. Threats from water sources are not discussed in the report.

21. "Oak Ridge," *Uranium Enrichment Newsletter*, October 2001 <http://www.earthisland.org/yggdrasil/UEN_oct_01.htm>.

22. William J. Kole, "Global Atomic Agency Confesses Little Can Be Done to Safeguard Nuclear Plants," Associated Press, September 19, 2001, from Nuclear Control Institute, Washington, DC <http://www.nci.org/01/09/19-11.htm> (accessed December 28, 2004).

23. "Security of the Nation's 103 Nuclear Reactors," transcript of News Conference, Nuclear Control Institute and Committee to Bridge the Gap, Washington, DC, September 25, 2001.

24. Daniel Hirsch, "The Truck Bomb and Insider Threats to Nuclear Facilities," Nuclear Control Institute, Washington, DC, 1987 <http://www.nci.org/g-h/hirschtb.htm>; *U.S. Nuclear Weapons Complex: Security at Risk*, p. 20.

25. Alden Meyer, "New UCS Fact Sheet on Spent Fuel Security," World Information Service on Energy, Washington, DC, October 23, 2001 <http://www.antenna.nl/wise/terrorism/10232001us.html>; "Nuclear Reactor Security," Union of

Concerned Scientists, Cambridge, MA, October 29, 2002 <http://www.ucsusa.org/clean_energy/nuclear_safety/page.cfm?pageID=176>; Paul Choiniere, "Officials Taking a Second Look at Plant Security," *TheDay.com*, September 19, 2001, from the Nuclear Control Institute website <http://www.nci.org/01/09/19-10.htm> n.d. (accessed December 28, 2004).

26. "Castor and Terror," World Information Service on Energy, Washington, DC, November 23, 2001 <http://www.antenna.nl/wise/terrorism/11222001wis.html>.

27. State of Nevada, Nuclear Waste Project Office, *Fact Sheet: Terrorism Considerations in the Transportation of Spent Nuclear Fuel and High-Level Radioactive Waste*, Carson City, NV, n.d. [2000] <http://www.state.nv.us/nucwaste/yucca/terrfact.htm>.

28. William Potter, "Less Well-Known Cases of Nuclear Terrorism and Nuclear Diversion in the Former Soviet Union," Nuclear Threat Initiative, Washington, DC, August 1997 <http://www.nti.org/db/nisprofs/over/nuccases.htm>.

29. "US to Probe IAEA Warning," *Indian Express*, October 13, 2004 <http://www.indianexpress.com/full_story.php?content_id=56857>.

30. Glenn E. Schweitzer with Carole Dorsch Schweitzer, *A Faceless Enemy: The Origins of Modern Terrorism* (Cambridge, MA: Perseus Publishing, 2002), pp. 51–81.

31. Jon B. Wolfsthal and Tom Z. Collina, "Nuclear Terrorism and Warhead Control in Russia," *Survival*, 44, 2 (Summer 2002), p. 71.

32. Cameron, *Nuclear Terrorism*, p. 2.

33. Ibid., pp. 2–13.

34. "'Russia Sitting on 70 Mn Tons of N-Waste,'" *Indian Express*, December 17, 2004 <http://www.indianexpress.com/full_story.php?content_id=61035>.

35. Wolfsthal and Collina, "Nuclear Terrorism and Warhead Control in Russia," p. 73.

36. Basrur and Rizvi, "Nuclear Terrorism and South Asia," pp. 52–55; and Gaurav Kampani, "Safety Concerns about the Command and Control of Pakistan's Strategic Forces, Fissile Material, and Nuclear Installations," Center for Nonproliferation Studies, Monterey Institute of International Studies, Monterey, CA, September 28, 2001 <http://www.cns.miis.edu/research/wtc01/spna.htm>.

37. On Pakistani proliferation, see Braun and Chyba, "Proliferation Rings"; and Sharon Squassoni, "Closing Pandora's Box: Pakistan's Role in Nuclear Proliferation," *Arms Control Today*, 34, 3 (April 2004), pp. 8–13.

38. A. Gopalakrishnan, "Evolution of the Indian Nuclear Power Program," *Annual Reviews: Energy and the Environment*, 27 (2002), pp. 369–95; and Government of India, Department of Atomic Energy, *Annual Report 2002–2003*. Official publications, however, are not informative with respect to the military and security aspects of the nuclear program.

39. The CISF's website at <http://cisf.nic.in/> does not even mention its role in the protection of nuclear facilities directly. For a more useful—but still sparse—overview, see Mallika Joseph A, "The Central Industrial Security Force," Article no. 687, Institute for Peace and Conflict Studies, Delhi, January 31, 2002 <http://www.ipcs.org/issues/newarticles/687-mi-mallika.html>.

40. For a review of these functions, see Nuclear Power Corporation of India

Limited, *Emergency Preparedness in Nuclear Power Plants,* n.d. <http://www.npcil.org/docs/emergency.htm> (accessed August 8, 2002).

41. Humphrey Hawksley, "India's Nuclear Muscle," *BBC News,* January 13, 2003 <http://news.bbc.co.uk/1/hi/world/south_asia/2646979.stm>.

42. P. R. Chari, "Protection of Fissile Material: The Indian Experience," ACDIS Occasional Paper, Program in Arms Control, Disarmament and International Security, University of Illinois at Urbana-Champaign, September 1998, p. 6.

43. "The Canadian Nuclear FAQ—Section D: Safety and Liability, D 1. Why is the CANDU Design One of the Safest in the World?" n.d., <http://www.nuclearfaq.ca/cnf_sectionD.htm#q> (accessed February 15, 2003).

44. "The Canadian Nuclear FAQ—Section D: Safety and Liability, D 11. How Are Nuclear Plants Protected from Terrorist Attacks?" n.d. <http://www.nuclearfaq.ca/cnf_sectionD.htm#q> (accessed February 15, 2003).

45. Helmut Hirsch, "Vulnerability of VVER-1000 Nuclear Power Plants to Passenger Aircraft Crash," World Information Service on Energy, Amsterdam, November 2001 <http://www.antenna.nl/wise/terrorism/112001vver.html>.

46. "Uranium Racket Unearthed," *Indian Express,* July 24, 1998 <http://www.indian-express.com/archive_frame.php>.

47. "Radiation Scare in Assam," *Hindustan Times,* July 21, 2002 <http://www.hindustantimes.com/news/printedition/220702/detNAT13.shtml>.

48. "Radioactive Material Stolen from Jamshedpur Tisco Plant," *Hindustan Times,* August 17, 2003 <http://www.hindustantimes.com/news/printedition/170803/detFRO03.shtml>.

49. Hirsch, "The Truck Bomb and Insider Threats to Nuclear Facilities."

50. "Nuclear Terrorism," *Three Mile Island Alert,* n.d. <http://www.tmia.com/sabter.html> (accessed February 15, 2003).

51. *U. S. Nuclear Weapons Complex,* pp. 21–23.

52. Lalit Kumar and Rajat Pandit, "Secret Military Codes Stolen from DRDO," *Times of India,* June 3, 2004 <http://timesofindia.indiatimes.com/articleshow/718209.cms>.

53. Aman Sharma, "Scientist Couple Held for Selling Data," *Indian Express,* September 25, 2004 <http://www.indianexpress.com/full_story.php?content_id=55787>.

54. Herbert L. Abrams, "Human Reliability and Safety in the Handling of Nuclear Weapons," *Science and Global Security,* 2 (1991), pp. 1–26.

55. "Titanium Rings Stolen from ISRO," *Deccan Herald,* February 14, 2004 <http://www.deccanherald.com/deccanherald/feb142004/i11.asp>.

56. Nilanjana Bhaduri Jha, "Is Stress Taking a Toll on CISF Personnel?" *Times of India,* September 19, 2003 <http://timesofindia.indiatimes.com/cms.dll/html/uncomp/articleshow?msid=190906>. The problem continues. In January 2005, a CISF soldier killed two of his colleagues in the Indian Embassy in Kathmandu, Nepal. See "2 CISF Men Shot Allegedly by Colleague," *Hindu,* January 19, 2005 <http://www.thehindu.com/2005/01/19/stories/2005011904841200.htm>.

57. "Day Two of Summit: 34 Die in Valley," *Tribune,* July 17, 2001 <http://www.tribuneindia.com/2001/20010717/main6.htm>.

58. Mukhtar Ahmad, "Militants Storm J & K Army Camp, 4 Jawans Killed," *Rediff.com,* November 4, 2001 <http://indiaabroad.com/news/2001/nov/04jk.htm>.

59. Mukhtar Ahmad, "Militants Attack Army Transit Camp, 13 Killed," *Rediff.com*, November 18, 2001 <http://indiaabroad.com/news/2001/nov/18kash.htm>.

60. "Morning Terror in Jammu Casts Shadow on Days Ahead," *Indian Express*, May 15, 2002 <http://www.indianexpress.com/archive_frame.php>.

61. "Army Officer, Four Rebels Dead in Kashmir Clash," *New York Times*, August 1, 2002 <http://www.nytimes.com/reuters/international/international-kashmir.html>.

62. "Probe Ordered into Disarming of Cops by Militants," *Times of India*, February 15, 2003 <http://www.timesofindia.indiatimes.com/cms.dll/html/uncomp/articleshow?artid=37551001>.

63. Arun Joshi, "Complacency Making Army Vulnerable in J&K: Experts," *Hindustan Times*, August 8, 2003 <http://www.hindustantimes.com/news/printedition/030803/detNAT18.shtml>.

64. Vishal Thapar, "High Casualty Rate Worries Army," *Hindustan Times*, July 27, 2002 <http://www.hindustantimes.com/2002/Jul/27/printedition/270702/det/NAT10.shtml>.

65. Ranjit Bhushan, "Shock Therapy," *Outlook*, December 24, 2001 <http://www.outlookindia.com/full.asp?fodname=20011224&fname=Cover+Story&sid=1>.

66. "Blowing Up in Our Faces," *Hindustan Times*, May 2, 2001 <http://www.hindustantimes.com/nonfram/020501/editpage.asp#two>; and Vishal Thapar, "Ammo Fires: Not Quite Accidental," *Hindustan Times*, August 5, 2001 <http://www.hindustantimes.com/nonfram/050801/detFEA02.asp>.

67. Thapar, "Ammo Fires: Not Quite Accidental."

68. Chengappa, *Weapons of Peace*, p. 422.

69. Paul Schulte, "Motives and Methods of Future Political Violence: Landscapes of the Early 21st Century," in Alexander and Hoenig, eds., *Super Terrorism*, p. 46.

70. Martha Crenshaw, "The Logic of Terrorism: Terrorist Behavior as a Product of Strategic Choice," in Walter Reich, ed., *Origins of Terrorism: Psychologies, Ideologies, Theologies, States of Minds* (Cambridge: Cambridge University Press, 1990).

71. Jerrold M. Post, "Terrorist Psycho-Logic: Terrorist Behavior as a Product of Psychological Forces," in Reich, ed., *Origins of Terrorism*. See also Richard E. Rubenstein, "The Psycho-Political Sources of Terrorism," in Kegley, Jr., ed., *The New Global Terrorism*, pp. 139–50.

72. By one account, only four actual acts of WMD terrorism, none of them involving nuclear materials, have taken place: a salmonella poisoning incident in the United States in 1984; a chlorine gas attack on Sri Lankan forces by the Liberation Tigers of Tamil Eelam (LTTE) in 1990; the well-known Tokyo subway liquid sarin gas attack in 1995; and the 2001 anthrax attacks in the United States. John Parachini, "Putting WMD Terrorism into Perspective," *Washington Quarterly*, 26, 4 (Autumn 2003), pp. 37–50.

73. Falkenrath, Newman, and Thayer, *America's Achilles' Heel*, p. 47, Table 1.

74. Ibid., pp. 45–59.

75. Brian M. Jenkins, "Is Nuclear Terrorism Plausible?" in Leventhal and Alexander, eds., *Nuclear Terrorism*, p. 28.

76. Ibid., p. 29.

77. Ibid., p. 28.

78. Potter, "Less Well-Known Cases of Nuclear Terrorism and Nuclear Diversion in the Former Soviet Union." Some half a dozen other cases cited by Potter are of a criminal nature, and do not fall into the category of terrorism as defined above.

79. Vasiliy Golovnin, "Aum Cult Implicated in Nuclear Information Stealing," *Itaar-Tass News Agency*, March 29, 2000, reproduced on Federation of American Scientists website, n.d. <http://www.fas.org/sgp/news/2000/03/aum.html> (accessed February 15, 2003).

80. David Albright, "Al Qaeda's Nuclear Program: Through the Window of Seized Documents," *Policy Forum On-line, Special Forum*, no. 47, November 6, 2002, Nautilus Institute, Berkeley, CA <http://www.nautilus.org/fora/Special-Policy-Forum/47_Albright.html>.

81. Falkenrath, Newman, and Thayer, *America's Achilles' Heel*, pp. 168–215.

82. Ibid., p. 184.

83. Ehud Sprinzak, "The Lone Gunmen," *Foreign Policy*, 127 (November–December 2001), pp. 72–73.

84. Cited in Jim Puzzanghera, "Possibility for Nuclear Terror Too Real to Be Ignored," *Mercury News Washington Bureau*, October 14, 2001, reproduced at <http://www.ci-ce-ct.com/article/showquestion.asp?faq=14&fldAuto=1219> (accessed February 15, 2003).

85. For an overview, see Ved Marwah, "India," in Alexander, ed., *Combating Terrorism*. For a full list of terrorist groups in India, see "India—Terrorist, Insurgent and Extremist Groups," *South Asia Terrorism Portal*, n.d. <http://www.satp.org/satporgtp/countries/india/terroristoutfits/index.html> (accessed December 28, 2004).

86. K. P. S. Gill, "Endgame in Punjab: 1988–1993," in K. P. S. Gill, ed., *Terror and Containment Perspectives of India's Internal Security* (New Delhi: Gyan Publishing House, 2001).

87. K. Srinivas Reddy, "Red Terror," *Hindu*, February 4, 2003 <http://www.thehindu.com/2003/02/04/stories/2003020400571000.htm>.

88. Navnita Chadha Behera, *State, Identity and Violence: Jammu, Kashmir, and Ladakh* (New Delhi: Manohar, 2000), pp. 164–214.

89. Ajai Sahni, "Extremist Islamist Terror and Subversion," in K. P. S. Gill and Ajai Sahni, eds., *The Global Threat of Terror: Ideological, Material and Political Linkages* (New Delhi: Bulwark Books, 2002), p. 215, Table 1.

90. Ibid., pp. 185–96.

91. B. Raman, "The Hydra-Headed Monster," *Outlook*, October 4, 2002 <http://www.outlookindia.com/full.asp?fodname=20021004&fname=raman&sid=1>.

92. For an exception, see Kanti Bajpai, *Roots of Terrorism* (New Delhi: Penguin, 2002), pp. 18, 21–22.

93. Afsir Karim, "Religious Extremism and National Security," *Hindu*, February 6, 2003 <http://www.thehindu.com/2003/02/06/stories/2003020600031000.htm>.

94. Dionne Bunsha and Praveen Swami, "The Terror Trail," *Frontline*, October 12–25, 2002 <http://www.frontlineonnet.com/fl1921/stories/20021025007001200.htm>.

95. For a post–September 11 retrospective assessment, see Manoj Joshi, "Fight against Terrorists Has to Be Indivisible," *Economic Times*, September 13, 2001; reproduced on the Government of India, Ministry of External Affairs, website: <http://meadev.nic.in/OPn/2001sept/13et.htm> (accessed February 13, 2003).

96. On the Gujarat pogrom, see Anjali Mody, "Genocide in the Land of Gandhi," *Hindu*, March 10, 2002 <http://www.hinduonnet.com/thehindu/2002/03/10/stories/2002031000011600.htm>.

97. V. Sudarshan, "Cynical Gambit," *Outlook*, January 13, 2003 <http:www.outlookindia.com/full.asp?fodname=20030113&fname=Terrorism+%28F%29&sid>.

98. Nirupama Subramanian, "It's No More Tiger Country," *Hindu*, July 28, 2002 <http://www.hinduonnet.com/thehindu/2002/07/28/stories/2002072800151600.htm>.

99. Nora Boustany, "Sri Lankan Peace as a Long Term Investment," *Washington Post*, July 26, 2002 <http://www.washingtonpost.com/wp-dyn/articles/A2943-2002Jul25.html>.

100. Mandavi Mehta and Teresita Schaffer, *Islam in Pakistan: Unity and Contradictions* (Washington, DC: Center for Strategic and International Studies, October 7, 2002), p. 15.

101. Rohan Gunaratna, *Inside Al Qaeda: Global Network of Terror* (New York: Columbia University Press, 2002), pp. 208–9. There are reports that Al Qaeda may be on the decline, but that the threat from other Islamic terrorist groups remains high, particularly in South Asia, the Middle East, and Southeast Asia. Beth Gardiner, "Report Evaluates al-Qaida Risks Worldwide" *Washington Post*, November 10, 2003 <http://www.washingtonpost.com/wp-dyn/articles/A24571-2003Nov10.html>. Bruce Hoffman, however, argues that Al Qaeda remains a major threat. Bruce Hoffman, *Al Qaeda, Trends in Terrorism and Future Potentialities* (Santa Monica, CA: RAND, 2003).

102. Gunaratna, *Inside Al Qaeda*, p. 218.

103. Sahni, "Extremist Islamist Terror and Subversion," pp. 212–33. How close these links are is unclear.

104. Samina Ahmed, "The United States and Terrorism in Southwest Asia," *International Security*, 26, 3 (Winter 2001–2), pp. 79–93.

105. John L. Esposito, *Unholy War: Terrorism in the Name of Islam* (Oxford: Oxford University Press, 2002), pp. 104–17.

106. Ranjan Roy, "U.N. Says Al Qaeda's Afghan Camps Reopening," *Washington Post*, December 17, 2002 <http://www.washingtonpost.com/wp-dyn/articles/A1467-2002Dec17.html>.

107. Carlotta Gall, "Afghan Poppy Growing Reaches Record Level, U.N. Says," *New York Times*, November 19, 2004 <http://www.nytimes.com/2004/11/19/international/asia/19afghanistan.html?oref=login&th>.

108. Sudhi Ranjan Sen, "Lion's Share of Afghan Opium Headed for India," *Hindustan Times*, December 1, 2002 <http://www.hindustantimes.com/2002/Dec/01/printedition/011202/detFR003.shtml>.

109. B. Raman, "Control of Transnational Crime and War against Terrorism: An Indian Perspective," *Outlookindia.com*, May 6, 2002 <http://www.outlookindia.com/specialfeaturerem.asp?fodname=20020506&fname=raman&sid=1>.

110. Mehta and Schaffer, *Islam in Pakistan*; S. V. R. Nasr, "The Rise of Sunni Militancy in Pakistan: The Changing Role of Islamism and the Ulema in Society and Politics," *Modern Asian Studies*, 34, 1 (January 2000), pp. 139–80. Nasr notes (p. 179) that the militant Deobandi School in Pakistan exercises a geographically wide influence, since its students come from as far away as Malaysia, Indonesia, and Thailand.

111. Chalk, "Pakistan's Role in the Kashmir Insurgency"; and Tim Judah, "The Taliban Papers," *Survival*, 44, 1 (Spring 2002), pp. 69–80. Judah (p. 75) provides in-

contestable evidence of Pakistan's active role in supporting what a Pakistani official refers to as the "proxy guerilla war" in Kashmir.

112. Owen Bennett Jones, *Pakistan: Eye of the Storm* (New Haven and London: Yale University Press, 2002), pp. 285–90.

113. Jessica Stern, "Pakistan's Jihad Culture," in Kushner, ed., *Essential Readings on Political Terrorism*. See also Esposito, *Unholy War*, pp. 109–11. According to Esposito (p. 109), the number of Pakistani *madrasas*, religious schools that often nurture Islamic radicalism, has increased from 147 in 1947 to over 9,000 today.

114. Qudssia Aklaque, "18m Illegal Weapons in Country: Small Arms Survey 2002," *Dawn*, January 14, 2003 <http://www.dawn.com/2003/01/14top6.htm>.

115. "Banned Groups Still Terrorizing Pakistan," *Washington Post*, January 30, 2003 <http://www.washingtonpost.com/wp-dyn/articles/A2313-2003Jan30.html>; and "Unfulfilled Promises: Pakistan's Failure to Tackle Extremism," International Crisis Group, Asia Report No. 73, Islamabad and Brussels, January 16, 2004 <http://www.crisisweb.org/home/index.cfm?id=2472&l=1>.

116. "Islamic Militants Freed in Baluchistan," *BBC News*, December 4, 2002 <http://news.bbc.co.uk/1/hi/world/south_asia/2541565.stm>.

117. James Dao, "Afghans Raise Concern that Taliban Forces Are Reorganizing in Pakistan," *New York Times*, November 3, 2002 <http://www.nytimes.com/2002/11/03/international/asia/03AFGH.html>.

118. John J. Lumpkin, "Al-Qaida Leaders Said in Pakistan," *Washington Post*, November 11, 2002 <http://www.washingtonpost.com/wp-dyn/articles/A39482-2002Nov11.html>.

119. John Lancaster and Kamran Khan, "Extremist Groups Renew Activity in Pakistan," *Washington Post*, February 8, 2003 <http://www.washingtonpost.com/wp-dyn/articles/A42370-2003Feb7.html>.

120. On the latter point, see Navnita Chadha-Behera, "A Relationship at Odds," *Hindu*, February 14, 2003 <http://www.thehindu.com/2003/02/14/stories/2003021400041000.htm>.

121. James Risen and David Rohde, "A Hostile Land Foils the Quest for bin Laden," *New York Times*, December 13, 2004 <http://www.nytimes.com/2004/12/13/international/asia/13osama.html?oref=login&th>.

122. Bertil Lintner, "Bangladesh: Extremist Islamicist Consolidation," *Faultlines*, 14 (n. d.) <http://www.satp.org/satporgtp/publication/faultlines/volume14/Article1.htm> (accessed December 14, 2004); and Gunaratna, *Inside Al Qaeda*, pp. 219–20.

123. Gunaratna, *Inside Al Qaeda*, p. 219.

124. B. Raman, "'We All Will Become Taliban...'" *Outlookindia.com*, December 9, 2002 <http://www.outlookindia.com/full.asp?fodname=20021209&fname=raman&sid=2>.

125. "India for New Approach to Relations with Bangladesh," *Hindu*, February 14, 2003 <http://www.thehindu.com/2003/02/14/stories/2003021403391200.htm>.

126. Bibhuti Bhusan Nandy, "Space Invaders," *Hindustan Times*, February 14, 2003 <http://www.hindustantimes.com/news/printedition/140203/detIDE01.shtml>.

127. Sharvani Pandit, "Terrorists Vow to Hit Indian N-Sites," *Rediff.com*, September 12, 2001 <http://www.rediff.com/news/2001/sep/12ter.htm>.

128. Albright, "Al Qaeda's Nuclear Program."

129. "Laden's Aides Reveal How They Masterminded Sep 11 Attacks," *Times of*

India, August 9, 2002 <http://www.timesofindia.com/cms.dll/articleshow?artid=21549242&sType=1>.

130. "Pak Scientist Son Says Osama Met Dad for Nuke Help," *Indian Express*, December 31, 2002 <http://www.indianexpress.com/full_story.php?content_id=15756>; "Pakistan Holds Nuclear Scientists," *BBC News*, October 25, 2001 <http://news.bbc.co.uk/1/hi/world/south_asia/1619252.stm>; and Julian West, "Al Qaeda Sought Nuclear Scientists," *Washington Times*, April 11, 2002 <http://www.washtimes.com/world/20020411-76849160.htm>.

131. "Nine Nuclear Scientists Slip out of Pakistan," *South Asia Tribune*, December 30, 2002–January 5, 2003 <http://www.satribune.com/archives/dec30_jan05_03/P1_Chashma.htm>.

132. Braun and Chyba, "Proliferation Rings"; Squassoni, "Closing Pandora's Box"; Gaurav Kampani, "Proliferation Unbound: Nuclear Tales from Pakistan," CNS Research Story, Center for Nonproliferation Studies, Monterey Institute of International Studies, Monterey, CA, February 23, 2004 <http://cns.miis.edu/pubs/week/040223.htm>; and David E. Sanger, "The Khan Network," paper presented at the Conference on South Asia and the Nuclear Future, Center for International Security and Cooperation, Institute for International Studies, Stanford University, Stanford, CA, June 4–5, 2004.

133. Jerrold M. Post, Keven G. Ruby, and Eric D. Shaw, "From Car Bombs to Logic Bombs: The Growing Threat from Information Terrorism," *Terrorism and Political Violence*, 12, 2 (Summer 2000), p. 114.

134. An exceptional situation might arise if a terrorist group obtains physical control over a geographic area. But unless the area is devoid of a civilian population, the use of nuclear capabilities (say, small nuclear weapons) against them is politically undoable. Even in such an unusual situation, a state would find it extraordinarily difficult to use nuclear weapons since that would, in a sense, justify the terrorists' use of nuclear force against it at a time and place of their choosing.

135. Schelling, "Thinking about Nuclear Terrorism," pp. 71–72.

136. Mohamed ElBaradei, "Dirty Bombs: Assessing the Threat," *Washington Post*, July 2, 2002 <http://www.washingtonpost.com/wp-dyn/articles/A11202-2002Jul1.html>.

137. Among WMD threats, chemical terrorism is the easiest to carry out owing to the wide availability of materials and technology and poor security. Joby Warrick, "An Easier, but Less Deadly, Recipe for Terror," *Washington Post*, December 31, 2004 <http://www.washingtonpost.com/wp-dyn/articles/A37519-2004Dec30.html>.

138. For a more detailed review, see Basrur and Rizvi, "Nuclear Terrorism and South Asia."

139. Government of India, Ministry of Home Affairs, *Annual Report, 2003–2004*.

140. The American NEST pulls together seventeen categories of personnel, including four types of physicists (nuclear, infrared, atmospheric, and health), engineers, chemists, and mathematicians, as well as specialists in communications, logistics, management, and public information. See Jeffrey T. Richelson, "Defusing Nuclear Terror," *Bulletin of the Atomic Scientists*, 58, 2 (March–April 2002), pp. 38–43.

141. Sonu Jain, Ashok Malik, and Royden D'Souza, "26 Countries Alerted in 15 Minutes, India Not One of Them," *Indian Express*, December 28, 2004 <http://www.indianexpress.com/full_story.php?content_id=61674>.

142. "Amid Grief, India Asks, 'Why Weren't We Warned?'" *Expressindia.com*, January 1, 2005 <http://www.expressindia.com/fullstory.php?newsid=40222>.

143. Scott D. Sagan, "The Problem of Redundancy Problem: Why More Nuclear Security Forces May Produce Less Nuclear Security," *Risk Analysis*, 24, 4 (2004), pp. 935–46. Sagan identifies three ways in which this can happen: common-mode errors (the failure of one component in a complex system causes systemic collapse), social shirking (a tendency to leave responsibility or decisions to others), and overcompensation (the acceptance of risks in the belief that security features will prevent failure, when they may not).

144. Erin E. Harbaugh, "The Proliferation Security Initiative: Counterproliferation at the Crossroads," *Strategic Insights*, 3, 7 (July 2004) <http://www.ccc.nps.navy.mil/si/2004/jul/harbaughJul04.asp>; Jofi Joseph, "The Proliferation Security Initiative: Can Interdiction Stop Proliferation?" *Arms Control Today*, 34, 5 (June 2004), pp. 6–13; and Rebecca Weiner, *Proliferation Security Initiative to Stem Flow of WMD Matériel* (Monterey, CA: Center for Nonproliferation Studies, Monterey Institute of International Studies, July 16, 2003) <http://cns.miis.edu/pubs/week/030716.htm>.

145. Benjamin Friedman, *The Proliferation Security Initiative: The Legal Challenge* (Washington, DC: Bipartisan Security Group, September 2003).

146. Varadarajan, "India Signals Wariness on Missile Defence."

147. G. Balachandran, "Nuclear Safety," in Chari, Gupta, and Rajain, eds., *Nuclear Stability in South Asia*, pp. 96–98.

148. For useful discussions from an American standpoint, see Rose Gottemoeller and Rebecca Longsworth, *Enhancing Nuclear Security in the Counter-Terrorism Struggle: India and Pakistan as a New Region for Cooperation* (Washington, DC: Carnegie Endowment for International Peace, August 2002); and Arian Pregenzer, "Securing Nuclear Capabilities in India and Pakistan: Reducing the Terrorist and Proliferation Risks," *Nonproliferation Review*, 10, 1 (Spring 2003), pp. 124–31.

149. Azfar-ul-Ashfaq, "Terrorists Tried to Kill Musharraf," *Dawn*, July 9, 2002 <http://www.jang-group.com/thenews/index.html>; "Musharraf Plot Suspect Arrested," *BBC News*, May 19, 2004 <http://news.bbc.co.uk/2/hi/south_asia/3728937.stm>; and "3 JeM Terrorists Held for Bid against Pak PM," *Hindustan Times*, January 20, 2005 <http://www.hindustantimes.com/news/181_1204325,000 50002.htm>.

Chapter 7. Minimum Deterrence and Democracy

1. A seminal discussion of the problem can be found in Rajesh M. Basrur, "Towards Democratization of Nuclear Policy," in Nawaz B. Mody, Kannamma Raman, and Louis D'Silva, eds., *Revitalizing Indian Democracy* (Mumbai: Allied Publishers, 2001).

2. For a collection of Gandhi's views on nuclear weapons, see Anand, *What Mahatma Gandhi Said about the Bomb*.

3. See, e.g., Bidwai and Vanaik, *South Asia on a Short Fuse*, pp. 151–52. Here, the collection put together by Anand is cited, but no mention is made of Gandhi's ambiguity about the use of military force. For a view that highlights Gandhi's ambivalence, see Karnad, *Nuclear Weapons and Indian Security*, pp. 30–65.

4. Katherine K. Young, "Hinduism and the Ethics of Weapons of Mass Destruc-

tion," in Sohail H. Hashmi and Stephen P. Lee, eds., *Ethics and Weapons of Mass Destruction* (Cambridge: Cambridge University Press, 2004).

5. Bidwai and Vanaik, *South Asia on a Short Fuse*, pp. 126–58; and Amulya Reddy, "The Immorality of Nuclear Weapons," in Kothari and Mian, eds., *Out of the Nuclear Shadow*.

6. It goes without saying that the terms "Indian" and "Hindu" are not identical. This is at best an approximation of reality in that Hindus constitute well over 80 percent of India's population and dominate its political life. There is no work that comprehensively analyzes the evolution of Indian thinking with respect to the relationship between ethics and security.

7. Young, "Hinduism and the Ethics of Weapons of Mass Destruction," pp. 291–95.

8. Paul Ramsey, *The Just War* (New York: Charles Scribner's Sons, 1968), p. 250.

9. While the "just war tradition" originates in Western Christianity, its contemporary manifestation, as embodied in international law, is secular-legal rather than religio-moral. Nicholas Rengger, "On the Just War Tradition in the Twenty-First Century," *International Affairs*, 78, 2 (April 2002), pp. 353–63.

10. Batcher, "Consequences of an Indo-Pakistani Nuclear War," Table 9, p. 155.

11. Ramsey, *Just War*, p. 213.

12. Clark, *Limited War*, p. 200. See also Herbert Scoville, Jr., "Flexible Madness? The Case against Counterforce," in Harold P. Ford and Francis X. Winters, SJ, eds., *Ethics and Nuclear Strategy?* (Maryknoll, NY: Orbis Books, 1977).

13. Arundhati Roy, "The End of Imagination," *Outlook*, August 3, 1998, p. 64.

14. Ashis Nandy, "Nuclearism, Genocidal Mentality and Psychic Numbing," *Himal*, 11, 7 (July 1998), pp. 14–15.

15. James Turner Johnson, *Just War Tradition and the Restraint of War* (Princeton, NJ: Princeton University Press, 1981), pp. 330–38.

16. Cited in ibid., p. 333.

17. Roy, "The End of Imagination," p. 62.

18. Michael Walzer, *Just and Unjust Wars* (New York: Basic Books, 1977), p. 268 (emphasis added).

19. *Legality of the Use by a State of Nuclear Weapons in Armed Conflict* (The Hague: International Court of Justice, July 8, 1996); reprinted in John Baylis and Robert O'Neill, eds., *Alternative Nuclear Futures: The Role of Nuclear Weapons in the Post-Cold War World* (Oxford: Oxford University Press, 2000). For the view that the weight of the Court's opinion went against legitimizing nuclear weapons, see Siddharth Mallavarapu, "A Mandate for Nuclear Prudence: International Court of Justice on Nuclear Weapons," in M. V. Ramana and Rammanohar Reddy, eds., *Prisoners of the Nuclear Dream* (New Delhi: Orient Longman, 2003).

20. Geoffrey Goodwin, "Deterrence and Détente: The Political Environment," in Geoffrey Goodwin, ed., *Ethics and Nuclear Deterrence* (New York: St. Martin's Press, 1982), p. 36 (emphasis original).

21. John Finnis, Joseph M. Boyle, Jr., and Germain Grisez, *Nuclear Deterrence, Morality and Realism* (Oxford: Clarendon Press, 1987), p. 294.

22. Michael Novak, "The Moral Implications of Strategic Deterrence," in James E. Dougherty, *Ethics, Deterrence and National Security* (Maclean, VA: Pergamon-Brassey's, 1985), p. 66.

23. Krepon et al., eds., *Handbook of Confidence Building Measures for Regional Security*, pp. 189–210.

24. Sumantra Bose, "'Hindu Nationalism' and the Crisis of the Indian State: A Theoretical Perspective," in Sugata Bose and Ayesha Jalal, eds., *Nationalism, Democracy and Development* (Delhi: Oxford University Press, 1997). Other—less successful—attempts to refashion the nation's identity were through language (Hindi) and caste ("backward castes"). See Sudipta Kaviraj, "Crisis of the Nation-State in India," in John Dunne, ed., *Contemporary Crisis of the Nation State?* (Oxford and Cambridge, MA: Blackwell, 1995), esp. pp. 127–28.

25. Kanti Bajpai, "Hinduism and Weapons of Mass Destruction: Pacifist, Prudential and Political," in Hashmi and Lee, eds., *Ethics and Weapons of Mass Destruction*.

26. Achin Vanaik, "Crossing the Rubicon," *Economic and Political Weekly* (June 13, 1998), pp. 1435–36.

27. Sumit Sarkar, "The BJP Bomb and Aspects of Nationalism," *Economic and Political Weekly* (July 4, 1998), pp. 1725–30.

28. For a nonnuclear example, see Carlos Egan, "National Security Regimes and Human Rights Abuse: Argentina's Dirty Wars," in Edward E. Azar and Chung-in Moon, eds., *National Security in the Third World* (Aldershot: Edward Alger, 1988).

29. Praful Bidwai, "New Security Mantra: Perils of a Paranoid Mentality," *Times of India*, July 2, 1996, p. 12.

30. Shrikant Rao, "Atomic Energy Dept Nukes Anti-N Scientist," *Sunday Mid-Day*, November 22, 1998, p. 1.

31. Bhaskar Roy, "Censor Board Bombards Peace Film," *Times of India*, June 22, 2002 <http://www.timesofindia.indiatimes.com/articleshow.asp?art_id13704229>; and M. V. Ramana, "Censorship in the Nuclear Age," *Hindu*, July 19, 2002 <http://www.thehindu.com/2002/07/19/stories/2002071900931000.htm>.

32. Richard Falk, *The Promise of World Order* (Philadelphia: Temple University Press, 1987), p. 81.

33. For a review of the nascent movement, see Praful Bidwai, "Nuclear Disarmament and Peace," *Economic and Political Weekly*, December 9, 2000 <http://www.epw.org.in/showArticles.php?root=2000&leaf=12&filename=2462&filetype=html>; and Achin Vanaik, "Developing the Anti-Nuclear Movement," *Economic and Political Weekly*, May 5–11, 2001 <http://www.epw.org.in/showArticles.php?root=2000&leaf=05&filename=2963&filetype=html>.

34. Falk, *Promise of World Order*, p. 82.

35. Robert Jay Lifton, "The World of the Bomb," in Robert Jay Lifton and Richard Falk, eds., *Indefensible Weapons: The Political and Psychological Case against Nuclearism* (New York: Basic Books, 1982), p. 3.

36. See the statement by General S. Padmanabhan, former Chief of Army Staff, in "'About the Nuclear Threat, Musharraf Isn't Irrational,'" (Interview), *Hindustan Times*, February 11, 2004 <http://www.hindustantimes.com/2004/Feb/11/181_567823,00120003.htm>.

37. Cited in Robert C. Aldridge, "A Scary Nuclear 'Loophole'," *Strategic Digest*, 10, 9 (September 1980), p. 651.

38. Richard Ned Lebow and Janice Gross Stein, *We All Lost the Cold War* (Princeton, NJ: Princeton University Press, 1994), pp. 303–4.

39. Robert Dahl, *Controlling Nuclear Weapons: Democracy versus Guardianship* (Syracuse, NY: Syracuse University Press, 1985).

40. Ibid., p. 31.

41. Ibid., p. 42.

42. Rahul Sagar, "Watchdog Needed: Weaponisation and Civil Society," *Times of India*, August 19, 2000, p. 12.

43. Dahl, *Controlling Nuclear Weapons*, p. 64.

44. Ibid., pp. 86–89.

45. Erich Fromm, *Escape from Freedom* (New York: Holt, Rinehart & Winston, 1941).

46. Debi Chatterjee, "Pokhran-II: A Socio-political View," in Majumdar, ed., *Nuclear India into the New Millennium*, pp. 149–50; Jean Drèze, "Militarism, Development and Democracy," in Ramana and Reddy, *Prisoners of the Nuclear Dream*.

47. For typically one-sided views that fail to consider the latter, see Bidwai and Vanaik, *South Asia on a Short Fuse*, pp. 159–67; and Mohammed Ahmedullah, "Let 'Em Eat Nukes," *Bulletin of the Atomic Scientists*, 56, 5 (September–October 2000), pp. 52–57.

48. For a review, see Kanwal, *Nuclear Defence*, pp. 192–201.

49. Stephen I. Schwartz, ed., *Atomic Audit: The Costs and Consequences of U.S. Nuclear Weapons since 1940* (Washington, DC: Brookings Institution Press, 1998).

50. Ibid., p. 5, Figure 2.

51. Ibid., p. 3.

52. Peter R. Lavoy, "The Costs of Nuclear Weapons in South Asia," in D. R. SarDesai and Raju G. C. Thomas, eds., *Nuclear India in the Twenty-First Century* (New York and Basingstoke: Palgrave-Macmillan, 2002), pp. 264–65.

53. Kanwal, *Nuclear Defense*, pp. 200–201.

54. Schwartz, ed., *Atomic Audit*, pp. 519–43.

55. Feaver, *Guarding the Guardians*.

56. Sundarji, *Blind Men of Hindoostan*.

57. The influence of the armed forces can sometimes be negative. More than seven years after the official adoption of nuclear deterrence as national strategy, India still had no fully unified nuclear command and control system. The decision to appoint a Chief of Defense Staff (CDS) was held up in part by prolonged squabbles among the services. Atul Aneja, "Govt in a Bind over Naming CDS," *Hindu*, May 21, 2001 <http://www.the-hindu.com/stories/01210003.htm>; and Atul Aneja, "India Has 'Problems' Managing Nuclear Arms," *Hindu*, August 14, 2001 <http://www.hinduonnet.com/thehindu/2001/08/14/stories/02140003.htm>. Evidently, the government's commitment to democratic norms—civilian control over the military—was not strong enough to enforce discipline on its service chiefs.

58. Itty Abraham, "Science and Secrecy in Making of Colonial State," *Economic and Political Weekly* (August 16–23, 1997), pp. 2136–46.

59. Dhirendra Sharma, *India's Nuclear Estate* (New Delhi: Lancer International, 1983).

60. Rajiv Wagh, "Dr. Subbarao: The Spy Who Never Was?" *Times of India*, June 13, 1993, p. 7; Burjor Taraporewala, "Dr. K. Subbarao's Quest for Justice," *Lawyers*, 9, 7–8 (July–August 1994), pp. 8–24, 33–36.

61. B. Krishnakumar, "An Epic Battle," *The Week*, August 17, 1997 <http://www.the-week.om/97aug17/events1.htm>.

62. For an equally infamous case in the nonnuclear sphere, the so-called "Samba spy case," see "After 25 Yrs, Samba Spy Case Thrown Out," *Indian Express*, December 22, 2000, p. 1.

63. "SC Raps Nayanar Govt in ISRO Case, Acquits All," *Expressindia.com*, April 30, 1998 <http:www.expressindia.com/ie/daily/19980430/12050514.html>; and R. Krishnakumar, "Requiem for a Scandal," *Frontline*, May 9–22, 1998 <http://www.flonnet.com/fl1510/15101140.htm>.

64. "NHRC Asks Kerala Govt to Pay Rs One Million to ISRO Scientist," *Rediff.com*, March 16, 2001 <http://www.rediff.com/news/2001/mar/16/nhrc.htm>.

65. One recent example is that of the Taiwan-born American scientist, Wen Ho Lee, who was subjected to legal harassment for allegedly leaking nuclear secrets to China. Another is that of the Israeli scientist, Mordechai Vanunu, who was abducted from Italy and jailed in Israel for "blowing the whistle" on the Israeli nuclear program.

66. Shekhar Gupta, "Afraid of One's Shadow," *Indian Express*, December 30, 2000 <http://www.indian-express.com/columnists/shek/20001230.html>.

67. J. Venkatesan, "NHRC Denounces POTO as 'Draconian'," *Hindu*, November 19, 2001 <http://www.hinduonnet.com/stories/02200003.htm>.

68. "'Terrorists Not Entitled to Rights,'" *Hindu*, October 30, 2001 <http://www.hinduonnet.com/stories/02300003b.htm>.

69. Rajiv Dhawan, "The Makings of a Police State?" *Hindu*, January 11, 2002 <http://www.hinduonnet.com/stories/2002111101271000.htm>.

70. "Whither Nuclear Safety?" *Hindu*, July 4, 2000 <http://www.indiaserver.com/thehindu/2000/07/04/stories/05042512.htm>.

71. A. Gopalakrishnan, "Issues of Safety," *Frontline*, March 13–26, 1999 <http://www.frontlineonnet.com/fl1606/16060820.htm>; and R. Ramachandran, "In the Name of National Security," *Frontline*, July 8–21, 2000 <http://www.frontlineonnet.com/fl1714/17140890.htm>.

72. Herbert L. Abrams, "Sources of Human Instability in the Handling of Nuclear Weapons," in Fred Solomon and Robert Q. Marston, eds., *The Medical Implications of Nuclear War* (Washington, DC: National Academies Press, 1986).

73. Herbert L. Abrams, "Who's Minding the Missiles?" *Sciences*, 26, 4 (July–August 1986), pp. 22–28.

74. Ibid., p. 23.

75. Chuck Hansen, "The Oops List," *Bulletin of the Atomic Scientists*, 56, 6 (November–December 2000), pp. 65–66.

76. M. V. Ramana, "The Concorde and the Nuclear Reactor," *Himal*, September 2000 <http://www.himalmag.com/sep2000/content/Analysis.html>.

77. Gopalakrishnan, "Issues of Safety"; and Ramana, "The Concorde and the Nuclear Reactor."

78. Ibid.

79. "31 Pilots Killed in Three Years," *Hindustan Times*, February 21, 2003 <http://www.hindustantimes.com/news/printedition/210203/detNAT05.shtml>.

80. "Rocket Explodes in Navy Ship, Crew Safe," *Indian Express*, February 7, 2004 <http://www.indianexpress.com/full_story.php?content_id=40614>.

81. V. Geetanath, "One Killed as Missile Fires Accidentally," *Hindu*, January 5, 2001 <http://www.hinduonnet.com/thehindu/2001/01/05/stories/01050006.htm>.

82. T. S. Subramanian, "6 Killed in Explosion at Sriharikota Space Centre," *Hindu*, February 24, 2004 <http://www.thehindu.com/2004/02/24/stories/2004022406180100.htm>. One report cited officials as saying that the accident occurred when an Agni motor was being tested. Ashok Das, "Agni Engine Fire Kills 6 in Sriharikota," *Hindustan Times*, February 24, 2004 <http://www.hindustantimes.com/news/printedition/240204/detFRO02.shtml>. However, this was denied by the ISRO Chairman G. Madhavan Nair. T. S. Shankar, "'No Setback to ISRO Programmes,'" *Hindu*, February 25, 2004 <http://www.thehindu.com/2004/02/25/stories/2004022504750100.htm>.

83. For a discussion on allegiance and nuclear weapons, see Stephen Toulmin, "The Limits of Allegiance in a Nuclear Age," in Avner Cohen and Steven Lee, eds., *Nuclear Weapons and the Future of Humanity* (Totowa, NJ: Rowman & Allanheld, 1986).

Chapter 8. Conclusion: Shaping the Uncertain Future

1. Sea-based and air-launched weapons would require earlier delegation of authority and would thus be more vulnerable to unauthorized launch or errors of perception.

2. For two interesting attempts, the first focusing on conflict scenarios, the second on alternative force postures, see *Nuclear Futures—Asia: Final Report* (San Diego, CA: Strategic Assessment Center, Science Applications International Corporation, October 2001); and Tellis, *India's Emerging Nuclear Posture*, pp. 117–249.

3. The section below draws partly upon Rajesh M. Basrur and Stephen P. Cohen, "Bombs in Search of a Mission: India's Uncertain Nuclear Futures," in Michael R. Chambers, ed., *South Asia in 2020: Future Strategic Balances and Alliances* (Carlisle Barracks, PA: U.S. Army War College, 2002).

4. See, e.g., Ahmar, ed., *Challenge of Confidence-Building in South Asia*; Dipankar Banerjee, ed., *Confidence-Building in South Asia* (Colombo: Regional Center for Strategic Studies, 1999); Zafar Nawaz Jaspal, *Nuclear Risk Reduction Measures and Restraint Regime in South Asia*, RCSS Policy Studies, 25 (Colombo: Regional Centre for Strategic Studies, 2004); Feroz Hasan Khan, "Challenges to Nuclear Stability in South Asia," *Nonproliferation Review*, 10, 1 (Spring 2003), pp. 59–74; Rafi uz Zaman Khan, *Pakistan and India: Can NRRCs Help Strengthen Peace?* (Washington, DC: Henry L. Stimson Center, December 2002); *Nuclear Risk Reduction Centers in South Asia: Working Group Report* (Washington, DC: Center for Strategic and International Studies, May 2004); Gaurav Rajen and Kent Biringer, "Nuclear-Related Agreements and Cooperation in South Asia," *Disarmament Diplomacy*, 55 (March 2001) <http://www.acronym.org.uk/dd/dd55/55rajen.htm>; and W. P. S. Sidhu, Brian Cloughley, John H. Hawes, and Teresita C. Schaffer, *Nuclear Risk-Reduction Measures in South Asia* (Washington, DC: Henry L. Stimson Center, November 1998).

5. On continuing cross-border terrorism, see Rajat Pandit, "Valley LOCked in Terror, Insurgency," *Times of India*, September 18, 2003 <http://timesofindia.indiatimes.com/cms.dll/html/uncomp/articleshow?msid=187385>.

6. For a review of the concept of learning in interstate relations, see Jeffrey W. Knopf, "The Importance of International Learning," *Review of International Studies*,

29, 2 (April 2003), pp. 187–209. For an empirical study of learning from crises, see Leng, *Bargaining and Learning in Recurring Crises*.

7. George W. Breslauer and Philip E. Tetlock, "Introduction," in George W. Breslauer and Philip E. Tetlock, eds., *Learning in U.S. and Soviet Foreign Policy* (Boulder, CO: Westview Press, 1991), pp. 6–8.

8. Banning Garrett, "The Need for Strategic Reassurance in the 21st Century," *Arms Control Today*, 31, 2 (March 2001) <http://www.armscontrol.org/act/2001_03/garrett.asp>; Andrew Kydd, "Trust, Reassurance and Cooperation," *International Organization*, 54, 2 (Spring 2000), pp. 325–57; Janice Gross Stein, "Deterrence and Reassurance," in Philip E. Tetlock, Jo L. Husbands, Robert Jervis, Paul C. Stern, and Charles Tilly, eds., *Behavior, Society and Nuclear War*, vol. 2 (New York and Oxford: Oxford University Press); and John Steinbruner, *Principles of Global Security* (Washington, DC: Brookings Institution Press, 2000), pp. 126–32.

9. Stein, "Deterrence and Reassurance," pp. 35–56.

10. Ibid., pp. 42–45.

11. Ibid., p. 56.

12. I thank M. V. Ramana for drawing my attention to the distinction between transparency and limitations.

13. For an elaboration on this point, see Rajesh M. Basrur, "Nuclear India at the Crossroads," *Arms Control Today*, 33, 7 (September 2003), pp. 7–11.

14. Sony Devabhaktuni and Matthew C. J. Rudolph, "Key Developments in the Indo-Pak Development Process," in Krepon et al., eds., *Handbook of Confidence-Building Measures for Regional Security*.

15. The first major round in the 1960s was spurred by the Cuban Missile Crisis, the second in the 1980s by the fear of war caused by the conjunction of two developments: the sudden rise in tensions during the early Reagan years, and the deployment of intermediate ballistic missiles in Europe.

16. Hagerty, *Consequences of Nuclear Proliferation*; Saira Khan, *Nuclear Proliferation Dynamics in Protracted Conflict Regions: A Comparative Study of South Asia and the Middle East* (Aldershot: Ashgate Publishing, 2002), pp. 151–65.

Index

In this index an "f" after a number indicates a separate reference on the next page, and an "ff" indicates separate references on the next two pages. A continuous discussion over two or more pages is indicated by a span of page numbers, e.g., "57–59."

ABM, see Antiballistic Missile Treaty
ABNES, see Akhil Bharatiya Nepali Ekta Samaj
Abrams, Herbert, 132, 231n72
Accidents: nuclear, 166–67
Accountability, 145, 148, 161
Advani, L. K., 93
AEC, see Atomic Energy Commission
AERB, see Atomic Energy Regulatory Board
AEW, see Airborne early warning platform
Afghanistan, 40, 83, 174, 176; terrorism in, 84, 137f; U.S. intervention in, 91f, 100; Soviet war in, 104f
Agni missiles, 60, 70, 89, 105, 203n83, 232n82
Agra summit, 82, 85, 174, 180
Ahamed, E., 107
Airborne early warning (AEW) platform, 105
Airplanes: as terrorist weapons, 128
Akash missile, 105
Akhil Bharatiya Nepali Ekta Samaj (ABNES), 136
Alami, al-, 147

Albright, Madeleine, 106, 109
Al-Jazeera, 139
Al Qaeda, 97, 135, 137–38, 139, 144, 224n101
Ammunition dumps: fires in, 133–34
Anarchy, 2, 13; systemic, 19, 55; and world politics, 22, 23–24
Andhra Pradesh, 136f
Antiballistic Missile (ABM) Treaty, 107ff, 115, 118
Antitactical ballistic missiles (ATBMs), 105
Arab-Israeli War, 104
Armed forces, 104, 135, 151, 161, 179f, 230n57
Armenian Scientific Group, 135
Armitage, Richard, 93
Arms build-up, 61, 109–10
Arms control, 22, 46, 50, 74–75, 107, 178; transparency in, 180–81; pressure for, 181–82
Arms races, 100, 111; defensive, 102–3, 113; types of, 115–16
Arrow ATBM, 105
Arsenals, 42, 160; first strike vulnerability of, 31–32; stockpiles, 109–10; sizes of, 140–41
Arunachalam, V. S., 62, 66

Arunachal Pradesh, 174
Assam, 132, 136, 221n47
Assassinations, 133, 136f
Assured destruction, 26
Asymmetry: nuclear and conventional, 87–88
ATBMs, see Antitactical ballistic missiles
Atomic audit, 159–60
Atomic bomb, 26, 152–53
Atomic Energy Commission (AEC), 130, 162, 165
Atomic Energy Regulatory Board (AERB), 131, 165
Aum Shinrikyo, 135, 144
Australia, 146
Authority: centralized, 148

Babri Masjid, 137
Bajpai, Kanti, 57, 190n55, 193n9, 195n24, 197n76, 201n27, 202n43, 223n92, 229n25
Baluchistan, 139
Ballistic missiles, see by type
Bangalore, 133
Bangladesh, 61, 137, 139
BARC, see Bhabha Atomic Research Centre
Belarus, 9
Bentham, Jeremy, 12
Berry, Nicholas, 106–7
Bhabha, Homi, 61, 67, 162
Bhabha Atomic Research Centre (BARC), 131, 162, 165
Bharat Dynamics Limited, 166
Bharatiya Janata Party (BJP), 15f, 63–64, 66, 73f, 87, 93, 155
Bharatpur, 133
Bhatia, V. K., 98
Bhopal, 166
Bhutan, 13, 137
Bhutto, Benazir, 63
Bihar, 136
BJP, see Bharatiya Janata Party
Bombs: atomic, 26, 152–53; terrorist-built, 127–28
Border issues, 37; Chinese-Soviet, 39, 95–96; India-Pakistan, 75, 80, 84f, 86–87, 98f. See also Kashmir
Bosnia, 13, 115, 135
BrahMos cruise missile, 70
Brodie, Bernard, 18, 31, 185n2, 191n66, 196n37
Buk-MI system, 105
Bundy, McGeorge, 36f, 39, 112, 188n39, 216n60
Bush, George W., 92f, 102, 106f, 110f, 115

Cadogan, Alexander, 45
C&C, see Command and control
Canada Deuterium Uranium (CANDU), 131
Caste system, 56, 136, 229n24
CBI, see Central Bureau of Investigation
CBMs, see Confidence-building measures
Central Bureau of Investigation (CBI), 163
Central Industrial Security Force (CISF), 130–31, 133, 145
Cesium-137, 125, 135
Chakra, INS, 70
Chandra, Naresh, 84
Chandra, Satish, 107
Chari, P. R., 45, 131, 199n3, 209n53, 215n51
Chechen rebellion, 115, 135
Chellaney, Brahma, 72, 198n87, 218n3
Chelyabinsk complex, 130
Chenab River, 89
Chernobyl, 166
Chidambaram, R., 166
Chief of Defence Staff, 71
Chiefs of Staff Committee, 71
China, 32, 40, 53, 56, 78, 112, 147, 154; nuclear weapons in, 15, 29, 38, 43; nuclear program in, 16–17, 65, 67; limited deterrence of, 26–27; and Soviet Union, 39, 95–96; and Pakistan, 61ff, 66, 194nn17, 18; as threat, 73, 76;

arms build up and, 100, 115f; missile systems in, 104f; and United States, 107f, 110, 114; relations with, 117–18, 174–75, 176, 179
CISF, *see* Central Industrial Security Force
Civil-military relations, 160–61, 207n32
Civil wars, 61f
Clinton, Bill, 102
Cold War, 5, 8–9, 14, 16, 21, 36, 46, 60, 117, 157
Command and control (C&C), 46–47
Compellence, 2, 7, 45, 80, 100, 142–43; threat of, 88–90; trilateral, 90–93; and deterrence, 94–95; reversibility of, 95–96
Comprehensive Test Ban Treaty (CTBT), 102, 109
Confidence-building measures (CBMs), 56, 75, 154, 172f, 181
Conflict: levels of, 37–38; India-Pakistan, 88–89; preparation for, 89–90; controlling, 98–99
Congress party, 16, 61, 63f, 66–67
Congress system, 21
Constructivism, 11, 186n19
Continuous Behavior Observation Program, 145
Cooperation, 3, 13; international, 146–47
Counterforce strategy, 43f, 72, 151
Counterterrorism, 163–64
Covert infiltration, 37
Credibility, 38, 50, 169; and Draft Nuclear Doctrine, 40–41; nuclear capability and, 41–42
Cruise missiles, 31, 70, 112
CTBT, *see* Comprehensive Test Ban Treaty
Cuban Missile Crisis, 21, 39, 46, 98, 157, 197n67, 233n15
Cultural Revolution, 95

DAE, *see* Department of Atomic Energy

Dahl, Robert, 157, 158
Damage, 25, 197n70; unacceptable, 38–40, 53
Damansky Island, 95f
Dasgupta, Sunil, 77
DBT, *see* Design Basis Threat
Decapitating strike, 45f
Defence Research and Development Organization (DRDO), 132
Defense, 3, 7, 14; national system of, 103–4; missile, 108–9, 110–13, 170
Defense Nuclear Facilities Safety Board (DNFSB), 165
Delivery systems, 30f, 41, 70, 72
Democracy, 3, 7, 148ff, 156f, 159, 164, 167–68; and national security, 162–63
Democratization, 149
Denuclearization, 16
Department of Atomic Energy (DAE), 131, 155, 165
Department of Energy (DOE), 165
Deployment, 69ff, 76, 171; absence of active, 45–46; minimum deterrence and, 141–42
Desai, Morarji, 62, 64, 66, 74, 150, 202n53
Design Basis Threat (DBT), 128
Deterrence, 3, 6f, 17f, 47f, 78, 108, 118–19, 151, 156, 208n49, 230n57; types of, 26–29; stages of, 29–30; weapons and, 34–35; politics of, 35–36; numbers of weapons and, 41–43; as official policy, 63–64; strategic culture of, 67–69; and compellence, 94–95; missile defense systems and, 111–17; terrorists and, 143–44; morality of, 153–54; alternative models of, 171–77. *See also* Minimum deterrence
Dhanush, 70
Disarmament, 50, 61, 66, 75, 108, 118, 180
Dirty bomb, 125, 144, 219n14 226n136

Disaster Management Division (Ministry of Home Affairs), 145
DND, see Draft Nuclear Doctrine
DNFSB, see Defense Nuclear Facilities Safety Board
DOE, see Department of Energy
Doomsday cults, 135
Draft Nuclear Doctrine (DND), 30, 50, 59, 68, 72, 74, 81; credibility and, 40–41; retaliation, 51–52
DRDO, see Defence Research and Development Organization

Economic development, 159
Economics: interdependence and, 19–20
Eisenhower, Dwight, 35
11 Army Corps, 151
Elites, 59, 72, 158
Escalation, 43, 44–45, 98–99
Espionage: accusations of, 162–63
Ethics, 149–54
Europe, 13, 176. See also various countries
Executive Council (NCA), 30, 71, 77
Existential deterrence, 36, 38

Falk, Richard, 156, 229n35
Federation of American Scientists, 126
Fernandes, George, 83, 86f, 89, 93, 106, 166, 203n83
Finnis, John, 153
First strike, 31–32, 36–37, 42
First World War, 21, 33
Fissile material: protection of, 128–29
Fissile Material Cutoff Treaty (FMCT), 52, 109
France, 27, 29, 32, 117, 146, 193n9, 200n17

Gadwal, 130
Gandhi, Indira, 61–62, 105, 133, 136, 155, 194n20; nuclearization, 65–66, 67
Gandhi, Mahatma, 60, 150

Gandhi, Rajiv, 15–16, 17, 62–63, 64, 66, 137
Ganguly, Sumit, 44, 185n1, 189n43, 189–90n50, 195n40, 198n100, 207n7, 209n52
Germany, 26, 29, 146
Ghauri missile, 95
Glaser, Charles, 112, 191n67, 192n3, 216n57
Globalization, 2, 8f, 13
Golra, 130
Goodwin, Geoffrey, 153
Gorbachev, Mikhail, 8–9
Gordon, Sandy, 56
Gowda, H. D. Deve, 63, 67
Gradual reciprocation in tension reduction (GRIT), 180
Gray, Colin, 54
Gray War, 14
Great Britain, 27, 29, 32, 65
GRIT, see Gradual reciprocation in tension reduction
Gujarat, 137
Gujral, I. K., 63
Gulf War, 104

Haq, Inamul, 118
Harkat-ul-Ansar, 139
Harkat-ul-Jihad-al-Islami (HUJI), 139
Harkat-ul-Muahideen (HuM), 136f, 139, 147
Harknett, Richard, 34, 156, 195n35
HEU, see Highly enriched uranium
Highly enriched uranium (HEU), 127
Hijacking: Indian Airlines, 83, 86
Hindu Army, 136
Hinduism, 137, 149–50, 155
Hindus, 137, 228n6
Hindutva (Hindu-ness), 155, 190n59
Hiroshima, 62, 152
Hizb-ul-Mujahideen (HM), 137
Hobbes, Thomas, 20, 187n23
HUJI, see Harkat-ul-Jihad-al-Islam
HuM, see Harkat-ul-Muahideen
Human rights, 153, 163f
Hyderabad, 137

IAF, *see* Indian Air Force
ICBMs, *see* Intercontinental ballistic missiles
Identity: national, 154–55, 229n24
Indian Air Force (IAF), 166
Indian Airlines: hijacking, 83, 86
Indian Army, 86, 89, 99, 131
Indian Censor Board, 156
Indian Institute of Mathematical Sciences, Chennai, 155
Indian Institute of Technology, 162
Indian Navy, 62, 70, 89
Indian Parliament, 50, 67, 105, 145, 161, 166; terrorist attack on, 38, 80, 84, 86, 91f, 100, 164
Indian Space Research Organization (ISRO), 133, 163, 166
India-Pakistan agreement (1988), 75
India-Pakistan wars, 27
Indira Gandhi Centre for Atomic Research, 132
Indus River, 13, 208n44
Insurgency, 77, 81, 90; in Kashmir, 82–83, 96–97
Intercontinental ballistic missiles (ICBMs), 27, 30, 176
Integrated Guided Missile Development Program, 62, 105
Interdependence, 2, 11, 13, 23; economic, 19–20
International Court of Justice, 153
International relations theory, 9–11
Internet, 122, 141, 165
Intervention, 175
Iran, 9, 16, 28f
Iran-Iraq War, 104
Iraq, 9, 16, 104, 117, 121, 129, 176
Islam, 92, 225n113; terrorism and, 135, 136–38, 224n101
Isolationism, 13, 21–22
Israel, 28, 105, 120, 179, 231n65
ISRO, *see* Indian Space Research Organization
Italy, 146
Ivanov, Igor, 107

Jaish-e-Mohammed (JeM), 92, 136f, 147
Jammu and Kashmir, 85, 94, 136
Jammu and Kashmir legislature: terrorist attack on, 84, 86, 91, 133, 136
Jammu city, 133
Jamshedpur, 132
Janata Dal, 63
Japan, 6, 13, 16, 26f, 29, 56, 104, 135, 146; atomic bomb in, 135, 152–53
Jayaraman, T. K.: harassment of, 155–56
JeM, *see* Jaish-e-Mohammed
Jenkins, Brian, 134
Jervis, Robert, 13, 186n8, 186–87n19, 191n67, 191n75, 233n8
Jharkhand, 136
Jihadis, 136, 137–40
Joint Intelligence Committee, 82

Kahuta, 130
Kaluchak massacre, 92–93, 133
Kanchanbagh, 166
Kandahar, 83
Kant, Immanuel, 20
Kanwal, Gurmeet, 40, 68, 71f
Karachi, 42, 89, 130
Karakoram highway, 174
Kargil conflict, 64, 73, 81f, 83–84, 85f, 97, 119, 170, 174, 206n6, 207n22; Pakistan's role in, 90–91, 93; impacts of, 179–80
Kargil Review Committee Report, 82f
Karnad, Bharat, 59–60, 68, 71f, 201n37
Kashmir, 39, 64, 72, 80, 174, 179, 181; terrorism in, 16, 77, 94, 97, 136, 137–38, 139, 178; conflict over, 73–74, 81, 84ff; Pakistan and, 82–83, 90, 96; massacres in, 92–93, 133
Kashmiriyat, 136
Kashmir Valley, 80, 136
Kautilya, 12, 56
Kazakhstan, 9
Kerala, 163

Khan, A. Q., 140
Khan Research Laboratories, 130
Khushab, 130
Koodankulam, 131
Kosovo, 105, 115
Kraig, Michael, 77, 205n105
Krepon, Michael, 32, 190n50, 191n62, 201n24, 206n15, 212n1, 216n58, 22923
Krishnamurthy, Jana, 87
Kumar, Sushil, 88
Kuwait, 117

Laden, Osama bin, 135, 139
Lahore Memorandum/Declaration, 64, 75, 78, 81, 147, 154, 180
Lashkar-e-Taiba (LeT), 92, 137
Latham, Andrew, 56
Law enforcement: counterterrorism and, 163–64
League of Nations, 21
Leng, Russell, 99, 198n95
LeT, see Lashkar-e-Taiba
Liberalism, 11, 12–13, 20
Liberation Tigers of Tamil Eelam (LTTE), 137, 222n72
Libya, 29
Lilienthal, David, 35
Limited deterrence, 26–27, 30–31, 32, 172, 173
Line of Control (LoC), 73–74, 84f, 86, 98f, 182; Kargil crisis and, 90f; Pakistan and, 93, 95
Liquid Propulsion Systems Centre, 133
LoC, see Line of Control
Loonda Post, 99
LTTE, see Liberation Tigers of Tamil Eelam
Lucknow, 132

MAD, see Mutual assured destruction
Madrasas, 138, 225n113
Maharashtra, 136
Maldives, 77, 163
Marginalization of nuclear weapons, 9, 15

Marxian approach, 11
Massacres: Kaluchak, 92–93, 133
M-11 missiles, 105
Menon, Raja, 68, 71f, 198n98, 215n50
Menon, V. K. Krishna, 60
Militarization of Indian strategy, 76–77, 93–94
Military, 15, 19, 26, 31, 62f, 83, 104; defensive realism and, 22–23; force and nuclear weapons, 33–36; and politics, 76–77, 93–94; border issues, 80, 85–87, 99; mobilization of, 89–90; terrorist attacks against, 133–34; nuclear policy and, 160–61
Military culture, 55, 57
Military facilities: threats to, 132–33
Mill, James, 12
Minimalism, 6, 58–59, 61, 65–66, 70, 77
Minimum deterrence, 1f, 4f, 23, 25, 27–28, 30ff, 72, 119, 154, 157, 172f, 177, 182; risk and, 36–38; damage and, 38–40; benefits of, 140–43; domestic dilemmas and, 148–49; secrecy and, 161–63
Minipopulus, 158
Ministry of Defence, 77, 86
Ministry of Home Affairs, 130–31, 145
Mishra, Brajesh, 93
Missile defense, and stability, 102–3, 111–17; Indian development of, 105–6; Indian debate on, 109–11
Missiles, 70, 95, 201n35, 233n15. See also by name and type
Missile systems, Indian, 70
MMA, see Muttahida Majlis-e-Amal
Mobilization: Indian military, 89–90
Mohan, C. Raja, 84, 210n72
Moral issues, 113–14, 149–50, 167–68; and nuclear weapons, 58, 60–61, 62, 148, 150–54
Moral Man and Immoral Society (Niebuhr), 152

Mountain Strike Corps, 99
MUD, *see* Mutual unacceptable damage
Muhammad, Abdul Salam, 139
Mujjaid, Nazeer Ahmed, 138
Mumbai, 118, 125, 126, 131, 137, 166
Musharraf, Pervez, 82, 92f, 96, 100, 118, 138, 206n6
Muslim fundamentalists, 92, 135, 138
Muttahida Majlis-e-Amal (MMA), 138–39
Mutual assured destruction (MAD), 38f, 105f, 108, 110, 112, 117f, 121, 172f
Mutual unacceptable damage (MUD), 39
Myanmar, 13, 137

Nagaland, 136
Nagasaki, 34, 62, 127, 152
Naidu, Venkaiah, 164
Nair, Vijai K., 68, 71f
Nambinarayan, S., 163
Nanavatty, R. K., 86
Nandy, Ashis, 152
National Command Authority (Pakistan), 130
National Emergency Response Force, 145
National Human Rights Commission, 163f
National Security Advisory Board (NSAB), 50, 68
NCA, *see* National Command Authority
NCBMs, *see* Nuclear confidence building measures
Nehru, Jawaharlal, 15, 59–61, 66f, 69, 154–55, 162, 202n42
Nepal, 62, 137, 222n56
Neorealism, 12
NEST, *see* Nuclear Emergency Search Team
Netherlands, 146
New Lab, 130
NFU, *see* No first use

Niebuhr, Reinhold: *Moral Man and Immoral Society*, 152
Nilhore, 130
Nimitz, USS, 165
NMD, *see* National missile defense
No first use (NFU), 30, 44, 52, 70; commitment to, 50–51
Nonalignment, 121
Nonviolence, 60, 149, 152
Northeast: insurgency in, 77
Northern Command, 86, 133
North Korea, 9, 16, 28f
North West Frontier Province (NWFP) (Pakistan), 139
NPT, *see* Nuclear Nonproliferation Treaty
NSAB, *see* National Security Advisory Board
Nuclear capability, India's attainment of, 54, 61
Nuclear Command Authority, 30, 52, 71, 77, 156
Nuclear confidence building measures (NCBMs), 119–20
Nuclear doctrine, Indian, 50–53
Nuclear Emergency Search Team (NEST), 145
Nuclear infrastructure, 139, 145; monitoring, 164–65; internal security of, 165–66
Nuclearism, 152
Nuclearization, 65–66, 67f, 100
Nuclear materials: sources of, 129–32
Nuclear minimalism, 58–59
Nuclear Nonproliferation Treaty (NPT), 16, 28, 61f, 181
Nuclear plants, 124, 130, 139, 166; threats against, 128–29
Nuclear scientists and terrorism, 139–40
Nuclear weapons, 1, 4, 15, 33, 54, 68f, 73, 156; possession and nonpossession of, 2–3; politics of, 34–36, 78–79, 100–101, 118; risk and, 36–38, 169–70; deterrence and, 36–48; strategic culture and, 57–59; moral opposition to, 60–61,

151–52; terrorism and, 123–24, 124–27, 127–29; opposition to, 151–52; costs of, 159–60; as defensive, 167–68
NWFP, see North West Frontier Province

Official Secrets Act, 162
Opaque deterrence, 28
Operational bias: strategic culture and, 75–77
Operational drift, 49
Operationalization, 70–71
Operation Brasstacks, 62, 92, 179
Operation Desert Storm, 105
Operation Enduring Freedom, 138
Operation Parakram, 80, 84, 88, 90, 91–92, 94f, 98, 100, 156, 170, 178, 180

Padmanabhan, S., 86f, 229n36
Pakistan, 2, 13, 39, 46, 56, 61, 65, 105, 119, 130, 154, 171, 174, 176, 181, 194n17; conflict with, 11, 73f, 80ff, 84f, 88–89, 97–98, 99, 179, 194nn17, 18; nuclear program in, 16–17, 29, 62f, 66; deterrence in, 27, 28–29, 40, 42, 147; nuclear weapons in, 38, 43; escalation and, 44–45; negotiation with, 64, 78; as threat, 73, 76; terrorism, 74, 94, 137, 138–40; and Kashmir, 82–83, 94, 96; border issues, 86–87; nuclear and conventional asymmetry of, 87–88; U.S. pressures on, 90–93, 209n51; and U.S. missile defense, 107, 118, 120
Pakistan Nuclear Regulatory Authority (PNRA), 130
Pan-Islamism, 136
Paramilitary forces, 130–31
Patwardhan, Anand: *War and Peace*, 156
Peace, commitment to, 179
Peace constituency, 109, 156
Peace movement, 158–59

Pentagon, 14
People's War Group (PWG), 136
Perestroika, 9
Perkovich, George, 66, 189n50, 194n13
Personnel: reliability of, 165–66
Personnel Assurance Program, 165
Peshawar, 151
Phalcon airborne early warning platform, 105
Plutonium, 123, 126ff, 130
PNRA, see Pakistan Nuclear Regulatory Authority
Poland, 146
Polaris system, 31
Political Council (NCA), 71
Political parties, 66–67
Politics, 2, 4, 7, 10, 66–67, 68, 97, 134, 178; world, 11, 22, 23–24; war and, 18–19; nuclear weapons and, 34–35, 54, 78–79, 100–101, 118; deterrence, 35–36; military, 76–77; missile defense, 111, 114
Portugal, 146
Potter, William, 129, 218n3, 223n78
Poverty, 17, 67, 136
Powell, Colin, 92f
Powell, Robert, 113
Power, 3, 7; distribution of, 14, 19; asymmetry of, 87–88
Pragmatism, 60, 110
Prasad, Hari, 133
Preemption, 45, 108
Prevention of Terrorism Act, 164
Prithvi missile, 63, 70, 89, 105
Proliferation, 17–18, 113, 130, 139–40, 146
Proliferation Security Initiative (PSI), 146
Public Accounts Committee (Parliament), 145
Public opinion, 67, 93
Punitive retaliation school, 31
Punjab, 16, 77, 83, 155, 130, 136
Pushtun, 174
Putin, Vladimir, 115, 130
PWG, see People's War Group

Quetta, 151

Radar systems, 32, 103, 105, 107
Radiation: terrorism, 123–24
Radioactive materials: sources of, 129–32
Radiological dispersion device (RDD), 125f, 128f, 141f, 218n8
Rahman, Fazlur, 139
Rajendra phased array, 105
Ramana, M. V., 166, 197n65, 219n13, 228n19, 233n12
R&D, see Research and development
Rao, P. V. Narasimha, 63f, 67
Rasheeda, Mariam, 163
Rashtriya Swayamsevak Sangh (RSS), 93
RDD, see Radiological dispersion device
Realism, 11, 12–13, 20, 65; defensive, 22–23; strategic culture and, 54–55, 59–60
Reassurance, 8, 114, 116, 119f, 172, 178–80, 182
Redundancy, 32, 51, 70, 72–73, 173
Rehman, Jamilur, 139
Religion: terrorism and, 135f, 138–39
Remote Sensing Applications Centre, 132
Research and development (R&D), 160
Retaliation, 31, 44, 47, 50, 51–52, 53, 73, 78, 84, 89, 112, 150, 169
Reversibility: of compellence, 95–96
Risk, 25; and minimum deterrence, 36–38; escalation of, 44–45; terrorism, 124–27; nuclear weapons and, 169–70
Rousseau, Jean Jacques, 12, 21–22
Roy, Arundhati, 152
RSS, see Rashtriya Swayamsevak Sangh
Rule of law: violations of, 162–64
Russia, 13f, 16, 26, 35, 70, 105, 120, 131, 135, 176; arms control in, 107, 111f; and NMD, 114–15; nuclear materials, in, 129–30
Russian-American relations, 20

Sabotage, 129, 131f, 134
Sadat, Anwar, 179
Sagan, Scott, 5, 31, 98, 190n54, 191n60, 227n43
Sagarika, 70
Saha, Meghnad, 161
Salal dam, 89
Saudi Arabia, 138
Schelling, Thomas, 94, 123, 143
Scud missiles, 104
Secessionists: in Kashmir, 81–83, 179
Second strike capability and use, 30, 32, 41f, 70, 72, 112, 140
Second World War, 20f, 26f, 33, 36, 38
Secrecy, 7; nuclear policy and, 148f, 161–63
Security, 3, 5f, 9, 13f, 19, 69, 171, 227n143; nuclear weapons and, 58–59; deterrence policy and, 63–64, 148–49; facilities and organizations, 132–34; international cooperation in, 146–47; nuclear infrastructure, 165–66
Separatism: Islamic, 136
September 11, 2001, attacks, 8, 14, 84, 104, 113, 122, 135, 138f, 176f
SFC, see Strategic Forces Command
Shaheen missile, 95
Sharif, Nawaz, 82
Shastri, Lal Bahadur, 61, 65f
Shekhar, Chandra, 63
Shoko Asahara, 135
Sihala, 130
Sikhs, 136
Simla Agreement, 92
Singh, Jasjit, 68, 71f, 85
Singh, Jaswant, 56, 81, 93, 100, 106f; on retaliation, 51–52
Singh, Manmohan, 64–65, 107
Singh, Natwar, 65
Singh, V. P., 63

SLBMs, *see* Submarine-launched ballistic missiles
SNEP, *see* Subterranean Nuclear Explosion Project
Snyder, Jack, 55
Solid Propellant Booster Plant, 166
South Africa, 9
South Korea, 104
Soviet Union, 8–9, 16, 40, 65, 66, 70, 166; United States and, 20, 46, 60, 81, 98; nuclear arsenal in, 31–32, 36, 38, 141, 157; and China, 39, 95–96; in Afghanistan, 104–5
Spain, 146
Sriharikota Island, 166
Sri Lanka, 40, 62, 77, 137
Standing Committee on Defence, 105
S-300V system, 105
Strategic culture, 49–50, 205n100; realism in, 54–55; theory of, 55–56; nuclear weapons and, 57–59; India's, 59–75; beliefs in, 67–69; operational bias in, 75–77
Strategic doctrine, 145–46
Strategic Forces Command (SFC), 71
Strategic theory, 31–32
Subbarao, B., 162–63
Submarine-launched ballistic missiles (SLBMs), 31, 41, 47–48, 70, 195n32, 201n35
Submarines, 31, 41, 70, 89
Subrahmanyam, K., 39, 68, 71f, 185n1, 189n44, 207n27
Subterranean Nuclear Explosion Project (SNEP), 61
Sundarji, Krishnaswamy, 30, 40, 46, 68, 71f, 161, 195n32
Surveillance data: U.S., 107
Survivability, 25, 30, 32, 41–42, 50ff, 75, 169, 171, 195n32
Sweden, 6, 13, 29

Tactical nuclear weapons (TNW), 30
Taepodong missile, 104
Taiwan, 15, 104, 116, 175–76
Taiwan Straits, 104

Talbott, Strobe, 106
Taliban, 84, 91, 97, 138f, 175
Tamil Nadu, 131
Tamil Nadu Liberation Army (TNLA), 136
Tamils, 137
Tanham, George, 56
Tanzim Islah-ul-Mumineen, 137
Targeting, 43, 69, 70, 72, 150f
Technical capability, 18, 28
Technology, 43, 67, 103, 144, 173; of nuclear weapons, 127–29
Tehrik-ul-Mujahideen, 139
Tellis, Ashley, 32, 190n52, 193n9, 207n178
Tenet, George, 92
Terrorism, terrorists, 2, 7, 11, 16, 21, 74, 77, 83, 86, 97, 122–23, 141, 222n72, 226n134; Parliament attack by, 80, 100; in Kashmir, 82, 96, 133, 178; cross-border, 84, 94; Pakistan and, 81–82, 88, 92ff, 138–39; nuclear, 123–27, 144–46; and nuclear materials, 129–32; motivations of, 134–35; in India, 135–36; Islamic, 136–38, 224n101; as deterrers, 143–44
Theater missile defense (TMD), 103–4
Think tanks, 158–59
Third World, 10
Threat perception, 18, 65, 123
Threats: technological, 127–29
Tibet, 105, 175
TMD, *see* Theater missile defense
TNLA, *see* Tamil Nadu Liberation Army
TNW, *see* Tactical nuclear weapons
Tomahawk missiles, 105
ToR-M1, 105
Torture, 163
Transparency, 180–81
Triad, 26, 30, 32, 43, 51f, 72–73, 76, 140, 172
Tripura, 136
Truman, Harry, 31, 35, 152
Turkey, 135

12 Army Corps, 151
2 Corps, 98

Ukraine, 9
United Front, 63
United Kingdom, 146
United Nations, 21, 63, 107
UN Conference on Disarmament, 118
United Progressive Alliance, 64–65
United States, 8, 10, 13f, 26, 65, 97, 100, 120, 138, 165, 175; and nuclear weapons, 15, 30, 31–32, 35, 38; and Soviet Union, 20, 46, 60, 81; and Pakistan, 61, 63, 66, 98, 209n51; compellence in, 90–93; national missile defense in, 102, 103–4, 106–9, 110, 116–17; and regional politics, 114, 115–16; and Russian nuclear materials, 129–30; defense measures in, 145f; nuclear weapons costs in, 159–60
U.S. National Intelligence Council, 129
U.S. Navy, 21, 61, 63, 107
Uranium: sources of, 130
Ussuri River, 95

Vajpayee, Atal Behari, 16, 44, 50, 52, 63–64, 73, 82, 90, 100, 106, 178–79, 180, 203n62; and Pakistan, 93, 95
VHP, see Vishwa Hindu Parishad

Vietnam, 40, 175
Vij, Kapil, 98
Violence: terrorist, 122, 133–35; nuclear explosions and, 126–27
Virtual deterrence, 28–29, 153
Vishwa Hindu Parishad (VHP), 93
Voice of America, 138

Wagner, Harrison, 44
Waltz, Kenneth, 12, 36, 41, 191n60
War(s), 13–14, 27, 33, 40, 60, 113, 141; and state politics, 18–19; risk and, 36–37; limited nuclear, 43–44; limited, 85–87; just cause in, 150–51, 228n9
War and Peace (Patwardhan), 156
War-avoidance, 4–5, 19, 21
Warheads, 70; storage of, 45–46, 109
Weaponization, 46, 63–64, 66, 70, 119
Weapons, 33, 34–35, 181, 232n1; defensive, 3, 7. *See also* Nuclear weapons
Weapons of mass destruction (WMD), 122, 222n72, 226n137
World Islamic Front against the Jews and the Crusaders, 139
World Trade Center, 14, 128, 135
Wright, Quincy, 23

Yusuf, Ramsey, 135

Zhenbao Island, 95

STUDIES IN ASIAN SECURITY

A series sponsored by the East-West Center
Muthiah Alagappa, Chief Editor
Director, East-West Center Washington

Minimum Deterrence and India's Nuclear Security. By Rajesh M. Basrur. 2006
Unifying China, Integrating with the World: Securing Chinese Sovereignty in the Reform Era. By Allen Carlson. 2005
Rising to the Challenge: China's Grand Strategy and International Security. By Avery Goldstein. 2005
Rethinking Security in East Asia: Identity, Power, and Efficiency. Edited by J. J. Suh, Peter J. Katzenstein, and Allen Carlson. 2004

The authorized representative in the EU for product safety and compliance is:
Mare Nostrum Group
B.V Doelen 72
4831 GR Breda
The Netherlands

www.ingramcontent.com/pod-product-compliance
Lightning Source LLC
Chambersburg PA
CBHW030340240426
43661CB00052B/1693